The Aims of Argument

FOURTH EDITION

The Aims of Argument
A BRIEF GUIDE

Timothy W. Crusius
Southern Methodist University

Carolyn E. Channell
Southern Methodist University

Boston   Burr Ridge, IL   Dubuque, IA   Madison, WI   New York
San Francisco   St. Louis   Bangkok   Bogotá   Caracas   Kuala Lumpur
Lisbon   London   Madrid   Mexico City   Milan   Montreal   New Delhi
Santiago   Seoul   Singapore   Sydney   Taipei   Toronto

McGraw-Hill Higher Education

*A Division of The **McGraw-Hill** Companies*

The Aims of Argument: A Brief Guide

Published by McGraw-Hill, an imprint of The McGraw-Hill Companies, Inc., 1221 Avenue of the Americas, New York, NY 10020. Copyright © 2003, 2000, 1998, 1995 by The McGraw-Hill Companies, Inc. All rights reserved. No part of this publication may be reproduced or distributed in any form or by any means, or stored in a database or retrieval system, without the prior written consent of The McGraw-Hill Companies, Inc., including, but not limited to, in any network or other electronic storage or transmission, or broadcast for distance learning.

This book is printed on acid-free paper.

1 2 3 4 5 6 7 8 9 0 FGR/FGR 0 9 8 7 6 5 4 3 2

ISBN 0-07-286343-9

Vice president and Editor-in-chief: *Thalia Dorwick*
Senior developmental editor: *Renée Deljon*
Senior marketing manager: *David S. Patterson*
Senior production editor: *David M. Staloch*
Senior production supervisor: *Richard DeVitto*
Design manager: *Violeta Díaz*
Interior and cover designer: *Ellen Pettengell*
Photo researcher: *Holly Rudelitsch*
Art editor: *Cristin Yancey*
Compositor: *G & S Typesetters, Inc.*
Typeface: *10.25/12 Giovanni Book*
Paper: *45# New Era Matte*
Printer and binder: *Quebecor Printing, Fairfield*

Text and photo credits begin on page C1 and constitute an extension of the copyright page.

LIBRARY OF CONGRESS CATALOGING-IN-PUBLICATION DATA

Crusius, Timothy W., 1950–
    The aims of argument: a brief guide / Timothy W. Crusius,
Carolyn E. Channell.— 4th ed.
        p. cm.
    Includes index.
    ISBN 0-07-286343-9
    1. English language—Rhetoric.   2. Persuasion (Rhetoric)   3. Report writing.
I. Channell, Carolyn E.   II. Title.

    PE1431.C778 2002
    808'.0427—dc21   2002023046

www.mhhe.com

For W. Ross Winterowd

Preface

As its first three editions were, the fourth edition of *The Aims of Argument* is different from other argumentation texts because it remains the only one that focuses on the aims, or purposes, of argument. That this book's popularity increases from edition to edition tells us that our approach does in fact satisfy the previously unmet need that moved us to become textbook authors. We're gratified that our approach has proven useful — and seemingly more effective than others available.

NOTES ON THIS TEXT'S ORIGINS

With over thirty years of teaching experience between us, we had tried most of the available argument books. Many of them were quite good, and we learned from them. However, we found ourselves adopting a text not so much out of genuine enthusiasm but rather because it had fewer liabilities than any of the others we were considering. True, all textbook selection involves comparisons of the "lesser evil" sort. But we wondered why we were so lukewarm about even the best argumentation textbooks. We found many problems, both major and minor, that explained our dissatisfaction, and we boiled them down to a few major criticisms:

- Most treatments were too formalistic and prescriptive.
- Most failed to integrate class discussion and individual inquiry with written argumentation.
- Apart from moving from simple concepts and assignments to more complicated ones, no book offered a learning sequence.
- Despite the fact that argument, like narrative, is clearly a mode or means of development, not an end in itself, no book offered a well-developed view of the aims or purposes of argument.

We thought that these shortcomings had many undesirable results in the classroom, including the following:

- The overemphasis on form confused students with too much terminology, made them doubt their best instincts, and drained away energy and interest from the process of inventing and discovering good arguments. Informal argumentation is not cut-and-dried but open-ended and creative.
- The separation of class discussion from the process of composition created a hiatus (rather than a useful distinction) between oral and written argument so that students had difficulty seeing the relation between the two and using the insights learned from each to improve the other.
- The lack of a learning sequence—of assignments that begin by refining and extending what students can do without help and that then build on these capacities with each subsequent assignment—meant that courses in argumentation were less coherent and less meaningful than they could be. Students did not understand why they were doing what they were doing and could not envision what might reasonably come next.
- Finally, inattention to what people actually use argument to accomplish resulted in too narrow a view of the functions of argument and thus in unclear purposes for writing. Because instruction was mainly limited to what we call arguing to convince, too often students saw argument only as a monologue of advocacy. Even when their viewpoint was flexible, too often they assumed a pose of dogmatism and ignored any true spirit of inquiry.

We set out consciously to solve these problems—or at least to render them less problematical—when we wrote the first edition of this book. The result was a book different in notable respects from any other argument text available because it focuses on the four aims of argument:

Arguing to inquire, the process of questioning opinions
Arguing to convince, the process of making cases
Arguing to persuade, the process of appealing to the whole person
Arguing to negotiate, the process of mediating between or among
     conflicting positions

COMMON QUESTIONS ABOUT THE AIMS OF ARGUMENT

We have found that instructors have certain questions about these aims, especially in terms of how they relate to one another. No doubt we have yet to hear all the questions that will be asked, but we hope that by answering the ones we have heard, we can clarify some of the implications of our approach.

1. *What is the relative value of the four aims? Because mediation comes last, is it the best or most valued?* Our answer is that no aim is "better" than any other aim. Given certain needs or demands for writing and certain audiences, one aim can be more appropriate than an-

other for the task at hand. We treat mediation last because it involves inquiry, convincing, and persuading and thus comes last in the learning sequence.

2. *Must inquiry be taught as a separate aim?* Not at all. We have designed the text so that it may be taught as a separate aim (the use of argument Plato and Aristotle called *dialectic*), but we certainly do not intend this "may" to be interpreted as a "must." We do think that teaching inquiry as a distinct aim has certain advantages. Students need to learn how to engage in constructive dialogue, which is more disciplined and more focused than class discussion usually is. Once they see how it is done, students seem to enjoy dialogue with one another and with texts. Dialogue helps students think through their arguments and imagine reader reaction to what they say, both of which are crucial to convincing and persuading. Finally, as with the option of teaching negotiation, teaching inquiry offers instructors another avenue for assignments other than the standard argumentative essay.

3. *Should inquiry come first?* For a number of reasons, inquiry has a certain priority over the other aims. Most teachers are likely to approach inquiry as a prewriting task, preparatory to convincing or persuading. And very commonly, we return to inquiry when we find something wrong with a case we are trying to construct, so the relationship between inquiry and the other aims is as much recursive as it is a matter of before and after.

   However, we think inquiry also has psychological, moral, and practical claims to priority. When we are unfamiliar with an issue, inquiry comes first psychologically, often as a felt need to explore existing opinion. Regardless of what happens in the "real world," convincing or persuading without an open, honest, and earnest search for the truth is, in our view, immoral. Finally, inquiry goes hand-in-hand with research, which, of course, normally precedes writing in the other aims of argument.

   In sum, we would not defend Plato's concept of the truth. Truth is not simply "out there" in some wordless realm waiting to be discovered; rather, our opinion is that we discover or uncover truth as we grapple with a controversial issue and that it results largely from how we interpret ourselves and our world. We agree, therefore, with Wayne Booth that truth claims ought to be provisional and subject to revision, held for good reasons until better ones change our minds. Moreover, we agree with Plato that rhetoric divorced from inquiry is dangerous and morally suspect. The truth (if always provisional — some person's, some group's, or some culture's version of the truth) must count for more than sheer technical skill in argumentation.

4. *Isn't the difference between convincing and persuading more a matter of degree than of kind?* Fairly sharp distinctions can be drawn between inquiry and negotiation and between either of these two aims and the

monologues of advocacy: convincing and persuading. But convincing and persuading do shade into one another so that the difference is only clear at the extremes, with carefully chosen examples. Furthermore, the "purest" appeal to reason — a legal brief, a philosophical or scientific argument — appeals in ways beyond the sheer cogency of the case being made. Persuasive techniques are typically submerged but not absent in arguing to convince.

Our motivation for separating convincing from persuading is not so much theoretical as pedagogical. Students usually have so much difficulty with case-making that individual attention to the logical appeal by itself is justified. Making students focally conscious of the appeals of character, emotion, and style while they are struggling to cope with case-making is too much to ask and can overburden them to the point of paralysis.

Regardless, then, of how sound the traditional distinction between convincing and persuading may be, we think it best to take up convincing first and then persuasion, especially because what students learn in the former can be carried over more or less intact into the latter. And, of course, it is not only case-making that carries over from convincing into persuading. Because one cannot make a case without unconscious appeal to character, emotional commitments (such as values), and style, teaching persuasion is really a matter of exposing and developing what is already there in arguing to convince.

The central tenets of an approach based on aims of argument may be summarized as follows:

- *Argumentation is a mode or means of discourse, not an aim or purpose of discourse;* consequently, our task is to teach the aims of argument.
- *The aims of argument are linked in a learning sequence so that convincing builds on inquiry, persuasion on convincing, and all three contribute to mediation;* consequently, we offer this learning sequence as an aid to conceiving a course or courses in argumentation.

We believe in the learning sequence as much as we do in the aims of argument. We think that anyone giving it an honest chance will come to prefer this way of teaching argument over any other ordering currently available.

At the same time, we recognize that textbooks are used selectively, as teachers and programs need them for help in achieving their own goals. As with any other text, this one can be used selectively, ignoring some parts, playing up others, designing other sequences, and so on. If you want to work with our learning sequence, it is there for creative adaptation. If not, the text certainly does not have to be taught as a whole and in sequence to be useful and effective.

A FINAL WORD ABOUT THE APPROACH

Some reviewers and users have called our approach innovative. But is it better? Will students learn more? Will instructors find the book more satisfying and more helpful than what they currently use? Our experience—both in using the book ourselves and in listening to the responses of those who have read it or tested it in the classroom or used it for years—is that they will. Students complain less about having to read this book than about having to read others used in our program. They do seem to learn more. Teachers claim to enjoy the text and find it stimulating, something to work with rather than around. We hope your experience is as positive as ours has been. We invite your comments and will use them in the process of perpetual revision that constitutes the life of a text and of our lives as writing teachers.

NEW TO THE FOURTH EDITION

On the whole, we think this revision has made *Aims* more user-friendly and more diverse in its appeal while maintaining its attempt not to dodge or gloss over the genuine complexities and special challenges of argumentation. As always, we invite your comments and suggestions, as we continue to learn a great deal from the students and teachers who use this book.

The major changes from the third edition are as follows:

New Organization

In an effort to make materials easier to locate and more accessible, we've reorganized the book into four parts and changed the format, including the addition of a much-needed second color. We now have up front, in Part One, all the materials we think of as "basic training": understanding rhetoric and argumentation, reading arguments, analyzing them, doing research. The popular chapter on visual rhetoric is here as well because visuals are especially useful for teaching reading and analysis and because they are often used as an aid for making arguments, regardless of aim.

Among other important topics, Chapter 1, Understanding Argument, confronts the popular notions of rhetoric and argument and moves students immediately into working with both. Reading an Argument, Chapter 2, addresses the problems students have in reading arguments and provides detailed strategies for overcoming those challenges. Because many contemporary students are not used to processing uninterrupted blocks of prose that advance sustained arguments, we see this greatly enhanced coverage as part of our continuing effort to develop still better ways to help students become critical readers. This chapter includes an analytical writing assignment and a student example of the completed assignment.

Entirely Rewritten Inquiry Chapter

Part Two groups together what has been and will always be the foundation of the book: the sequence of the four aims. The only significant change in this part is an extensive overhaul of the inquiry chapter. Most composition texts focus on helping students find sources rather than showing them what to do once sources are located. Making useful note cards is important but only a small part of the problem students face in analyzing and assessing sources. Therefore, the fourth edition of *The Aims of Argument* now offers more detailed guidance, with illustrations, in thinking critically about sources and relating them to the issues connected with controversial topics. Included is a section on how to assess sources defending opposing theses on the same issue, a challenge students typically encounter in research but which is rarely addressed sufficiently in composition textbooks. We also show students, complete with examples and exercises, the difference between conversation and dialogue and especially how to move from merely asserting opinions to questioning them. Finally, we've designed a new assignment for this chapter, one we think will contribute significantly to making the exploratory essay a more rewarding experience for both students and instructors.

New Boxes

In response to reviewers' suggestions, we added numerous boxes throughout Parts One and Two, and to help students get the most out of them, we identify the majority of the boxes as one of two types: Concept Close-Up or Best Practices. We intend each type to achieve a different purpose. The contents of Concept Close-Up boxes provide, as the boxes' name suggests, a summary or an expanded discussion of a covered concept or topic. Best Practices boxes offer guidelines for successfully completing reading, writing, and thinking tasks; employing the full range of argumentation strategies; and writing effective arguments.

New Web Site

In addition to the many changes the fourth edition offers in the text itself, and in addition to the text's print instructor resources manual, this edition of *Aims* is also accompanied by a new Web site that provides not only a wealth of links to relevant sites but also interactive activities to help students develop skills such as evaluating online sources. The Web site's address is <www.mhhe.com/crusius>.

Online Course Delivery and Distance Learning

In addition to the supplements described previously (the print *Instructor's Resources to Accompany The Aims of Argument,* Fourth Edition and the book's new Web site), McGraw-Hill also offers the following technology products for composition classes. The online content of *The Aims of Argument* is supported by WebCT, Blackboard, eCollege.com, and most other course systems. Additionally, McGraw-Hill's PageOut service is available to get you and your course up and running online in a matter of hours—at no cost! To find out more, contact your local McGraw-Hill representative or visit <http://www.pageout.net>.

PageOut

McGraw-Hill's widely used click-and-build Web site program offers a series of templates and many design options, requires no knowledge of HTML, and is intuitive and easy to use. With PageOut, anyone can produce a professionally designed course Web site in very little time.

AllWrite!

Available online or on CD-ROM, *AllWrite!* offers over 3,000 exercises for practice in basic grammar, usage, punctuation, context spelling, and techniques for effective writing. The popular program is richly illustrated with graphics, animations, video, and Help screens.

Webwrite

This online product, available through our partner company Meta Text, makes it possible for writing teachers and students to, among other things, comment on and share papers online.

Teaching Composition Faculty Listserv at <www.mhhe.com/tcomp>

Moderated by Chris Anson at North Carolina State University and offered by McGraw-Hill as a service to the composition community, this listserv brings together senior members of the college composition community with newer members—junior faculty, adjuncts, and teaching assistants—in an online newsletter and accompanying discussion group to address issues of pedagogy, in both theory and in practice.

ACKNOWLEDGMENTS

We have learned a great deal from the comments of both teachers and students who have used this book, so please continue to share your thoughts with us.

We wish to acknowledge the work of the following reviewers who guided our work on the first, second, and third editions: Linda Bensel-Meyers, University of Tennessee, Knoxville; Lisa Canella, DePaul University; Mary F. Chen-Johnson, Tacoma Community College; Matilda Cox, University of Maryland—College Park; Margaret Cullen, Ohio Northern University; Richard Fulkerson, Texas A&M University—Commerce; Judith Gold Stitzel, West

Virginia University; Matthew Hearn, Valdosta State University; Elizabeth Howard Borczon, University of Kansas; Peggy B. Jolly, University of Alabama at Birmingham; James L. Kastely, University of Houston; William Keith, Oregon State University; Dr. Charles Watterson Davis, Kansas State University; Anne Williams, Indiana University-Purdue University Indianapolis.

We are grateful to the reviewers whose helpful comments guided our work on this edition: Joel R. Brouwer, Montcalm Community College; Amy Cashulette Flagg, Colorado State University; Lynee Lewis Gaillet, Georgia State University; Cynthia Haynes, University of Texas at Dallas; Lisa J. McClure, Southern Illinois University, Carbondale; Rolf Norgaard, University of Colorado at Boulder; Julie Robinson, Colorado State University; Gardner Rogers, University of Illinois, Urbana-Champaign; Cara-Lynn Ungar, Portland Community College; N. Renuka Uthappa, Eastern Michigan University.

The work of David Staloch, our production editor, and April Wells-Hayes, our copyeditor, went far beyond the call of duty in helping us refine and complete the revised manuscript. At McGraw-Hill, Marty Granahan's work with permissions and Holly Rudelitsch's photo research also deserve special recognition and our deepest gratitude. Finally, Renée Deljon, our editor, showed her usual brilliance and lent her unflagging energy throughout the process that led to this new edition of *Aims*.

Timothy Crusius
Carolyn Channell
Dallas, Texas

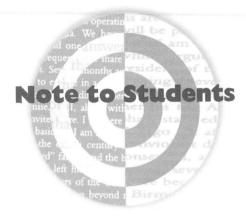

Note to Students

Our goal in this book is not just to show you how to construct an argument but also to make you more aware of why people argue and what purposes that argument serves in our society. Consequently, Part Two of this book introduces four specific aims that people may have in mind when they make arguments: to inquire, to convince, to persuade, and to negotiate. Part One precedes the chapters on the aims of argument and consists of relatively short chapters that focus on understanding argumentation in general, reading and analyzing arguments, doing research, and working with forms of visual persuasion such as advertising.

As examples of the aims of argument, the selections in Parts One and Two offer something for you to emulate. All writers learn from studying the strategies of other writers. The object is not so much to imitate what a more experienced writer does as it is to understand the range of approaches and strategies you might use in your own way and for your own purposes.

Included in this range of approaches are arguments made not only with words but also with images. Part One therefore includes some examples of editorial cartoons, advertisements, and photographs.

This book concludes with an appendix that focuses on editing, the art of polishing and refining prose, and on proofreading for some common errors. We suggest that you consult this reference repeatedly as you work through the text's assignments.

Arguing well is difficult for anyone. For many college students it is especially challenging because they have had little experience writing arguments. We have tried to write a text that is no more complicated than it has to be, and we welcome your comments so that we may improve future editions. Please write us at the following address:

The Rhetoric Program
Dallas Hall
Southern Methodist University
Dallas, Texas 75275

You may also e-mail us at the following address:
cchannel@mail.smu.edu

About the Authors

Timothy W. Crusius is professor of English at Southern Methodist University, where he teaches beginning and advanced composition. He's also the author of books on discourse theory, philosophical hermeneutics, and Kenneth Burke. He resides in Dallas with his wife, Elizabeth, and their children, Micah and Rachel.

Carolyn E. Channell taught high school and community college students before coming to Southern Methodist University, where she is now a senior lecturer and a specialist in first-year writing courses. She resides in Richardson, Texas, with her husband, David, and her "child"—a boxer named Heidi.

Contents

BOXES BY TYPE

Concept Close-Up Boxes

Best Practices Boxes

Part One Resources for Reading and Writing Arguments

Part One # Resources for Reading and Writing Arguments

Chapter 1

Understanding
Argument

The *Aims of Argument* is based on two key concepts: argument and rhetoric. These days, unfortunately, the terms *argument* and *rhetoric* have acquired bad reputations. The popular meaning of *argument* is *disagreement;* we
think of raised voices, hurt feelings, winners and losers. Most people think of
rhetoric, too, in a negative sense — as language that sounds good but evades or
hides the truth. In this sense, rhetoric is the language we hear from the politician who says whatever will win votes, the public relations person who puts
"positive spin" on dishonest business practices, the buck-passing bureaucrat
who blames the foul-up on someone else, the clever lawyer who counterfeits
passion to plead for the acquittal of a guilty client.

The words *argument* and *rhetoric,* then, are commonly applied to the
darker side of human acts and motives. This darker side is real — arguments
are often pointless and silly, ugly and destructive; all too often, rhetoric is
empty words contrived to mislead or to disguise the desire to exert power.
But this book is not about that kind of argument or that kind of rhetoric.
Here we develop the meanings of *argument* and *rhetoric* in an older, fuller,
and far more positive sense — as the language and art of mature reasoning.

WHAT IS ARGUMENT?

In this book, **argument** means *mature reasoning.* By *mature,* we mean an attitude and approach to argument, not an age group. Some older adults are incapable of mature reasoning, whereas some young people reason very well.
And all of us, regardless of age, sometimes fall short of mature reasoning —
when we are tired, bored, on edge, or when a situation pushes all the wrong
buttons. What is "mature" about the kind of argument we have in mind? One
meaning of *mature* is "worked out fully by the mind" or "considered" (*American Heritage Dictionary*). Mature decisions, for example, are thoughtful ones,
reached slowly after full consideration of all the consequences. And this is
true also of mature reasoning.

We also consider the second term in this definition of argument: *reasoning*. If we study logic in depth, we find many definitions of reasoning, but for practical purposes, *reasoning* here means *an opinion plus a reason (or reasons) for holding that opinion*. As we will see in detail later in this chapter, good arguments require more than this; to be convincing, reasons must be developed with evidence like specific facts and examples. However, understanding the basic form of opinion-plus-a-reason is the place to begin when considering your own and other people's arguments.

One way to understand argument as mature reasoning is to contrast it with *debate*. In debate, opponents take a predetermined, usually assigned, side and attempt to defend it, in much the same way that an army or a football team must hold its ground. The point is to win, to best one's opponent. In contrast, rather than starting with a position to defend, mature reasoners work toward a position. If they have an opinion to start with, mature reasoners think it through and evaluate it rather than rush to its defense. To win is not to defeat an opponent but rather to gain insight into the topic at hand. The struggle is with the problem, question, or issue we confront. Rather than seeking the favorable decision of the judges, as in debate, we are after a sound opinion in which we can believe—an opinion consistent with the facts and that other people will respect and take seriously.

Of course, having arrived at an opinion that seems sound to us, we still must *make our case*—argue in the sense of providing good reasons and adequate evidence in support of them. But whereas debaters must hold their positions at all costs, mature reasoners may not. The very process of making a case will often show us that what we thought was sound really isn't. We try to defend our opinion and find that we can't—or at least, not very well. And so we rethink our position until we arrive at one for which we *can* make a good case. From beginning to end, therefore, mature reasoning is a process of discovery. We find out what we really think about something and whether what we think holds water. It's a learning process. It's what makes argument worthwhile, not merely a test of our cleverness.

One other important difference from debate is this: Once we have arrived at a position we want to defend, the goal of mature reasoning is not to score points to impress an outside observer or judge. Our goal is to convince or persuade a real-life opponent to see the issue as we do. Mature reasoning takes into consideration those who disagree and their reasons for disagreeing. We must offer them reasons and evidence they can accept, and we must argue in a way that shows respect and charity, not aggression and anger. (See page 5.)

WHAT IS RHETORIC?

Over time, the meanings of most words in most languages change—sometimes only a little, sometimes a lot. The word *rhetoric* is a good example of a big change. As indicated already, the popular meaning of *rhetoric* is empty verbiage—the art of sounding impressive while saying little—or the art of

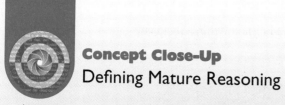

Concept Close-Up
Defining Mature Reasoning

Argument as mature reasoning means:

- Defending *not the first position* you might take on an issue *but the best position*, determined through open-minded inquiry
- Providing reasons for holding that position that can earn the respect of an opposing audience

verbal deception. This meaning of *rhetoric* confers a judgment, and not a positive one.

In contrast, in ancient Greece, where rhetoric was invented about 2,500 years ago, *rhetoric* referred to the art of public speaking. The Greeks recognized that rhetoric could be abused, but, for their culture in general, it was not a negative term. They had a goddess of persuasion (see Figure 1.1), and they respected the power of the spoken word to move people. It dominated their law courts, their governments, and their public ceremonies and events. As an art, the spoken word was an object of study. People enrolled in schools of rhetoric to become effective public speakers. Further, the ancient rhetoricians put a high value on good character. Not just sounding ethical but being known as an ethical person contributed to a speaker's persuasive power.

This old, highly valued meaning of rhetoric as oratory survived well into the nineteenth century. In Abraham Lincoln's day, Americans assembled by the thousands to hear speeches that went on for hours. For them, a good speech held the same level of interest as a big sporting event does for people today.

In this book, we are interested primarily in various ways of using *written* argument, but the rhetorical tradition informs our understanding of mature reasoning. Mature reasoning has nothing to do with the current definition of rhetoric as speech that merely sounds good or deceives people. The ancient meaning of *rhetoric* is more relevant, but we update it here to connect it directly with mature reasoning.

If argument is mature reasoning, then rhetoric is its *art*—that is, how we go about arguing with some degree of success. Just as there is an art of painting or sculpture, so is there an art of mature reasoning. Since the time of Aristotle, teachers of rhetoric have taught their students *self-conscious* ways of reasoning well and arguing successfully. The study of rhetoric, therefore, includes both what we have already defined as reasoning *and* ways of appealing to an audience. These include self-conscious efforts to project oneself as a good and intelligent person as well as efforts to connect with the audience through humor, passion, and image.

Note the emphasis on self-consciousness, which means awareness of what we are doing. Rhetoric teaches us how to make the best conscious choices when we put together an argument.

Figure 1.1   Peitho, the goddess of Persuasion, was often involved in seductions and love affairs. On this piece (a detail from a terracota kylix, c. 410 B.C.), Peitho, the figure on the left, gives advice to a dejected-looking woman, identified as Demonassa. To the right, Eros, the god of Love, stands with his hands on Demonassa's shoulder, suggesting the nature of this advice.

There's a sense in which no one has to teach anyone else how to argue; it's human nature. From the time they can talk, kids argue with other kids and with their parents. But the fact that we know how to argue doesn't mean that we do it well, as you probably know from looking at the daily letters to the editor in your local newspaper. To master the rhetorical arts, we need good models, much as we do when we work with conscious awareness on our serve in tennis or on our batting in baseball. And we must develop the habits and skills of good rhetoric, just as we do to gain proficiency in any art, whether it's singing, drawing, or cooking.

AN EXAMPLE OF ARGUMENT

So far, we've been talking about argument in the abstract — definitions and explanations. To really understand argument, especially as we define it here, we need a concrete example. One thing mature reasoning does is to challenge unexamined belief, the stances people take out of habit without much thought. The following argument by a syndicated columnist would have us consider more carefully our notion of "free speech."

Defining Rhetoric

Rhetoric is the art of argument as mature reasoning. The study of rhetoric develops self-conscious awareness of the principles and practices of mature reasoning and effective arguing.

You Also Have the Right to Tell a Bigot What You Think

Leonard Pitts

For the record, I have no idea who let the dogs out. I didn't even know the gate was open.

We Americans get hooked on saying some pretty silly things, you know? "Where's the beef?" "Make my day."

Generally, it is pretty harmless stuff. Granted, after the fifteenth time someone avows that he feels your pain, you probably are ready to inflict some of your own. But overall, yeah—pretty harmless.

There is, however, one expression that never fails to make me nuts. Truth be told, it is less a catchphrase than a cop-out, a meaningless thing people say—usually when accusations of racism, sexism, anti-Semitism or homophobia have been leveled and they are being asked to defend the indefensible.

"Entitled to my opinion," they say. Or "entitled to his opinion," as the   5
case may be. The sense of it is the same even when the words vary: People clamber atop the First Amendment and remind us that it allows them or someone they decline to criticize to say or believe whatever they wish.

It happened again just the other day, on the eve of the Grammys. One of the entertainment news programs did an informal poll of musicians, asking them to comment on the rapper Eminem's violently homophobic and misogynistic music. You would have sworn they all were reading from the same script: "He is entitled to say what he feels," they said.

In that, they echoed the folks who thought John Rocker was unfairly maligned for his bigotry: "He is entitled to his opinion," the ballplayer's defenders told us. And that, in turn, was an echo of what happened in 1993 when a reporter asked a student at City University of New York about Dr. Leonard Jeffries' claim of a Jewish conspiracy against black people. "He had a right to say whatever he chooses to say," the student replied.

As I said, it makes me crazy—not because the observation isn't correct, but because it is beside the point.

Anybody who is a more ardent supporter of the First Amendment than I probably ought to be on medication. I believe the liberties it grants are meaningless unless extended as far as possible into the ideological hinterlands. Only in this way can you preserve and defend those liberties for the rest of us. So, as far as I am concerned, every sexist, homophobe, communist, flag burner, Jew baiter, Arab hater and racist must be protected in the peaceful expression of his or her beliefs.

But after acknowledging the right of the hateful to be hateful and the 10
vile to be vile, it seems to me that the least I can do is use my own right of free speech to call those people what they are. It seems to me, in fact, that I have a moral obligation to do so. But many people embrace moral cowardice instead and blame it on the First Amendment.

It is a specious claim. The First Amendment is violated when the government seeks to censor expression. That didn't happen to Eminem. That didn't happen to John Rocker, either. What did happen was that the media and private citizens criticized them and demanded that some price—public condemnation or professional demotion—be extracted as a penalty for the stupid things they said.

Friends and neighbors, that isn't a violation of free speech. That *is* free speech. And if some folks confuse the issue, well, that is because too many of us believe freedom of speech means freedom from censure, the unfettered right to say whatever you please without anyone being allowed to complain. Worse, many of us accept that stricture for fear of seeming "judgmental." These days, of course, "judgmental" is a four-letter word.

I make no argument for being closed-minded. People ought to open themselves to the widest possible variety of ideas and expressions. But that doesn't mean losing your ability to discern or abdicating your responsibility to question, criticize . . . *think*. All ideas aren't created equal. To pretend otherwise is to create a rush from judgment—to free a bigot from taking responsibility for his beliefs and allow him a facade of moral validity to hide behind.

So I could happily live the rest of my life without being reminded that this fool or that has the right to say what he thinks. Sure, he does. But you know what? We all do.

Discussion of "You Also Have the Right [. . .]"

Leonard Pitts's argument is an example of a certain type or *genre* of written argument, the opinion column we find in the editorial section of newspapers. Arguments of this genre are usually brief and about some issue of general public concern, often an issue prominent in recent news stories. Most arguments written for college assignments are longer and deal with academic topics, but if we want to grasp the basics of mature reasoning, it's good to begin with the concise and readable arguments of professional columnists. Let's consider both the argument Pitts makes and his rhetoric—the art he uses to make his argument appealing to readers.

Pitts's Reasoning

In defining argument as mature reasoning, we stressed the process of arriving at an opinion as much as defending it. Arriving at an opinion is part of the aim of argument we call *inquiry,* and it's clearly very important for college writers who must deal with complex subjects and digest much information. Unfortunately, we can't see how authors arrived at their opinions by reading their finished work. As readers, we "come in" at the point where the writer states and argues for a position; we can't "go behind" it to appreciate how he or she got there. Consequently, all we can do with a published essay is discover how it works. That is, we can study its reasoning, its author's appeal to the readers' need for logical thinking.

Let's ask the first question we must ask of any argument we're analyzing: What is Pitts's opinion, or claim? If a piece of writing is indeed an argument, we should be able to see that the author has a clear position or opinion. We can call this the **claim** of the argument. It is what the author wants the audience to believe or to do.

All statements of opinion are answers to questions, usually **implied questions** because the question itself is too obvious to need spelling out. But when we study an argument, we must be willing to be obvious and spell it out anyway to see precisely what's going on. The question behind Pitts's argument is: What should we do when we hear someone making clearly bigoted remarks? His answer to the question is this: We have the right and even the moral obligation to "call those people what they are." That is his claim.

What reasons does he give his readers to convince them of his claim? He tells them that the common definition of freedom of speech is mistaken. Freedom of speech does not give everyone the right to say whatever he or she wants without fear of consequences, without even the expectation of being criticized. He thinks people use this definition as an excuse not to speak up when they hear or read bigotry.

In developing his reason, Pitts explains that this common definition is beside the point because no one is suggesting that people aren't entitled to their opinions. Of course they are, even if they are uninformed and full of hatred for some person or group of people. But freedom of speech is not the right to say anything without suffering consequences; rather, as Pitts says, it's a protection against government censorship, what's known in law as *prior restraint.* In other words, if a government authority prevents you from saying or printing something, that is censorship and a violation of the First Amendment in most cases. Nor should we feel that someone's rights have been taken away if a high price—for instance, "public condemnation or professional demotion" (paragraph 11)—must be paid for saying stupid things. The First Amendment does not protect us from the social or economic consequences of what we say or write. "All ideas aren't created equal," as Pitts maintains. Some deserve the condemnation they receive.

Now that we understand what Pitts is arguing, we can ask another question: What makes Pitts's argument mature, an example of the kind of reasoning worth learning how to do? First, it's mature in contrast to the opinion about free speech he criticizes, which clearly does not result from a close examination of what free speech means. Second, it's mature because it assumes civic responsibility. It's not a cop-out. It argues for doing the difficult thing because it is right and good for our society. It shows mature reasoning when it says: "People ought to open themselves to the widest possible variety of ideas and expressions. But that doesn't mean losing your responsibility to question, criticize . . . *think*." Finally, it's mature in contrast to another common response to bigotry that Pitts doesn't discuss—the view that "someone ought to shut that guy up" followed by violence or the threat of violence directed at the offending person. Such an attitude is neither different from nor better than the attitude of a playground bully, and the mature mind does not accept it.

In recognizing the maturity of Pitts's argument, we should not be too respectful of it. Ultimately, the point of laying out an argument is to respond to it maturely ourselves, and that means asking our own questions. For instance, we might ask:

When we say, "He's entitled to his opinion," are we *always* copping out, or is such a response justified in some circumstances?

Does it do any good to call a bigot a bigot? Is it wiser sometimes to just ignore hate speech?

How big a price is too big for stating a foolish opinion? Does it matter if a bigot later retracts his opinion, admits he was wrong, and apologizes?

One of the good things about mature arguments is that we can pursue them at length and learn a lot from discussing them.

Following Through

Select an opinion column on a topic of interest to your class from your local city or campus newspaper. Choose an argument that you think exemplifies mature reasoning. Discuss its reasoning as we have here with Pitts's essay. Can you identify the claim or statement of the author's opinion? The claim or opinion is what the author wants his or her readers to believe or to do. If you can find no exact sentence to quote, can you nevertheless agree on what it is he or she wants the readers to believe or to do? Can you find in the argument one or more reasons for doing so?

Other Appeals in Pitts's Argument

Finally, we ask, what makes Pitts's argument effective? That is, what makes it succeed with his readers? We have said that reasoning isn't enough when it comes to making a good argument. A writer, like a public speaker, must employ more than reason and make a conscious effort to project personality, to connect with his or her readers. Most readers seem to like Leonard Pitts because of his T-shirt-and-shorts informality and his conversational style, which includes remarks like "it makes me crazy" and sentence fragments like "But overall, yeah—pretty harmless."

We can't help forming impressions of people from reading what they write, and often these impressions correspond closely to how authors want us to perceive them anyway. Projecting good character goes all the way back to the advice of the ancient rhetoric teachers. Showing intelligence, fairness, and other signs of maturity will help you make an argument effectively, at least to an intelligent audience.

Pitts also makes a conscious effort to appeal to his readers (that is, to gain their support) by appealing to their feelings and acknowledging their attitudes. Appreciating Pitts's efforts here requires first that we think for a moment about who these people probably are. Pitts writes for the *Miami Herald*, but his column appears in many local papers across the United States. It's safe to say that the general public—those with time to read the newspaper and an interest in reactions to events in the news—are his readers. Because he is writing an argument, we assume he envisions them as not already seeing the situation as he sees it. They might be "guilty" of saying, "Everyone's entitled to an opinion." But he is not angry with them. He just wants to correct their misperception. Note that he addresses them as "friends and neighbors" in paragraph 12.

He does speak as a friend and neighbor, opening with some small talk, alluding to a popular song that made "Who let the dogs out" into a catch phrase. Humor done well is subtle, as here, and it tells the readers he knows they are as tired of this phrase as he is. Pitts is getting ready to announce his serious objection to one particular catch phrase, and he wants to project himself as a man with a life, an ordinary guy with common sense, not some neurotic member of the language police about to get worked up over nothing. Even though he shifts to a serious tone in the fourth paragraph, he doesn't completely abandon this casual and humorous personality—for example, in paragraph 9, where he jokes about his "ardent" support of the First Amendment.

But Pitts also projects a dead serious tone in making his point and in presenting his perspective as morally superior. One choice that conveys this attitude is his comment about people in the "ideological hinterlands": "every sexist, homophobe, communist, flag burner, Jew baiter, Arab hater and racist must be protected in the peaceful expression of his or her beliefs."

Following Through

For class discussion: What else in Pitts's argument strikes you as particularly good, conscious choices? What choices convey his seriousness of purpose? Pay special attention to paragraphs 9 and 13. Why are they
(continues)

Following Through (continued)

there? How do they show audience awareness? Which of Pitts's strategies or choices seem particularly appropriate for op-ed writing? Which might not be appropriate in an academic essay? One reason for noticing the choices professional writers make in their arguments is to learn some of their strategies, which you can use when writing your own arguments.

FOUR CRITERIA OF MATURE REASONING

Students often ask, "What does my professor want?" Although you will be writing many different kinds of papers in response to the assignments in this textbook, your professor will most likely look for evidence of mature reasoning. When we evaluate student work, we look for four criteria that we consider marks of mature reasoning. They will give you a better idea of what instructors have in mind when they talk about "good writing" in argumentation.

Mature Reasoners Are Well Informed

Your opinions must develop from knowledge and be supported by reliable and current evidence. If the reader feels that the writer "doesn't know his or her stuff," the argument loses all weight and force.

You may have noticed that people have opinions about all sorts of things, including subjects they know little or nothing about. The general human tendency is to have the strongest opinions on matters about which we know the least. Ignorance and inflexibility go together because it's easy to form an opinion when few or none of the facts get in the way and we can just assert our prejudices. Conversely, the more we know about most topics, the harder it is to be dogmatic. We find ourselves changing or at least refining our opinions more or less continuously as we gain more knowledge.

Of course, being well informed is not an absolute. We can be relatively knowledgeable about something and still not know that much compared to someone who has studied it for years. We can't be experts on everything we argue about. We should, however, recognize and admit the limitations of our knowledge. We should listen to those who know more. When the situation calls for more than tossing out a casual opinion—and college writing assignments always call for much more—you need to be sufficiently informed to respond appropriately.

Mature Reasoners Are Self-Critical and Open to Constructive Criticism from Others

We have opinions about all sorts of things that don't matter much to us, casual opinions we've picked up somehow and may not even bother to defend if challenged. But we also have opinions in which we are heavily invested, sometimes to the point that our whole sense of reality, right and wrong, good and bad—our very sense of ourselves—is tied up in them. These opinions we defend passionately.

On this count, popular argumentation and mature reasoning are alike. Mature reasoners are often passionate about their convictions, as committed to them as the fanatic on the street corner is to his or her cause. A crucial difference, however, separates the fanatic from the mature reasoner. The fanatic is all passion; the mature reasoner is able and willing to step back and examine even deeply held convictions. "I may have believed this for as long as I can remember," the mature reasoner says to him- or herself, "but is this conviction really justified? Do the facts support it? When I think it through, does it really make sense? Can I make a coherent and consistent argument for it?" These are questions that don't concern the fanatic and are seldom posed in the popular argumentation we hear on talk radio.

In practical terms, being self-critical and open to well-intended criticism boils down to this: Mature reasoners can and do change their minds when they have good reasons to do so. In popular argumentation, changing one's mind can be taken as a weakness, as "wishy-washy," and so people tend to go on advocating what they believe, regardless of what anyone else says. But there's nothing wishy-washy about, for example, confronting the facts, about realizing that what we thought is not supported by the available evidence. In such a case, far from being a weakness, changing one's mind is a sign of intelligence and the very maturity mature reason values. Nor is it a weakness to recognize a good point made against one's own argument. If we don't listen and take seriously what others say, they won't listen to us.

You may agree with all this and yet still feel uncomfortable. Perhaps you think that being critical is a fault. Perhaps, when you've been criticized in the past, you felt "picked on" or embarrassed. But there is such a thing as *constructive* and *friendly* criticism. The hostile sort is as out of place in mature reasoning as refusal to listen to any criticism, no matter how well intentioned. Let's look at it this way: We all have blind spots and prejudices. We all argue badly sometimes. We need others to help us see and correct our shortcomings. The golden rule certainly applies to mature reasoning.

Mature Reasoners Argue with Their Audience or Readers in Mind

Nothing drains energy from argument more than the feeling that it will accomplish nothing. As one student put it, "Why bother? People just go on thinking what they want to." This attitude is understandable. Popular, undisciplined argument often does seem futile: minds aren't changed; no progress is made; it's doubtful that anyone learned anything. Sometimes the opposing positions only harden, and the people involved are more at odds than before.

Why does this happen so often? One reason we've already mentioned—nobody's really listening to anyone else. We tend to hear only our own voices and see only from our own points of view. But there's another reason: The people making the arguments have made no effort to reach their audience. This is the other side of the coin of not listening—when we don't take other points of view seriously, we can't make our points of view appealing to those who don't already share them.

To have a chance of working, arguments must be *other-directed*, attuned to the people they want to reach. This may seem obvious, but it's also commonly ignored and not easy to do. We have to imagine the other guy. We have to care about other points of view, not just see them as obstacles to our own. We have to present and develop our arguments in ways that won't turn off the very people for whom we're writing. In many ways, *adapting to the audience* is the biggest challenge of argument.

Note that the challenge is *adapting to*, not manipulating. Mature reasoning is not a bag of tricks or a slick way to fool people into agreeing with us. Rather, *adapting to* means that we want a fair hearing, and so we "talk the talk," making a sincere effort to understand and connect with other people, other points of view.

Mature Reasoners Know Their Arguments' Contexts

All arguments are part of an ongoing conversation. We think of arguments as something individuals make. We think of our opinions as *ours*, almost like private property. But arguments and opinions have pasts: Other people argued about more or less the same issues and problems before—often long before—we came on the scene. They have a present: Who's arguing what now, the current state of the argument. And they have a future: What people will be arguing about tomorrow, in different circumstances, with knowledge we don't have now.

So most arguments are not the isolated events they seem to be. Part of being well informed is knowing something about the history of an argument. By understanding an argument's past, we learn about patterns that will help us develop our own position. To some extent, we must know what's going on now and what other people are saying to make our own reasoning relevant. And although we can't know the future, we can imagine the drift of the argument, where it might be heading. In other words, there's a larger context we need to join—a big conversation of many voices to which our few belong.

Throughout this book, we'll emphasize the backgrounds or contexts of arguments and try to heighten your awareness of them. For now, remember this: Arguments are living things, and like all living things, they evolve. When we argue, we are part of a flow of life, part of a conversation going on in many places and among many people. The more aware we are of the big conversation, the better we'll argue in our smaller ones.

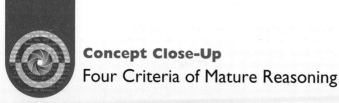

Concept Close-Up
Four Criteria of Mature Reasoning

Mature Reasoners Are Well Informed
Their opinions develop out of knowledge and are supported by reliable and current evidence.

Mature Reasoners Are Self-Critical and Open to Constructive Criticism
They balance their passionate attachment to their opinions with willingness to evaluate and test them against differing opinions, acknowledge when good points are made against their opinions, and even, when presented with good reasons for doing so, change their minds.

Mature Reasoners Argue with Their Audiences in Mind
They make a sincere effort to understand and connect with other people and other points of view because they do not see differences of opinion as obstacles to their own points of view.

Mature Reasoners Know Their Arguments' Contexts
They recognize that what we argue about now was argued about in the past and will be argued about in the future, that our contributions to these ongoing conversations are influenced by who we are, what made us who we are, where we are, what's going on around us—just as those arguing about the topic before and after us were and will be subject to similar influences.

Following Through

Look again at the article by Leonard Pitts on pages 7–8. Do you see mature reasoning in his essay? Cite passages you think are especially indicative of our criteria.

WHAT ARE THE AIMS OF ARGUMENT?

The heart of this book is the section entitled "The Aims of Argument." In conceiving this book, we worked from one basic premise: Mature reasoners do not argue just to argue; rather, they use argument to accomplish something: *to inquire* into a question, problem, or issue (commonly part of the research process); *to convince* their readers to assent to an opinion, or claim; *to persuade* readers to take action, such as buying a product or voting for a candidate; and *to mediate* conflict, as in labor disputes, divorce proceedings, and so on.

Let's look at each of these aims in more detail.

Arguing to Inquire

Arguing to **inquire** is using reasoning to determine the best position on an issue. We open the "Aims" section with inquiry because mature reasoning is not a matter of defending what we already believe but of questioning it. Arguing to inquire helps us form opinions, question opinions we already have, and reason our way through conflicts or contradictions in other people's arguments on a topic. Inquiry is open minded, and it requires that we make an effort to find out what people who disagree think and why.

The ancient Greeks called argument as inquiry **dialectic;** today we might think of it as dialogue or serious conversation. There is nothing confrontational about such conversations; they are friendly. We have them with friends, family, and colleagues, even with ourselves. We have these conversations in writing, too, as we make notations in the margins of the arguments we read. Listserv groups engage in inquiry about subjects of mutual interest.

Inquiry centers on questions and involves some intellectual legwork to answer them—finding the facts, doing research. This is true whether you are inquiring into what car to buy, what major to choose in college, what candidate to vote for, or what policy our government should pursue on any given issue. A research scientist may devote years, even a lifetime, to formulating, testing, and reformulating hypotheses that explore a single set of phenomena, like black holes. Businesspeople must find solutions to practical problems, such as how to increase sales in a region of the country or how to anticipate changes in societal attitudes. Inquiry takes work, but without it the world would stall. What kind of world would we live in if no one questioned what they already knew or believed? Through inquiry, we don't just take a position—we earn it.

Arguing to Convince

We've seen that the goal of inquiry is to reach some kind of conclusion on an issue. This conclusion can go by many names, but we'll call it a **conviction** and define it as "an earned opinion, achieved through careful thought, research, and discussion." Once we arrive at a conviction, we usually want others to share it. The aim of further argument is to secure the assent of people who do not share our conviction (or who do not share it fully). Such assent is an agreement of minds secured by reason rather than by force.

Argument to **convince** centers on making a case, which means offering reasons and evidence in support of our opinion. Arguments to convince are all around us. In college, we find them in scholarly and professional writing. For example, one historian has just concluded that the dancer known during World War I as Mata Hari was not a dangerous spy and should not have been executed by the French. His book presents his case for this conclusion. In everyday life, we find arguments to convince in editorials, in the courtrooms, and in political speeches. Whenever we encounter an opinion supported by reasons and asking us to agree, we are dealing with argument to convince. Whenever we as writers intend to gain the intellectual agreement of our readers, to get them to say, "You're right," we are arguing to convince.

Arguing to Persuade

Like convincing, persuasion attempts to earn agreement, but it aims further. **Persuasion** attempts to influence not just thinking but also behavior. It motivates. An advertisement for Mercedes-Benz aims to convince us not only that the company makes a high-quality car but also that we should go out and buy one. A Sunday sermon asks for more than agreement with some interpretation of a biblical passage; the minister wants the congregation to live according to its message. Persuasion asks us to do something—spend money, give money, join a demonstration, recycle, vote, enlist, acquit. Because we don't always act on our convictions, persuasion cannot rely on reasoning alone. It must appeal in broader, deeper ways.

Persuasion appeals to readers' emotions. It tells stories about individual cases of hardship that move us to pity. It often uses photographs, as when charities confront us with pictures of poverty or suffering. Visual persuasion plays a role in architecture, from cathedrals to shopping malls. Persuasion uses many of the devices of poetry, such as patterns of sound, repetitions, metaphors, and similes to arouse a desired emotion in the audience.

Persuasion also relies on the personality of the writer to an even greater degree than does convincing. The persuasive writer attempts to represent something "higher" or "larger" than him- or herself—some ideal with which the reader would like to be associated. For example, a war veteran and hero like John McCain naturally brings patriotism to the table when he makes a speech.

Persuasion is one form of argument that some people distrust, and with good reason. It's important to note the difference between ethical persuasion and manipulation or even propaganda. We believe persuasion's role in the world cannot be denied. We need to study it so that we can make intelligent responses to it wherever it occurs—in the marketplace, the political arena, or the jury room. But we also need to study it to use it effectively in our work and public lives.

Arguing to Negotiate

By the time we find ourselves in a situation where our aim is to **negotiate,** we will have already attempted to convince an opponent of our case and to persuade that opponent to settle a conflict or dispute to our satisfaction. Our opponent will no doubt also have used convincing and persuading in an attempt to move us similarly. Yet neither side will have been able to secure the assent of the other, and "agreeing to disagree" is not a practical solution because the participants must come to some agreement in order to pursue a necessary course of action.

In most instances of negotiation, the parties involved try to work out the conflict themselves because they have some relationship they wish to preserve—as employer and employee, business partners, family members, neighbors, even coauthors of an argument textbook. Common differences requiring negotiation include the amount of a raise or the terms of a contract, the wording of a bill in a congressional committee, and trade agreements among nations. In private life, negotiation helps roommates live together and families decide on everything from budgets to vacation destinations.

Just like other aims of argument, arguing to negotiate requires sound logic and the clear presentation of positions and reasons. However, negotiation challenges our interpersonal skills more than do the other aims. Each side must listen closely to understand not just the other side's case but also the other side's emotional commitments and underlying values. Initiating such a conversation and keeping it going sometimes can be so difficult that an outside party, a mediator, must assist in the process. With or without a mediator, when negotiation works, the opposing sides begin to converge. Exchanging viewpoints and information and building empathy enable all parties to make concessions, to loosen their hold on their original positions, and finally to reach consensus—or at least a resolution that all participants find satisfactory.

As Chapter 6 makes clear, this final aim of argument brings us full circle, back to *dialogue*, to the processes involved in arguing to inquire. The major difference is that in negotiation we are less concerned with our own claims to truth than we are with overcoming conflict, with finding some common ground that will allow us to live and work together.

WHERE ARE THE AIMS OF ARGUMENT USED?

Although most college writing assignments in other courses will ask you to argue to convince, we think it's important to learn to argue with a full range of aims. In the future, you will need to argue well not just for academic purposes but also about public issues and problems you'll encounter "out there," in public meetings, in business settings, and so on. The first two aims are therefore most appropriate for college argumentation; the last two are for public or civic argumentation. (See the Concept Close-Up box on page 19.) By structuring the book in this way, we intend to offer specific guidance toward arguing well as both a student and a citizen.

A GOOD TOOL FOR UNDERSTANDING AND WRITING ARGUMENTS: THE WRITER'S NOTEBOOK

As you've probably already noticed, argumentation places unique demands on readers and writers. One of the most helpful tools that you can use to meet these demands is a writer's notebook.

Concept Close-Up
Comparing the Aims of Argument

The aims of argument have much in common. For example, besides sharing argument, they all tend to draw on sources of knowledge (research) and to deal with controversial issues. But the aims also differ from one another, mainly in terms of purpose, audience, situation, and method, as summarized here and on the inside front cover.

	Purpose	Audience	Situation	Method
Inquiry	Seeks truth	Oneself, friends, and colleagues	Informal; a dialogue	Questions
Convincing	Seeks assent to a thesis	Less intimate; wants careful reasoning	More formal; a monologue	Case-making
Persuading	Seeks action	More broadly public, less academic	Pressing need for a decision	Appeals to reason and emotions
Negotiating	Seeks consensus	Polarized by differences	Need to cooperate, preserve relations	"Give-and-take"

We offer this chart as a general guide to the aims of argument. Think of it as the "big picture" you can always return to as you work your way through Part Two, which deals with each of the aims in detail.

We hope you will explore on your own how the aims converge and diverge and how they overlap and interact in specific cases.

The main function of a writer's notebook is to help you sort out what you read, learn, accomplish, and think as you go through the stages of creating a finished piece of writing. A writer's notebook contains the writing you do before you write; it's a place to sketch out ideas, assess research, order what you have to say, and determine strategies and goals for writing.

Why Keep a Notebook?

Some projects require extensive research and consultation, which involve compiling and assessing large amounts of data and working through complex chains of reasoning. Under such conditions, even the best memory will fail without the aid of a notebook. Given life's distractions, we often forget too much and imprecisely recall what we do manage to remember. With a writer's notebook, we can preserve the idea that come to us as we walk across campus or stare into space over our morning coffee. Often, a writer's notebook even provides sections of writing that can be incorporated into your papers and so can help you save time.

Any entry that helps or that you may want to use for future reference is appropriate to make in your writer's notebook. It's for private exploration, for your eyes only—so don't worry about organization, spelling, or grammar. Following are some specific possibilities.

To Explore Issues You Encounter in and out of Class

Bring your notebook to class each day. Use it to respond to ideas presented in class and in every reading assignment. When you're assigned a topic, write down your first impressions and opinions about it. When you're to choose your own topic, use the notebook to respond to controversial issues in the news or on campus. Your notebook then becomes a source of ideas for your essays.

To Record and Analyze Assignments

Staple your instructors' handouts to a notebook page, or write the assignment down word for word. Take notes as your instructor explains the assignment. Later, look it over more carefully, circling and checking key words, underlining due dates and other requirements. Record your questions, ask your instructor as soon as possible, and jot down the answers.

To Work Out Timetables for Completing Assignments

To avoid procrastination, schedule. Divide the task into blocks—preparing and researching, writing a first draft, revising, editing, final typing and proofreading—and work out how many days you can devote to each. Your schedule may change as you complete the assignment, but making a schedule and attempting to stick to it should help you avoid last-minute scrambling.

To Make Notes As You Research

Record ideas, questions, and preliminary conclusions that occur to you as you read, discuss your ideas with others, conduct experiments, compile surveys and questionnaires, consult with experts, and pursue information on your topic. Keep your notebook handy at all times; write down ideas as soon as possible and assess their value later.

To Respond to Arguments You Hear or Read

To augment the notes you make in the margins of books, jot down more extended responses in your notebook. Evaluate the strengths and weaknesses of texts, compare an argument with other arguments; make notes on how to use what you read to build your own arguments. Note page numbers to make it easier to use this information later.

To Write a Rhetorical Prospectus

A *prospectus* details a plan for proposed work. A **rhetorical prospectus** will start you thinking about *what, to whom, how,* and *why* you are writing. In your notebook, explore and then briefly outline:

Your thesis: What are you claiming?

Your aim: What do you want to accomplish?

Your audience: Who should read this? Why? What are these people like?

Your persona: What is your relationship to the audience? How do you want them to perceive you?

Your subject matter: What does your thesis obligate you to discuss? What do you need to learn more about? How do you plan to get the information?

Your organizational plan: What should you talk about first? Where might that lead? What might you end with?

To Record Useful Feedback

Points in the writing process when it is useful to seek feedback from other students and the instructor include:

When your *initial ideas* have taken shape, to discover how well you can explain your ideas to others and how they respond

After you and other students have *completed research* on similar topics, to share information and compare evaluations of sources

Upon completion of a *first draft,* to uncover what you need to do in a second draft to accommodate readers' needs, objections, and questions

At the end of the *revising process,* to correct surface problems such as awkward sentences, usage errors, misspellings, and typos

Prepare specific questions to ask others, and use your notebook to jot them down; leave room to sum up the comments you receive.

To Assess a Graded Paper

Look over your instructor's comments carefully, and write down anything useful for future reference. For example, what did you do well? What might you carry over to the next assignment? Is there a pattern in the shortcomings your instructor has pointed out? If so, list the types of problems you discover. Refer to these notes when you compose the next essay.

In the chapters that follow, we refer frequently to your writer's notebook. Whether or not you keep one may depend on your instructor's requirements, but we hope you'll try out this excellent tool.

Following Through

What issues do you currently have strong opinions about? Although you can look to today's newspaper or the evening news for inspiration, also think about events you've noticed on campus, at your job, or around your town — a change in course requirements for your planned major, a conflict over some aspect of your work environment, or a proposed land development near your house. Write a notebook entry in which you list several possible topics for written arguments. Then pick one or two, and create the briefest of arguments — a statement of your position followed by a statement of your best reason for holding that position. Think about who the audience for such an argument could be. Think also about your aim: Would you be arguing to inquire, convince, persuade, or negotiate?

Chapter 2

Reading an Argument

In a course in argumentation, you will read many arguments. Our book contains a wide range of argumentative essays, some by students, some by established professionals. In addition, you may find arguments on your own in books, newspapers, and magazines, or on the Internet. You'll read them to develop your understanding of argument. That means you will analyze and evaluate these texts—known as **critical reading.** Critical reading involves special skills and habits that are not essential when you read a book for information or entertainment. This chapter discusses skills and habits that are essential when an assignment involves writing an analysis of an argument or researching an argument of your own.

By the time most students get to high school, reading as a subject has dropped out of the curriculum. While there's plenty to read in high school and college, any advice on *how to read* is usually about increasing vocabulary or reading speed, not reading critically. This is too bad, because in high school and college you are called upon to read more critically than ever, and doing it well is not just a matter of time or intuition.

So have patience with yourself and with the texts you work with in this course. Reading each text will involve much more than reading it through once, no matter how careful that single reading may be. You will go back and look at the text again and again, asking new questions each time. That takes patience; but we ourselves read and reread a text, analyzing it thoroughly, when we prepare to teach it in class. Just as when one sees a film a second time, one notices new details, so it is with critical reading, whether one is a student or a teacher. We suggest three different encounters to have with a text in the process of reading it critically—not three linear, line-by-line readings, but three visits to the text in which you practice different critical-reading skills and habits.

Before we start, a bit of advice: Attempt critical reading only when your mind is fresh. Some experts on reading half-jokingly have suggested "rules" for reading when your purpose is to put yourself to sleep: "Get into bed in a comfortable position, make sure the light is inadequate. . . ." Conversely, when your purpose is to stay alert, find a time and place conducive to that goal—such as a table in the library. As you will see, critical reading is about being an active reader, not a passive one.

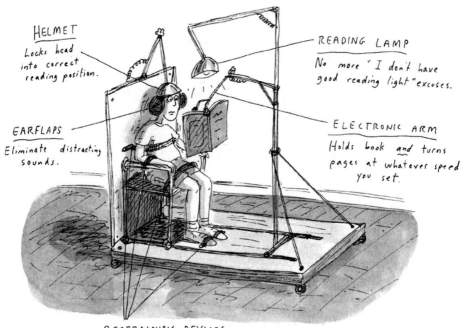

HELMET
Locks head into correct reading position.

READING LAMP
No more "I don't have good reading light" excuses.

EARFLAPS
Eliminate distracting sounds.

ELECTRONIC ARM
Holds book and turns pages at whatever speed you set.

RESTRAINING DEVICES
Prevent reader from leaving machine for snacks, phone calls, quick channel flip-throughs, etc.

THE FIRST ENCOUNTER: SEEING THE TEXT IN CONTEXT

Critical reading begins not with a line-by-line reading but with a fast over-view of the whole text, followed by some thinking about how the text fits into a bigger picture, or *context,* which we describe shortly.

We like to use the word *sampling* to explain the first critical encounter with a text. Sampling can be fast, superficial, and not even sequential. Look at how long the text is. Look at the headings and subdivisions, if such exist. Get a sense of how the text is organized. Note what parts look interesting and which ones look boring or hard to understand. Note any information about the author appearing before or after the text itself, as well as any publication information (where and when the piece was originally published). Most im-portant, look at the opening and closing paragraphs to discern the author's main point or view.

Experts have found that reading comprehension depends less on a large vocabulary than on the ability to see how the text fits into contexts. Sampling will help you consider the text in light of two contexts that are particularly important:

1. *The general climate of opinion* surrounding the topic of the text. This includes debate on the topic both before and since the text's publication.
2. *The rhetorical context* of the text. This includes facts about the au-thor, the intended audience, and the setting in which the argument takes place.

Considering the Climate of Opinion

Your familiarity with the topic of an argument and the climate of opinion surrounding it naturally will help you read critically. Imagine trying to cri-tique an argument written over two hundred years ago protesting the condi-tion of the poor in Ireland if you had no knowledge of social conditions in Ireland at the time or of the politics of English rule over Ireland. Yet many high school students are asked to analyze Jonathan Swift's "A Modest Pro-posal" without the knowledge of history—the context—that would enable them to understand it. The arguments reproduced in this text are more recent than Swift's essay; their topics are likely to have caught your attention already through TV, reading, or personal experience. But thinking about the climate of opinion surrounding them, including your own preconceptions, is still necessary.

Familiarity with the climate of opinion will help you view any argu-ment critically, recognize a writer's biases and assumptions, and spot gaps or errors in the information. Your own perspective, too, will affect your interpretation of the text. So think about what you know, how you know it, what your opinion is, and what might have led to its formation. The text is not just "out there"—you will interact with it, so be aware of yourself as a participant.

We suggest that before reading an assigned argument, you and your classmates discuss the topic and the climate of opinion surrounding it so that all can learn what others know about the context of the essay. More formally, your instructor may ask you to write in your writer's notebook a summary of your prior knowledge of topic and the climate of opinion surrounding it.

Following Through

An argument on the topic of body decoration (tattoos and piercing) appears later in this chapter. More specifically, "On Teenagers and Tattoos" is about motives for decorating the body. Imagine that you are about to read this argument, and practice identifying the climate of opinion surrounding this topic. Think about what people say about motives for tattooing and piercing. Have you heard people argue that it is "low-class"? a rebellion against middle-class conformity? immoral? an artistic expression? a fad? an affront to school or parental authority? an expression of individuality? If you would not want a tattoo, why not? If you have a tattoo or a piercing, why did you get it? In your writer's notebook, jot down some positions you have heard debated, and state your own viewpoint. Why do you feel as you do? If you have no opinions on the topic, why hasn't it become an issue for you?

Considering the Rhetorical Context

Critical readers also are aware of the **rhetorical context** of an argument. They do not see the text merely as words on a page but as a contribution to some debate among interested people. When you look at rhetorical context, you are considering the text as communication and identifying its elements: the author, to whom he or she was writing and why, as well as where and when the argument was written (its date and place of publication). The reader who knows in advance something about the author's politics or affiliations will have an advantage over the reader who does not. For example, knowing if the periodical that printed it was liberal, like *The Nation,* or conservative, like *National Review,* will also enable you to read more intelligently.

An understanding of rhetorical context comes from both external and internal clues—information outside the text and information you gather as you read and reread it. You can gather a lot of information about rhetorical

To determine an argument's rhetorical context, answer the following questions:

Who wrote this argument, and what are his or her occupation, personal background, and political leanings?

To whom do you think the author is writing? Arguments are rarely aimed at "the general public" but rather at a definite target audience, such as "entertainment industry moguls," "drivers in Dallas," or "parents of teenagers."

Where does the article appear? If it is reprinted, where did it appear originally? What do you know about the publication?

When was the argument written? If not recently, what do you know about the time during which it appeared?

Why was the article written? What prompted its creation, and what purpose does the author have for writing? (In order to answer this last question, you will probably have to read the argument.)

context from external evidence such as publishers' notes about the author or about a magazine's editorial board or sponsoring foundation. You can usually find this information in a column in the first few pages or by following an information link on the homepage of an online publication. On the Internet, though, check out the homepage for this kind of background before you waste time reading something because much material on the Internet is propaganda rather than serious argument.

You may also have prior knowledge of rhetorical context—for example, you may have heard of the author. Or you can look in a database such as *Info-Trac* (see pages 110, 117–118) to see what else the author has written. Later, when you read the argument more thoroughly, you will enlarge your understanding of rhetorical context as you discover what the text itself reveals about the author's bias, character, and purpose for writing.

One of the biggest differences between high school research and college research is knowledge of rhetorical context. This awareness deepens with repeated encounters with the text, but as you sample an argument, you should begin to see it as an act of communication, taking place at a certain time, for a reason, between an author and an audience.

In sum, the first encounter with a text is preliminary to a careful, close reading. It prepares you to get the most out of the second encounter. If you are researching a topic and looking for good sources of information and viewpoints about it, the first encounter with any text will help you decide whether you want to read it at all. A first encounter can be a time-saving last encounter if the text does not seem appropriate or credible.

Following Through

Read the following information about "On Teenagers and Tattoos."

> *When* published: First published in 1997, reprinted in fall 2000.
> *Where* published: First in the *Journal of Child and Adolescent Psychiatry,* which is published by the American Academy of Child and Adolescent Psychiatry, then reprinted in a journal entitled *Reclaiming Children and Youth.*
> Written by *whom:* Andres Martin, MD. Martin is identified as an assistant professor of child psychiatry at the Yale Child Study Center in New Haven, CT.

Then do a fast sampling of the text itself, which appears on pages 28–32. In your writer's notebook, make some notes about what you expect to find in this argument. What do you expect the author's perspective to be on the topic, and why? How might it differ from that of a teen, a parent, a teacher? Do the subheadings give you any idea of the main point? Do you notice at the opening or closing any repeated ideas that might give a clue to the author's claim? To whom do you imagine the author was writing, and what might be the purpose of an essay in a journal such as the one that published his argument?

On Teenagers and Tattoos
Andres Martin

The skeleton dimensions I shall now proceed to set down are copied verbatim from my right arm, where I had them tattooed: as in my wild wanderings at that period, there was no other secure way of preserving such valuable statistics.

—MELVILLE, *Moby Dick*

Tattoos and piercing have become a part of our everyday landscape. They are ubiquitous, having entered the circles of glamour and the mainstream of fashion, and they have even become an increasingly common feature of our urban youth. Legislation in most states restricts professional tattooing to adults older than 18 years of age, so "high end" tattooing is rare in children and adolescents, but such tattoos are occasionally seen in older teenagers. Piercings, by comparison, as well as self-made or "jailhouse" type tattoos, are not at all rare among adolescents or even among school-age children. Like hairdo, makeup, or baggy jeans, tattoos and piercings can be subject to fad influence or peer pressure in an effort toward group affiliation. As with any other fashion statement, they can be construed as bodily aids in the inner struggle toward identity consolidation, serving as adjuncts

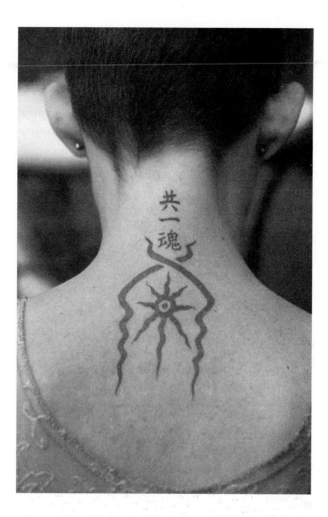

to the defining and sculpting of the self by means of external manipulations. But unlike most other body decorations, tattoos and piercings are set apart by their irreversible and permanent nature, a quality at the core of their magnetic appeal to adolescents.

Adolescents and their parents are often at odds over the acquisition of bodily decorations. For the adolescent, piercing or tattoos may be seen as personal and beautifying statements, while parents may construe them as oppositional and enraging affronts to their authority. Distinguishing bodily adornment from self-mutilation may indeed prove challenging, particularly when a family is in disagreement over a teenager's motivations and a clinician is summoned as the final arbiter. At such times it may be most important to realize jointly that the skin can all too readily become but another battleground for the tensions of the age, arguments having less to do with tattoos and piercings than with core issues such as separation from the family matrix. Exploring the motivations and significance [underlying] tattoos (Grumet, 1983) and piercings can go a long way toward resolving such differences and can become a novel and additional way of getting to know teenagers. An interested and nonjudgmental appreciation of teenagers' surface presentations may become a way of making contact not only in their terms but on their turfs: quite literally on the territory of their skins.

The following three sections exemplify some of the complex psychological underpinnings of youth tattooing.

Identity and the Adolescent's Body

Tattoos and piercing can offer a concrete and readily available solution for many of the identity crises and conflicts normative to adolescent development. In using such decorations, and by marking out their bodily territories, adolescents can support their efforts at autonomy, privacy, and insulation. Seeking individuation, tattooed adolescents can become unambiguously demarcated from others and singled out as unique. The intense and often disturbing reactions that are mobilized in viewers can help to effectively keep them at bay, becoming tantamount to the proverbial "Keep Out" sign hanging from a teenager's door.

Alternatively, feeling prey to a rapidly evolving body over which they have no say, self-made and openly visible decorations may restore adolescents' sense of normalcy and control, a way of turning a passive experience into an active identity. By indelibly marking their bodies, adolescents can strive to reclaim their bearings within an environment experienced as alien, estranged, or suffocating or to lay claim over their evolving and increasingly unrecognizable bodies. In either case, the net outcome can be a resolution to unwelcome impositions: external, familial, or societal in one case; internal and hormonal in the other. In the words of a 16-year-old girl with several facial piercings, and who could have been referring to her body just as well as to the position within her family: "If I don't fit in, it is because I say so."

Incorporation and Ownership

Imagery of a religious, deathly, or skeletal nature, the likenesses of fierce animals or imagined creatures, and the simple inscription of names are some of the time-tested favorite contents for tattoos. In all instances, marks become not only memorials or recipients for dearly held persons or concepts: they strive for incorporation, with images and abstract symbols gaining substance on becoming a permanent part of the individual's skin. Thickly embedded in personally meaningful representations and object relations, tattoos can become not only the ongoing memento of a relationship, but at times even the only evidence that there ever was such a bond. They can quite literally become the relationship itself. The turbulence and impulsivity of early attachments and infatuations may become grounded, effectively bridging oblivion through the visible reality to tattoos.

Case Vignette: "A," a 13-year-old boy, proudly showed me his tattooed deltoid. The coarsely depicted roll of the dice marked the day and month of his birth. Rather disappointed, he then uncovered an immaculate back, going on to draw for me the great "piece" he envisioned for it. A menacing figure held a hand of cards: two aces, two eights, and a card with two sets of dates. "A's" father had belonged to Dead Man's Hand, a motorcycle gang named after the set of cards (aces and eights) that the legendary Wild Bill Hickock had held in the 1890s when shot dead over a poker table in Deadwood, South Dakota. "A" had only the vaguest memory of and sketchiest information about his father, but he knew he had died in a motorcycle accident: The fifth card marked the dates of his birth and death.

The case vignette also serves to illustrate how tattoos are often the culmination of a long process of imagination, fantasy, and planning that can start at an early age. Limited markings, or relatively reversible ones such as piercings, can at a later time scaffold toward the more radical commitment of a permanent tattoo.

The Quest of Permanence

The popularity of the anchor as a tattoo motif may historically have had to do less with guild identification among sailors than with an intense longing for rootedness and stability. In a similar vein, the recent increase in the popularity and acceptance of tattoos may be understood as an antidote or counterpoint to our urban and nomadic lifestyles. Within an increasingly mobile society, in which relationships are so often transient — as attested by the frequencies of divorce, abandonment, foster placement, and repeated moves, for example — tattoos can be a readily available source of grounding. Tattoos, unlike many relationships, can promise permanence and stability. A sense of constancy can be derived from unchanging marks that can be carried along no matter what the physical, temporal, or geographical vicissitudes at hand. Tattoos stay, while all else may change.

Case Vignette: A proud father at 17, "B" had had the smiling face of his 4-month-old baby girl tattooed on his chest. As we talked at a tattoo convention, he proudly introduced her to me, explaining how he would "always know how beautiful she is today" when years from then he saw her semblance etched on himself.

The quest for permanence may at other times prove misleading and offer premature closure to unresolved conflicts. At a time of normative uncertainties, adolescents may maladaptively and all too readily commit to a tattoo and its indefinite presence. A wish to hold on to a current certainty may

10

lead the adolescent to lay down in ink what is valued and cherished one day but may not necessarily be in the future. The frequency of self-made tattoos among hospitalized, incarcerated, or gang-affiliated youths suggests such motivations: A sense of stability may be a particularly dire need under temporary, turbulent, or volatile conditions. In addition, through their designs teenagers may assert a sense of bonding and allegiance to a group larger than themselves. Tattoos may attest to powerful experiences, such as adolescence itself, lived and even survived together. As with Moby Dick's protagonist, Ishmael, they may bear witness to the "valuable statistics" of one's "wild wandering(s)": those of adolescent exhilaration and excitement on the one hand; of growing pains, shared misfortune, or even incarceration on the other.

Adolescents' bodily decorations, at times radical and dramatic in their presentation, can be seen in terms of figuration rather than disfigurement, of the natural body being through them transformed into a personalized body (Brain, 1979). They can often be understood as self-constructive and adorning efforts, rather than prematurely subsumed as mutilatory and destructive acts. If we bear all of this in mind, we may not only arrive at a position to pass more reasoned clinical judgment, but become sensitized through our patients' skins to another level of their internal reality.

References[1]

Brain, R. (1979). *The decorated body.* New York: Harper & Row.

Grumet, G. W. (1983). Psychodynamic implications of tattoos. *American Journal of Orthopsychiatry, 53,* 482–92.

THE SECOND ENCOUNTER: READING AND ANALYZING THE TEXT

We turn now to suggestions for reading and analyzing. These are our own "best practices," what we writing instructors ourselves do when we prepare to discuss or write about a written text. Remember, when you read critically, your purpose goes beyond reading merely to find out what an argument says and to agree or disagree. The critical reader is different from the target audience. As a critical reader, you are more like the food critic who dines not merely to eat but to evaluate the chef's efforts.

In the second encounter, you will read the text through carefully, rereading difficult passages and attempting to clarify in your own mind not only what the text says but also how it works as an argument. Here again, we emphasize the difference between reading and critical reading.

---

[1] These references are formatted in the style recommended by the American Psychological Association, the style used by many scholarly journals in the social sciences.

To see the difference, consider the different perspectives that an ant and a bird would have when looking at the same suburban lawn. The ant is down among the blades of grass, climbing one and then the next. It's a close look, but the view is limited. The bird in the sky above looks down, noticing the size and shape of the yard, the brown patches, the difference between the grass in this yard and the grass in the surrounding yards. The bird has the big picture, the ant the close-up. Critical readers move back and forth between the perspective of the ant and the perspective of the bird, each perspective enriching the other. The big picture helps one notice the larger details, even as the details offer clues to the big picture.

Because critical reading means interacting with the text, be ready with pencil or pen to mark up the text to help yourself understand what it says and how it works. Highlighting or underlining are not the most helpful marks you can make; all they tell you later is that you read those lines and for some reason thought that passage was important. Later, we suggest more useful ways to mark up an argument. Finally, the observations you made in your first encounter with the text are not just so many facts to file away. As you read, keep in mind what you know about the topic, its climate of opinion, and the rhetorical context for this specific argument. All of this information will aid you in comprehending the text.

Wrestling with Difficult Passages

Because one goal of the second encounter is to understand the argument fully, you will need to figure out the meanings of unfamiliar words and difficult passages. In most college-level texts, you will find some difficult passages, especially if you are not part of the original audience, the one you identified as part of the rhetorical context. You may encounter new words. You may find allusions or references to other books or authors that you have not read. You may find that an author speaks figuratively rather than directly, using metaphors. The author may speak ironically or for another person. The author may assume that readers have lived through all that he or she has or that readers share the same political viewpoint. All of this can make reading harder. Following are some features that often make reading difficult.

Unfamiliar Contexts

If the author and his or her intended audience are removed from your own experiences, perspectives, and store of knowledge about the world, you will find the text difficult. Texts from a distant culture or period in history will necessarily include concepts familiar to the original writer and readers but not to you. This is true also of contemporary writing intended for a group of specialists. Even a general newspaper such as the *New York Times* publishes articles and editorials aimed at audiences familiar with certain scholarly theories, such as postmodernism in literature, art, and philosophy. And if you have lived a life removed from much discussion of politics or ideologies, you may miss the political agenda in a piece of writing. The role of college is to increase your store of such concepts and introduce you to new (and ancient) perspectives on the world. Accepting the challenge of difficult texts is part of that education. Seek help when you are confused. Your instructors are there to help you bridge the gaps between your world and that of your texts.

Contrasting Voices and Views

Authors often put into their texts viewpoints that contradict their own. They may concede that part of an opposing argument is true, or they may put in an opposing view in order to refute it. These voices and viewpoints may be in the form of direct quotations or paraphrases. In order to avoid misreading these views as the author's, be alert to words that signal contrast. The most common are *but* and *however*. Much confusion can result from failure to note these turning points in a text.

Allusions

Allusions are brief references to things outside the text—to people, works of art, songs, events in the news—anything in the culture that the author assumes he or she shares knowledge of with the readers. Allusions are one way for an author to form a bond with readers—provided the readers' and authors' opinions are the same about what is alluded to. Allusions influence readers. They are persuasive devices that can provide positive associations with the author's viewpoint.

In "On Teenagers and Tattoos," the epigraph (the quotation that appears under the title of the essay) is an allusion to the classic novel *Moby Dick*. Martin alludes to the novel again in paragraph 11 (we might say that here he alludes to his own earlier allusion). Martin assumes that his readers know the work—not just its title but also its characters, in particular, the narrator, Ishmael. And he assumes his readers would know that the "skeleton dimensions" of a great whale were important and that readers would therefore understand the value of preserving these statistics. The allusion predisposes readers to see that there are valid reasons for permanently marking the body.

Specialized Vocabulary

If an argument is aimed at an audience of specialists, it will undoubtedly contain vocabulary peculiar to that group or profession. Martin's essay contains social science terminology: "family matrix" and "surface presentations" (paragraph 2), "individuation" (paragraph 4), "grounded" (paragraph 6), "sense of constancy" (paragraph 9) and "normative uncertainties" (paragraph 11).

The text surrounding these terms provides enough help for most lay readers to get a fair understanding. For example, the text surrounding *individuation* suggests that the person would stand out as a separate physical presence; this is not quite the same meaning as *individuality*, which refers more to one's character. Likewise, the text around *family matrix* points to something the single word *family* does not; it emphasizes the family as the surroundings in which one develops.

If you need to look up a term and a dictionary does not seem to offer an appropriate definition, go to one of the specialized dictionaries available on the library reference shelves. (See pages 113–119 for more on these.)

If you encounter an argument with more jargon than you can handle, you may have to accept that you are not an appropriate reader for it. Some readings are aimed at people with highly specialized graduate degrees or training. Without advanced courses, no one could read these articles with full comprehension, much less critique their arguments.

Following Through

Find other words in Martin's essay that sound specific to the field of psychology. Use the surrounding text to come up with laymen's terms for these concepts.

Missing Persons

A common difficulty with scientific writing is that it can sound disembodied and abstract. You won't find a lot of people doing things in it. Generally, a sentence is clearer if the subject is a person or thing that performs the action of the verb. Sentences are easiest to read when they take a "who-does-what" form. A technical term for this kind of sentence is **agent-action**. (*"Agent:* one who has the power or authority to act," *American Heritage Dictionary.*) But in many of Martin's sentences, we have a hard time seeing exactly who does what. His subjects tend to be abstractions, like the long phrase italicized below, and he uses many nonaction verbs like *to be* and *to become:*

> *An interested and nonjudgmental appreciation of teenagers' surface presentations* may become a way of making contact not only in their terms but on their turfs . . .

In this sentence, Martin is being indirect rather than saying, "Psychiatrists who take an interest in teenagers' tattoos can make contact with their patients." In at least one other sentence, Martin goes so far in leaving people out that his sentence is grammatically incorrect, as in this example of a dangling modifier, which we have italicized:

> Alternatively, *feeling prey to a rapidly evolving body over which they have no say,* self-made and openly visible decorations may restore adolescents' sense of normalcy and control, a way of turning passive experience into active identity.

The italicized phrase describes adolescents, not decorations. We wonder, "Where was Martin's editor?" If you have trouble reading passages like this, take comfort in the fact that the difficulty is not your fault. But recasting the idea into who-does-what form can clear things up. We offer the following paraphrase:

> Teens may feel like helpless victims of the changes taking place in their bodies. They may mark themselves with highly visible tattoos and piercings to regain a sense of control over their lives.

Passive Voice

Passive voice is another common form of the missing-person problem. In an active-voice sentence, we see our predictable who-does-what pattern:

> *Active voice:* The rat ate the cheese.

In passive-voice sentences, the subject of the verb is not an agent; it does not act. Here, the cheese is the subject but not the agent (actor).

> *Passive voice:* The cheese was eaten by the rat.

At least in this sentence, we know who the agent is — it's the rat. But scientists often leave out any mention of agents. Thus, in Martin's essay we have sentences like this one, in which we have italicized the passive verb:

> Adolescents' bodily decorations [. . .] *can be seen* in terms of figuration rather than disfigurement. [. . .]

Who can see them? Martin really means that *psychiatrists should see tattoos* as figuration rather than disfigurement. But that would sound too committed, not scientific. Passive-voice sentences are common in the sciences and social sciences as part of an effort to sound objective. However, Martin is nowhere near as objective as he attempts to sound, as we note in our third encounter with this text.

You might note other places in the essay where a switch to active voice would heat up the rhetoric. However, our point here is that passive voice generally makes sentences abstract, disembodied, and harder to read for those not accustomed to scientific writing. Rhetorically, however, passive voice may be effective with the target audience, who might think active voice sounds unprofessional.

If you learn to recognize passive voice, you can often mentally convert the troublesome passage into active voice, making it clearer. Passive voice is explained in more detail on pages A3–A4, but it always takes this pattern:

> A helping verb in some form of the verb *to be: Is, was, were, has been, will be, will have been, could have been,* and so forth.

Followed by a main verb, a past participle: Past participles end in *ed,
en, g, k,* or *t.*

Some examples:

The car *was being driven* by my roommate when we had the wreck.

Infections *are spread* by bacteria.

The refrain *is sung* three times.

Following Through

Convert the following sentences into active voice. We have put the
passive-voice verbs in bold type, but you may need to look at the surrounding text to figure out who the agents are.

> A sense of constancy *can be derived* from unchanging marks that
> *can be carried* along no matter what the physical, temporal, or ge-
> ographical vicissitudes at hand. (paragraph 9) To edit this one,
> ask *who* can derive what and *who* can carry what.

> The intense and often disturbing reactions that *are mobilized* in
> viewers can help to effectively keep them at bay, becoming tanta-
> mount to the proverbial "Keep Out" sign hanging from a teen-
> ager's door. (paragraph 4) To edit, ask *what* mobilizes the reac-
> tions in other people.

Using Paraphrase to Aid Comprehension

As we all know, explaining something to someone else is the best way to
make it clear to ourselves. Putting an author's ideas into your own words,
that is, **paraphrasing** them, is like explaining the author to yourself—or to a
classmate who is having trouble understanding a passage in an argument.
(Because paraphrasing is an important skill in writing a researched essay, we
cover it in more detail in Chapter 5. See pages 128–131.)

Unlike summary (see pages 131–132 in Chapter 5), paraphrase makes
no effort to shorten. In fact, a paraphrase is often longer than the original, as
it tends to loosen up what is dense. Try to make both the language and the
syntax (word order) simpler. This could mean making two sentences where
there was one. It often means finding plainer, more everyday language, con-
verting passive voice to active voice, breaking a complicated sentence into
several shorter sentences, and making the subjects concrete rather than abstract. It is hard to write a good paraphrase of a difficult passage if you read it
out of context. Paraphrasing a passage is something you do after reading the
whole argument through twice—or more.

- Use your own words, but don't strain to find a different word for every single one in the original. Some of the author's plain words are clearer than what you might find as substitutes.
- If you take a phrase from the original, enclose the phrase in quotation marks.
- Don't use the sentence pattern of the original. Make a simpler pattern, even if it means making several short sentences. You are aiming for clarity.
- Check the surrounding sentences to make sure you understand the passage in its context. You may want to add an idea from the context.
- Aim for who-does-what sentences.

Wrestling with difficult passages means noting and checking allusions, writing out definitions, and writing paraphrases either in the margins or in your writer's notebook. All of these are better aids to comprehension than simply underlining a passage.

Following Through

Pair up with another member of your class. Together, select a passage of one or two sentences from Martin's essay that you both agree is not obvious or easy to say in your own words. Each work out a paraphrase of the passage, then compare your attempts, and combine what is best in each to make a good paraphrase. Discuss what makes the passage easier to read.

Analyzing the Reasoning of an Argument

As part of your second encounter with the text, you should be able to pick out its reasoning. The reasoning is the author's case, which consists of the *claim* (what the author wants the readers to believe or do) and the *reasons* and evidence offered in support of it. In the second reading, we want to be able to state the case, preferably in our own words, and also describe what else is going on the argument, such as the inclusion of opposing views or background information.

If a text is an argument, we ought to be able to find a sentence in the text (or create such a sentence ourselves) stating what the author wants the readers to believe or do. And we should be able to find another statement (or more) that tells us *why* they should believe it or do it. This is the essential structure of argument. A claim and a reason — or two, or more. (Don't expect to find many reasons. In a good argument, much space and effort may go toward developing and supporting only one reason.) Of course, we should also look for evidence presented to make the reasons seem good and believable. Marking claims and reasons in the margin is something we always do when preparing to teach an argument. We advise that you do it too (unless you are reading a library book).

For people not experienced at analyzing arguments, picking out a case can be challenging, unless the author has explicitly laid out the case with direct statements such as "My first reason for claiming . . . is. . . ." Not many mature writers make arguments so explicitly or arrange them in as simple a form as the five-paragraph essay pattern that teachers may have imposed on you. Although it's good to be clear and organized, most readers are likely to find such a heavy-handed approach insulting rather than persuasive. Then there is always the possibility that an author has failed to make a case — has written his or her opinions but failed to provide good reasoning to support them.

Therefore, most complex arguments require critical reading. Two critical-reading skills will help you rise to the challenge. Both ask you to take the perspective of the bird, who sees the big picture and its patterns, rather than the ant. One is **subdividing the text.** The other, already discussed, is **considering contexts.** Critical readers use these in combination simultaneously, but here we describe them one at a time.

Finding Parts

Critical readers develop the habit of breaking a text down into parts instead of seeing it as a monolith. By *parts of the text,* we mean groups of paragraphs that work together to perform some role in the essay. Examples of such roles are to introduce the essay, to provide background material, to give an opposing view, to conclude the piece, and so on. When we talk about the parts of the text, we mean how the essay itself is arranged.

Discovering the parts of a text can be simple. Authors often make them obvious with subheadings and blank space. Even without these, transitional expressions and clear statements of intention make subdividing a text almost as easy as breaking a Hershey bar into its already well-defined segments. However, other arguments are more loosely constructed, their subdivisions less readily discernible. But even with these, close inspection will usually reveal some fault lines that indicate subdivisions, and you should be able to see the roles played by the various chunks.

We have placed numbers next to every fifth paragraph in the essays reprinted in our text. Numbering makes it easier to refer to specific passages and to discuss parts. You too should number the paragraphs of essays you find, considering every single indention a new paragraph, no matter how short. (Block quotations, such as the epigraph at the beginning of Martin's essay, however, are part of the paragraphs that contain them.)

Martin helps us see the parts of his essay by announcing early on, in paragraph 3, that it will have three sections, each "[exemplifying] some of the complex psychological underpinnings of youth tattooing." Martin's essay can thus be subdivided into the following six parts:

1. Epigraph
2. Paragraphs 1, 2, and 3: the introduction
3. Paragraphs 4 and 5: an example
4. Paragaphs 6, 7, and 8: another example
5. Paragraphs 9, 10, and 11: a third example
6. Paragraph 12: the conclusion

When preparing to teach an argument, we write numbers next to each paragraph and draw lines across the page to mark the major subdivisions of the argument. Looking for transitional expressions as well as changes in topic or focus will help you mark a text this way. Again, this kind of marking up of the text is superior to underlining if your intention is to think analytically about the essay.

Using Context

Taking the bird's-eye view again, we can use surroundings or contexts to help pick out the reasoning. While a quick reading might suggest that Martin is arguing that teens have good reasons for decorating their bodies, we need to recall that the essay appeared in a journal for psychiatrists — doctors, not parents or teachers. Martin is writing to other psychiatrists and psychologists, clinicians who work with families. Reading carefully, we learn that his audience is an even smaller portion of this group: clinicians who have been "summoned as the final arbiter" in family disputes involving tattoos and other body decoration (paragraph 2). Because journals such as the *Journal of Child and Adolescent Psychiatry* are aimed at improving the practice of medicine, we can assume that Martin is trying to help his readers in their own practices. We want to look for sentences that tell these readers what they ought to do and how it will make them better doctors.

Identifying the Claim and Reasons

The claim: Martin is very clear about his claim, repeating it three times, using just slightly different wording:

> His readers should "[explore] the motivations and significance [underlying] tattoos and piercings. . . ." (paragraph 2)

> His readers should have "[a]n interested and nonjudgmental appreciation of teenagers' surface presentations. . . ." (paragraph 2)

His readers should see "[a]dolescents' bodily decorations . . . in terms of figuration rather than disfigurement. . . ." (paragraph 12)

Asked to identify Martin's claim, you could choose any one of these statements or write a paraphrase of the idea. Why might an author repeat the claim, or any key idea, as often as Martin does here? By using slightly different language in each version, he moves from a neutral claim to a more biased one—from just exploring the motives to seeing them in positive terms.

The reason: The reason is the "because" part of the argument. Why should the readers believe or do as he suggests? We can find the answer in paragraph 2, in the same sentences with his claim:

Because doing so "**can go a long way toward resolving . . . differences and can become a novel and additional way of getting to know teenagers.**"

Because doing so "**may become a way of making contact not only in their terms but on their turfs. [. . .]**"

And the final sentence of Martin's essay offers a third version of the same reason:

Because "**we may not only arrive at a position to pass more reasoned clinical judgment, but become sensitized through our patients' skins to another level of their internal reality.**"

Again, we could choose any one of these sentences or paraphrase his reason. Using paraphrase, we can begin to outline the case structure of Martin's argument:

Claim: Rather than dismissing tattoos as disfigurement, mental health professionals should take a serious interest in the meaning of and motivation behind the tattoos.

Reason: Exploring their patients' body decorations can help them gain insight and make contact with teenagers on teenagers' own terms.

What about the rest of the essay? Where is Martin's evidence? Martin tells us that the three subsections will "exemplify some of the complex psychological underpinnings of youth tattooing." In each, he offers a case, or vignette, as evidence.

Example and Evidence (paragraphs 4 and 5): Tattoos are a way of working out identity problems when teens need either to mark themselves off from others or to regain a sense of control of a changing body or an imposing environment. The sixteen-year-old-girl who chose not to fit in.

Example and Evidence (paragraphs 6, 7, and 8): Tattoos can be an attempt to make the intangible a tangible part of one's body. The thirteen-year-old boy remembering his father.

Example and Evidence (paragraphs 9, 10, and 11): Tattoos are an "antidote" to a society that is on the run. The seventeen-year-old father.

THE THIRD ENCOUNTER: RESPONDING CRITICALLY TO AN ARGUMENT

Once you feel confident that you have the argument figured out, you are ready to respond to it, which means evaluating it and comparing it with other perspectives, including your own. You already should have marked the text with lines, numbers, and highlighting or underlining, but only by *writing words* can you respond critically. As the reading expert Mortimer Adler says in his book entitled *How to Read a Book*,

> Reading, if it is active, is thinking, and thinking tends to express itself in words, spoken or written. The person who says he knows what he thinks but cannot express it in words usually does not know what he thinks. (49)

Annotation Is Key

So we suggest that you annotate heavily. *Annotation* simply means to make a note. You may use the margins for these notes of critical response, but you may also find you need to move to your writer's notebook. Many writers keep reading journals just for this purpose, to practice active interaction with what they read and to preserve the experience of reading a text they want to remember.

What should you write about? Think of questions you would ask the author if he or she were in the room with you. Think of your own experience with the subject. Note similarities and contrasts with other arguments you have read or experiences of your own that confirm or contradict what the author is saying. Write about anything you notice that seems interesting, unusual, brilliant, or wrong. Comment, question—the more you actually write on the page, the more the essay becomes your own. And you will write more confidently (that is, better) about a text you own than one you are just borrowing.

The list on the next page will give you ideas for annotations, but don't be limited by these suggestions.

- Paraphrase the claim and reasons next to where you find them stated.
- Does the author support his or her reasons with evidence? Is the evidence sufficient in terms of both quantity and quality?
- Circle the key terms. Note how the author defines or fails to define them.
- What does the author assume? Behind every argument, there are assumptions. For example, a baseball fan wrote to our local paper arguing that the policy of fouls after the second strike needs to be changed. His reason was that the fans would not be subjected to such a long game. The author assumed that a fast game of hits and outs is more interesting than a slow game of strategy between batters and hitters. Not every baseball fan would share that assumption.
- Do you see any contradictions, either within the text itself or with anything else you've read or learned?
- What are the implications of the argument? If we believe and/or do what the author argues, what is likely to happen?
- Think of someone who would disagree with this argument, and say what that person might object to.
- If you see any opposing views in the argument, has the author been fair in presenting them? Consider whether the author has represented opposing views fairly or has set them up to be easily knocked down.
- What is the author overlooking or leaving out, in your opinion?
- Where does the argument connect with anything else you have read?
- Does the argument exemplify mature reasoning as explained in Chapter 1, "Understanding Argument"?
- What aim does the argument seem to pursue? One of the four in the box on page 19, or some other aim?
- What about the character or projected personality of the author? What kind of person does he or she sound like? Mark places where you hear the author's voice. Describe the tone. How does the author establish credibility—or fail to?
- What about the author's values and biases? Note places where the author sounds liberal or conservative, religious or materialistic, and so on.
- Note places where you see clues about the intended audience of the argument and where the author has made an effort to appeal to their interests, values, tastes, and so on. Maybe you see manipulation or pandering—note it!

There are no margins wide enough to let you write about all the points we raise here, but pick out what is salient to the argument before you, and if you run out of space, you can always turn to your notebook to do more free-writing in response to the argument.

A concluding comment about responses: Even if you agree with an argument, think about who might oppose it and what their objections might be. It may be easier (and more fun) to challenge arguments you disagree with, but if you are studying arguments as claims to truth, it is even more important to challenge the views you find most sympathetic.

As an example of annotation, we offer here our annotations of some paragraphs from Martin's argument.

Sample Annotations

How is he defining "solution"? Do tattoos solve a problem or just indicate one?

Tattoos and piercing can offer a concrete and readily available solution for many of the identity crises and conflicts normative to adolescent development. In using such decorations, and by marking out their bodily territories, adolescents can support their efforts at autonomy, privacy, and insulation. Seeking individuation, tattooed adolescents can

It seems like there are more mature ways to do this.

become unambiguously demarcated from others and singled out as unique. The intense and often disturbing reactions that are mobilized in viewers can help to effectively

Or would it cause parents to pay attention to them rather than leave them alone?

keep them at bay, becoming tantamount to the proverbial "Keep Out" sign hanging from a teenager's door.

Alternatively, feeling prey to a rapidly evolving body over which they have no say, self-made and openly visible decorations may restore adolescents' sense of normalcy and control, a way of turning a passive experience into an active

What is normal?

Is he implying that the indelible mark is one they will not outgrow? What if they do?

identity. By indelibly marking their bodies, adolescents can strive to reclaim their bearings within an environment experienced as alien, estranged, or suffocating or to lay claim over their evolving and increasingly unrecognizable bodies. In either case, the net outcome can be a resolution to unwelcome impositions: external, familial, or societal in one case, internal and hormonal in the other. In the words of a 16-year-old girl with several facial piercings, and who could have been referring to her body just as well as to the position within her family: "If I don't fit in, it is because I say so."

Would he say the same about anorexia?

5

Does he assume this family needs counseling — or will not need it? He says the problem is "resolved."

WRITING ASSIGNMENT: A CRITICAL RESPONSE TO A SINGLE ARGUMENT

This assignment asks you to write an essay about your critical reading of an argument. Writing about your encounters with the text will make you self-conscious about your critical thinking, bringing to your own attention the habits and practices of critical reading. However, we think you should have your classmates in mind as an audience for this paper. The goal of your paper can be twofold: to help your classmates better comprehend and criticize an essay you have all read and to demonstrate the steps involved in giving any argument a thorough critical reading.

In Part One

The project will have two parts. In Part One (2–4 paragraphs), explain the rhetorical context, including who the author is and where he or she is coming from, as well as the intended audience for the argument as you infer it from clues both outside and inside the text. Describe the reasoning, explaining what you see as the claim and reasons. You should comment on the organization of the argument, referring to sections or groups of paragraphs, and on how well the argument is organized. Also in Part One, tell about your experience of reading the essay—whether you found it easy, difficult, confusing in parts, and why. Be specific, and refer to actual passages from the argument when you talk about what made the difficult parts difficult or what made the ideas accessible.

In Part Two

In Part Two (3–4 paragraphs), evaluate the argument. Say how effective it may have been for its target audience and also whether you think it is a good example of mature reasoning. Remember to focus on the text of the argument. Don't make an argument of your own, but talk about the strengths and weaknesses of the argument about which you have chosen to write. Your point is not to agree or disagree with the author; instead, show your understanding of the qualities of good argumentation based on what you have learned so far from *The Aims of Argument*. In developing Part Two, use the suggestions for annotation on pages 42–44 as well as the criteria for mature reasoning on pages 11–15. Although your responses may be critical in the sense of negative criticisms of the text, we use the term *critical* here in the broader sense of film or literary criticism, "a careful and exact evaluation and judgment" (*American Heritage Dictionary*). So support your judgments.

This can be a very informal paper. Many scholars keep journals about the things they read, both as a way of preserving what they learned about a text and as a way to do some thinking of their own about it. Think of this paper as a cleaned-up journal entry, but use first person to describe your experiences of reading and responding.

Other Advice for Both Parts

Be specific. Refer to paragraphs in the text by number.

If you use direct quotations, make sure they are exact, and enclose them in quotation marks. Indicate in parentheses what paragraph they come from.

Use paraphrase when talking about key ideas in the essay, and cite the paragraph in which the original passage appeared. It is important to demonstrate that you can state these key ideas in your own words.

Use first person. This will help keep your writing clear.

Refer to the author by full name on first mention and by last name only from there on.

STUDENT SAMPLE ESSAY: CRITICAL RESPONSE TO A SINGLE ARGUMENT

Here we have reproduced another argument on the topic of tattoos and body decorations. Following it is one student's critical response to this essay.

The Single Argument

The Decorated Body
France Borel

Nothing goes as deep as dress nor as far as the skin; ornaments have the dimensions of the world.

—MICHEL SERRES, *The Five Senses*

Human nakedness, according to social custom, is unacceptable, unbearable, and dangerous. From the moment of birth, society takes charge, managing, dressing, forming, and deforming the child—sometimes even with a certain degree of violence. Aside from the most elementary caretaking concerns—the very diversity of which shows how subjective the motivation is—an unfathomably deep and universal tendency pushes families, clans, and tribes to rapidly modify a person's physical appearance.

One's genuine physical makeup, one's given anatomy, is always felt to be unacceptable. Flesh, in its raw state, seems both intolerable and threatening. In its naked state, body and skin have no possible existence. The organism is acceptable only when it is transformed, covered with signs. The body only speaks if it is dressed in artifice.

For millennia, in the four quarters of the globe, mothers have molded the shape of their newborn babies' skulls to give them silhouettes conforming to prevalent criteria of beauty. In the nineteenth century, western children were tightly swaddled to keep their limbs straight. In the so-called primitive world, children were scarred or tattooed at a very early age in rituals which were repeated at all the most important steps of their lives. At a very young age, children were fitted with belts, necklaces, or bracelets; their lips, ears, or noses were pierced or stretched.

Some cultures have designed sophisticated appliances to alter physical structure and appearance. American Indian cradleboards crushed the skull to flatten it; the Mangbetus of Africa wrapped knotted rope made of bark around the child's head to elongate it into a sugar-loaf shape, which was considered to be aesthetically pleasing. The feet of very young Chinese girls were bound and spliced, intentionally and irreversibly deforming them, because this was seen to guarantee the girls' eventual amorous and matrimonial success.[1]

Claude Lévi-Strauss said about the Caduveo of Brazil: "In order to be a man, one had to be painted; whoever remained in a natural state was no different from the beasts."[2] In Polynesia, unless a girl was tattooed, she would not find a husband. An unornamented hand could not cook, nor dip into the communal food bowl. Pink lips were despicable and ugly. Anyone who refused the test of the tattoo was seen to be marginal and suspect.

Among the Tivs of Nigeria, women called attention to their legs by means of elaborate scarification and the use of pearl leg bands; the best decorated calves were known for miles around. Tribal incisions behind the ears of Chad men rendered the skin "as smooth and stretched as that of a drum." The women would laugh at any man lacking these incisions, and they would never accept him as a husband. Men would subject themselves willingly to this custom, hoping for scars deep enough to leave marks on their skulls after death.

At the beginning of the eighteenth century, Father Laurent de Lucques noted that any young girl of the Congo who was not able to bear the pain of scarification and who cried so loudly that the operation had to be stopped was considered "good for nothing."[3] That is why, before marriage, men would check to see if the pattern traced on the belly of their intended bride was beautiful and well-detailed.

The fact that such motivations and pretexts depend on aesthetic, erotic, hygienic, or even medical considerations has no influence on the result, which is always in the direction of transforming the appearance of the body. Such a transformation is wished for, whether or not it is effective.

The body is a supple, malleable, and transformable prime material, a kind of modeling clay, easily molded by social will and wish. Human skin is an ideal subject for inscription, a surface for all sorts of marks which make it possible to differentiate the human from the animal. The physical body offers itself willingly for tattooing or scarring so that, visibly and recognizably, it becomes a social entity.

The absolutely naked body is considered as brutish, reduced to the level of nature where no distinction is made between man and beast. The decorated body, on the other hand, dressed (if even only in a belt), tattooed, or mutilated, publicly exhibits humanity and membership in an established group. As Theophile Gautier said, "The ideal disturbs even the roughest nature, and the taste for ornamentation distinguishes the intelligent being from the beast more exactly than anything else. Indeed, dogs have never dreamed of putting on earrings."

So, it is by their categorical refusal of nakedness that human beings are distinguished from nature. The "mark makes unremarkable"—it creates an interval between what is biologically and brutally given in the animal realm and what is won in the cultural realm. The body is tamed continuously; social custom demands, at any price—including pain, constraint, or discomfort—that wildness be abandoned.

Each civilization chooses—through a network of elective relationships which are difficult to determine—which areas of the body deserve transformation. These areas are as difficult to define and as shifting as those of eroticism or modesty. An individual alone eludes bodily modifications; they are the expression of a homogeneous collectivity which, at a chosen moment, comes to a tacit agreement to attack one or another part of the anatomy.

Whatever the choices, options, or differences may be, that which remains constant is the transformation of appearance. In spite of our contemporary western belief that the body is perfect as it is, we are constantly changing it: clothing it in musculature, suntan, or makeup; dying its head hair or pulling out its bodily hair. The seemingly most innocent gestures for taking care of the body very often hide a persistent and disguised tendency to make it adhere to the strictest of norms, reclothing it in a veil of civilization. The total nudity offered at birth does not exist in any region of the world. Man puts his stamp on man. The body is not a product of nature, but of culture.

10

Notes

1. Of course, there are also many different sexual mutilations, including excisions and circumcisions, which we will not go into at this time as they constitute a whole study in themselves.
2. C. Lévi-Strauss, Tristes Tropiques (Paris: Plon, 1955), p. 214.
3. J. Cuvelier, Relations sur le Congo du Père Laurent de Lucques (Brussels: Institut royal colonial belge, 1953), p. 144.

From France Borel, *Le Vêtement incarné: Les Métamorphoses du corps* (Paris: Calmann-Lévy, 1992), pp. 15–18. Copyright © Calmann-Lévy, 1992. Translated by Ellen Dooling Draper with the permission of the publisher.

A SAMPLE STUDENT RESPONSE

ANALYSIS OF "THE DECORATED BODY"
Katie Lahey

Part One

"The Decorated Body" by France Borel addresses the idea of external body manipulation not only as an issue prevalent to our own culture
and time but also as a timeless concept that exists beyond cultural boundaries. It was published in *Parabola,* a magazine supported by the Society
for the Study of Myth and Tradition. Borel discusses the ways in which
various cultures both ancient and modern modify the natural body. Borel,
who has written books on clothing and on art, writes with a style that is
less a critique than an observation of his populations. This style suggests
an anthropological approach rather than a psychological one, focusing on
the motivations of people as a whole and less on the specific individuals
within the societies. It seems, therefore, that he may be targeting an academic audience of professional anthropologists or other readers who are
interested in the similarities of both "primitive" and "modern" cultures
and the whole idea of what it means to be human.

Borel makes the claim that "social custom" dictates that all
humans manipulate their bodies to brand themselves as humans. He
says in the first paragraph that "an unfathomably deep and universal tendency pushes families, clans, and tribes to rapidly modify a person's physical appearance." He restates the idea in paragraph 2: The body
"is acceptable only when it is transformed, covered with signs." He believes that in all cultures this type of branding or decorating is essential
to distinguish oneself as legitimate within a civilization. Man has evolved
from his original body; he has defied nature. We are no longer subject to
what we are born with; rather, we create our bodies and identities as we
see fit.

Borel reasons that this claim is true simply because all cultures conform to this idea and do so in such diverse ways. As he says, "the very
diversity . . . shows how subjective the motivation is . . ." (paragraph 1).
He provides ample evidence to support this reasoning in paragraphs 3
through 7, citing various cultures and examples of how they choose to
decorate the body.

Part Two

However, Borel does not provide a solid explanation as to why the
human race finds these bodily changes necessary to distinguish itself as
human. It serves his argument to state that the various specific motivations behind these changes are irrelevant. All he is interested in proving

is that humans must change their bodies, and he repeats this concept continually throughout the essay, first saying that a man remaining "in a natural state was no different from the beasts" in paragraph 5 and again in paragraphs 9 and 10. Maybe some readers would think this reiteration makes his point stronger, but I was unsatisfied.

I found myself trying to provide my own reasons why humans have this need to change their bodies. What makes this essay so unsatisfying to me is that, once I thought about it, it does in fact matter why cultures participate in body decoration. For example, why did the Chinese find it necessary to bind the feet of their young girls, a tradition so painful and unhealthy and yet so enduring? In such traditions, it becomes obvious that ulterior motives lie beneath the surface. The binding of the feet is not simply a tradition that follows the idea of making oneself human. In fact, it methodically attempts to put women below men. By binding the feet, a culture disables the young women not only physically but emotionally as well. It teaches them that they do not deserve the same everyday comforts as men and belittles them far beyond simply having smaller feet. Borel, however, fails to discuss any of these deeper motives. He avoids supplying his own opinion because he does not want to get into the politics of the practices he describes. He wants to speak in generalizations about body modification as a mark of being human, even though people in modern Western culture might see some of these activities as violations of human rights.

Borel barely touches on modern Western civilization. He really only addresses our culture in the final paragraph, where he alleges that everyday things we do to change ourselves, whether it be shaving, tanning, toning, dying, or even applying makeup, are evidence that we have the same need to mark ourselves as human. He challenges our belief that "the body is perfect as it is" by showing that "we are constantly changing it" (paragraph 13). But many people today, especially women, *do* doubt that their individual bodies are perfect and would concede that they are constantly trying to "improve" them. What does Borel mean by "perfect as it is?" Is he talking about an ideal we would like to achieve?

His placement of this paragraph is interesting. I wondered why he leaves this discussion of our own culture until the very end of the essay so that his ideas of European and American culture appear as an afterthought. He spends the majority of the essay discussing other, more "primitive cultures" that yield many more examples of customs, such as the American Indian cradleboards, that clearly mark one as a member of a tribe. Perhaps Borel tends to discuss primitive cultures as opposed to our modern Western culture because primitive cultures generally back up his thesis, whereas American culture, in particular, veers from his claim that people decorate themselves in order to demonstrate what they have in common.

Borel ignores any controversy over tattoos and piercing, which people in Western culture might do to mark themselves as different from other

people in their culture. In America, we value individualism, where everyone tries to be unique, even if in some small way. Other authors like An-
dres Martin, who wrote "On Teenagers and Tattoos," look at American
culture and claim that we use body decoration as a means to show and
celebrate our individuality. Martin says one good reason for teens to tattoo themselves is for "individuation"—to mark themselves as distinct
from their peers and their families. This goes completely opposite from
Borel's claim that "[a]n individual alone eludes bodily modifications; they
are the expression of a homogeneous collectivity . . ." (paragraph 12).

Borel makes a sound argument for his claim that human existence is
something more complex or more unnatural than simply being alive. But
we know this already through humans' use of speech, social organization,
and technology. Before I read his argument and even after the first time
I read it, I wasn't swayed by Borel. I was looking for something more
specific than what he is saying. In fact, all he is showing is that we decorate to symbolize our humanity. He does support this claim with good evidence. In this sense, the argument holds. But I cannot help but prefer to
think about the other, more specific things we symbolize through our body
decorations.

Chapter 3

Analyzing Arguments: A Simplified Toulmin Method

In Chapter 2, we discussed the importance of reading arguments critically: breaking them down into their parts to see how they are put together, noting in the margins key terms that are not defined, and raising questions about the writer's claims or evidence. Although these general techniques are sufficient for analyzing many arguments, sometimes—especially with intricate arguments and with arguments we sense are faulty but whose weaknesses we are unable to specify—we need a more systematic technique.

In this chapter, we explain and illustrate such a technique based on the work of Stephen Toulmin, a contemporary philosopher who has contributed a great deal to our understanding of argumentation. This method will allow you to analyze the logic of any argument, whether written or spoken; you will also find it useful in examining the logic of your own arguments as you draft and revise them. Keep in mind, however, that because it is limited to the analysis of logic, the Toulmin method is not sufficient by itself. It is also important to question an argument through dialogue (see Chapter 6) and to look at the appeals of character, emotion, and style (see Chapter 8).

A PRELIMINARY CRITICAL READING

Before we consider Toulmin, let's first explore the following argument carefully, using the general process for critical reading we described in Chapter 2.

Rising to the Occasion of Our Death
William F. May

William F. May (b. 1927) is a distinguished professor of ethics at Southern Methodist University. The following essay appeared originally in The Christian Century *(1990).*

For many parents, a Volkswagen van is associated with putting children to sleep on a camping trip. Jack Kevorkian, a Detroit pathologist, has now linked the van with the veterinarian's meaning of "putting to sleep." Kevorkian conducted a dinner interview with Janet Elaine Adkins, a 54-year-old Alzheimer's patient, and her husband and then agreed to help her commit suicide in his VW van. Kevorkian pressed beyond the more generally accepted practice of passive euthanasia (allowing a patient to die by withholding or withdrawing treatment) to active euthanasia (killing for mercy).

Kevorkian, moreover, did not comply with the strict regulations that govern active euthanasia in, for example, the Netherlands. Holland requires that death be imminent (Adkins had beaten her son in tennis just a few days earlier); it demands a more professional review of the medical evidence and the patient's resolution than a dinner interview with a physician (who is a stranger and who does not treat patients) permits; and it calls for the final, endorsing signatures of two doctors.

So Kevorkian-bashing is easy. But the question remains: Should we develop a judicious, regulated social policy permitting voluntary euthanasia for the terminally ill? Some moralists argue that the distinction between allowing to die and killing for mercy is petty quibbling over technique. Since the patient in any event dies—whether by acts of omission or commission—the route to death doesn't really matter. The way modern procedures have made dying at the hands of the experts and their machines such a prolonged and painful business has further fueled the euthanasia movement, which asserts not simply the right to die but the right to be killed.

But other moralists believe that there is an important moral distinction between allowing to die and mercy killing. The euthanasia movement, these critics contend, wants to engineer death rather than face dying. Euthanasia would bypass dying to make one dead as quickly as possible. It aims to relieve suffering by knocking out the interval between life and death. It solves the problem of suffering by eliminating the sufferer.

The impulse behind the euthanasia movement is understandable in an age when dying has become such an inhumanly endless business. But the movement may fail to appreciate our human capacity to rise to the occasion of our death. The best death is not always the sudden death. Those forewarned of death and given time to prepare for it have time to engage in acts of reconciliation. Also, advanced grieving by those about to be bereaved may ease some of their pain. Psychiatrists have observed that those who lose a loved one accidentally have a more difficult time recovering from the loss than those who have suffered through an extended period of illness before the death. Those who have lost a close relative by accident are more likely to experience what Geoffrey Gorer has called limitless grief. The community, moreover, may need its aged and dependent, its sick and its dying, and the virtues which they sometimes evince—the virtues of humil-

5

ity, courage, and patience—just as much as the community needs the virtues of justice and love manifest in the agents of care.

On the whole, our social policy should allow terminal patients to die, but it should not regularize killing for mercy. Such a policy would recognize and respect that moment in illness when it no longer makes sense to bend every effort to cure or to prolong life and when one must allow patients to do their own dying. This policy seems most consonant with the obligations of the community to care and of the patient to finish his or her course.

Advocates of active euthanasia appeal to the principle of patient autonomy—as the use of the phrase "voluntary euthanasia" indicates. But emphasis on the patient's right to determine his or her destiny often harbors an extremely naïve view of the uncoerced nature of the decision. Patients who plead to be put to death hardly make unforced decisions if the terms and conditions under which they receive care already nudge them in the direction of the exit. If the elderly have stumbled around in their apartments, alone and frightened for years, or if they have spent years warehoused in geriatrics barracks, then the decision to be killed for mercy hardly reflects an uncoerced decision. The alternative may be so wretched as to push patients toward this escape. It is a huge irony and, in some cases, hypocrisy to talk suddenly about a compassionate killing when the aging and dying may have been starved for compassion for many years. To put it bluntly, a country has not earned the moral right to kill for mercy unless it has already sustained and supported life mercifully. Otherwise we kill for compassion only to reduce the demands on our compassion. This statement does not charge a given doctor or family member with impure motives. I am concerned here not with the individual case but with the cumulative impact of a social policy.

I can, to be sure, imagine rare circumstances in which I hope I would have the courage to kill for mercy—when the patient is utterly beyond human care, terminal, and in excruciating pain. A neurosurgeon once showed a group of physicians and an ethicist the picture of a Vietnam casualty who had lost all four limbs in a landmine explosion. The catastrophe had reduced the soldier to a trunk with his face transfixed in horror. On the battlefield I would hope that I would have the courage to kill the sufferer with mercy.

But hard cases do not always make good laws or wise social policies. Regularized mercy killings would too quickly relieve the community of its obligation to provide good care. Further, we should not always expect the law to provide us with full protection and coverage for what, in rare circumstances, we may morally need to do. Sometimes the moral life calls us out into a no-man's-land where we cannot expect total security and protection under the law. But no one said that the moral life is easy.

A STEP-BY-STEP DEMONSTRATION
OF THE TOULMIN METHOD

The Toulmin method requires an analysis of the claim, the reasons offered to support the claim, and the evidence offered to support the reasons, along with an analysis of any refutations offered.

Analyzing the Claim

Logical analysis begins with identifying the *claim,* the thesis or central contention, along with any specific qualifications or exceptions.

Identify the Claim

First ask yourself, *What statement is the author defending?* In "Rising to the Occasion of Our Death," for example, William May spells out his claim in paragraph 6:

> [O]ur social policy should allow terminal patients to die, but it should not regularize killing for mercy.

In his claim, May supports passive euthanasia (letting someone die by withholding or discontinuing treatment) but opposes "regularizing" (making legal or customary) active euthanasia (administering, say, an overdose of morphine to cause a patient's death).

Much popular argumentation is sometimes careless about what exactly is being claimed: Untrained arguers too often content themselves with merely taking sides ("Euthanasia is wrong"). Note that May, a student of ethics trained in philosophical argumentation, makes a claim that is both specific and detailed. Whenever an argument does not include an explicit statement of its claim, you should begin your analysis by stating the writer's claim yourself. Try to state all claims fully and carefully in sentence form, as May's claim is stated.

Look for Qualifiers

Next, ask, *How is the claim qualified?* Is it absolute, or does it include words or phrases to indicate that it may not hold true in every situation or set of circumstances?

May qualifies his claim in paragraph 6 with the phrase "on the whole," indicating that he recognizes possible exceptions to the application of his claim. Other possible qualifiers include "typically," "usually," and "most of the time." Careful arguers are generally wary of making absolute claims. Although unqualified claims are not necessarily faulty, they do insist that there are no cases or circumstances in which the claim might legitimately be contradicted. Qualifying words or phrases are often used to restrict a claim and improve its defensibility.

Find the Exceptions

Finally, ask, *In what cases or circumstances would the writer not press his or her claim?* Look for any explicit exceptions the writer offers to qualify the claim.

May, for example, is quite clear in paragraph 8 about when he would not press his claim:

> I hope I would have the courage to kill for mercy—when the patient is utterly beyond human care, terminal, and in excruciating pain.

Once he has specified these conditions in abstract terms, he goes further and offers a chilling example of a case in which he believes mercy killing would be appropriate. Nevertheless, he insists that such exceptions are rare and thus do not justify making active euthanasia legal or allowing it to become common policy.

Critical readers respond to unqualified claims skeptically—by hunting for exceptions. With qualified claims, they look to see what specific exceptions the writer will admit and what considerations make restrictions necessary or desirable.

Summarize the Claim

At this point it is a good idea to write out in your writer's notebook the claim, its qualifiers, and its exceptions so that you can see all of them clearly. For May, they look like this:

> (qualifier)   "On the whole"
>
> (claim)   "our social policy should allow terminal patients to die, but it should not regularize killing for mercy"
>
> (exception)   "when the patient is utterly beyond human care, terminal, and in excruciating pain"

Record the claim and its qualifiers and exceptions in whatever way that helps you see them best, but do not skip this step. Not only will it help you remember the results of your initial claim analysis, but you will also be building on this summary when you analyze the argument in more detail.

Analyzing the Reasons

Once you have analyzed the claim, you should next identify and evaluate the reasons offered for the claim.

List the Reasons

Begin by asking yourself, *Why is the writer advancing this claim?* Look for any statement or statements that are used to justify the thesis. May groups all of his reasons in paragraph 5:

> The dying should have time to prepare for death and to reconcile with relatives and friends.

Those close to the dying should have time to come to terms with the
impending loss of a loved one.

The community needs examples of dependent but patient and courageous people who sometimes do die with dignity.

The community needs the virtues ("justice and love") of those who care
for the sick and dying.

When you list reasons, you need not preserve the exact words of the arguer; often doing so is impossible because reasons are not always explicit but
may have to be inferred. Be very careful, however, to adhere as closely as possible to the writer's language. Otherwise, your analysis can easily go astray,
imposing a reason of your own that the writer did not have in mind.

Note that reasons, like claims, can be qualified. May does not say, for instance, that "the aged and dependent" *always* show "the virtues of humility,
courage, and patience." He implicitly admits that they can be ornery and cow-
ardly as well. But for May's purposes it is enough that they sometimes manifest the virtues he admires.

Use your writer's notebook to list the reasons following your summary
of the claim, qualifiers, and exceptions. One possibility is to list them beneath the summary of the claim in the form of a tree diagram (see the model
diagram in the Concept Close-Up box on page 60).

Examine the Reasons

There are two questions to ask as you examine the reasons. First ask, *Are they
really good reasons?* A reason is only as good as the values it invokes or implies.
A value is something we think is good—that is, worth pursuing for its own
sake or because it leads to attaining other goods. For each reason, you should
specify the values involved and then determine whether you accept those values as generally binding.

Second, ask, *Is the reason relevant to the thesis?* In other words, does the relationship between the claim and the reason hold up to examination? For example, the claim "You should buy a new car from Fred Freed" cannot be supported by the reason "Fred is a family man with three cute kids" unless you
accept a relationship between an auto dealer's having cute children and his
or her reliability in dealing with customers.

Be careful and deliberate as you examine whether reasons are good and
whether they are relevant. No other step is as important in assessing the logic
of an argument, and no other can be quite as tricky.

To illustrate, consider May's first reason: Those who know they are about
to die should have time to prepare for death and to seek reconciliation with
people from whom they have become estranged. Is this a good reason? Most
of us would probably think so, valuing the chance to prepare for death and
to reconcile ourselves with estranged friends or family members. Not to do
so would seem immature, irresponsible, unforgiving.

But is the reason relevant? May seems to rule out the possibility that a dying person seeking active euthanasia would be able to prepare for death and reconcile with others. But this is obviously not the case. Terminally ill people who decide to arrange for their own deaths may make any number of preparations beforehand, so the connection between this reason and May's claim is really quite weak. To accept a connection, we would have to assume that active euthanasia necessarily amounts to a sudden death without adequate preparation. Because we cannot do so, we are entitled to question the relevance of the reason, no matter how good it might be in itself.

Following Through

Now examine May's second, third, and fourth reasons on your own, as we have just examined the first one. Make notes about each reason, evaluating how good each is in itself and how relevant it is to the thesis. In your writer's notebook, create your own diagram based on the model on page 60.

Analyzing the Evidence

Once you have finished your analysis of the reasons, the next step is to consider the evidence offered to support any of those reasons.

List the Evidence

Ask, *What kinds of evidence (data, anecdotes, case studies, citations from authority, and so forth) are offered as support for each reason?* Some arguments advance little in the way of evidence. May's argument is a good example of a moral argument from and about principles; such an argument does not require much evidence to be effective. Lack of evidence, then, is not always a fault. For one of his reasons, however, May does offer some evidence: After stating his second reason in paragraph 5 — the chance to grieve before a loved one dies can be helpful for those who must go on living after the patient's death — he invokes authorities who agree with him about the value of advanced grieving.

Examine the Evidence

Two questions apply. First, ask, *Is the evidence good?* That is, is it sufficient, accurate, and credible? Second, ask, *Is it relevant to the reason it supports?* Clearly, the evidence May offers in paragraph 5 is sufficient; any more would probably be too much. We assume his citations are accurate and credible as well.

Model Toulmin Diagram for Analyzing Arguments

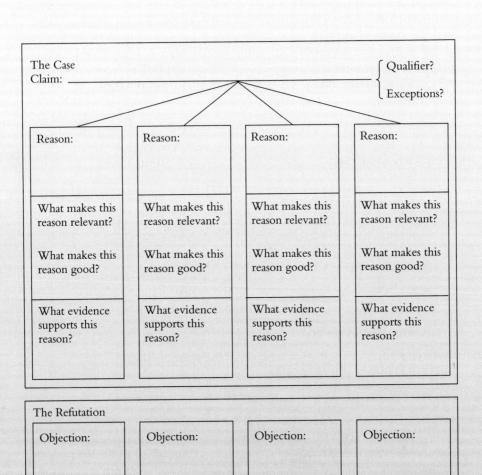

The Case
Claim: _____ { Qualifier?

{ Exceptions?

Reason:	Reason:	Reason:	Reason:
What makes this reason relevant?	What makes this reason relevant?	What makes this reason relevant?	What makes this reason relevant?
What makes this reason good?	What makes this reason good?	What makes this reason good?	What makes this reason good?
What evidence supports this reason?	What evidence supports this reason?	What evidence supports this reason?	What evidence supports this reason?

The Refutation

Objection:	Objection:	Objection:	Objection:
Rebuttal:	Rebuttal:	Rebuttal:	Rebuttal:

We would generally also accept them as relevant because apart from our own experience with grieving, we have to rely on expert opinion. (See Chapter 5 for a fuller discussion of estimating the adequacy and relevance of evidence.)

Noting Refutations

A final—and optional—step is to assess an arguer's refutations. In a refutation, a writer anticipates potential objections to his or her position and tries to show why they do not undermine the basic argument. Refutations do not relate directly to claims, reasons, and evidence. A skilled arguer typically uses them not as part of the main logic of an argument but as a separate step to deal with any obvious objections a reader is likely to have.

First, ask, *What refutations does the writer offer?* Summarize all refutations and list them on your tree diagram of claims, reasons, and evidence. Then, ask, *How does the writer approach each objection?* May's refutation occupies paragraph 7. He recognizes that the value of free choice lends weight to the pro-euthanasia position, and so he relates this value to the question of "voluntary euthanasia." Because in our culture individual freedom is so strong a value, May doesn't question the value itself; rather, he leads us to question whether voluntary euthanasia is actually a matter of free choice. He suggests that unwanted people may be subtly coerced into "choosing" death or may be so isolated and neglected that death becomes preferable to life. Thus, he responds to the objection that dying people should have freedom of choice where death is concerned.

Summarizing Your Analysis

Once you have completed your analysis, it is a good idea to summarize the results in a paragraph or two. Be sure to set aside your own position on the issue, confining your summary to the argument the writer makes. In other words, whether or not you agree with the author, attempt to assess his or her logic fairly.

Although May's logic is strong, it doesn't seem fully compelling. He qualifies his argument and uses exceptions effectively, and his single use of refutation is skillful. However, he fails to acknowledge that active euthanasia need not be a sudden decision leading to sudden death. Consequently, his reasons for supporting passive euthanasia can be used to support at least some cases of active euthanasia as well. It is here—in the linkage between reasons and claim—that May's argument falls short. Furthermore, we may question whether the circumstances under which May would permit active euthanasia are in fact as rare as he suggests. Experience tells us that many people are beyond human care, terminal, and in pain, and many others suffer acute anguish for which they might legitimately seek the relief of death.

A. Analyze the Claim

1. **Find the claim.** In many arguments, the claim is never explicitly stated. When it isn't, try to make the implied claim explicit by stating it in your own words. (Note: If, after careful analysis, you aren't sure *exactly* what the writer is claiming, you've found a serious fault in the argument.)
2. **Look for qualifiers.** Is the claim absolute? Or is it qualified by some word or phrase like *usually* or *all things being equal*? If the claim is absolute, can you think of circumstances in which it might not apply? If the claim is qualified, why is it not absolute? That is, is there any real thought or content in the qualifier — good reasons for qualifying the claim?
3. **Look for explicit exceptions to the claim.** If the writer has pointed out conditions in which he or she would *not* assert the claim, note them carefully.

Summarize steps 1–3. See the diagram on page 60.

B. Analyze the Reasons

1. **Find the reason or reasons advanced to justify the claim.** All statements of reason will answer the question, "Why are you claiming what you've claimed?" They can be linked to the claim with *because*. As with claims, reasons may be implied. Dig them out and state them in your own words. (Note: If, after careful analysis, you discover that the reasons aren't clear or relevant to the claim, you should conclude that the argument is either defective and in need of revision or invalid and therefore unacceptable.)
2. **Ponder each reason advanced.** Is the reason good in itself? Is the reason relevant to the thesis? Note any problems.

List the reasons underneath the claim. See the diagram on page 60.

C. Analyze the Evidence

1. **For each reason, locate all evidence offered to back it up.** Evidence is not limited to hard data. Anecdotes, case studies, and citations from authorities also count as evidence. (Note: Not all reasons require extensive evidence. But we should be suspicious of reasons without evidence, especially when it seems that evidence ought to be available. Unsupported reasons are often a sign of bad reasoning.)
2. **Ponder each piece of evidence.** Is it good? That is, is it sufficient, accurate, believable? Is it relevant to the reason it supports? Note any problems.

List the evidence underneath the claim. See the diagram on page 60.

D. Examine the Refutations

If there are refutations — efforts to refute objections to the case — examine them. If not, consider what objections you think the writer should have addressed.

Following Through

Following is a student-written argument on capital punishment. Read it through once, and then use the Toulmin method as described in this chapter to analyze its logic systematically.

STUDENT SAMPLE: *An Argument for Analysis*

CAPITAL PUNISHMENT: SOCIETY'S SELF-DEFENSE

Amber Young

Just after 1:00 A.M. on a warm night in early June, Georgeann, a pretty college student, left through the back door of a fraternity house to walk the ninety feet down a well-lighted alley to the back door of her sorority house. Lively and vivacious, Georgeann had been an honor student, a cheerleader, and Daffodil Princess in high school, and now she was in the middle of finals week, trying to maintain her straight A record in college. That evening, several people saw Georgeann walk to within about forty feet of the door of her sorority house. However, she never arrived. Somewhere in that last forty feet, she met a tall, handsome young man on crutches, his leg in a cast, struggling with a brief case. The young man asked Georgeann if she could help him get to his car, which was parked nearby. Georgeann consented. Meanwhile, a housemother sleeping by an open window in a nearby fraternity house was awakened by a high-pitched, terrified scream that suddenly stopped. That was the last anyone ever heard or saw of Georgeann Hawkins. Her bashed skull and broken body were dumped on a hillside many miles away, along with the bodies of several other young female victims who had also been lured to their deaths by the good looking, clean-cut, courteous, intelligent, and charming Ted Bundy.

By the time Ted Bundy was caught in Utah with his bashing bar and other homemade tools of torture, he had bludgeoned and strangled to death at least thirty-two young women, raping and savaging many of them in the process. His "hunting" trips had extended into at least five Western states, including Washington, Oregon, Idaho, Utah, and Colorado, where he randomly selected and killed his unsuspecting victims.

Bundy was ultimately convicted of the attempted kidnapping of Carol DeRonche and imprisoned. For this charge he probably would have been paroled within eighteen months. However, before parole could be approved, Bundy was transferred to a jail in Colorado to stand trial for the murder of Caryn Campbell. With Bundy in jail, no one died at his hands or at the end of his savagely swung club. Young women could go about their lives normally, "safe" and separated from Ted Bundy by prison walls. Yet any number of things could have occurred to set Bundy free—an acquittal, some sympathetic judge or parole board, a psychiatrist pronouncing him rehabilitated and safe, a state legislature passing shorter sentencing or earlier parole laws, inadequate prison space, a federal court ruling abolishing life in prison without any possibility for parole, or an escape.

In Bundy's case, it was escape—twice—from Colorado jails. The first time, he was immediately caught and brought back. The second time, Bundy made it to Florida, where fifteen days after his escape he bludgeoned and strangled Margaret Bowman, Lisa Levy, Karen Chandler, and Kathy Kleiner in their Tallahassee sorority house, tearing chunks out of Lisa Levy's breast and buttock with his teeth. Ann Rule, a noted crime writer who became Bundy's confidant while writing her book *The Stranger Beside Me,* described Bundy's attack on Lisa Levy as like that of a rabid animal. On the same night at a different location, Bundy sneaked through an open window and so savagely attacked Cheryl Thomas in her bed that a woman in the apartment next door described the clubbing as seeming to reverberate through the whole house for about ten seconds. Then, three weeks later, less than forty days after his escape from the Colorado jail, Bundy went hunting again. He missed his chance at one quarry, junior high school student Leslie Ann Parmenter, when her brother showed up and thwarted her abduction. But Bundy succeeded the next day in Lake City, where he abducted and killed twelve-year-old Kimberly Diane Leach and dumped her strangled, broken body in an abandoned pig barn.

The criminal justice system and jails in Utah and Colorado did not keep Margaret Bowman, Lisa Levy, Karen Chandler, Kathy Kleiner, Cheryl Thomas, Leslie Ann Parmenter, or little Kimberly Leach safe from Ted Bundy. The state of Florida, however, with its death penalty, has made every other young woman safe from Ted Bundy forever. Capital punishment is society's means of self-defense. Just as a person is justified in using deadly force in defending herself or himself against a would-be killer, so society also has a right to use deadly force to defend itself and its citizens from those who exhibit a strong propensity to kill whenever the opportunity and the urge arise.

However, while everyone wants a safe society, some people would say that capital punishment is too strong a means of ensuring it. Contemporary social critic Hendrick Hertzberg often attacks the death penalty, using arguments that are familiar, but not compelling, to those who do not share his absolute value-of-life position. For example, in one article he tries to paint a graphic picture of how horrible and painful even the most modern execution methods, such as lethal injection, are to the prisoner ("Premeditated"). Elsewhere he dismisses the deterrence argument as "specious," since "[n]o one has ever been able to show that capital punishment lowers the murder rate" ("Burning" 4). But the Florida death penalty has, in fact, made certain that Ted Bundy will never again go on one of his hunting trips to look for another young woman's skull to bash or body to ravage. A needle prick in the arm hardly conjures up images of excruciating pain so great as to be cruel and unusual. Thousands of good people with cancer and other diseases or injuries endure much greater pain every day until death. Therefore, waiting for death, even in pain, is more a part of a common life experience than a cruel or unusual punishment.

Of course, the possibility of mistakenly executing an innocent person is a serious concern. However, our entire criminal justice system is tilted heavily toward the accused, who is protected from the start to the end of the criminal justice procedure by strong individual-rights guarantees in the Fourth, Fifth, Sixth, and Seventh Amendments of the U.S. Constitution. The burden of proof in a criminal case is on the government, and guilt must be proved beyond a reasonable doubt. The chances of a guilty person going free in our system are many times greater than those of an innocent person being convicted. Those opposed may ask, "How do we know that the number of innocent people found guilty is really that low?" The number must be low because when the scandal of an innocent person being convicted comes to light, the media covers it from all angles. The movie *The Thin Blue Line* is an example of such media attention. In addition, the story of *The Thin Blue Line* is illustrative in that the U.S. Supreme Court caught the error and remanded the case, and Randall Adams is no longer subject to the death penalty.

If, however, such a mistake should occur in spite of all the protections guaranteed to the accused, such an innocent death would certainly be tragic, just as each of the nearly 50,000 deaths of innocent people each year on our highways are tragic. As much as we value human life, we inevitably weigh and balance that value against social costs and benefits, whether we like to admit it or not. If the rare, almost nonexistent, chance that an innocent person might be executed is such a terrible evil as to require abolition of capital punishment, then why don't we also demand the abolition of automobiles as well? Because we balance the value of those lives lost in traffic accidents against the importance of automobiles in society. In doing so, we choose to accept the thousands of automobile deaths per year in order to keep our cars. It is interesting to note that even opponents of capital punishment like Hertzberg do not demand abolition of the automobile, which leads to the observation that even they may not be at the extreme, absolute end of the life-value scale, where preservation of life takes precedence over *all* other social concerns.

Just as we as a society have decided that the need for automobiles outweighs their threat to innocent life, we can decide that capital punishment is necessary for the safety and well-being of the general populace. The most legitimate and strongest reason for capital punishment is not punishment, retribution, or deterrence, but simply society's right to self-defense. Society has a right to expect and demand that its government remove forever those persons who have shown they cannot be trusted to circulate in society, even on a limited basis, without committing mayhem. First degree murderers, like Bundy, who hunt and kill their victims with premeditation and malice aforethought must be removed from society permanently as a matter of self-defense.

Having made that decision, there are only two alternatives available—life in prison or death. We base our approval or disapproval of capital punishment as an option on fundamental values and ideals relating to life itself, rather than on statistics or factual evidence. Most of us are a long way from the extreme that considers life to have no value; instead, we crowd more closely to the other side, where life is viewed as inviolable. However, few in our society go so far as to believe that life is sacrosanct, that its preservation is required above all else. Our founding fathers wrote in the Declaration of Independence that all men are endowed by their Creator with unalienable rights, including "life, liberty, and the pursuit of happiness." However, there is no indication that life was more sacred to them than liberty. In fact, Patrick Henry, who would later be instrumental in the adoption of the Bill of Rights to the U.S. Constitution, is most famous for his defiant American Revolutionary declaration, "I know not what course others may take, but as for me, give me liberty or give me death!"

The sentiment that some things are worse than death remains pervasive in this country where millions of soldiers and others have put themselves in harm's way and even sacrificed their lives to preserve and defend freedom for themselves or for the people they leave behind. Many people will readily or reluctantly admit to their willingness to use deadly force to protect themselves or their families from a murderer. The preservation of life, any life, regardless of everything else, is not an absolute value that most people in this country hold.

In fact, many prisoners would prefer to die than to languish in prison. While some might still want to read and expand their minds even while their bodies are confined, for those who are not intellectually or spiritually oriented, life in prison would be a fate worse than death. Bundy himself, in his letters from prison to Ann Rule, declared, "My world is a cage," as he tried to describe "the cruel metamorphosis that occurs in captivity" (qtd. in Rule 148). After his sentencing in Utah, Bundy described his attempts to prepare mentally for the "living hell of prison" (qtd. in Rule 191). Thus, some condemned prisoners, including Gary Gilmore, the first person to be executed after the U.S. Supreme Court found that Utah's death penalty law met Constitutional requirements, refused to participate in the appeals attempting to convert his death sentence to life in prison because he preferred death over such a life. In our society, which was literally founded and sustained on the principle that liberty is more important than life, the argument that it is somehow less cruel and more civilized to deprive someone of liberty for the rest of his or her life than just to end the life sounds hollow. The Fifth Amendment of the U.S. Constitution prohibits the taking

10

of either life or liberty without due process of law, but it does not place one at a higher value than the other.

The overriding concerns of the Constitution, however, are safety and self-defense. The chance of a future court ruling, a release on parole, a pardon, a commutation of sentence, or an escape—any of which could turn the murderer loose to prey again on society—creates a risk that society should not have to bear. Lisa Levy, Margaret Bowman, Karen Chandler, Kathy Kleiner, Cheryl Thomas, and Kimberly Leach were not protected from Bundy by the courts and jails in Utah and Colorado, but other young women who were potential victims are now absolutely protected from Bundy by the Florida death penalty.

The resolutions of most great controversies are, in fact, balancing acts, and capital punishment is no exception. There is no perfect solution; rather, the best answer lies on the side with the greatest advantages. It comes down to choosing, and choosing has a price. Capital punishment carries with it the slight risk that an innocent person will be executed; however, it is more important to protect innocent, would-be victims of already convicted murderers. On balance, society was not demeaned by the execution of Bundy in Florida, as claimed by Hertzberg ("Burning" 49). On the contrary, society is, in fact, better off with Ted Bundy and others like him gone.

Works Cited

Hertzberg, Hendrick. "Burning Question." <u>The New Republic</u> 20 Feb. 1989: 4+.

---. "Premeditated Execution." <u>Time</u> 18 May 1992: 49.

Rule, Ann. <u>The Stranger Beside Me</u>. New York: Penguin, 1989.

<u>The Thin Blue Line</u>. Dir. Errol Morris. HBO Video, 1988.

A FINAL NOTE ABOUT LOGICAL ANALYSIS

No method for analyzing arguments is perfect, and no method can guarantee that everyone using it will assess an argument the same way. Uniform results are not especially desirable anyway. What would be left to talk about? The point of argumentative analysis is to step back and examine an argument carefully, to detect how it is structured, to assess the cogency and power of its logic. The Toulmin method helps us move beyond a hit-or-miss approach to logical analysis, but it cannot yield a conclusion as compelling as mathematical proof.

Convincing and persuading always involve more than logic, and, therefore, logical analysis alone is never enough to assess the strength of an argument. For example, William May's argument attempts to discredit those like Dr. Jack Kevorkian who assist patients wishing to take their own lives. May depicts Kevorkian as offering assistance without sufficient consultation with the patient. Is his depiction accurate? Clearly, we can answer this question only by finding out more about how Kevorkian and others like him work. Because such questions are not a part of logical analysis, they have not been of concern to us in this chapter. But any adequate and thorough analysis of an argument must also address questions of fact and the interpretation of data.

Chapter 4

Reading and Writing about Visual Arguments

We live in a world awash in pictures. We turn on the TV and see not just performers, advertisers, and talking heads but dramatic footage of events from around the world, commercials as visually creative as works of art, and video images to accompany our popular music. We boot up our computers and surf the Net; many of the waves we ride are visual swells, enticing images created or enhanced by the very machines that take us out to sea. We drive our cars through a gallery of street art — on billboards and buildings and on the sides of buses and trucks. We go to movies, video stores, arcades, and malls and window-shop, entertained by the images of fantasy fulfillment each retailer offers. Print media are full of images; in our newspapers, for instance, photos, drawings, and computer graphics appear in color and vie with print for space. Even college textbooks, once mostly blocks of uninterrupted prose with an occasional black-and-white drawing or photo, now often have colorful graphics and elaborate transparency overlays.

If a picture is indeed worth a thousand words, then perhaps our image-saturated world is all to the good. Or perhaps, as some argue, all this rapid-fire, reality-manipulating technology yields jaded people with short attention spans who haven't the patience for the slower thought needed to understand words in print. But no matter how we assess it, the technology rolls on, continually extending its range and reach, filling our minds and, more importantly, *forming* them. Visual images are not just "out there" clamoring for our attention but also "in here," part of how we attend to and judge experience. Like language, visual images are rhetorical. They persuade us in obvious and not-so-obvious ways. And so we need some perspective on visual rhetoric; we need to learn how to recognize its power and how to use it effectively and responsibly.

UNDERSTANDING VISUAL ARGUMENTS

Visual rhetoric is *the use of images, sometimes coupled with sound or appeals to the other senses, to make an argument or persuade us to act as the image-maker would have us act.* Probably the clearest examples are advertisements and political cartoons, a few of which we will examine shortly. But visual rhetoric is as ubiquitous and as old as human civilization. We do not ordinarily think, say, of a car's body style as "rhetoric," but clearly it is, because people are persuaded to pay tens of thousands of dollars for the sleekest new body style when they could spend a few thousand for an older car that would get them from home to work or school just as well. Consider also the billions of dollars we spend on clothes, hairstyles, cosmetics, diets, and exercise programs—all part of the rhetoric of making the right "visual statement" in a world that too often judges us solely by how we look. We spend so much because our self-images depend in part on others' responses to our cars, bodies, offices, homes—to whatever appears to represent "us." No doubt we all want to be liked and loved for our true selves, but distinguishing this "inside" from the "outside" we show the world has never been easy. Because we tend to become the image we cultivate, the claim that "image is everything" may not be as superficial as it sounds. Even if it isn't everything, image certainly is important enough to preoccupy us, and we would be hard pressed to name a significant human activity that is not entangled in visual rhetoric.

We might imagine that visual rhetoric is something peculiarly modern—that without photography, computers, and Madison Avenue it wouldn't amount to much. But we would be mistaken. The pharaohs of ancient Egypt didn't build the pyramids merely to have a place to be buried; these immense structures "proclaim" the power and status of the rulers who had them built, as well as the civilization and empire they symbolize, and they "argue" against a view of human existence as merely transitory. Even now, millennia after ancient Egypt's decline, we can only stand before the pyramids in awe and wonder. The impact of visual rhetoric is not always as fleeting as the clever new commercial on television.

As old as the pyramids are, visual rhetoric is still older. We will never find its origins, for it began with natural places that prehistoric people invested with sacred power, with the earliest drawings and paintings, with natural and sculpted objects used in religious rites and festivals. When a culture disappears, most visual rhetoric is lost, leaving only a few fragments that archaeologists dig up and speculate about thousands of years later. There is no way to know exactly what these artifacts meant and no way to even estimate what remains undiscovered or lost beyond any possibility of recovery.

Although there is much that we cannot know about visual rhetoric—where and why it began, or what it might be like hundreds or thousands of years in the future, in cultures we cannot imagine, using technologies we cannot envision—we can still study how it works now, in our culture and time. We can learn to appreciate the art that goes into making potent images. We can learn how to interpret and evaluate images. We can reflect on the ethics of visual argumentation and persuasion. We can create visual rhetoric ourselves, in images that stand alone or in visuals combined with text. This chapter analyzes some common forms of visual rhetoric. The assignments will give you practice in analyzing images and creating visual rhetoric of your own.

"READING" IMAGES

Rhetorical analysis of visual rhetoric involves examining images to see how they attempt to convince or persuade an audience. We must first recognize that "reading" an image demands interpretive skills no less than does reading a written text. Pictures, even photographs, do not merely reflect reality, as many people assume. Pictures are symbols that must be read, just as language is read; this becomes clear when we look at art from different cultures. The bodies in Egyptian paintings seem distorted to us, flattened onto a geometrical plane in a combination of full frontal and profile views, but the Egyptians understood these figures as representing the human form as timeless and ideal. Also, visual symbols operate within a culture—the color white, for example, suggests purity in one culture, death in another. To read an argument made through images, a critic must be able to recognize visual allusions to other aspects of the culture. For example, initially Americans knew that the white mustaches on the celebrities in the milk commercials alluded to children's milk-drinking style; but more recently, the milk mustache has become an allusion to the ad campaign itself, which has become part of our culture.

As with inquiry into any argument, we ought to begin with questions about rhetorical context: When was the visual argument created and by whom? To what audience was it originally aimed and with what purpose? Then we can ask what claim a visual argument makes and what reasons it offers in support of that claim. "Reading" the claims and reasons of purely visual arguments requires greater interpretive skills than does reading verbal arguments, simply because pictures are even more ambiguous than words—they mean different things to different people. Then, as with verbal texts that make a case, we can examine the visual argument for evidence, assumptions, and bias, and we can ask what values it favors and what will be the implications of accepting the argument—for instance, if we buy the Jaguar, what kind of debt will we incur?

Although it is possible to make a claim and support it with no words at all, most arguments that use images do not rest their cases entirely on the images. If the visual argument includes some verbal text, some of the reasoning usually appears in the words. Either way, if we see that an argument is offered, we can inquire into it as we have done with verbal texts: What is the claim?

the reason(s)? the evidence? the assumptions? the bias? the implications? What values are being promoted? We cannot, however, expect a visual argument to make a fully developed argument to convince.

Many visual arguments do not even attempt to persuade through reasoning; they rely instead on ethical and emotional appeals. Appeals to emotions and character are frequent and powerful in visual arguments. They are most obvious in advertising, where the aim is to move a target audience to buy a service or product. In many advertisements, especially for products like beer, cigarettes, and perfume, where the differences are subjective or virtually nonexistent, emotional appeal and character identification are all there is. Although some images make us fear what will happen if we don't buy the product, vote for the candidate, or at least believe the argument's claim, most emotional appeals work by promising to reward our desires for love, status, peace of mind, or escape from everyday responsibilities.

Advertisements and other forms of visual argument use ethical appeals as well, associating their claim with values the audience approves of and wants to identify with — such as images that show nature being preserved, races living in harmony, families staying in touch, and people attaining the American dream of upward mobility. However, some advertisements appeal to counter-culture values through images of rebellion against conventional respectability. Such ads project an ethos of "attitude" and rule-breaking.

In evaluating the ethics of visual rhetoric, we need to consider whether the argument appeals to logic and, if so, whether the case is at least reasonable: Does the image encourage good reasoning, or does it oversimplify and even mislead? Most likely, we will want to look for the emotional and ethical appeals as well and decide if the argument panders to the audience by playing to their weaknesses and prejudices or manipulates them by playing to their fantasies and fears. We can ask what values the image seems to endorse or wants the audience to identify with, and we can question the implications of widespread acceptance of such values and behavior.

ANALYSIS: FIVE COMMON TYPES OF VISUAL ARGUMENT

In the next pages, we analyze some specific visual arguments in various genres: advertisements, editorial cartoons, public sculpture, and news photographs. We show how "reading" visual texts requires interpretive skills and how interpretive skills, in turn, depend on the critic's knowledge of the context in which the image appears. Practice in analyzing visual rhetoric helps us appreciate the role of culture and context in all communication.

Advertisements

In the arguments made by advertisements, the claims, if not the reasons, are usually clear. And because advertisers aim carefully at target audiences, we can readily see how strategy comes into play in making a persuasive case and in choosing ethical and emotional appeals. Here we examine some advertisements to see how visual images and verbal texts combine to sell products and services to specific audiences.

An advertisement for Pentax (see Figure C-1 in the color section) appeared originally in *Sierra* magazine, published by the environmentalist Sierra Club. *Sierra*'s readership is primarily middle-class adults who love nature and are concerned about preserving the environment. It is not a radical environmental group, however, and most of the ads and articles are of interest to parents planning family trips and wanting to ensure that wilderness will be around for their children and grandchildren to enjoy.

The logical appeal of the ad is obvious. The ad argues that readers should buy a Pentax IQZoom 140M because it is a convenient, light camera with many features that will help them take great pictures. The features of the camera are the reasons for buying it, and these are clearly indicated by the large photo of the camera itself and the text in red print. The small, tacked-on snapshot of the boys is evidence in support of the reasons. Readers who want a user-friendly camera would find the argument persuasive. They want good pictures with minimal fussing. However, rather than letting the argument rest on the technological features of the camera, the advertisers depend heavily on ethical and emotional appeals to sell it to the *Sierra* readers.

The ad features the image of a stock character in mainstream American culture: the soccer mom — although in this case she is the Badger den mother. The choice of this figure shows the strategy of ethical appeal targeted at parents: a wholesome, friendly, young mother reaches out — literally — and "testifies" to how successfully she uses the camera. The advertiser expects *Sierra* readers would trust such a character and admire her values. Her affectionate descriptions of the "scrappy champions" and her reference to the "box of bandages" show that she is loving and nurturing. The Band-Aid on her right knee shows that she is a participant in the action. She is energetic and cheerful in her bright yellow uniform as she smiles up at the readers. They would find nothing in this ad to intimidate them or challenge their ideas about traditional gender roles for women and boys. In short, she confirms middle-American values.

None of what we have said so far addresses the real appeal of the ad, however. The advertisers wanted to get the audience laughing, and the eye-catching image of the woman does just that as it plays with photographic effects. The knowledge of how to "read" a two-dimensional photograph as a realistic image of three-dimensional space is nearly universal, but this image distorts even that "reality," providing some ridiculous relationships in size, such as between the woman's head and the cap that should fit it. The camera and the woman's hand seem grossly out of proportion as they float above her tiny hiking boots. These distortions of reality are funny, not threatening or disorienting, as images in serious art photography can be. Most Americans know that such distorted effects occur when a wide-angle lens is used for a close-up or when the dog decides to sniff the wide-angle lens. Like the exaggeratedly childish uniform on the woman, the wide-angle distortions are merely for fun.

The direct, friendly relationship between the viewer and the woman in the ad is supported by the angle of the camera that took her photograph. The camera angle puts the viewers above her in the position of power. There is nothing intimidating or pretentious about this ad, which suggests through both visual images and verbal text that the Pentax IQZoom 140M is a way for ordinary people to capture fun on film.

You may not think of postage as a form of advertising, but the stamp that appears as Figure C-2 in the color section has raised over $22.3 million for breast cancer research since it was first issued on July 29, 1998. Its fundraising success makes it a compelling example of visual rhetoric, despite the tiny dimensions of its actual size. Called a "semi-postal" stamp, because a percentage of its sale price is donated to fund the cause it represents, it and other stamps in the postal service's "social awareness" stamp category rely on all of the appeals — logical, ethical, emotional, and stylistic.

That you need to buy stamps anyway, and for just a few cents more can get an attractive stamp *and* contribute to a good cause, is a logical reason to buy such a stamp. But the breast cancer stamp persuades people to buy it because all postage stamps confer honor on the subjects they represent. "Getting your face on a stamp" is a highly desirable form of social validation, as not just stamp collectors notice who, or what, has "gotten a stamp": Malcolm X got a stamp; the Sonoran Desert got a stamp. That they did confirms their importance and credibility — their worthiness of our consideration and respect. Furthermore, every time we buy a stamp because of its subject, we reconfirm the subject's value, and, in a sense, participate in our country's shared values as well as reinforce the federal government's inherent authority, since it decides who or what gets a stamp.

Is it, however, just federal validation that has sold more than 377.2 million copies of this stamp? No, its success as a product and rhetorical appeal also has a lot to do with how its image works visually. Designed by breast cancer survivor Ethel Kessler of Bethesda, Maryland, and illustrated by Whitney Sherman of Baltimore, the stamp depicts a goddess. While we may not consciously recognize the female figure as a goddess, we do recognize the image's combination of femaleness and strength: Non-angular lines dominate, suggesting softness, traditionally considered a female attribute; however, the stamp's colors are bold — suggesting vitality and even triumph — and exclude the traditionally feminine color pink. The stamp's minimal main text, "Fund the Fight. Find a Cure," furthers its rhetorical effectiveness by beginning at the left edge of the image, moving in a straight line, and then curving down sharply and encircling the area where the figure's right breast would be. The visual effect is that of highlighting, or circling, an important point.

We may not have noticed the feelings the US postal service evokes or how those feelings contribute to the credibility and appeal of the postal service's products. Nor may we have thought about what an effective advertisement its tiniest product can be, even if it's not specifically helping to raise money for a social cause. That organizations like the Human Genome Project are aggressively competing to get their "faces" on a stamp, however, is evidence that it is.

As the postage stamp shows, visual images with little or no accompanying text can be powerfully persuasive by implying an argument rather than stating it explicitly. Consider the poster reproduced as Figure C-3 of the color section, created by an advertising agency for the Southampton Anti-Bias Task Force. It shows a line of five sharp new crayons, each labeled "flesh." On one level, a viewer may see the poster as an eye-catching message for racial tolerance. However, anyone old enough to recall a now-discontinued Crayola crayon called "flesh" that was the color of the center crayon will see a more complicated argument. This prior knowledge allows viewers to read the image as an argument against the cultural bias that allowed millions of children to grow up thinking that "flesh" was the color skin was supposed to be — and all other skin colors were deviations from the norm. While white people might remember thinking that this "flesh" didn't quite match their own, they knew it approximated the color of white people's skin. Children of other races or mixed races knew that "flesh" was not their flesh.

Because an image invites interpretation rather than blatantly stating a message, it opens a space for contemplation, just as we may contemplate the implied message of any work of art — fiction, film, poetry, painting. Our own reading of this poster led us to wonder if other examples of bias, invisible to all except the victims, exist in American culture. As we noted earlier in this chapter, studying visual rhetoric reminds us of the reader's contribution to the meaning of any text, visual or verbal.

Following Through

1. Although the advertisement for the Volkswagen Beetle shown in Figure C-4 of the color section features an image of the product, as is customary with car ads, the lack of background, the size of the image relative to the white space surrounding it, and the unusual wording of the text all contribute to making this an unconventional piece of visual rhetoric. Consider these elements and any other aspect of the ad as you discuss how it might appeal to a specific audience of car buyers.

2. An advertisement for Comstock, Inc., a company that rents out photographs for commercial purposes, promotes its service with a striking example of its own product. The company wishes to persuade potential clients that it can supply a visual image for any idea. Discuss how the image of the goldfish bowl, (Figure C-5 of the color section) conveys the feeling of being "stuck." Do you find the image and accompanying text persuasive?

(continues)

Following Through (continued)

3. The Adidas advertisement shown as Figure C-7 of the color section is an example of the creative effects possible with photographic techniques. How do you "read" the image of the man in relation to the image of the shadow? How does the entire picture convey the idea of speed? Why do you think the advertisers chose to identify the celebrity athlete in such fine print?

Editorial Cartoons

Editorial cartoons comment on events and issues in the news. At times they can be riotously funny, but more often they offer serious arguments in a concise and witty form. Many political cartoons rely on captions and on dialogue spoken by characters in the picture to make their argument, so they combine visual and verbal argument. Like advertisements, editorial cartoons are not ambiguous in their purpose; their arguments are clearly stated or at least easily inferred. However, as they age, editorial cartoons may become harder to "read" because they usually allude to current events. But some cartoons have longer lifespans, like the one by Mike Keefe (Figure 4.1. See page 77.) that comments on a general condition of contemporary culture—how computers are affecting people's ideas of knowledge.

This cartoon illustrates how "reading" a visual argument depends on a shared knowledge of symbols and visual metaphors within a culture. The image of a thirsty man crawling on hands and knees through a desert is a common visual metaphor suggesting any environment that denies humans something they need to sustain themselves. Other treatments of this metaphor suggest that sustenance could be anything from love to religion to the music of Mozart. In Keefe's cartoon, a highway labeled "information" runs through the desert. The cartoon takes our common metaphor for the Internet, as "information superhighway," and depicts it in a graphic way. The man is literally on the Internet, and he is desperate for wisdom. To read the argument of the cartoon and appreciate its humor, the viewer has to know something about what can be found on the Internet—the advertising, the data, the opinions, and especially the overwhelming glut of information, as suggested by the size of the letters on the road. The cartoon argues that relying on the Internet for knowledge will deprive a civilization of the wisdom it needs to sustain itself.

We might question how convincing political cartoons can be. Can they change people's views on an issue? A picture may indeed be worth a thousand words, but visual arguments must present a concise argument, not a fully reasoned case. Anthony Blair, one critic of visual arguments, has written that "visual arguments tend to be one-dimensional; they present the case for one side only, without including arguments against it. [. . .] Visual arguments,

Figure 4.1

then, must always be suspect in this respect and their power countered by a degree of skepticism and a range of critical questions: 'Is that the whole story?' 'Are there other points of view?' 'Is the real picture so black and white?'"

Cartoons also may fail to change people's minds because their humor comes at the expense of the side they oppose—they satirize and often exaggerate the opposition's view. In fact, political cartoons are usually arguments that "preach to the choir." Believers will applaud having their position cleverly portrayed, while nonbelievers will be more annoyed or offended than persuaded by cartoons that ridicule their position. Consider the two cartoons in Figure 4.2 (page 78), which use both language and visual images to make cases about what the cartoonists see as misplaced priorities in the pro-life and the pro-choice movements.

The McCloskey cartoon (top) argues that the pro-choice demonstrators are hypocritical in their protests about murdered doctors, for they ignore the death of the fetus. The lower half of the drawing emphasizes the fetus by putting it in a black background and giving it wings to symbolize its human soul. This half of the cartoon stands in stark contrast to the "noisy" upper half, in which the protesters look deranged. In the Luckovich cartoon (bottom), the contrast is between the shapeless fetus and the more fully depicted corpse of the doctor, both preserved in specimen bottles. One is a person; the other clearly is not. Viewers on either side of this issue would argue that these portraits misrepresent their positions through oversimplification.

Public Sculpture

Public sculptures, such as war memorials, aim to teach an audience about a nation's past and to honor the values for which its citizens were willing to die.

Figure 4.2

Figure 4.3

Following Through

1. The above cartoon by Gary Varvel (Figure 4.3) comments on attempts in Oregon to legalize doctor-assisted suicide. This is not a funny topic, but Varvel makes a humorous comment on it by exploiting a stock situation in American comedy—that of the ledge-jumper and the would-be rescuer. How does the humor work here to poke fun at the idea of doctor-assisted suicide? What aspects of the larger issue does the cartoon leave out?
2. Find a recent editorial cartoon on an issue of interest to you. Bring it to class, and be prepared to elaborate on its argument and explain its persuasive tactics. Do you agree or disagree with the cartoonist's perspective? Discuss the fairness of the cartoon. Does it minimize the complexity of the issue it addresses?

An example of a public sculpture that can be read as an argument is the Marine Corps Memorial (better known as the Iwo Jima Memorial), which was erected in 1954 on the Mall in Washington, DC (see Figure 4.4, the photograph on page 80). The memorial honors all Marines who gave their lives for their country through a literal depiction of one specific act of bravery, the planting of the American flag on Iwo Jima, a Pacific island that the United States captured from the Japanese in 1945. The claim that the sculpture makes

Figure 4.4

to American audiences is clear: Honor your country. The image of the soldiers straining every muscle to raise the American flag gives the reason: "These men made extreme sacrifices to preserve the values symbolized by this flag." Interpreting the memorial is not difficult for Americans who associate the flag with freedom and who know not only the military custom of raising flags in victory but also the history of the fierce Iwo Jima battle. But the sculpture has more to say. It communicates an emotional appeal to patriotism through details like the wind-whipped flag and the angles of the men's arms and legs, which suggest their supreme struggle.

The Iwo Jima sculpture is indeed a classic war memorial, glorifying a victory on enemy soil. We might therefore compare its argument with the argument of a very different memorial, the Vietnam War Memorial, which was dedicated in Washington in November 1982. Maya Lin designed what has come to be known simply as "the Wall" while she was an undergraduate architecture student at Yale. Her design was controversial because the monument was so untraditional in its design (see Figures 4.5 and 4.6, page 81) and in its argument, which is ambiguous and more difficult to interpret than most public sculpture. With its low, black granite slates into which are etched the names of the war casualties, the Wall conveys a somber feeling; it honors not a victory but the individuals who died in a war that tore the nation apart.

News Photographs

While some news photographs seem merely to record an event, the camera is not an objective machine. The photographer makes many "editorial"

Figure 4.5

Figure 4.6

decisions—whether to snap a picture, when to snap it, what to include and exclude from the image—and artistic decisions about light, depth of field, and so on. Figure 4.7 (see page 83), a photograph that appeared in the *New York Times*, shows one scene photographer Bruce Young encountered when covering a snowstorm that hit Washington, DC, in January 1994. The storm was severe enough to shut down the city and all government operations. Without the caption supplied by the *New York Times*, readers might not have recognized the objects in the foreground as human beings, homeless people huddled on benches, covered by undisturbed snow.

The picture argues that homelessness in America is a national disgrace, a problem that must be solved. The composition of the picture supports this claim. The White House in the background is our nation's "home," a grand and lavishly decorated residence symbolic of our national wealth. In juxtaposition in the foreground, the homeless people look like bags of garbage; they mar the beautiful picture of the snow-covered landscape. Viewers are unlikely to find in this picture evidence to blame the homeless for their condition: they are simply too pathetic, freezing under their blankets of snow. True, there is no in-depth argument here taking into account causes of the problem such as unemployment or mental illness, or solutions such as shelters. The picture simply shows that homelessness is a fact of life in our cities, tarnishing the idealized image of our nation.

Following Through

1. The Vietnam War Memorial invites interpretation and analysis. Because it does not portray a realistic scene or soldiers as does the Iwo Jima Memorial, readings of it may vary considerably—and this was the source of the controversy surrounding it. Look at the two photographs on page 82, and if you have visited the Wall, try to recall your reaction to it. What specific details—the low black wall, its shape, its surfaces—lead to your interpretation? Could you characterize the Wall as having logical, ethical, and emotional appeals?

2. Even if you do not live in Washington, DC, or New York City, where the Statue of Liberty serves as another outstanding example of visual rhetoric, you can probably find public sculpture or monuments to visit and analyze. Alone or with some classmates, take notes and photographs. Then develop your interpretation of the sculpture's argument, specifying how visual details contribute to the case, and present your analysis to the class. Compare your interpretation with those of your classmates.

Graphics

Visual supplements to a longer text such as an essay, article, or manual are known as *graphics*. Given the ubiquity of visual appeals in almost everything

(continues on page 84)

Figure 4.7

Following Through

1. A color news photograph of the October 1998 launch of the space shuttle *Discovery* is reproduced as Figure C-6 of the color section. This was the flight that carried John Glenn into space for the second time. Photographer Gregg Newton captured this image well into the launch, when the plume of smoke was all that was visible. Although some Americans were skeptical that Glenn's flight was merely a clever public relations ploy by NASA, most people celebrated Glenn's accomplishment. Media images such as this contributed to Americans' perspective on the launch. How do you "read" the photo's argument?

2. In a recent newspaper or news magazine, find a photograph related to an issue in the news, something people may have differing opinions about. What perspective or point of view does the photograph offer? Explain your "reading" of the photograph through an analysis of the content, composition, and any other details that contribute to your interpretation.

we read and the widespread use of them in business and industry, it is odd how few school writing assignments require graphics or multimedia support. When students want to use photos, drawings, graphs, and the like in a paper, they tend to ask permission, as if they fear violating some unspoken rule. We believe that the pictorial should not be out of bounds in English papers or other undergraduate writing. Many texts could be more rhetorically effective with visual supplements, and we encourage you to use them whenever they are appropriate and helpful.

Most graphics fall into one of the following categories:

Tables and charts (typically an arrangement of data in columns and
    rows that summarizes the results of research)
Graphs (including bar, line, and pie graphs)
Photographs
Drawings (including maps and cartoons)

Although charts and tables are not technically images or figures, they present data in the form of visual arrangement rather than linear prose. Tables are used to display data economically in one place so that readers can find the information easily, both as they read and afterward if they want to refer to the table again. Consider Figure 4.8, which combines a table with bar graphs. It comes from a study of poverty in the United States. Note how much information is packed into this single visual. Note also how easy it is to read, moving from top to bottom and left to right through the categories. Finally, consider how many long and boring paragraphs it would take to say the same thing in prose.

Graphs are usually no more than tables transformed into visuals we can "read" and interpret more easily. Bar graphs are one example. They allow us to compare subcategories within the major categories almost at a glance. Making the comparisons would be much more difficult if we had only the percentages listed in a table. Bar graphs are best at showing comparisons at some single point in time. In contrast, line graphs allow us to see trends—for example, the performance of the stock market. Pie graphs highlight relative proportions well. When newspapers or news magazines want to show us how the federal budget is spent, for example, they typically use pie graphs with the pieces labeled in some way to represent categories such as national defense, welfare, entitlement programs, and the like. Who gets the biggest pieces of the pie becomes instantly clear and easier to remember—the two major purposes all graphs try to achieve. Graphs in themselves may not make arguments, but they are powerful deliverers of evidence and in that sense fall into the category of visual rhetoric.

As graphics, photographs represent people, objects, and scenes realistically and concretely. They give us a "human's eye" view of something as nothing else can. Thus, for instance, owner's manuals for cars often have a shot of the engine compartment that shows where fluid reservoirs are located. Clearly,

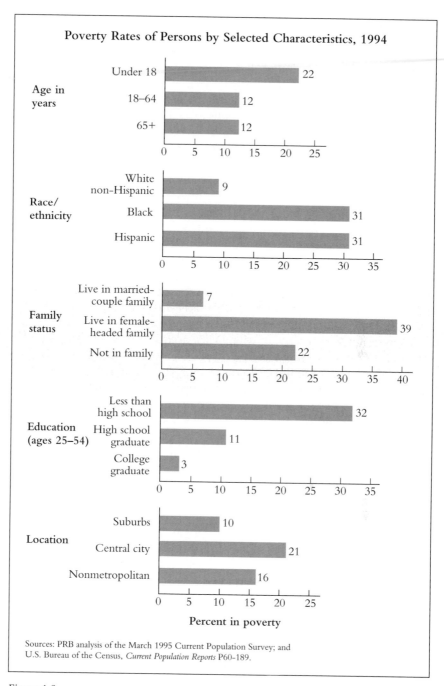

Poverty Rates of Persons by Selected Characteristics, 1994

Figure 4.8

such photos serve highly practical purposes, such as helping us locate the dipstick. But they're also used, for example, in biographies; we get a better sense of, say, Abraham Lincoln's life and times when pictures of him, his family, his home, and so on are included. But photographs can do much more than merely inform. They can also be highly dramatic and powerfully emotional in ways that only the best writers can manage with prose—hence their inclusion to generate interest and excitement or to communicate an overall impression of a subject matter or theme. Photos are powerful persuaders.

But photogaphs are not very analytical—by their nature, they give us the surface of things, only what the camera can "see." A different type of graphic, drawings, are preferable when we want to depict how something is put together or structured. For instance, instructions for assembling and installing a ceiling fan or a light fixture usually have many diagrams—a large one showing how all the parts fit together and smaller ones that depict steps in the process in more detail. Corporate publications often include diagrams of the company's organizational hierarchy or chain of command. Scientific articles and textbooks are often full of drawings or illustrations created with computer graphics; these publications use drawings because science writers want us to understand structures, particularly internal structures, that often are difficult to capture on film and difficult to interpret when they are so captured. For example, our sense of what DNA looks like and our understanding of its double helix structure comes almost entirely from diagrams.

The following article illustrates how a variety of graphics can contribute to the effectiveness of a written text that informs readers about a complicated and often misunderstood subject, attention-deficit hyperactivity disorder (ADHD). ADHD afflicts millions of people the world over, most in their youth, during the years of formal education. We have taught many college students diagnosed with ADHD, and you probably have friends whose intense struggle for self-control and focus makes coping with college especially difficult. This article both informs us about ADHD and argues two theses about it: (1) that self-control is the primary problem and (2) that the disorder is genetic, related to smaller-than-usual structures in the brain that regulate attention. As you read, notice how the graphics support the author's informative and argumentative purposes. (In our textbook's reproduction of the article, the original page layout has been changed. You may wish to consult a copy of the magazine or access it via the Net at <www.sciam.com>.)

Attention-Deficit Hyperactivity Disorder
Russell A. Barkley

This article appeared in the September 1998 issue of Scientific American; *its author, Russell Barkley, is a professor of psychiatry and neurology at the University of Massachusetts Medical Center in Worcester and an internationally recognized expert on ADHD.*

My Pentax IQZoom 140M

This is the print format switch. I chose to get a panorama print of all my scrappy champions.

This is the compact, lightweight design. Smaller to carry than your average box of bandages.

[My Photo]

How I captured my little Badgers, after they emerged victorious from "Capture the Flag."

This is the six-segment multi-pattern metering system that shed a winning light on the whole bunch, from persistent Pete to wild William.

This is the 38-140mm power zoom lens. A handy zoom to have when your subjects are wielding live snakes or suspicious bugs.

Aren't
your
pictures
worth
a
PENTAX
?

Pentax Corporation
35 Inverness Drive East
Englewood, CO 80112
www.pentax.com

Source: Thomas & Perkins Advertising

Figure C-1

Figure C-2

Source: AP Photo/U.S. Postal Service

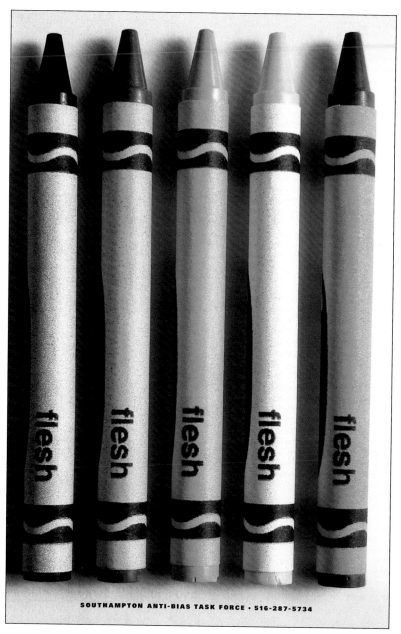

SOUTHAMPTON ANTI-BIAS TASK FORCE · 516-287-5734

Figure C-3   Source: Holzman & Kaplan Worldwide, Bret Wills-Photographer.

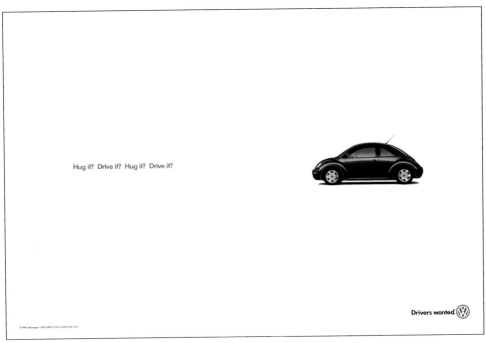

Figure C-4

Source: By permission of Volkswagen of America, Inc.

Figure C-5

Source: www.comstock.com

Source: Reuters/Gregg Newton Archive Photos

Figure C-6

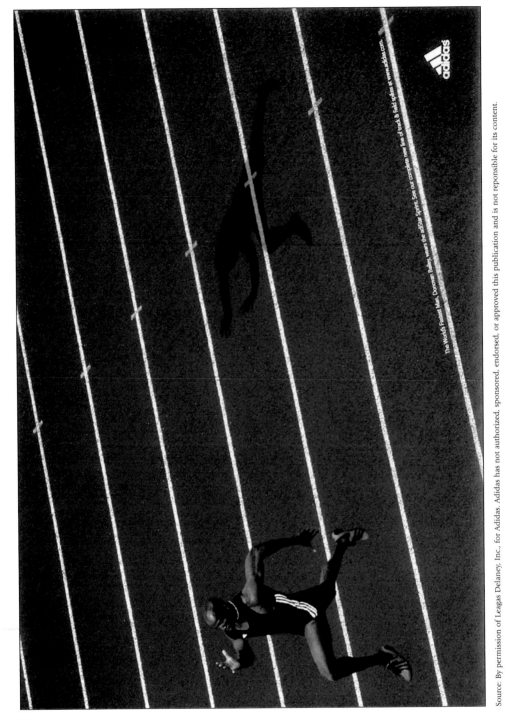

Source: By permission of Leagas Delaney, Inc., for Adidas. Adidas has not authorized, sponsored, endorsed, or approved this publication and is not reponsible for its content.

Figure C-7

Children with ADHD cannot control their responses to their environment. This lack of control makes them hyperactive, inattentive, and impulsive.

As I watched five-year-old Keith in the waiting room of my office, I could see why his parents said he was having such a tough time in kindergarten. He hopped from chair to chair, swinging his arms and legs restlessly, and then began to fiddle with the light switches, turning the lights on and off again to everyone's annoyance — all the while talking nonstop. When his mother encouraged him to join a group of other children busy in the playroom, Keith butted into a game that was already in progress and took over, causing the other children to complain of his bossiness and drift away to other activities. Even when Keith had the toys to himself, he fidgeted aimlessly with them and seemed unable to entertain himself quietly. Once I examined him more fully, my initial suspicions were confirmed: Keith had attention-deficit hyperactivity disorder (ADHD).

Since the 1940s, psychiatrists have applied various labels to children who are hyperactive and inordinately inattentive and impulsive. Such youngsters have been considered to have "minimal brain dysfunction," "brain-injured child syndrome," "hyperkinetic reaction of childhood," "hyperactive child syndrome" and, most recently, "attention-deficit disorder." The frequent name changes reflect how uncertain researchers have been about the underlying causes of, and even the precise diagnostic criteria for, the disorder.

Within the past several years, however, those of us who study ADHD have begun to clarify its symptoms and causes and have found that it may have a genetic underpinning. Today's view of the basis of the condition is strikingly different from that of just a few years ago. We are finding that ADHD is not a disorder of attention per se, as had long been assumed. Rather it arises as a developmental failure in the brain circuitry that underlies inhibition and self-control. This loss of self-control in turn impairs other important brain functions crucial for maintaining attention, including the ability to defer immediate rewards for later, greater gain.

ADHD involves two sets of symptoms: inattention and a combination of hyperactive and impulsive behaviors (see table on page 89). Most children are more active, distractible and impulsive than adults. And they are more inconsistent, affected by momentary events and dominated by objects in their immediate environment. The younger the children, the less able they are to be aware of time or to give priority to future events over more immediate wants. Such behaviors are signs of a problem, however, when children display them significantly more than their peers do.

Boys are at least three times as likely as girls to develop the disorder; indeed, some studies have found that boys with ADHD outnumber girls with the condition by nine to one, possibly because boys are genetically more prone to disorders of the nervous system. The behavior patterns that typify ADHD usually arise between the ages of three and five. Even so, the age of onset can vary widely: some children do not develop symptoms until late childhood or even early adolescence. Why their symptoms are delayed remains unclear.

Huge numbers of people are affected. Many studies estimate that between 2 and 9.5 percent of all school-age children worldwide have ADHD; researchers have identified it in every nation and culture they have studied. What is more, the condition, which was once thought to ease with age, can persist into adulthood. For example, roughly two thirds of 158 children with ADHD my colleagues and I evaluated in the 1970s still had the disorder in their twenties. And many of those who no longer fit the clinical description of ADHD were still having significant adjustment problems at work, in school or in other social settings.

To help children (and adults) with ADHD, psychiatrists and psychologists must better understand the causes of the disorder. Because researchers have traditionally viewed ADHD as a problem in the realm of attention,

Diagnosing ADHD

Psychiatrists diagnose attention-deficit hyperactivity disorder (ADHD) if the individual displays six or more of the following symptoms of inattention or six or more symptoms of hyperactivity and impulsivity. The signs must occur often and be present for at least six months to a degree that is maladaptive and inconsistent with the person's developmental level. In addition, some of the symptoms must have caused impairment before the age of seven and must now be causing impairment in two or more settings. Some must also be leading to significant impairment in social, academic or occupational functioning; none should occur exclusively as part of another disorder.

Inattention	Hyperactivity and Impulsivity
Fails to give close attention to details or makes careless mistakes in schoolwork, work or other activities	Fidgets with hands or feet or squirms in seat
Has difficulty sustaining attention in tasks or play activities	Leaves seat in classroom or in other situations in which remaining seated is expected
Does not seem to listen when spoken to directly	Runs about or climbs excessively in situations in which it is inappropriate (in adolescents or adults, subjective feelings of restlessness)
Does not follow through on instructions and fails to finish schoolwork, chores or duties in the workplace	
Has difficulty organizing tasks and activities	Has difficulty playing or engaging in leisure activities quietly
Avoids, dislikes or is reluctant to engage in tasks that require sustained mental effort (such as schoolwork)	Is "on the go" or acts as if "driven by a motor"
Loses things necessary for tasks or activities (such as toys, school assignments, pencils, books or tools)	Talks excessively
	Blurts out answers before questions have been completed
Is easily distracted by extraneous stimuli	Has difficulty awaiting turns
Is forgetful in daily activities	Interrupts or intrudes on others

Source: Reprinted with permission from the *Diagnostic and Statistical Manual of Mental Disorders,* Fourth Edition, Text Revision. © 2000, American Psychiatric Association.

some have suggested that it stems from an inability of the brain to filter competing sensory inputs, such as sights and sounds. But recently scientists led by Joseph A. Sergeant of the University of Amsterdam have shown that children with ADHD do not have difficulty in that area; instead they cannot inhibit their impulsive motor responses to such input. Other researchers have found that children with ADHD are less capable of preparing motor responses in anticipation of events and are insensitive to feedback about errors made in those responses. For example, in a commonly used test of re-action time, children with ADHD are less able than other children to ready themselves to press one of several keys when they see a warning light. They also do not slow down after making mistakes in such tests in order to im-prove their accuracy.

The Search for a Cause

No one knows the direct and immediate causes of the difficulties experi-enced by children with ADHD, although advances in neurological imaging techniques and genetics promise to clarify this issue over the next five years. Already they have yielded clues, albeit ones that do not yet fit together into a coherent picture.

Imaging studies over the past decade have indicated which brain re-gions might malfunction in patients with ADHD and thus account for the symptoms of the condition. That work suggests the involvement of the prefrontal cortex, part of the cerebellum, and at least two of the clus-ters of nerve cells deep in the brain that are collectively known as the basal ganglia (see illustration on page 91). In a 1996 study F. Xavier Castellanos, Judith L. Rapoport and their colleagues at the National Insti-tute of Mental Health found that the right prefrontal cortex and two basal ganglia called the caudate nucleus and the globus pallidus are significantly smaller than normal in children with ADHD. Earlier this year Castellanos's group found that the vermis region of the cerebellum is also smaller in ADHD children.

The imaging findings make sense because the brain areas that are re-duced in size in children with ADHD are the very ones that regulate atten-tion. The right prefrontal cortex, for example, is involved in "editing" one's behavior, resisting distractions and developing an awareness of self and time. The caudate nucleus and the globus pallidus help to switch off auto-matic responses to allow more careful deliberation by the cortex and to co-ordinate neurological input among various regions of the cortex. The exact role of the cerebellar vermis is unclear, but early studies suggest it may play a role in regulating motivation.

10

What causes the structures to shrink in the brains of those with ADHD? No one knows, but many studies have suggested that mutations in several genes that are normally very active in the prefrontal cortex and basal ganglia might play a role. Most researchers now believe that ADHD is a polygenic disorder—that is, that more than one gene contributes to it.

Early tips that faulty genetics underlie ADHD came from studies of the relatives of children with the disorder. For instance, the siblings of children with ADHD are between five and seven times more likely to develop the

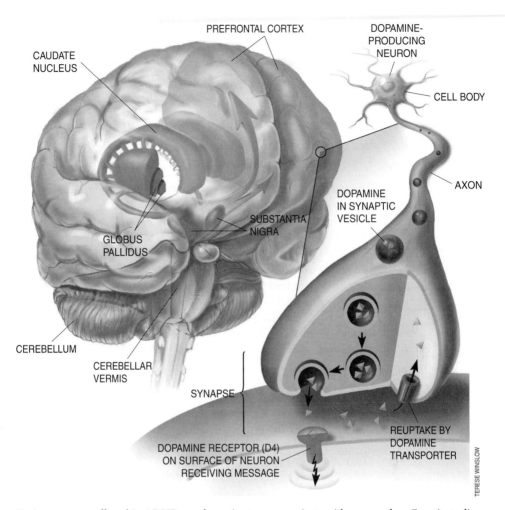

Brain structures affected in ADHD use dopamine to communicate with one another. Genetic studies suggest that people with ADHD might have alterations in genes encoding either the D4 dopamine receptor, which receives incoming signals, or the dopamine transporter, which scavenges released dopamine for reuse. The substantia nigra, where the death of dopamine-producing neurons causes Parkinson's disease, is not affected in ADHD.

syndrome than children from unaffected families. And the children of a parent who has ADHD have up to a 50 percent chance of experiencing the same difficulties.

The most conclusive evidence that genetics can contribute to ADHD, however, comes from studies of twins. Jacquelyn J. Gillis, then at the University of Colorado, and her colleagues reported in 1992 that the ADHD risk of a child whose identical twin has the disorder is between 11 and 18 times greater than that of a nontwin sibling of a child with ADHD; between 55 and 92 percent of the identical twins of children with ADHD eventually develop the condition.

One of the largest twin studies of ADHD was conducted by Helene Gjone and Jon M. Sundet of the University of Oslo with Jim Stevenson of the University of Southampton in England. It involved 526 identical twins, who inherit exactly the same genes, and 389 fraternal twins, who are no more alike genetically than siblings born years apart. The team found that ADHD has a heritability approaching 80 percent, meaning that up to 80 percent of the differences in attention, hyperactivity and impulsivity between people with ADHD and those without the disorder can be explained by genetic factors.

Nongenetic factors that have been linked to ADHD include premature birth, maternal alcohol and tobacco use, exposure to high levels of lead in early childhood and brain injuries — especially those that involve the prefrontal cortex. But even together, these factors can account for only between 20 and 30 percent of ADHD cases among boys; among girls, they account for an even smaller percentage. (Contrary to popular belief, neither dietary factors, such as the amount of sugar a child consumes, nor poor child-rearing methods have been consistently shown to contribute to ADHD.)

Which genes are defective? Perhaps those that dictate the way in which the brain uses dopamine, one of the chemicals known as neurotransmitters that convey messages from one nerve cell, or neuron, to another. Dopamine is secreted by neurons in specific parts of the brain to inhibit or modulate the activity of other neurons, particularly those involved in emotion and movement. The movement disorders of Parkinson's disease, for example, are caused by the death of dopamine-secreting neurons in a region of the brain underneath the basal ganglia called the substantia nigra.

Some impressive studies specifically implicate genes that encode, or serve as the blueprint for, dopamine receptors and transporters; these genes are very active in the prefrontal cortex and basal ganglia. Dopamine receptors sit on the surface of certain neurons. Dopamine delivers its message to those neurons by binding to the receptors. Dopamine transporters protrude from neurons that secrete the neurotransmitter; they take up unused dopamine so that it can be used again. Mutations in the dopamine receptor gene can render receptors less sensitive to dopamine. Conversely, mutations in the dopamine transporter gene can yield overly effective transporters that scavenge secreted dopamine before it has a chance to bind to dopamine receptors on a neighboring neuron.

In 1995 Edwin H. Cook and his colleagues at the University of Chicago reported that children with ADHD were more likely than others to have a particular variation in the dopamine transporter gene *DAT1*. Similarly, in 1996 Gerald J. LaHoste of the University of California at Irvine and his co-

15

workers found that a variant of the dopamine receptor gene *D4* is more common among children with ADHD. But each of these studies involved 40 or 50 children—a relatively small number—so their findings are now being confirmed in larger studies.

From Genes to Behavior

How do the brain-structure and genetic defects observed in children with ADHD lead to the characteristic behaviors of the disorder? Ultimately, they might be found to underlie impaired behavioral inhibition and self-control, which I have concluded are the central deficits in ADHD.

Self-control—or the capacity to inhibit or delay one's initial motor (and perhaps emotional) responses to an event—is a critical foundation for the performance of any task. As most children grow up, they gain the ability to engage in mental activities, known as executive functions, that help them deflect distractions, recall goals and take the steps needed to reach them. To achieve a goal in work or play, for instance, people need to be able to remember their aim (use hindsight), prompt themselves about what they need to do to reach that goal (use forethought), keep their emotions reined in and motivate themselves. Unless a person can inhibit interfering thoughts and impulses, none of these functions can be carried out successfully. 20

In the early years, the executive functions are performed externally: children might talk out loud to themselves while remembering a task or puzzling out a problem. As children mature, they internalize, or make private, such executive functions, which prevents others from knowing their thoughts. Children with ADHD, in contrast, seem to lack the restraint needed to inhibit the public performance of these executive functions.

The executive functions can be grouped into four mental activities. One is the operation of working memory—holding information in the mind while working on a task, even if the original stimulus that provided the information is gone. Such remembering is crucial to timeliness and goal-directed behavior: it provides the means for hindsight, forethought, preparation and the ability to imitate the complex, novel behavior of others— all of which are impaired in people with ADHD.

The internalization of self-directed speech is another executive function. Before the age of six, most children speak out loud to themselves frequently, reminding themselves how to perform a particular task or trying to cope with a problem, for example. ("Where did I put that book? Oh, I left it under the desk.") In elementary school, such private speech evolves into inaudible muttering; it usually disappears by age 10 [see "Why Children Talk to Themselves," by Laura E. Berk; *Scientific American*, November 1994]. Internalized, self-directed speech allows one to reflect to oneself, to follow

A Psychological Model of ADHD

A loss of behavioral inhibition and self-control leads to the following disruptions in brain functioning:

Impaired Function	Consequence	Example
Nonverbal working memory	Diminished sense of time Inability to hold events in mind Defective hindsight Defective forethought	Nine-year-old Jeff routinely forgets important responsibilities, such as deadlines for book reports or an after-school appointment with the principal
Internalization of self-directed speech	Deficient rule-governed behavior Poor self-guidance and self-questioning	Five-year-old Audrey talks too much and cannot give herself useful directions silently on how to perform a task
Self-regulation of mood, motivation and level of arousal	Displays all emotions publicly; cannot censor them Diminished self-regulation of drive and motivation	Eight-year-old Adam cannot maintain the persistent effort required to read a story appropriate for his age level and is quick to display his anger when frustrated by assigned schoolwork
Reconstitution (ability to break down observed behaviors into component parts that can be recombined into new behaviors in pursuit of a goal)	Limited ability to analyze behaviors and synthesize new behaviors Inability to solve problems	Fourteen-year-old Ben stops doing a homework assignment when he realizes that he has only two of the five assigned questions; he does not think of a way to solve the problem, such as calling a friend to get the other three questions

Source: Lisa Burnett

rules and instructions, to use self-questioning as a form of problem solving and to construct "meta-rules," the basis for understanding the rules for using rules—all quickly and without tipping one's hand to others. Laura E. Berk and her colleagues at Illinois State University reported in 1991 that the internalization of self-directed speech is delayed in boys with ADHD.

A third executive mental function consists of controlling emotions, motivation and state of arousal. Such control helps individuals achieve goals by enabling them to delay or alter potentially distracting emotional reactions to a particular event and to generate private emotions and motiva-

Psychological tests used in ADHD research include the four depicted here. The tower-building test (upper left), *in which the subject is asked to assemble balls into a tower to mimic an illustration, measures forethought, planning and persistence. The math test* (upper right) *assesses working memory and problem-solving ability. In the auditory attention test* (lower left), *the subject must select the appropriate colored tile according to taped instructions, despite distracting words. The time estimation test* (lower right) *measures visual attention and subjective sense of time intervals. The subject is asked to hold down a key to illuminate a lightbulb on a computer screen for the same length of time that another bulb was illuminated previously.*

tion. Those who rein in their immediate passions can also behave in more socially acceptable ways.

The final executive function, reconstitution, actually encompasses two separate processes: breaking down observed behaviors and combining the parts into new actions not previously learned from experience. The capacity for reconstitution gives humans a great degree of fluency, flexibility and creativity; it allows individuals to propel themselves toward a goal without having to learn all the needed steps by rote. It permits children as they mature to direct their behavior across increasingly longer intervals by combining behaviors into ever longer chains to attain a goal. Initial studies imply that children with ADHD are less capable of reconstitution than are other children.

25

I suggest that like self-directed speech, the other three executive functions become internalized during typical neural development in early childhood. Such privatization is essential for creating visual imagery and verbal thought. As children grow up, they develop the capacity to behave covertly, to mask some of their behaviors or feelings from others. Perhaps because of faulty genetics or embryonic development, children with ADHD have not attained this ability and therefore display too much public behavior and speech. It is my assertion that the inattention, hyperactivity and impulsivity of children with ADHD are caused by their failure to be guided by internal instructions and by their inability to curb their own inappropriate behaviors.

Prescribing Self-Control

If, as I have outlined, ADHD is a failure of behavioral inhibition that delays the ability to privatize and execute the four executive mental functions I have described, the finding supports the theory that children with ADHD might be helped by a more structured environment. Greater structure can be an important complement to any drug therapy the children might receive. Currently children (and adults) with ADHD often receive drugs such as Ritalin that boost their capacity to inhibit and regulate impulsive behaviors. These drugs act by inhibiting the dopamine transporter, increasing the time that dopamine has to bind to its receptors on other neurons.

Such compounds (which, despite their inhibitory effects, are known as psychostimulants) have been found to improve the behavior of between 70 and 90 percent of children with ADHD older than five years. Children with ADHD who take such medication not only are less impulsive, restless and distractible but are also better able to hold important information in mind, to be more productive academically, and to have more internalized speech and better self-control. As a result, they tend to be liked better by other children and to experience less punishment for their actions, which improves their self-image.

My model suggests that in addition to psychostimulants—and perhaps antidepressants, for some children—treatment for ADHD should include training parents and teachers in specific and more effective methods for managing the behavioral problems of children with the disorder. Such methods involve making the consequences of a child's actions more frequent and immediate and increasing the external use of prompts and cues about rules and time intervals. Parents and teachers must aid children with ADHD by anticipating events for them, breaking future tasks down into smaller and more immediate steps, and using artificial immediate rewards. All these steps serve to externalize time, rules and consequences as a replacement for the weak internal forms of information, rules and motivation of children with ADHD.

In some instances, the problems of ADHD children may be severe   30
enough to warrant their placement in special education programs. Although
such programs are not intended as a cure for the child's difficulties, they
typically do provide a smaller, less competitive and more supportive environment in which the child can receive individual instruction. The hope
is that once children learn techniques to overcome their deficits in self-
control, they will be able to function outside such programs.

There is no cure for ADHD, but much more is now known about
effectively coping with and managing this persistent and troubling developmental disorder. The day is not far off when genetic testing for
ADHD may become available and more specialized medications may be
designed to counter the specific genetic deficits of the children who suffer
from it.

Analyzing Barkley's Graphics

Barkley's article contains the following graphics, listed in order of
appearance:

A cartoon depicting the whirling, chaotic world of the ADHD sufferer
A chart of the symptoms of the disorder entitled "Diagnosing ADHD"
A computer-generated, three-dimensional graphic depicting the brain
    and processes having to do with neural activity
Another chart entitled "A Psychological Model of ADHD"
A set of photographs showing tests used in ADHD research

Thus, in a relatively short article, we have a wide range of graphics, each one
of which we could comment on at far greater length than we do here. The following comments are designed to stimulate thinking about how graphics
function rhetorically in a text, not to exhaust what could be said about any
of the graphics.

Turning to the first graphic on page 87, we should notice what it "says"
about the intended audience. *Scientific American*'s readership is mixed; it is
not limited to scientists, but it includes scientists who enjoy reading about
the work of other scientists in other fields. Thus, the articles must be "real science" but also must have broad appeal. The cartoonlike image we first encounter would almost certainly not appear in a "hard-core" science journal
written by specialists for specialists. We might also consider how well the
graphic works to "predict" the content of the article and to represent the
problem of ADHD.

We might compare the opening graphic with the drawing of the brain on
page 91. Clearly, the cartoon is intended for the more "pop" side of *Scientific
American*'s readership, whereas the drawing targets those who want a more detailed understanding of the "hard science" involved in ADHD research. The

article itself moves from knowledge that can be widely shared to information more specialized and harder to grasp, returning at the end to its broader audience's interests. The movement from the cartoon to the drawing mirrors the text's development from the relatively accessible to the more specialized. The drawing assists Barkley in presenting essential information about the disorder itself.

The four photos near the end of the article (page 95) reflect a turning from brain structures and neural processes to a humanistic concern for the welfare of ADHD children. The role of these photographs is less informative than it is persuasive. Because this article from *Scientific American* seems more informative than argumentative, we need to consider how it fits into the general context of debate about ADHD. Although less controversial than it once was, when even its existence was in dispute, ADHD remains a disputed topic. Some contend that the syndrome is diagnosed too often and too easily, perhaps in part at the urging of parents who know that laws mandate special treatment for ADHD cases in schools, such as more time to complete tests. Others argue that the disorder is more environmental than genetic and trace its source to a chaotic family life, too much TV, bad eating habits, and factors other than (or in addition to) brain abnormalities. Finally, among other doubts and criticism are questions often raised by teachers: When a child is properly treated for ADHD, just how impaired is he or she? Is special treatment really warranted? up to what age?

Barkley's article hardly alludes to the controversies surrounding ADHD, probably because the view he develops represents an emerging consensus among researchers. But if we read the article with its unspoken context in mind, we see much in it intended to refute dissenters and skeptics. Clearly, the genetic hypothesis is advanced by both text and graphics, and the concluding four photos claim, in effect, that actual and reliable testing is part of the diagnostic process.

We turn now to another graphic, the charts. Surely the chart entitled "Diagnosing ADHD" on page 89 is included to confirm the existence of definite criteria for diagnosis and to insist that, once made, diagnosis should be neither hasty nor uncertain. Note especially the sentence "The signs must occur often and be present for at least six months to a degree that is maladaptive and inconsistent with the person's developmental level." A similar implicit argument can be found in the second chart, "A Psychological Model of ADHD." It "says" that the disorder is thoroughly conceived, that we know much about it, and that we can be concrete about how the symptoms manifest themselves. These charts, then, although they may appear to be merely information to a casual reader, are actually arguments—claims about the solid, objective reality of the syndrome we call ADHD. They are definitely not merely decorative throw-ins but rather serve complex rhetorical purposes that become especially clear in the larger context of debate about ADHD.

Following Through

1. Discuss the first graphic in the article as an introduction to the article's topic and argument. What function does this graphic serve? What message is conveyed by the assortment of items swirling around the child? Into what categories do the items fall? Why is the child male? How would you characterize his expression? What attitude about his plight does this image suggest that readers will find in the article?

2. Consider these questions as you examine the drawing of the brain on page 91 and the enlarged drawing of the connections between nerve cells, or neurons. What purposes do these visuals serve? For what part of the audience are they intended? Do they help you understand the physiology of the disorder? Can you explain how perspective comes into play in the drawing of the two neurons? Without these graphics, how much would you understand about the complex brain and neural processes discussed?

3. Discuss the four concluding photographs in the article as persuasion. How much information about psychological testing is conveyed by the photos themselves? Why are the adult figures women? How are they dressed? (Suppose they were men in white lab coats. What different impression would this create?) How would you characterize the office or clinical environment in which the child performs the tests? What messages are sent by the child's gender, age, race, clothes, hair, and cast on his left arm? by his body language and facial expressions? What might the persuasive intent be? If there is an implicit argument, what would it be, and why is it necessary?

4. Discuss why Barkley decided to present the material in the two charts in this tabulated form rather than incorporating it into the body of the article.

5. As an exercise in considering the role of graphics, bring to class a paper you have written recently for a college or high school assignment. If you didn't use graphics, ask yourself the following questions: Could the paper be improved with graphic support? If so, given your audience and purpose(s), what graphic types would you use and why? How would you go about securing or creating the graphics? If you did use graphics, be prepared to discuss them—what you did and why, how you went about creating the visuals, and so on. If you now see ways to improve the graphics, discuss your revision strategies as well.

WRITING ASSIGNMENTS

Assignment 1: Analyzing an Advertisement or Editorial Cartoon

Choose an ad or cartoon from a current magazine or newspaper. First, inquire into its rhetorical context: What situation prompted its creation? What purpose does it aim to achieve? Where did it originally appear? Who is its intended audience? What would they know or believe about the product or issue? Then inquire into the argument being made. To do this, you should consult the questions for inquiry on pages 177–178 to the extent that they apply to visual rhetoric. You should also consider some of the points we have made in this chapter that pertain to visual images in particular: What visual metaphors or allusions appear in the ad or cartoon? What prior cultural knowledge and experiences would the audience have to have to "read" the image? Consider how the visual argument might limit the scope of the issue or how it might play to the audience's biases, stereotypes, or fears. After thorough inquiry, reach some conclusion about the effectiveness or ethics of this particular visual argument. Write up your conclusion as a thesis or claim. Write up your analysis as an argument to convince, using the evidence gathered during the inquiry as material to support and develop your claim. Be sure to be specific about the visual details of the ad or cartoon.

STUDENT SAMPLE: *Analysis of Visual Rhetoric*

The following student essay by Kelly Williams serves as an example of the foregoing assignment. Before you begin your own essay, you might want to read the essay and discuss the conclusions Kelly reached about an advertisement for Eagle Brand condensed milk. Unfortunately, we were unable to obtain permission to reprint the advertisement itself, but the descriptions of the ad's text and visual images should make Kelly's analysis easy to follow.

A MOTHER'S TREAT

Kelly Williams

Advertisements are effective only if they connect with their audiences. Advertisers must therefore study the group of people they hope to reach and know what such groups value and what images they like to have of themselves. Often these images come from societal expectations that tell businessmen, mothers, fathers, teens that they should look or act a certain way. Most people have a hard time deviating from these images or stereotypes because adhering to them gives social status. Advertisers tend to look to these stereotypes as a way to sell their products. For example, an ad depicts a man in an expensive suit driving a luxury car, and readers assume he is a lawyer, physician, or business executive. Therefore, doctors,

lawyers, and businessmen will buy this car because they associate it with
the image of status that they would like to project. Likewise, some advertisements try to manipulate women with children by associating a product
with the ideal maternal image that society places on mothers.

An advertisement for Eagle Brand condensed milk typifies the effort
to persuade mothers to buy a product to perform the ideal maternal role.
The advertisement appeared in magazines aimed at homemakers and in
People magazine's "Best and Worst Dressed" issue of September 1998.
The readers of this issue are predominantly young females; those with
children are probably second-income producers or maybe even single
mothers. These readers are struggling to raise a family, and they have
many demands on their time. They may feel enormous pressure to fulfill
ideal corporate and domestic roles. These readers may be susceptible to
pressure to invest in an image that is expected of them.

The advertisement itself creates a strong connection with a maternal audience. The black-and-white photograph depicts a young girl about
kindergarten age. The little girl's facial expression connotes hesitation and
sadness. In the background is a school yard. Other children are walking
toward the school, their heads facing down, creating a feeling of gloom.
All readers will recognize the situation taking place. The little girl is about
to attend her first day of school. One could easily guess that she is looking
back to her mother with a sense of abandonment, pleading for support.
Without a mother pictured, the audience assumes the maternal perspective. The girl's eyes stare at the reader. Her expression evokes protectiveness, especially in an audience of young mothers.

The wording of the text adds some comic relief to the situation. The
ad is not intended to make the readers sad. The words seem to come from
the mind of the child's mother: "For not insisting on bunny slippers for
shoes, for leaving Blankie behind, for actually getting out of the car. . . ."
These words also show that the mother is a good mother, very empathetic
to her daughter's situation. Even the type of print for these words is part
of an effective marketing strategy. The font mimics a "proper" mother's
handwriting. The calligraphy contains no sharp edges, which reinforces
the generalization that mothers are soft, feminine, and gentle.

The intent of the advertisement is to persuade mothers that if they   5
buy Eagle Brand milk and make the chocolate bar treat, they will be good
mothers like the speaker in the ad. It tells women that cooking such treats
helps alleviate stressful situations that occur in everyday family life.
The little girl in the ad is especially effective in reminding maternal figures of their duty to care for and comfort their kids. She evokes the ideal
maternal qualities of compassion, empathy, and protectiveness. Indirectly,
the girl is testing her mother's maternal qualities. The expectations for her
mother (and the reader) to deliver on all of these needs are intense. Happily, there is an easy way to do it. By making these treats, she can fulfill
the role of a genuine mother figure.

The ad also suggests that good mothers reward good behavior. The statements listing the girl's good behavior suggest that it would be heartless not to reward her for her willingness to relinquish her childhood bonds. As the ad says, "It's time for a treat." But good mothers would also know that "Welcome Home Chocolate Bars" are very sweet and rich, so this mother has to say, "I'll risk spoiling your dinner." The invisible mother in the ad is still ideal because she does care about her child's nutrition, but in this case she will make an exception out of her concern for the emotional state of her child. The ad succeeds in selling the product by triggering mothers' maternal instincts to respond to their children's needs.

In many ways this ad is unethical. It pressures women to fit certain ideals so that Eagle Brand can sell more condensed milk. The ideal "mommy" makes the home a warm, safe, comforting place, and the ad suggests that using Eagle Brand is the way to do it. While the ad looks harmless and cute, it actually reinforces social pressures on women to make baked goods as part of their maternal duties. If you don't bake a treat to welcome your child back to the home after school, you are failing as a mother. The recipe includes preparation time, showing that the treat can be made with minimal effort. It gives mothers no excuse for not making it. Moreover, the advertisement exploits children to sell their product. All children have anxieties about new situations, but putting this into the ad just makes women feel guilty about unavoidable stresses their children have to deal with. The ad works by manipulating negative emotions in the readers.

Desserts do not have much nutritional value. It would be hard to make a logical case for making the Welcome Home Bars, so Eagle Brand used an emotional approach and an appeal to the image of the nurturing mother. There is nothing wrong with spoiling a child with a treat once in a while, but it is wrong to use guilt and social pressures to persuade mothers to buy a product.

Assignment 2: Using Visual Rhetoric to Promote Your School

Colleges and universities compete fiercely for students and are therefore as concerned about their image as any corporation or politician. As a class project, collect all the images your school uses to promote itself, including brochures for prospective students, catalogs, class lists, and Web homepages. Choose three or four of the best ones, and in class discussions subject them to careful scrutiny as we did in the previous section with ads and cartoons. Then, working in groups of three or four students or individually, do one or all of the following:

1. Find an aspect of your college or university that has been overlooked in the publications put out by the admissions office but that you believe is a strong selling point. Employing photographs, drawings,

paintings, or some other visual medium, create an image appropriate for one of the school publications you have collected to write an appropriate and appealing short text to go with the image. Then, in a page or two, explain why you think your promotional image would work as well as or better than some of the ones presently in circulation.

2. If someone in the class has the computer knowledge to do so, create an alternative to your school's homepage, or make changes that would make it more appealing to prospective students, their parents, and other people who might use the Web.

3. Imagine that for fun or for purposes of parody or protest you wanted to call attention to aspects of your school that the official images deliberately omit. Proceed as in item 1. In a one- or two-page statement, explain why you chose the image you did and what purpose(s) you want it to serve.

4. Select a school organization (a fraternity or sorority, a club, etc.) whose image you think could be improved. Create a promotional image for it either for the Web or for some other existing or desirable publication.

5. As in item 3, create a visual parody of the official image of a school organization, perhaps as an inside joke intended for other participants in the organization.

No matter which of the preceding you or your group chooses, be sure to consult with other class members as you create and discuss the final results, including how revision or editing might enhance the impact. Remember that visual rhetoric can be altered in many ways; photos, for instance, can be taken from different angles and in different lighting conditions, processed in different ways, enlarged, reduced, trimmed, and so on.

Assignment 3: Analyzing Your Own Visual Rhetoric

Study all the images your class created as argument and/or persuasion in the previous assignment. Select an image to analyze in depth. Write an essay that addresses the following questions:

What audience does the image intend to reach?
What goal did the creator of the image seek to accomplish?

If something is being argued, ask:

What thesis is advanced by the image or its accompanying text?
Are there aspects of the image or text functioning as reasons for holding the thesis?

If an image persuades more than it argues, attempt to discover and understand its major source or sources of appeal. Persuasion appeals to the whole person in an effort to create **identification,** a strong linking of the reader's interests and values with the image that represents something desired or potentially desirable. Hence, we can ask:

How do the images your class created appeal to the audience's interests and values?
Do the images embody emotional appeals? How?

Assignment 4: Writing to Convince

Newspapers have been criticized for printing pictures that used to be considered too personal or gruesome for publication. The famous picture of the firefighter carrying the baby killed in the Oklahoma City bombing is an example, as are pictures of victims of war atrocities in Kosovo and elsewhere. Highly respected newspapers like the *New York Times* have offered defenses for their decisions on this issue. Look into what publishers, readers, and critics have to say on this topic. What issues and questions come up in these debates? Draw a conclusion of your own on this topic, and write an essay supporting it.

Assignment 5: Using Graphics to Supplement Your Own Writing or Other Texts

Select an essay from the preceding assignment that could be improved either by adding graphics or by revising the graphics used. (If none of the papers seems appropriate for visual supplementation or revision, you may want to use one provided by your instructor.) Working alone or collaboratively with a writing group, rewrite/revise one of the papers. Pay attention to purpose and audience. Graphics should be efficient and memorable, designed to achieve a definite purpose and to have impact on a definite audience. For help with using graphics effectively in your writing, see the Best Practices box on page 105, "Guidelines For Using Visuals."

Recall that the best way to learn how to use graphics is by studying how others use them in respected publications. After reading and analyzing the graphics in the article from *Scientific American,* you may want to examine other examples of graphics in news magazines, scholarly books and articles, technical journals, institutional or business reports, and so on. You have many options: Besides adding visuals, you can cut unneeded ones, redesign existing ones, change media (for example, from a photo to a drawing), change types (for example, from a table to a graph), and so on. Working with graphics always means reworking the text as well. Expect changes in one to require changes in the other.

If more than one group works with the same paper, do not consult until rewriting or revising is complete. Then compare the results and discuss the strategies used. Which changes seem to improve the paper most? Why?

Graphics come in a variety of useful forms: as tables to display numerical data economically, as graphs to depict data in a way that permits easy comparison of proportions or trends, as photographs to convey realism and drama, and as drawings to depict structures. Whatever graphics you use, be sure to do the following:

- Make sure every graphic has a definite function. Graphics are not decorative and should never be "thrown" into an essay.
- Choose the kind or form best suited to convey the point you are trying to make.
- Design graphics so that they are easy to "read" and interpret. That is, keep them simple, make them large enough to be read without strain, and use clear labeling.
- Place graphics as close as possible to the text they explain or illustrate. Remember, graphics should be easier to understand than the text they supplement.
- Refer to all your graphics in the text. Readers usually need both the graphic and a text discussion for full understanding.
- Acknowledge the creator or source of each graphic next to the graphic itself. As long as you acknowledge the source or creator, you can borrow freely, just as you can with quotations from texts. Of course, if you wish to publish an essay that includes borrowed graphics, you must obtain written permission.

Chapter 5

Writing Research-Based Arguments

This chapter is intended to help you with any argument you write. Research, which simply means "careful study," is essential to serious inquiry and most well-constructed cases. Before you write, you need to investigate the ongoing conversation about your issue. As you construct your argument, you will need specific evidence and the support of authorities to make a convincing case to a skeptical audience.

Your high school experience may have led you to regard the research paper as different from other papers, but this distinction between researched and nonresearched writing does not usually apply to argumentation. An argument with no research behind it is generally a weak one. Many of the arguments you read may not appear to have been researched because the writers have not cited their sources—most likely because they were writing for the general public rather than for an academic or professional audience. In college writing, however, students are usually required to document all sources of ideas. Although documentation is important for many reasons, perhaps the two most important are these: (1) It allows readers to look up source material for themselves, should they wish to, and (2) it protects both the source and the writer of the paper from **plagiarism,** the presenting of another's words as one's own. (See the Concept Close-Up box on page 108.)

Research for argumentation usually begins not as a search for evidence but as inquiry into an issue you have chosen or been assigned. Your task in inquiry is to discover information about the issue and, what is more important, to find arguments that address the issue and to familiarize yourself with the range of positions and the cases people make for them. You should inquire into these arguments, using your critical-reading skills and entering into dialogues with the authors until you feel satisfied with and confident about the position you take.

Sometimes, however, research must begin at an even earlier stage—for example, when your instructor asks you to select an issue to write about. So we begin with suggestions for finding an issue.

Concept Close-Up

Defining Plagiarism

Plagiarism: From the Latin *plagiarius*, a plunderer, kidnapper, literary thief.

> The appropriating and putting forth as one's own the ideas, language, or designs of another.—*New Grolier Webster International Dictionary*

> Act or instance of taking and passing off as one's own someone else's work or ideas.—*Scribner Dictionary*

Plagiarism is not limited to copying a source or having someone else write a paper for you. These are just the worst cases. It also includes taking an idea from a source without acknowledgment or using a source's actual words without quotation marks. All are serious violations of academic honesty.

FINDING AN ISSUE

Let's say you have been assigned to write an essay on any issue of current public concern, ranging from one debated on your campus to one rooted in international affairs. If you have no idea what to write about, or if you want to follow up on an idea from your writer's notebook, what should you do?

Understand that an Issue Is More Than Just a Topic

You must look for a subject about which people genuinely disagree. For example, homelessness is a **topic:** you could report on many different aspects of it—from the number of homeless people in our country to profiles of individual homeless people. But homelessness in itself is not really an issue, because virtually everyone agrees that the problem exists. However, once you start considering solutions to the problem of homelessness, you are dealing with an **issue,** because people will disagree about how to solve the problem.

Keep Abreast of Current Events and Research the News

Develop the habit of regularly reading newspapers and magazines in print or online to keep informed of debates on current issues. It has become easy to browse the day's news stories when you first turn on your computer. Many newspapers are available online. Major daily newspapers, such as the *New York Times* and the *Wall Street Journal*, maintain commercial Web sites. Here are several:

> *Chicago Tribune* <http://www.chicagotribune.com>
> *Los Angeles Times* <http://www.latimes.com>
> *New York Times* <http://www.nytimes.com>

Wall Street Journal <http://www.wsj.com>
Washington Post <http://www.washingtonpost.com>

Another site, *Newslibrary,* <http://www.newslibrary.com>, allows you to search approximately thirty-five different newspapers. It is best to write on issues of genuine concern to you rather than to manufacture concern at the last minute because a paper is due. In your writer's notebook, record your responses to your reading so that you have a readily available source of ideas.

Visit the current periodicals shelves of your library or local newsstand. Consult the front pages and the editorial/opinion columns of your city's daily papers. In addition, most newsstands and libraries carry the *New York Times* and other large-city dailies that offer thorough coverage of national and international events. Remember that you are looking for an issue, not just a topic, so if you find an article on the front page that interests you, think about how people might disagree over some question it raises. For example, an article announcing that health care costs rose a record fourteen percent in the past year might suggest the issue of government control over the medical profession; a campus newspaper article about a traditionally African-American fraternity could raise the issue of colleges tolerating racial segregation in the Greek system. In addition to newspapers, such magazines as *Time, Newsweek,* and *U.S. News & World Report* cover current events; and others, such as *Harper's, Atlantic Monthly, New Republic, National Review,* and *Utne Reader,* offer essays, articles, and arguments on important current issues. With the growth of the Internet, new resources are now available online that allow quick and easy access to a broad range of information sources.

Research Your Library's Periodicals Indexes

Indexes are lists of articles in specific publications or groups of publications. Your school's library probably has a number of periodicals indexes in print, online, or in other electronic formats. You may be familiar with one index, the *Readers' Guide to Periodical Literature.* (For names of other indexes, see the section "Finding Sources," which begins on page 110.) If you have a vague subject in mind, such as gender discrimination, consulting an index for articles and arguments on the topic can help you narrow your focus. However, if you don't have an issue in mind, looking through the *Readers' Guide* won't be very helpful, so we offer some suggestions for using indexes more efficiently.

You can look, for example, in a newspaper index (some are printed and bound; others are computerized) under "editorial" for a list of topics on which the editors have stated positions, or you can look under the name of a columnist—such as William F. Buckley, Anna Quindlen, or A. M. Rosenthal—whose views on current issues regularly appear in that paper. The bonus for using a newspaper index in this way is that it will lead you directly to arguments on an issue.

Another resource for finding arguments on an issue when you have a topic in mind is *InfoTrac*, a computerized index to magazines, journals, and selected current articles in the *New York Times*. After you type in an appropriate subject word or key word, *InfoTrac* allows you to narrow your search further. If you type in the key word of your subject followed by "and editorial" or "and opinion," only argumentative columns and editorials will appear on your screen. *InfoTrac* now also includes online many full texts of articles.

A further possibility is to browse through an index dedicated solely to periodicals that specialize in social issues topics, such as the *Journal of Social Issues* and *Vital Speeches of the Day*. Finally, *Speech Index* will help you find speeches that have been printed in books.

Inquire into the Issue

Once you have chosen an issue, you can begin your inquiry into positions already articulated in the public conversation. You may already hold a position of your own, but during inquiry you should be open to the full range of viewpoints on the issue; you should look for informative articles and arguments about the issue. This attitude of inquiry is central to the mature reasoning discussed in Chapter 1 (see pages 11–15).

Inquiring into an issue also involves evaluating sources. Remember that research means "careful study," and being careful as you perform these initial steps will make all the difference in the quality of the argument you eventually write. And, the more care you take now, the more time you'll save in the overall preparation of your paper.

Before you read further, take a moment to read the Concept Close-Up box, "Understanding the Ethics of Plagiarism," on page 111. In all writing — but especially in research writing, where you examine, evaluate, and record views and ideas from many different sources — a grasp of the full importance of plagiarism is crucial.

FINDING SOURCES

Sources for developing an argument can be found through several kinds of research. Library and Internet research will lead you to abundant sources, but don't overlook what social scientists call *field research*. All research requires time and patience as well as a knowledge of tools and techniques.

Field Research

Research "in the field" means studying the world directly through observations, questionnaires, and interviews.

Concept Close-Up
Understanding the Ethics of Plagiarism

A student who plagiarizes faces severe penalties: a failing grade on a paper, perhaps failure in a course, even expulsion from the university and an ethics violation recorded on his or her permanent record. Outside of academe, in the professional world, someone who plagiarizes may face public humiliation, loss of a degree, rank, or job, perhaps even a lawsuit. Why is plagiarism such a serious offense?

Plagiarism is theft. If someone takes our money or our car, we rightly think that person should be punished. Stealing ideas or the words used to express them is no less an act of theft. That's why we have laws that protect *intellectual property* such as books and essays.

Plagiarism is a breach of ethics. In our writing, we are *morally obligated* to distinguish between our ideas, information, and language and somebody else's ideas, information, and language. If we don't, it's like taking someone else's identity, pretending to be what we're not. Human society cannot function without trust and integrity—hence the strong condemnation of plagiarism.

Plagiarism amounts to taking an unearned and unfair advantage. You worked hard to get that "B" on the big paper in your political science class. How would you feel if you knew that another student had simply purchased an "A" paper, thereby avoiding the same effort? At the very least, you'd resent it. We hope you would go beyond resentment to actually report the plagiarism. For plagiarism is not just a moral failure with potentially devastating consequences for an individual. *Plagiarism, like any form of dishonesty intended to gain an unfair advantage, damages human society and hurts us.*

Observations

Do not discount the value of your own personal experiences as evidence in making a case. You will notice that many writers of arguments offer as evidence what they themselves have seen, heard, and done. Such experiences may be from the past.

Alternatively, you may seek out a specific personal experience as you inquire into your topic. For example, one student writing about the homeless in Dallas decided to visit a shelter. She called ahead to get permission and schedule the visit. Her paper was memorable because she was able to include the stories and physical descriptions of several homeless women, with details of their conversations.

Questionnaires and Surveys

You may be able to get information on some topics, especially if they are campus related, by doing surveys or questionnaires. This can be done very efficiently in electronic versions (Web-based or e-mail). Be forewarned, however, that it is very difficult to conduct a reliable survey.

First, there is the problem of designing a clear and unbiased instrument. If you have ever filled out an evaluation form for an instructor or a course, you will know what we mean about the problem of clarity. For example, one evaluation might ask whether an instructor returns papers "in a reasonable length of time"; however, what is "reasonable" to some students may be far too long for others. As for bias, consider the question, "Have you ever had trouble getting assistance from the library's reference desk?" To get a fair response, this questionnaire had better also ask how many requests for help were handled promptly and well. If you do decide to draft a questionnaire, we suggest you do it as a class project so that students on all sides of the issue can contribute and troubleshoot for ambiguity.

Second, there is the problem of getting a representative response. For the same reasons we doubt the results of certain magazine-sponsored surveys of people's sex lives, we should be skeptical about the statistical accuracy of surveys targeting a group that may not be representative of the whole. For example, it might be difficult to generalize about all first-year college students in the United States based on a survey of only your English class — or even the entire first-year class at your college. Consider, too, that those who respond to a survey often have an ax to grind on the topic.

We don't rule out the value of surveys here, but we caution you to consider the difficulties of designing, administering, and interpreting such research tools.

Interviews

You can get a great deal of current information about an issue, as well as informed opinions, by talking to experts. As with any kind of research, the first step in conducting an interview is to decide exactly what you want to find out. Write down your questions, whether you plan to conduct the interview over the telephone, in person, or through e-mail.

The next step, which can take some effort and imagination, is to find the right person to interview. As you read about an issue, note the names (and the possible biases) of any organizations mentioned; these may have local offices, the telephone numbers of which you could find in the directory. In addition, institutions such as hospitals, universities, and large corporations have information and public relations offices whose staffs are responsible for providing information. An excellent source of over 30,000 names and phone numbers of experts in almost any field is a book by Matthew Lesko, *Lesko's Info-Power.* Finally, do not overlook the expertise available from faculty members at your own school.

Once you have determined possible sources for interviews, you must begin a patient and courteous round of telephone calls, continuing until you are connected with the right person; according to Lesko, this can take as many as seven calls. Remain cheerful and clear in your pursuit. If you have a subject's e-mail address, you might write to introduce yourself and schedule an appointment for a telephone interview.

Whether your interview is face to face or over the telephone, begin by being sociable but also by acknowledging that the interviewee's time is valuable. Tell the person something about the project you are working on, but withhold your own position on any controversial matters. Try to sound neutral, and be specific about what you want to know. Take notes, and include the title and background of the person being interviewed and the date of the interview, which you will need when citing this source in the finished paper. If you want to tape the interview, be sure to ask permission first. Finally, if you have the individual's mailing address, it is thoughtful to send a follow-up note thanking him or her for the assistance.

If everyone in your class is researching the same topic and it is likely that more than one person will contact a particular expert on campus or in your community, avoid flooding that person with requests. Perhaps one or two students could be designated to interview the subject and report to the class, or, if convenient, the expert could be invited to visit the class.

Library and Online Research

University libraries are vast repositories of information in print and electronic form. To use them most efficiently, consult with professional librarians. Do not hesitate to ask for help. Even college faculty can discover new sources of information by talking with librarians about current research projects.

The Internet and its most popular component element, the World Wide Web, offer immediate access to millions of documents on almost any subject. The Internet provides currency and convenience, but it does not offer the reliability of most print sources. Do not overrely on the Internet; it is not a shortcut to the research process. We begin with a discussion of the resources available in your library or through its online network.

Library of Congress Subject Headings

Finding library sources will involve using the card or computerized catalog, reference books, and indexes to periodicals. Before using these, however, it makes sense first to look through a set of books every library locates near its catalog—the *Library of Congress Subject Headings.* This multivolume set will help you know what terms to look under when you move on to catalogs and indexes. The Library of Congress catalog is also available on the Internet at <http://catalog.loc.gov>. (See Figure 5.1.) Consulting these subject headings first will save you time in the long run: It will help you narrow your search and keep you from overlooking potentially good sources, because it also suggests related terms under which to look. For example, if you look under the

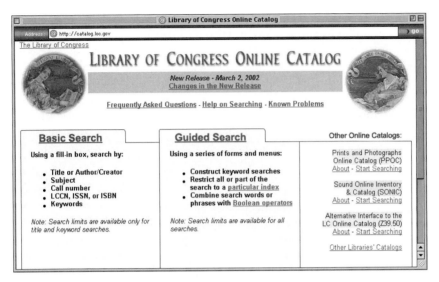

Figure 5.1

term "mercy killing," you will be directed to "euthanasia," where you can find the following helpful information:

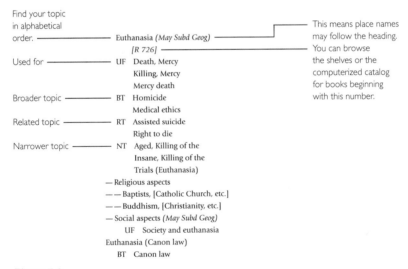

Figure 5.2

Your Library's Catalog

Use your library's catalog primarily to find books or government documents. (For arguments and information on very current issues, however, keep in mind that the card or computer catalog is not the best source; because books

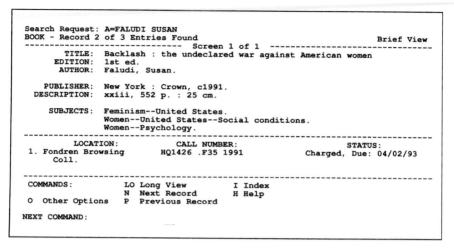

```
Search Request: A=FALUDI SUSAN
BOOK - Record 2 of 3 Entries Found                              Brief View
----------------------------- Screen 1 of 1 -----------------------------
        TITLE:  Backlash : the undeclared war against American women
      EDITION:  1st ed.
       AUTHOR:  Faludi, Susan.

    PUBLISHER:  New York : Crown, c1991.
  DESCRIPTION:  xxiii, 552 p. : 25 cm.

     SUBJECTS:  Feminism--United States.
               Women--United States--Social conditions.
               Women--Psychology.
--------------------------------------------------------------------------
        LOCATION:          CALL NUMBER:                    STATUS:
1. Fondren Browsing       HQ1426 .F35 1991          Charged, Due: 04/02/93
   Coll.


--------------------------------------------------------------------------
  COMMANDS:          LO Long View         I Index
                     N  Next Record       H Help
  O  Other Options   P  Previous Record

NEXT COMMAND:
```

Figure 5.3

take years to write and publish, they quickly become outdated.) Library catalogs list all holdings and are referenced according to author, title, and subject. With a computerized catalog, it is also possible to find works according to key words and by Library of Congress number. Look under the subject headings you find in the *Library of Congress Subject Headings.* Moreover, because the Library of Congress system groups books according to subject matter, you may want to browse in the catalog (or on the shelves) for other books in the same range of call numbers.

Typically, the library's catalog card or screen will appear as illustrated in Figure 5.3.

Indexes to Periodicals

Good libraries contain many indexes that list articles in newspapers, magazines, and journals. Some of these are printed and bound; others are online and on CD-ROM. Once again, the *Library of Congress Subject Headings* can help you determine the best words to search in these indexes.

Newspaper Indexes   The *New York Times Index* is printed and bound in volumes. Each volume indexes articles for one year, grouped according to subject and listed according to the month and day of publication. The subject headings in the *New York Times Index* tend to be very general. For example, we could not find the heading "euthanasia," the term for mercy killing used in the *Library of Congress Subject Headings.* We had to think of a more general term, so we tried "medicine." There we found the information in Figure 5.4.

MEDICINE AND HEALTH. See also
Abortion
Accidents and Safety
Acupuncture
Aged
Anatomy and Physiology
Anesthesia and Anesthetics
Antibiotics
Autopsies
Bacteria
Birth Control and Family Planning
Birth Defects
Blood
Death ————————————————————— The subject
Environment   heading most
Epidemics   likely to lead
Exercise   to articles on
Faith Healers   euthanasia
First Aid
Food Contamination and Poisoning
Handicapped
Hormones
Immunization and Immunity
Implants
Industrial and Occupational Hazards
Malpractice Insurance
Mental Health and Disorders
Nursing Homes
Pesticides and Pests
Population
Radiation
Smoking
Spas
Surgery and Surgeons
Teeth and Dentistry
Transplants
Vaccination and Vaccines
Veterinary Medicine
Viruses
Vitamins
Water Pollution
Workmen's Compensation Insurance
X-Rays

Figure 5.4

We decided the entry "death" on this list seemed most likely to lead us to articles on euthanasia, and we were correct. Figure 5.5 on page 117 shows a small selection of what we found.

You will also find a limited number of *New York Times* articles listed in the computerized periodicals index known as *InfoTrac*. Better yet, search the major newspapers' online archives. *The New York Times on the Web*, for example, provides access to all *NYT* articles published after 1996. Another excellent source of online articles from magazines and newspapers is *Lexis-Nexis*.

Other printed and bound newspaper indexes carried by most libraries are the *Christian Science Monitor Index*, the *Times Index* (to the London *Times*, a good source for international issues), the *Wall Street Journal Index*, and the *Washington Post Index* (good for federal government issues).

Topic headings are listed in alphabetical order.

DEATH. See also

Deaths

Several laws enacted in New York State in 1990 are set to take effect, including measure that will allow New Yorkers to designate another person to make health-care decisions on their behalf if they become unable to do so (M). Ja 1.1.32:1

Articles are listed in chronological order.

Another right-to-die case emerges in Missouri, where Christine Busalacchi had been in persistent vegetative state as result of auto accident on May 29, 1987, when she was 17-year-old high school junior: her father, Pete Busalacchi, who has been seeking unsuccessfully to have his daughter transferred to Minnesota, where feeding tube may possibly be removed, says that Christine never discussed matters of life or death; Nancy Cruzan case recalled; photo (M). Ja 2.A.12:1

Each entry contains an abstract.

Missouri state court dismisses order preventing Pete Busalacchi from moving his comatose daughter Christine to another state where less strict rules might allow removal of feeding tube (S). Ja S.A.16:1

(S), (M), or (L) before the date indicates whether an article is short, medium, or long.

In a case that medical ethicists and legal experts say is apparently a first, Minneapolis-based Hennapin County Medical Center plans to go to court for permission to turn off 37-year-old Helga Wanglie's life support system against her family's wishes; photos (L). Ja 10.A.1:1

Probate Judge Louis Kohn of St. Louis County rules that Pete Busalacchi may move his daughter, Christine, from Missouri hospital where she has lain for more than three years with severe brain damage and take her to Minnesota where law might allow removal of her feeding tube (S). Ja 17.3.5:1

Each entry concludes with the month, day, section, page, and column.

People wishing to avoid heroic medical treatment in event they become hopelessly ill and unable to speak for themselves are often poorly served by so-called "living wills" to achieve that end: many health care experts recommend a newer document, health care proxy, in which patients designate surrogate who has legal authority to make medical decisions if they are too sick to offer an opinion; others recommend combining living will with health care proxy; drawing (M). Ja 17.3.9:1

Missouri Judge Louis Kohn rules Pete Busalacchi had right to determine medical care of his daughter Christine, who has been severely brain-damaged for more than three years; gives him authority to have feeding tube removed (S). Ja 18.A.16:4

Missouri appeals court bars Pete Busalacchi from moving his comatose 20-year-old daughter Christine to Minnesota where laws governing removal of life-support systems are less restrictive (S). Ja 19.1.17:2

Editorial Notebook commentary by Fred M. Hechinger says his 94-year-old mother's last days were fiilled with needless suffering and fear because doctors ignored her, and her family's wish that no heroic efforts be taken to prolong her life; says inhumane legal restrictions have made doctors accomplices in torture, and medical profession has shown little courage in fighting them (M). Ja 24.A.22:1

Figure 5.5

Newsbank offers computerized indexes of hundreds of local and state newspapers. Your library is likely to subscribe to *Newsbank* for indexes of only one or two regional papers in your area. *Newsbank*'s CD-ROMs contain the entire text of each article indexed.

Indexes to Magazines, Journals, and Other Materials   Many libraries have CD-ROM databases indexing journals in business and academic fields. *InfoTrac,* one such database, indexes current articles from the *New York Times* and many other periodicals, so you may want to begin your search here rather than with the printed and bound indexes discussed previously. Be aware, however, that *InfoTrac* is a very selective index, far less comprehensive than the printed and bound indexes, which also go back much further in time. In addition, *InfoTrac* will not include many articles that can be found in the specialized indexes that follow. However, *InfoTrac* is constantly being upgraded, so check with your reference librarian to see how this database can help you research your issue.

1. General interest indexes:

   Readers' Guide to Periodical Literature
   Public Affairs Information Service (PAIS)
   Essay and General Literature Index
   Speech Index

2. Arts and humanities indexes:

   Art Index
   Film Literature Index
   Humanities Index
   Music Index
   Philosopher's Index
   Popular Music Periodical Index

3. Social science, business, and law indexes:

   Business Periodicals Index
   Criminology Index
   Education Index
   Index to Legal Periodicals
   Psychological Abstracts
   Social Sciences Index
   Sociological Abstracts
   Women's Studies Abstracts

4. Science and engineering indexes:

   Applied Science and Technology Index
   Biological and Agricultural Index
   Current Contents
   Environmental Index
   General Science Index

Reference Books

Students tend to overlook many helpful reference books, often because they are unaware of their existence. You may find reference books useful early in the process of inquiring into your issue, but they are also useful for locating supporting evidence as you develop your own argument. The following are some reference books you might find helpful:

> *First Stop: The Master Index to Subject Encyclopedias* (a subject index to 430 specialized encyclopedias—a good source of general background information)
> *Demographic Yearbook*
> *Facts on File*
> *Guide to American Law* (a reference work that explains legal principles and concepts in plain English)
> *Statistical Abstract of the United States*
> *World Almanac and Book of Facts*

Bibliographies

Books and articles sometimes include works-cited lists or bibliographies, which can reveal numerous additional sources. Library catalog entries and many indexes indicate whether a book or article contains a bibliography.

Internet Research

The *Internet* is a global network that links computers, and the files stored on them, to one another. It is a valuable research tool because it provides access to information in the computers of educational institutions, businesses, government bureaus, and nonprofit organizations all over the world. Most people now use the World Wide Web for access to the Internet. The Web is that portion of the Internet that uses HTML (hypertext mark-up language) to present information in the form of Web sites that contain individual Web pages.

The Internet also provides the connections for e-mail and real-time communications, such as ongoing discussions among groups with common areas of interest; the communication functions of the Internet can also be useful for researching a topic. Because nearly all college computer networks are linked to the Internet, as a student you will have access to it (even if you do not own a computer). Most schools have a department of computer and educational technology that can tell you where and how to get connected.

Just as we advise you to seek help from a librarian when beginning your library research, so we also suggest that you begin electronic or online research by consulting one of the librarians at your school who has specialized training in navigating the information superhighway. Because the Internet is so large and complex and—like most real highways—is perpetually "under construction," we will offer only general advice about what Internet resources would be most useful for undergraduate research on comtemporary public issues. One of the best online sources for help with the Internet is the Library of Congress Resource Page, at <http://lcweb.loc.gov/global/search.html>. Once you are connected to this page, you can link to any number of the following resources.

The World Wide Web

Of all the networks on the Internet, the *World Wide Web* is the friendliest and the most fun because it links files from various "host" computers around the world; from one site on the Web, you can click on highlighted words known as *hypertext links* that will take you to other sites on the Web where related information is stored. For example, an online article on euthanasia may highlight the words "Hippocratic oath"; clicking on the highlighted words will allow you to see a copy of the oath and learn a little more about it.

Although the Web continues to expand, finding useful sites is not always as easy as finding books and articles in the library because there is no system that neatly catalogs all the information as material is posted. However, technology to help users navigate the Internet is constantly improving. The Web does support a number of *search engines*, which index existing and newly posted information, usually through the use of key words. Once you connect to your school's Internet browser (such as Netscape or Microsoft Internet Explorer), you can type in the address of one of these engines, or you may be able to load the engine by simply clicking on an icon. Addresses on the Internet are known as *uniform resource locators (URLs)*. The following lists the names and URLs of search engines and metasearch engines that are recommended by the Librarians' Index to the Internet <http://www.lii.org>. World Wide Web URLs begin with "http," which stands for "hypertext transfer protocol."

Search Engines Recommended by Librarians

Google <http://www.google.com>
AllTheWeb <http://www.alltheweb.com>
AltaVista <http://www.altavista.com>
Excite <http://www.excite.com>
HotBot <http://www.hotbot.lycos.com>
NorthernLight <http://www.northernlight.com>

Recommended Metasearch Engines

Ixquick <http://www.ixquick.com>
MetaCrawler <http://www.metacrawler.com>

Once you access the search engine, enter key words describing the information you want. For example, by typing in "search engine," you can find the addresses of other search engines. We recommend that you try this because new search engines are being created all the time.

Surfing the Web, however, is not always a quick and easy way to do research. Be prepared to spend some time and to try a variety of search engines and metasearch engines, which, as their name suggests, search multiple search engine databases at once. Web searches can often take more time than library research because you will encounter so much irrelevant information. You will also find much information that is not suitable for use in academic writing.

Because anyone can post a document on the Web, you need to check the author's credentials carefully. (See "Evaluating Sources," pages 122–127.) The Internet is a tool that can provide new avenues for your research, but it will not replace the library as your primary research venue.

GopherSpace

Gopher, a program for accessing Internet information through hierarchical menus, is named for the Golden Gopher mascot at the University of Minnesota, where this software was developed. Gopher is an older system than the World Wide Web. Like other protocols such as FTP and telnet, Gopher looks different because it lacks a hypertext format. However, many documents are stored in *GopherSpace.* Once Gopher has retrieved a document for you, you can read it on your screen, save it to a disk, or even print out a copy of it. Instead of hypertext links, Gopher organizes hierarchical menus based on topic areas. For example, you may open a menu that lists major subject areas such as "government and politics." If you select this category, you will get another menu that may have the item "Supreme Court cases." Selecting that, you will find another list, and so on. Many of the Web search engines previously described include GopherSpace in their searches, so you may happen to find Gopher documents while you are searching the World Wide Web.

Listservs and Usenet Newsgroups

The Internet allows groups of people to communicate with one another on topics of common interest; observing and participating in such groups is another way to learn about a topic and find out what issues are being debated. *Listservs* are like electronic bulletin boards or discussion groups, where people with a shared interest can post or ask for information and simply converse about a topic. Listservs are supported by e-mail, so if you have an e-mail account, it will cost you nothing to join a group. You may find an appropriate listserv group by e-mailing <listserv@listserve.net> with a message specifying your area of interest, such as "list environmentalism" or "list euthanasia." You can also find listserv groups on the World Wide Web at <http://tile.net/lists>. *Usenet newsgroups* also act like electronic bulletin boards, which your college's system administrator may or may not make available on your school's server. To find lists of active newsgroups, type in "newsgroups" as a search term in one of the Web search engines, such as Yahoo! Newsgroups and listservs are often composed of highly specialized professionals who expect other participants to have followed their discussions for weeks and months before participating. They even post lists of *frequently asked questions (FAQs)* to avoid having to cover the same topics repeatedly. Finding the exact information you need in the transcripts of their discussions is like looking for the proverbial needle in a haystack, so Usenet is not likely to be as useful as the Web as a general research tool. However, while searching the Web, you may encounter links to some discussions relevant to your topic that have been archived on the Web. You may want to cite information gathered from these groups, but you need to be very careful about what you choose to use as a source because anyone can join in, regardless of his or her credentials and expertise. Most correspondents who have professional affiliations list them along with their name and "snail mail" (U.S. postal service) address. In addition to credentials, be sure to note the name of the group, the name of the individual posting the message, the date and time it was posted, and the URL if you have found it on the Web. (See the section "Creating Works-Cited and Reference Lists" on pages 144–157 for more information on citing electronic sources.)

EVALUATING SOURCES

Before you begin to read and evaluate your sources, you may need to reevaluate your issue. If you have been unable to find many sources that address the question you are raising, step back and consider changing the focus of your argument or at least expanding its focus.

For example, one student had the choice of any issue under the broad category of the relationship between humans and other animals. Michelle decided to focus on the mistreatment of circus animals, based on claims made in leaflets handed out at the circus by animal rights protestors. Even with a librarian's help, however, Michelle could find no subject headings that led to even one source in her university's library. She then called and visited animal rights activists in her city, who provided her with more materials written and published by the animal rights movement. She realized, however, that researching the truth of their claims was more than she could undertake, so she had to acknowledge that her entire argument was based on inadequate inquiry and heavily biased sources.

Once you have reevaluated your topic, use the following method to record and evaluate sources.

Eliminate Inappropriate Sources

If you are a first-year college student, you may find that some books and articles are intended for audiences with more specialized knowledge of the subject than you have. If you have trouble using a source—if it confuses you or shakes your confidence in your reading comprehension—put it aside, at least temporarily.

Also, carefully review any electronic sources you are using. While search engines make it easy to find source material on the Web, online documents often have met no professional standards for scholarship. Material can be "published" electronically without the rigorous review by experts, scholars, and editors that must occur in traditional publishing. Nevertheless, you will find legitimate scholarship on the Internet—many news reports, encyclopedias, government documents, and even scholarly journals appear online.

While the freedom of electronic publishing creates an exciting and democratic arena for discussion, it also puts a much heavier burden on students to ensure that the sources they use are worthy of readers' respect. You must exercise caution whenever you use a Web source as part of your research paper.

Carefully Record Complete Bibliographic Information

For every source you are even considering using, be sure to record full bibliographic information. You should take this information from the source itself, not from an index, which may be incomplete or even inaccurate. If you make a record of this information immediately, you will not have to go back later to fill in careless omissions. We recommend that you use a separate index card for each source, but whatever you write on, you must record the following:

1. For a book:

> Author's full name (or names)
> Title of book
> City where published
> Name of publisher
> Year published

For an article or essay in a book, record all of the information for the book, including the names of the book's author or editor and the title and the author(s) of the article; also record the inclusive page numbers of the article or chapter (for example, "pp. 100–150").

2. For a periodical:

> Author's full name (or names)
> Title of the article
> Title of the periodical
> Date of the issue
> Volume number, if given
> Inclusive page numbers

3. For a document found on the World Wide Web:

> Author's full name (or names)
> Title of the work
> Original print publication data, if applicable
> Title of the database or Web site
> Full URL
> Date you accessed the document

4. For a document found through Gopher:

> Author's full name (or names)
> Title of the work

Original print publication data, if applicable
Title of the database
Full Gopher search path that accessed the document
Date you accessed the document

5. For material found through listservs and Usenet newsgroups:

Author's full name (or names)
Author's e-mail address
Subject line from the posting
Date of the posting
Address of the listserv or newsgroups
Date you accessed the document

Read the Source Critically

As discussed in Chapter 2, critical reading depends on having some prior knowledge of the subject and the ability to see a text in its rhetorical context. As you research a topic, your knowledge naturally becomes deeper with each article you read. But your sources are not simply windows onto your topic, giving you a clear view; whether argumentative or informative, they present a bias. Before looking through them, you must look *at* your sources. Therefore, it is essential that you devote conscious attention to the rhetorical context of the sources you find. As you read, keep these questions in mind.

Who Is the Writer, and What Is His or Her Bias?

Is there a note that tells you anything about the writer's professional title or university or institutional affiliation? If not, a quick look in the *Dictionary of American Biographies* might help; or you can consult the *Biography and Genealogy Master Index*, which will send you to numerous specialized biographical sketches. If you are going to cite the writer as an authority in your argument, you need to be able to convince your audience of his or her credibility.

How Reliable Is the Source?

Again, checking for credibility is particularly important when you are working with electronic sources. For example, one student found two sites on the Web, both through a key word search on "euthanasia." One, entitled "Stop the Epidemic of Assisted Suicide," was posted by a person identified only by name, the letters MD, and the affiliation "Association for Control of Assisted Suicide." There was no biographical information, and the "snail mail" address was a post office box. The other Web site, entitled "Ethics Update: Euthanasia," was posted by a professor of philosophy at the University of San Diego whose homepage included a complete professional biography detailing his educational background and the titles and publishers of his many other books and articles. The author gave his address at USD in the Department of Philosophy. The student decided that although the first source had some interesting information — including examples of individual patients who were living with pain rather than choosing suicide — it was not a source that skeptical readers would find credible. Search engines often land you deep within a Web site, and you have to visit the site's homepage to get any background information about the source and its author. Be suspicious of sites that do not contain adequate source information; they may not be reliable.

When Was This Source Written?

If you are researching a very current issue, you need to decide what sources may be too old. Keep in mind, though, that arguments on current issues often benefit from earlier perspectives.

Where Did This Source Appear?

If you are using an article from a periodical, be aware of the periodical's readership and any editorial bias. For example, *National Review* has a conservative bent, whereas *The Nation* is liberal; an article in the *Journal of the American Medical Association* will usually defend the medical profession. Looking at the table of contents and scanning any editorial statements will help give you a feel for the periodical's political leanings. Also look at the page that lists the publisher and the editorial board. You would find, for example, that *New American* is published by the ultra-right-wing John Birch Society. If you need help determining political bias, ask a librarian. A reference book that lists periodicals by subject matter and explains their bias is *Magazines for Libraries*.

Why Was the Book or Article Written?

Although some articles are occasioned by events in the news, most books and arguments are written as part of an ongoing debate or conversation among scholars or journalists. Being aware of the issues and the participants in this conversation is essential, as you will be joining it with your own researched argument. You can check *Book Review Index* to find where a book has been reviewed, and then consult some reviews to see how the book was received.

What Is the Author's Aim?

First, be aware of whether the source is intended to inform or whether it is an argument with a claim to support. Both informative and argumentative sources are useful, and even informative works will have some bias. When your source is an argument, note whether it aims primarily to inquire, to convince, to persuade, or to mediate.

How Is the Source Organized?

If the writer does not employ subheadings or chapter titles, try to break the text into its various parts, and note what function each part plays in the whole.

1. Look at the last segment of the domain name, which will tell you who developed the site. The most reliable sites are those developed by colleges and universities (*.edu*) or by the government (*.gov*). Remember that commercial sites (*.com, .biz*) are usually profit-minded.
2. Check whether the name of the creator of the Web page or its Webmaster appears, complete with an e-mail address and the date of the last update, near either the top or the bottom of the page.
3. Check whether the source includes a bibliography; such inclusion indicates a scholarly page.
4. Ask yourself if the links are credible.
5. Remember that a tilde (˜) indicates a personal page; these pages must be evaluated carefully.

Inquire into the Source

Because we devote so much attention to inquiry in Chapters 3 and 6, we will not go into detail about this process here. However, you should identify any author's claim and evaluate the support offered for it. Look especially closely at arguments that support your own position; seeing weaknesses in such "friendly" arguments has caused many students to experience an epiphany, or moment of enlightenment, in which they change their whole stance on an issue. The box "Additional Guidelines for Evaluating Internet Sources," above, will help you evaluate Web sources for reliability.

Consider How You Might Use the Source

If you are fortunate, your research will uncover many authoritative and well-crafted arguments on your issue. The challenge you now face is to work out a way to use them in an argument of your own, built on your own structure and strategy and suited to your own aim and audience.

A good argument results from synthesizing, or blending, the results of your research. Your sources should help you come up with strong reasons and evidence as well as ideas about opposing views. But it is unlikely that all your reasons will come from one source or that each part of your argument will draw primarily upon a single source, and you don't want to create an argument that reads like a patchwork of other people's ideas. Thus, you must organize your sources according to your own argumentative strategy and integrate material from a variety of sources into each part of your argument.

We suggest that you review Chapter 7, where we discuss developing and refining a thesis (or claim) and constructing a brief of your argument. As you make your brief, identify those sources that will help you offer reasons or support, such as expert opinion or specific data.

Avoid plagiarism by being conscious of whether you are quoting or paraphrasing. Anytime you take exact words from a source, even if it is only a phrase or a significant word that expresses an author's opinion, you are quoting. You must use quotation marks in addition to documenting your source. If you make any change at all in the wording of a quotation, you must indicate the change with ellipses and/or brackets. Even if you use your own words to summarize or paraphrase portions of a source, you must still name that source in your text and document it fully. Be careful about using your own words when paraphrasing and summarizing.

1. At the very least, use an attributive tag such as "According to . . ." to introduce quotations both direct and indirect. Don't just drop them in to stand on their own.
2. Name the person whose words or idea you are using. Give the person's full name on first mention.
3. Identify the author(s) of your source by profession or affiliation so readers will understand the significance of what he or she has to say. Omit this if the speaker is someone readers would recognize without your help.
4. Use transitions into and out of quotations to link the ideas they express to whatever point you are making — that is, to the context of your essay.
5. If your lead-in to a quotation is a simple phrase, follow it with a comma. But if your lead-in can stand alone as a sentence, follow it with a colon.
6. Place the period at the end of a quotation or paraphrase after the parenthetical citation, except with block quotations. (See pages 141–142 for treatment of block quotations.)

USING SOURCES

How you use a source depends on what you need it for. After you have drafted an argument, you may simply need to consult an almanac for some additional evidence or, say, look up John F. Kennedy's inaugural address to find a stirring quotation. But at earlier stages of the writing process, you may be unsure of your own position and even in need of general background information on the issue. What follows is some advice for those early stages, in which you will encounter a great deal of information and opposing viewpoints. As you research, remember to write down all of the bibliographical information for every source you might use.

Taking Notes

Just as you can check out books from the library for your own use at home or in your dormitory, so you can photocopy entire articles for your personal

1. Note your source. Use the author's last name or an abbreviated title, or devise a code, such as "A," "B," "C," and so forth.
2. Note the exact page or pages where the information or quotation appears.
3. When you quote, be exact, and put quotation marks around the writer's words to avoid plagiarism if you use them later in your paper.
4. Paraphrase and summarize whenever possible; reserve quotations for passages in which the writer's words are strongly opinionated or especially memorable.

use away from the library. Likewise, if you are working with electronic sources, you can print out the entire text of many online documents. These various methods of gathering materials are helpful for doing research, but when it is time to use the sources in a paper of your own, the traditional writing skills of note-taking, paraphrasing, and summarizing will help you work efficiently and avoid plagiarism.

Whether you are working with a book, a photocopied article, or a document retrieved from the Internet, you will save time if you write down—preferably on a large notecard—anything that strikes you as important or useful. By taking notes, you will avoid having to sort through the entire text of your research materials to find the idea you thought would work in your paper two weeks ago. The box "Guidelines for Taking Notes," above, summarizes the process.

Paraphrasing

Paraphrasing, which means restating a passage in your own words, improves reading comprehension. When you put an idea, especially a complex one, into your own words, you are actually explaining the idea to yourself. When you have a firm grasp of an idea, you can write more confidently, with a sense of owning the idea rather than simply borrowing it. The box "Guidelines for Paraphrasing" on page 129 summarizes the technique.

We illustrate paraphrasing with an excerpt from a source selected by one student, Patrick Pugh, who was researching the topic of euthanasia and planning to defend active euthanasia, or assisted suicide. In the university library, Patrick found a book entitled *Suicide and Euthanasia: The Rights of Personhood*, a collection of essays written by doctors, philosophers, theologians, and legal experts. Published in 1981, the book was somewhat dated in 1991, when Patrick was doing his research, but he felt that the question of whether suicide is moral or immoral was a timeless one. He read an essay entitled "In Defense of Suicide" by Joseph Fletcher, a former professor at the Episcopal

1. Use a dictionary if any words in the original are not completely familiar to you.
2. Work with whole ideas—that is, remember that paraphrasing involves more than keeping the original word order and just plugging in synonyms. Don't be afraid to make your paraphrase longer than the original. Try to break a complex sentence into several simpler ones of your own; take apart a difficult idea and rebuild it, step by step. Don't just echo the original passage thoughtlessly.
3. Don't be a slave to the original—or to the thesaurus. Read the passage until you think you understand it, or a part of it. Then write your version without looking back at the original. Rearrange the order of ideas if doing so makes the passage more accessible.
4. Don't strain to find substitutes for words that are essential to the meaning of a passage.

Divinity School and president of the Society for the Right to Die. Before taking notes on Fletcher's essay, Patrick made a bibliography card recording all the necessary information about this source, like this:

Fletcher, Joseph. "In Defense of Suicide."
In Suicide and Euthanasia : The
Rights of Personhood. Eds. Samuel E.
Wallace and Albin Eser. Knoxville : U of
Tennessee P 1981

Fletcher's article : pp. 38–50.

The following passage from Fletcher's essay offers a crucial definition; it is the kind of passage that a researcher should paraphrase on a notecard rather than quote so that the idea becomes part of one's own store of knowledge.

> We must begin with the postulate that no action is intrinsically right or wrong, that nothing is inherently good or evil. Right and wrong, good and evil, desirable and undesirable — all are ethical terms and all are predicates, not properties. The moral "value" of any human act is always contingent, depending on the shape of the action in the situation. [. . .] The variables and factors in each set of circumstances are the determinants of what ought to be done — not prefabricated generalizations or prescriptive rules. [. . .] No "law" of conduct is always obliging; what we ought to do is whatever maximizes human well-being.
>
> —JOSEPH FLETCHER, "In Defense of Suicide"

Patrick paraphrased this passage on the following notecard. Note that he names the author of the essay, the editors of the book, and the exact pages on which the idea was found.

Fletcher's definition of ethical action:

The ethical value of any human action is not a quality inherent in the act itself. It is a judgment that we make about the act after examining the entire situation in which it takes place. Rather than relying on general rules about what is moral and immoral, we should make our decision on the basis of what is best for human well-being in any given set of circumstances.

Fletcher, pp. 38-39, in Wallace/Eser.

Following Through

From your own research, select a passage of approximately one paragraph that presents a complicated idea. Write a paraphrase of the passage.

Alternatively, write a paraphrase of the following paragraph, also from Joseph Fletcher's "In Defense of Suicide":

> What is called positive euthanasia—doing something to shorten or end life deliberately—is the form [of euthanasia] in which suicide is the question, as a voluntary, direct choice of death. For a long time the Christian moralists have distinguished between negative or indirectly willed suicide, like not taking a place in one of the *Titanic's* lifeboats, and positive or directly willed suicide, like jumping out of a lifeboat to make room for a fellow victim of a shipwreck. The moralists mean that we may choose to allow an evil by acts of omission but not to do an evil by acts of comission. The moralists contend that since all suicide is evil, we may only "allow" it; we may not "do" it. (47)

Your instructor may ask you to compare your paraphrase with that of a classmate's before revising it and handing it in.

Summarizing

Whereas a paraphrase may be longer or shorter than the original passage, a summary is always considerably shorter. It ought to be at least one-third of the length of the original and is often considerably less: you may, for example, reduce an entire article to one or two paragraphs.

A summary of an argument must contain the main idea or claim and the main points of support or development. The amount of evidence and detail you include depends on your purpose for summarizing: If you merely want to give your audience (or remind yourself of) the gist of the original, a bare-bones summary is enough; but if you plan to use the summary as part of making your case, you had better include the original's evidence as well. The box "Guidelines for Summarizing" on page 132 outlines the process.

For an example of using a summary as part of an argument, we return to Patrick Pugh's investigation of euthanasia. In another book, *The End of Life: Euthanasia and Morality* by James Rachels, Patrick found what Rachels describes as the chief religious objections to euthanasia, with Rachels' rebuttals for each. Patrick decided to include this material, in summary, in his paper. First read the passage from Rachels's book, then read Patrick's summarized version that follows immediately after.

1. Read and reread the original text until you have identified the claim and the main supporting points. You ought to be able to write a brief or outline of the case, using your own words. Depending on your purpose for summarizing and the amount of space you can devote to the summary, decide how much, if any, of the evidence you will need to include.
2. Make it clear at the start whose ideas you are summarizing.
3. If you are summarizing a long passage, break it down into subsections and work on summarizing each one at a time.
4. As with paraphrasing, work as independently as you can—from memory—as you attack each part. Then go back to the text to check your version for accuracy.
5. Try to maintain the original order of points, with this exception: If the author delayed presenting the thesis, you may want to refer to it earlier in your summary.
6. Use your own words as much as possible.
7. Avoid quoting entire sentences. If you want to quote key words and phrases, try to incorporate them into sentences of your own, using quotation marks around the borrowed words.
8. Write a draft summary, then summarize your draft.
9. Revise for conciseness and coherence; look for ways to combine sentences, using connecting words to show how ideas relate. (See the section in the appendix entitled "Use Transitions to Show Relationships between Ideas," pages A12–A13.)

The End of Life*

James Rachels

RELIGIOUS ARGUMENTS

Social observers are fond of remarking that we live in a secular age, and there is surely something in this. The power of religious conceptions was due, in some considerable measure, to their usefulness in explaining things. In earlier times, religious ideas were used to explain everything from the origins of the universe to the nature of human beings. So long as we had no other way of understanding the world, the hold of religion on us was powerful indeed. Now, however, these explanatory functions have largely been taken over by the sciences: physics, chemistry, and their allies explain physical nature, while evolutionary biology and psychology combine to tell us about ourselves. As there is less and less work for religious hypotheses to do, the grip of religious ideas on us weakens, and appeals to theological conceptions are heard only on Sunday mornings. Hence, the "secular age."

However, most people continue to hold religious beliefs, and they especially appeal to those beliefs when morality is at issue. Any discussion of mercy killing quickly leads to objections based on theological grounds, and "secular" arguments for euthanasia are rejected because they leave out the crucial element of God's directions on the matter.

Considering the traditional religious opposition to euthanasia, it is tempting to say: If one is not a Christian (or if one does not have some similar religious orientation), then perhaps euthanasia is an option; but for people who do have such a religious orientation, euthanasia cannot be acceptable. And the discussion might be ended there. But this is too quick a conclusion; for it is possible that the religious arguments against euthanasia are not valid *even for religious people.* Perhaps a religious perspective, even a conventional Christian one, does *not* lead automatically to the rejection of mercy killing. With this possibility in mind, let us examine three variations of the religious objection.

What God Commands

It is sometimes said that euthanasia is not permissible simply because God forbids it, and we know that God forbids it by the authority of either scripture or Church tradition. Thus, one eighteenth-century minister, Humphrey Primatt, wrote ironically that, in the case of aged and infirm animals,

> God, the Father of Mercies, hath ordained Beasts and Birds of Prey to do that distressed creature the kindness to relieve him his misery, by putting him to death. A kindness which *We* dare not show to our own species. If thy father, thy brother, or thy child should suffer the utmost pains of a long and agonizing sickness, though his groans should pierce through thy heart, and with strong crying and tears he should beg thy relief, yet thou must be deaf unto him; he must wait his appointed time till his charge cometh, till he sinks and is crushed with the weight of his own misery.

When this argument is advanced, it is usually advanced with great confidence, as though it were *obvious* what God requires. Yet we may well wonder whether such confidence is justified. The sixth commandment does not say, literally, "Thou shalt not *kill*" — that is a bad translation. A better translation is "Thou shalt not commit *murder*," which is different, and which does not obviously prohibit mercy killing. Murder is by definition *wrongful* killing; so, if you do not think that a given kind of killing is wrong, you will not call it murder. That is why the sixth commandment is not normally taken to forbid killing in a just war; since such killing is (allegedly) justified,

5

it is not called murder. Similarly, if euthanasia is justified, it is not murder, and so it is not prohibited by the commandment. At the very least, it is clear that we cannot infer that euthanasia is wrong *because* it is prohibited by the commandment.

If we look elsewhere in the Christian Bible for a condemnation of euthanasia, we cannot find it. These scriptures are silent on the question. We do find numerous affirmations of the sanctity of human life and the fatherhood of God, and some theologians have tried to infer a prohibition on euthanasia from these general precepts. (The persistence of the attempts, in the face of logical difficulties, is a reminder that people insist on reading their moral prejudices *into* religious texts much more often than they derive their moral views *from* the texts.) But we also find exhortations to kindness and mercy, and the Golden Rule proclaimed as the sum of all morality; and these principles, as we have seen, support euthanasia rather than condemn it.

We *do* find a clear condemnation of euthanasia in Church tradition. Regardless of whether there is scriptural authority for it, the Church has historically opposed mercy killing. It should be emphasized, however, that this is a matter of history. Today, many religious leaders favour euthanasia and think the historical position of the Church has been mistaken. It was an Episcopal minister, Joseph Fletcher, who in his book *Morals and Medicine* formulated the classic modern defence of euthanasia. Fletcher does not stand alone among his fellow churchmen. The Euthanasia Society of America, which he heads, includes many other religious leaders; and the recent "Plea for Beneficent Euthanasia," sponsored by the American Humanist Association, was signed by more religious leaders than people in any other category. So it certainly cannot be claimed that *contemporary* religious forces stand uniformly opposed to euthanasia.

It is noteworthy that even Roman Catholic thinkers are today reassessing the Church's traditional ban on mercy killing. The Catholic philosopher Daniel Maguire has written one of the best books on the subject, *Death by Choice*. Maguire maintains that "it may be moral and should be legal to accelerate the death process by taking direct action, such as overdosing with morphine or injecting potassium"; and moreover, he proposes to demonstrate that this view is "*compatible with historical Catholic ethical theory*," contrary to what most opponents of euthanasia assume. Historical Catholic ethical theory, he says, grants individuals permission to act on views that are supported by "good and serious reasons," even when a different view is supported by a majority of authorities. Since the morality of euthanasia *is* supported by "good and serious reasons," Maguire concludes that Catholics are permitted to accept that morality and act on it.

Thus, the positions of both scripture and Church authorities are (at least) ambiguous enough so that the believer is not bound, on these grounds, to reject mercy killing. The argument from "what God commands" should be inconclusive, even for the staunchest believer.

The Idea of God's Dominion

Our second theological argument starts from the principle that "The life   10
of man is solely under the dominion of God." It is for God alone to decide when a person shall live and when he shall die; we have no right to
"play God" and arrogate this decision unto ourselves. So euthanasia is
forbidden.

This is perhaps the most familiar of all the theological objections to euthanasia; one hears it constantly when the matter is discussed. However, it
is remarkable that people still advance this argument today, considering that
it was decisively refuted over 200 years ago, when Hume made the simple
but devastating point that *if it is for God alone to decide when we shall live and
when we shall die, then we "play God" just as much when we cure people as when
we kill them.* Suppose a person is sick and we have the means to cure him or
her. If we do so, then we are interfering with God's "right to decide" how
long the life shall last! Hume put it this way:

> Were the disposal of human life so much reserved as the peculiar providence
> of the Almighty that it were an encroachment on his right, for men to dispose
> of their own lives; it would be equally criminal to act for the preservation of
> life as for its destruction. If I turn aside a stone which is falling upon my head,
> I disturb this course of nature, and I invade the peculiar providence of the
> Almighty by lengthening out my life beyond the period which by the general
> laws of matter and motion he had assigned it.

We alter the length of a person's life when we save it just as much as when
we take it. Therefore, if the taking of life is to be forbidden on the grounds
that only God has the right to determine how long a person shall live, then
the saving of life should be prohibited on the same grounds. We would
then have to abolish the practice of medicine. But everyone (except, perhaps, Christian Scientists) concedes that this would be absurd. Therefore,
we may *not* prohibit euthanasia on the grounds that only God has the right
to determine how long a life shall last. This seems to be a complete refutation of this argument, and if refuted arguments were decently discarded, as
they should be, we would hear no more of it.

Suffering and God's Plan

The last religious argument we shall consider is based on the idea that suffering is a part of God's plan for us. God has ordained that people should
suffer; he never intended that life should be continually pleasurable. (If
he had intended this, presumably he would have created a very different
world.) Therefore, if we were to kill people to "put them out of their mis-
ery," we would be interfering with God's plan. Bishop Joseph Sullivan, a
prominent Catholic opponent of euthanasia, expresses the argument in
a passage from his essay "The Immorality of Euthanasia":

If the suffering patient is of sound mind and capable of making an act of divine resignation, then his sufferings become a great means of merit whereby he can gain reward for himself and also win great favors for the souls in Purgatory, perhaps even release them from their suffering. Likewise the sufferer may give good example to his family and friends and teach them how to bear a heavy cross in a Christlike manner.

As regard those that must live in the same house with the incurable sufferer, they have a great opportunity to practice Christian charity. They can learn to see Christ in the sufferer and win the reward promised in the Beatitudes. This opportunity for charity would hold true even when the incurable sufferer is deprived of the use of reason. It may well be that the incurable sufferer in a particular case may be of greater value to society than when he was of some material value to himself and his community.

This argument may strike some readers as simply grotesque. Can we imagine this being said, seriously, in the presence of suffering such as that experienced by Stewart Alsop's roommate? "We know it hurts, Jack, and that your wife is being torn apart just having to watch it, but think what a good opportunity this is for you to set an example. You can give us a lesson in how to bear it." In addition, some might think that euthanasia is exactly what *is* required by the "charity" that bystanders have the opportunity to practice.

But, these reactions aside, there is a more fundamental difficulty with   15
the argument. For if the argument were sound, it would lead not only to the condemnation of euthanasia but of *any* measures to reduce suffering. If God decrees that we suffer, why aren't we obstructing God's plan when we give drugs to relieve pain? A girl breaks her arm; if only God knows how much pain is right for her, who are we to mend it? The point is similar to Hume's refutation of the previous argument. This argument, like the previous one, cannot be right because it leads to consequences that no one, not even the most conservative religious thinker, is willing to accept.

We have now looked at three arguments that depend on religious assumptions. They are all unsound, but I have *not* criticized them simply by rejecting their religious presuppositions. Instead, I have criticized them on their own terms, showing that these arguments should not be accepted even by religious people. As Daniel Maguire emphasizes, the ethics of theists, like the ethics of all responsible people, should be determined by "good and serious reasons," and these arguments are not good no matter what world-view one has.

The upshot is that religious people are in the same position as everyone else. There is nothing in religious belief in general, or in Christian belief in particular, to preclude the acceptance of mercy killing as a humane response to some awful situations. So, as far as these arguments are concerned, it appears that Christians may be free, after all, to accept the Golden Rule.

STUDENT SAMPLE: *A Summary*

In the following paper, the numbers in parentheses indicate the original pages where material appeared. We explain this method of documentation later in this chapter.

SUMMARY OF EXCERPT FROM *THE END OF LIFE*

Patrick Pugh

According to James Rachels, in spite of the fact that we live in a secular age, many objections to active euthanasia focus on religion, and particularly Christianity. However, even religious people ought to be able to see that these arguments may not be valid. For example, one of the most often-stated objections is that in the Ten Commandments God forbids killing. Rachels counters by pointing out that the Sixth Commandment is more accurately translated as "Thou shalt not commit murder." Because we define murder as "wrongful killing," we will not call some killing murder if we do not see it as wrong. Thus, the Sixth Commandment "is not normally taken to forbid killing in a just war; since such killing is (allegedly) justified" (161–62). Rachels points out that although the scriptures do not mention euthanasia and in fact affirm the "sanctity of human life," one also finds "exhortations to kindness and mercy" for fellow humans, principles that "support active euthanasia rather than condemn it" (162).

To those who claim that "[i]t is for God alone to decide when a person shall live and when he shall die," Rachels responds that "if it is for God alone to decide when we shall live and when we shall die, then we 'play God' just as much when we cure people as when we kill them" (163). He notes that philosopher David Hume made this argument more than two hundred years ago.

A third common Christian argument is that because suffering is a part of God's plan for humans, we should not interrupt it by euthanasia. Rachels responds to this with the question, How can we then justify the use of any pain-relieving drugs and procedures? (165). He concludes that "[t]here is nothing in religious belief in general, or in Christian belief in particular, to preclude the acceptance of mercy killing as a humane response to some awful situations" (165).

Following Through

Write a summary of the argument opposing euthanasia entitled "Rising to the Occasion of Our Death" by William F. May, on pages 53–55. Or summarize any other argument that you are considering using as a source for a project you are currently working on.

Model Annotated Bibliography Entry

Ames, Katrine. "Last Rights." *Newsweek* 26 Aug. 1991: 40–41.

>This is a news article for the general public about the popu-
>larity of a book called *Final Exit,* on how to commit suicide.
>Ames explains the interest in the book as resulting from peo-
>ple's perception that doctors, technology, and hospital bureau-
>crats are making it harder and harder to die with dignity in this
>country. The article documents with statistics the direction of
>public opinion on this topic and also outlines some options, be-
>sides suicide, that are becoming available to ensure people of the
>right to die. Ames shows a bias against prolonging life through
>technology, but she includes quotations from authorities on both
>sides. This is a good source of evidence about public and profes-
>sional opinion.

Creating an Annotated Bibliography

To get an overview of the sources they have compiled, many writers find it useful to create an annotated bibliography. A **bibliography** is simply a list of works on a particular topic; it can include any kind of source—from news-paper articles to books to government documents. The basic information of a bibliography is identical to that of a works-cited list: author, title, publisher, date, and, in the case of articles, periodical name, volume, and page numbers. (See the section "Creating Works-Cited and Reference Lists" for examples.) Like a works-cited list, a bibliography is arranged in alphabetical order, based on each author's last name.

To **annotate** a bibliography means to include critical commentary about each work on the list, usually in one or two short paragraphs. Each annotation should contain the following:

- A sentence or two about the rhetorical context of the source. Is it an informative news article? an opinion column? a scholarly essay? Is it intended for lawyers? the public? students? the elderly? What is the bias?
- A capsule summary of the content.
- A note about why this source seems valuable and how you might use it.

Following Through

Write an annotated bibliography of the sources you are using for a re-searched argument of your own. Use the model above as a guide.

INCORPORATING AND DOCUMENTING SOURCE MATERIAL IN THE TEXT OF YOUR ARGUMENT

We turn now to the more technical matter of how to incorporate source material into your own writing and how to document the material you include. You incorporate material through direct quotation or through summary or paraphrase; you document material by naming the writer and providing full publication details of the source—a two-step process. In academic writing, documenting sources is essential, even for indirect references, with one exception: You do not need to document your source for factual information that could easily be found in many readily available sources, such as a Supreme Court decision or the number of women currently in the U.S. Senate.

Different Styles of Documentation

Different disciplines have specific formal conventions for documenting sources in scholarly writing. In the humanities, the most common style is that of the Modern Language Association (MLA). In the physical, natural, and social sciences, the American Psychological Association (APA) style is most often used. We will illustrate both in the examples that follow. Unlike the footnote style of documentation, MLA and APA use parenthetical citations in the text and simple, alphabetical bibliographies at the end of the text, making revision and typing much easier. (For a detailed explanation of these two styles, refer to the following manuals: *MLA Handbook for Writers of Research Papers.* 5th ed. New York: MLA, 1999; and the *Publication Manual of the American Psychological Association.* 5th ed. Washington, DC: APA, 2001. You may also visit Web sites for the MLA at <http://www.mla.org> and the APA at <http://apa.org>.)

In both MLA and APA formats, you provide some information in the body of your paper and the rest of the information under the heading "Works Cited" (MLA) or "References" (APA) at the end of your paper. The following summarizes the essentials of both systems.

Instructions for Using MLA and APA Styles

MLA Style

1. In parentheses at the end of both direct and indirect quotations, supply the last name of the author of the source and the exact page

number(s) where the quoted or paraphrased words appear. If the name of the author appears in your sentence that leads into the quotation, you can omit it in the parentheses.

> A San Jose State University professor who is black argues that affirmative action "does not teach skills, or educate, or instill motivation" (Steele 121).

> Shelby Steele, a black professor of English at San Jose State University, argues that the disadvantages of affirmative action for blacks are greater than the advantages (117).

2. In a works-cited list at the end of the paper, provide complete bibliographical information in MLA style, as explained and illustrated later in this chapter.

APA Style

1. In parentheses at the end of the directly or indirectly quoted material, place the author's last name, the date of the cited source, and the exact page number(s) where the material appears. If the author's name appears in the sentence, the date of publication should follow the name directly, in parentheses; the page number still comes in parentheses at the end of the sentence. Unlike MLA, the APA style uses commas between the parts of the citation and "p." or "pp." before the page numbers.

> A San Jose State University professor who is black argues that affirmative action "does not teach skills, or educate, or instill motivation" (Steele, 1990, p. 121).

> Shelby Steele (1990), a black professor of English at San Jose State University, argues that the disadvantages of affirmative action for blacks are greater than the advantages (p. 117).

2. In a reference list at the end of the paper, provide complete bibliographical information in APA style, as explained and illustrated later in this chapter.

Direct Quotations

Direct quotations are exact words taken from a source. The simplest direct quotations are whole sentences worked into your text, as illustrated in the following excerpt from a student essay.

MLA Style

> In a passage that echos Seneca, <u>Newsweek</u> writer Katrine Ames describes the modern viewpoint: "Most of us have some choices in how we live, certainly in how we conduct our lives" (40).

This source is listed in the works-cited list as follows:

> Ames, Katrine. "Last Rights." <u>Newsweek</u> 26 Aug. 1991: 40–41.

APA Style

> In a passage that echos Seneca, *Newsweek* writer Katrine Ames (1991) describes the modern viewpoint: "Most of us have some choices in how we live, certainly in how we conduct our lives" (p. 40).

This source is listed in the reference list as follows:

> Ames, K. (1991, August 26). Last rights. *Newsweek*, pp. 40–41.

Altering Direct Quotations with Ellipses and Brackets

Although there is nothing wrong with quoting whole sentences, it is often more economical to quote selectively, working some words or parts of sentences from the original into sentences of your own. When you do this, use *ellipses* (three evenly spaced periods) enclosed in brackets to signify the omission of words from the original; use brackets to substitute words, to add words for purposes of clarification, and to change the wording of a quotation so that it fits gracefully into your own sentence. (If an omission is not your own—that is, if ellipses already appear in the material you are quoting—it is not necessary to place the ellipses in brackets.)

The following passage from a student paper illustrates quoted words integrated into the student's own sentence, using both ellipses and brackets. The citation is in MLA style.

> Robert Wennberg, a philosopher and Presbyterian minister, explains that "euthanasia is not an exclusively modern development, for it was widely endorsed in the ancient world. [It was] approved by such respected ancients as [. . .] Plato, Sophocles, [. . .] and Cicero" (1).

The source appears in the works-cited list as follows:

> Wennberg, Robert N. <u>Terminal Choices: Euthanasia, Suicide, and the Right to Die</u>. Grand Rapids: Eerdmans, 1989.

Using Block Quotations

If a quoted passage runs to four lines of text in your essay, indent it one inch (or ten spaces if typewritten) from the left margin, double-space it as with the rest of your text, and omit quotation marks. In block quotations, a period is placed at the end of the final sentence, followed by one space and the parenthetical citation.

> The idea of death as release from suffering was expressed by Seneca, a Stoic philosopher of Rome, who lived during the first century C.E.:
>
> > Against all the injuries of life, I have the refuge of death. If I can choose between a death of torture and one that is simple and easy, why should I not select the latter? As I chose the ship in which I sail and the house which I inhabit, so will I choose the death by which I leave life. [. . .] Why should I endure the agonies of disease [. . .] when I can emancipate myself from all my torments? (qtd. in Wennberg 42–43)

Note that the source of the Seneca quotation is the book by Wennberg. In the parenthetical citation, "qtd." is an abbreviation for "quoted." The entry on the works-cited page would be the same as for the previous example.

Indirect Quotations

Indirect quotations are paraphrases or summaries of material, either fact or opinion, taken from a source. The Concept Close-Up box on page 143 gives an example of a direct quotation on a student notecard.

Here is how this quotation might be incorporated into a paper as an indirect quotation. Note that the author of the book is the same as the person indirectly quoted, so it is not necessary to repeat his name in parentheses.

MLA Style

> One cannot help but agree with pioneer heart-transplant surgeon Christiaan Barnard that death should involve dignity and that society may have to accept the practice of euthanasia as a means to death with dignity (8).

The entry on the works-cited list would appear as follows:

> Barnard, Christiaan. <u>Good Life, Good Death</u>. Englewood Cliffs: Prentice, 1980.

APA Style

> One cannot help but agree with pioneer heart-transplant surgeon Christiaan Barnard (1980) that death should involve dignity and that

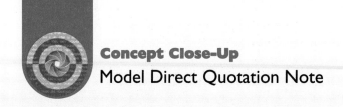
> Expert's opinion — pro:
>
> "It is time to rethink many of our attitudes toward death and dying.[...] I feel that society is ready to take a giant step toward a better understanding of the dignity of death, and in the attainment of that dignity, if necessary, through the acceptance of euthanasia."
>
> — Barnard in Barnard, p. 8

society may have to accept the practice of euthanasia as a means to death with dignity (p. 8).

The entry in the reference list would appear as follows.

Barnard, C. (1980). *Good life, good death.* Englewood Cliffs, NJ: Prentice-Hall.

In-Text References to Electronic Sources

Obviously, the conventions just described apply to print sources, but you should adapt the examples given, being as specific as you can, when you are using sources drawn from the Internet and other electronic communications. Because you will be including the electronic sources in your works-cited or reference list at the end of your paper, your in-text citations should help your readers make the connection between the material you are quoting or paraphrasing in your text and the matching citation on the list. Therefore, your in-text citation, whether parenthetical or not, should begin with the author's name or, in the absence of an author, the title of the work or posting. The APA format requires that you also include the date of the posting.

CREATING WORKS-CITED AND REFERENCE LISTS

At the end of your paper, include a bibliography of all sources that you quoted, paraphrased, or summarized. If you are using MLA style, your heading for this list will be *Works Cited*; if you are using APA style, your heading will be *References*. In either case, the list is in alphabetical order based on either the author's (or editor's) last name or — in the case of anonymously written works — the first word of the title, not counting the articles *a, an, the*. The entire list is double-spaced both within and between entries. See the works-cited page of the sample student paper at the end of this chapter for the correct indentation and spacing. Note that MLA format requires that the first line of each entry be typed flush with the left margin; subsequent lines of each entry are indented half an inch (or five spaces on a typewriter). The APA recommends that papers submitted in final form, such as student papers, use the same indentation.

The following examples illustrate the correct form for the types of sources you will most commonly use.

Books

Book by One Author

MLA: Crusius, Timothy W. <u>Discourse: A Critique & Synthesis of Major Theories</u>. New York: MLA, 1989.

APA: Crusius, T. W. (1989). *Discourse: A critique & synthesis of major theories.* New York: Modern Language Association.

(Note that APA uses initials rather than the author's first name and capitalizes only the first word and proper nouns in the titles and subtitles of books and articles.)

Two or More Works by the Same Author

MLA: Crusius, Timothy W. <u>Discourse: A Critique & Synthesis of Major Theories</u>. New York: MLA, 1989.

   ---. <u>A Teacher's Introduction to Philosophical Hermeneutics</u>. Urbana: NCTE, 1991.

(Note that MLA arranges works alphabetically by title and uses three hyphens to show that the name is the same as the one directly above.)

APA: Crusius, T. W. (1989). *Discourse: A critique & synthesis of major theories.* New York: Modern Language Association.

Crusius, T. W. (1991). *A teacher's introduction to philosophical hermeneutics*. Urbana, IL: National Council of Teachers of English.

(Note that APA repeats the author's name and arranges works in chronological order.)

Book by Two or Three Authors

MLA: Deleuze, Gilles, and Felix Guattari. <u>Anti-Oedipus: Capitalism and Schizophrenia</u>. New York: Viking, 1977.

APA: Deleuze, G., & Guattari, F. (1977). *Anti-Oedipus: Capitalism and schizophrenia*. New York: Viking.

(Note that MLA style inverts only the first author's name. APA style, however, inverts both authors' names and uses an ampersand (&) between authors instead of the word "and.")

Book by Four or More Authors

MLA: Bellah, Robert N., et al. <u>Habits of the Heart: Individualism and Commitment in American Life</u>. New York: Harper, 1985.

(Note that the Latin abbreviation *et al.,* meaning "and others," stands in for all subsequent authors' names. MLA style also accepts spelling out all authors' names instead of using *et al.*)

APA: Bellah, R., Madsen, R., Sullivan, W., Swidler, A., & Tipton, S. (1985). *Habits of the heart: Individualism and commitment in American life*. New York: Harper & Row.

(Note that APA uses *et al.* only for more than six authors.)

Book Prepared by an Editor or Editors

MLA: Connors, Robert J., ed. <u>Selected Essays of Edward P. J. Corbett</u>. Dallas: Southern Methodist UP, 1989.

APA: Connors, R. J. (Ed.). (1989). *Selected essays of Edward P. J. Corbett*. Dallas: Southern Methodist University Press.

Work in an Edited Collection

MLA: Jackson, Jesse. "Common Ground: Speech to the Democratic National Convention." <u>The American Reader</u>. Ed. Diane Ravitch. New York: Harper, 1991. 367–71.

APA: Jackson, J. (1991). Common ground: Speech to the Democratic National Convention. In D. Ravitch (Ed.), *The American reader*
(pp. 367–371). New York: HarperCollins.

Translated Book

MLA: Vattimo, Gianni. The End of Modernity: Nihilism and Hermeneutics in Postmodern Culture. Trans. Jon R. Snyder. Baltimore:
Johns Hopkins UP, 1988.

APA: Vattimo, G. (1988). *The end of modernity: Nihilism and hermeneutics in postmodern culture.* (J. R. Snyder, Trans.). Baltimore:
Johns Hopkins University Press.

Periodicals

Article in a Journal with Continuous Pagination

MLA: Herron, Jerry. "Writing for My Father." College English 54 (1992):
928–37.

APA: Herron, J. (1992). Writing for my father. *College English, 54,*
928–937.

(Note that in APA style the article title is not fully capitalized, but
the journal title is. Note also that the volume number is italicized in APA
style.)

Article in a Journal Paginated by Issue

MLA: McConnell, Margaret Liu. "Living with *Roe v. Wade*." Commentary
90.5 (1990): 34–38.

APA: McConnell, M. L. (1990). Living with *Roe v. Wade. Commentary,*
90(5), 34–38.

(In both these examples, "90" is the volume number and "5" is the number of the issue.)

Article in a Magazine

MLA: D'Souza, Dinesh. "Illiberal Education." Atlantic Mar.
1990: 51+.

(Note that the plus sign indicates that the article runs on nonconsecutive
pages.)

APA: D'Souza, D. (1990, March). Illiberal education. *Atlantic,* pp. 51–58,
          62–65, 67, 70–74, 76, 78–79.

(Note that APA requires all page numbers to be listed.)

Anonymous Article in a Newspaper

MLA: "Clinton Warns of Sacrifice." Dallas Morning News 7 Feb.
          1993: A4.

APA: Clinton warns of sacrifice. (1993, February 7). *The Dallas Morning
          News,* p. A4.

(In both these examples, the "A" refers to the newspaper section in which
the article appeared.)

Editorial in a Newspaper

MLA: Lewis, Flora. "Civil Society, the Police and Abortion." Editorial.
          New York Times 12 Sept. 1992, late ed.: A14.

APA: Lewis, F. (1992, September 12). Civil society, the police and abor-
          tion [Editorial]. *The New York Times,* p. A14.

(Note that in MLA style the edition of the newspaper must be specified.)

Nonprint Sources

Interview

MLA: May, William. Personal interview. 24 Apr. 1990.

(Note that APA style documents personal interviews only parenthetically
within the text: "According to W. May (personal interview, April 24, 1990), . . ."
Personal interviews are not included on the reference list.)

Sound Recording

MLA: Glass, Philip. Glassworks. CBS Sony, MK 37265, 1982.

APA: Glass, P. (1982). *Glassworks* [CD Recording No. MK 37265].
          Tokyo: CBS Sony.

Film

MLA: Scott, Ridley, dir. Thelma and Louise. Perf. Susan Sarandon,
          Geena Davis, and Harvey Keitel. MGM/UA Home Video,
          1991.

APA: Scott, R. (Director). (1991). *Thelma and Louise* [motion picture].
        Culver City, CA: MGM/UA Home Video.

(Note that with nonprint media, APA asks you to identify the medium —
CD, cassette, film, and so forth. MLA includes the principal actors, but APA
does not. APA specifies the place of production, but MLA does not.)

Electronic Sources

Although the documentation requirements for MLA and APA citations contain much of the same information, there are subtle format differences between the two styles. Use the following lists as general guides when you cite
Internet sources.

MLA Style: Citing Internet Sources

1. Author or editor name, followed by a period
2. The title of the article or short work (such as a short story or poem)
   enclosed by quotation marks
3. The name of the book, journal, or other longer work in italics
4. Publication information, followed by a period:

   > City, publisher, and date for books
   > Volume and year for journals
   > Date for magazines
   > Date for and description of government documents

5. The date on which you accessed the information (no period)
6. The URL, placed inside angle brackets, followed by a period

APA Style: Citing Internet Sources

1. Author or editor last name, followed by a comma and the initials
2. The year of publication, followed by a comma, with the month and
   day for magazine and newspaper articles, within parentheses and
   followed by a period
3. The title of the article, book, or journal (follow APA conventions for
   titles of works)
4. The volume number
5. Page numbers
6. The words "Retrieved from," followed by the date of access, followed
   by the source (such as the World Wide Web) and a colon
7. The URL, without a period

An Online Book

MLA: Strunk, William. The Elements of Style. 1st ed. Geneva:
        Humphrey, 1918. May 1995. Columbia U Academic
        Information Systems, Bartleby Lib. 12 Apr. 1999.

<http://www.Columbia.edu/acis/bartleby/strunk/
strunk100.html>.

APA: Strunk, W. (1918). *The elements of style* (1st ed.). [Online].
        Retrieved April 12, 1999, from the World Wide Web:
        http://www.Columbia.edu/acis/bartleby/strunk/
        strunk100.html

(Note that MLA requires that the original publication data be included if it is available for works that originally appeared in print. The APA, however, requires only an online availability statement.)

World Wide Web Site

MLA: Victorian Women Writers Project. Ed. Perry Willett. Apr. 1999.
        Indiana U. 12 Apr. 1999 <http://www.indiana.edu/
        ~letrs/vwwp>.

APA: Willett, P. (1999, April). *Victorian women writers project* [Web
        page]. Retrieved April 12, 1999, from http://www.indiana.
        edu/⌐letrs/vwwp

Article in an Electronic Journal

MLA: Harnack, Andrew, and Gene Kleppinger. "Beyond the MLA
        Handbook: Documenting Sources on the Internet." Kairos.
        1.2 (Summer 1996). 7 Jan. 1997 <http://english.ttu.edu/
        Kairos/1.2/index.html>.

APA: Harnack, A., & Kleppinger, G. (1996). Beyond the *MLA Handbook:*
        Documenting sources on the Internet. *Kairos* [Online], *1*(2).
        Retrieved January 7, 1997, from http://english.ttu.edu/
        Kairos/1.2/index.html

Encyclopedia Article on CD-ROM

MLA: Duckworth, George. "Rhetoric." Microsoft Encarta '95. CD-ROM.
        Redmond: Microsoft, 1995.

APA: Duckworth. G. (1995). Rhetoric. In *Microsoft encarta '95* [CD-ROM].
        Redmond, WA: Microsoft.

Encyclopedia Article Online

MLA: "Toni Morrison." Encyclopaedia Britannica Online. 1994–1999. En-
        cyclopaedia Britannica. 4 Mar. 1999

<http://members.eb.com/bol/
topic?eu=55183&sctn=#s_top>.

APA: (1994–1999). Toni Morrison. In *Encyclopaedia Britannica Online* [Online]. Retrieved March 4, 1999, from http://members.eb.com/bol/topic?eu=55183&sctn=#s_top

E-Mail, Listserv, and Newsgroup Citations

For MLA, give in this order the author's name, the title of the document (in quotation marks), followed by the description *Online posting,* the date when the material was posted, the name of the forum (if known), the date of access, and in angle brackets the online address of the list's Internet site or, if unknown, the e-mail address of the list's moderator.

MLA: Stockwell, Stephen. "Rhetoric and Democracy." Online posting. 13 Jan. 1997. 22 Jan. 1997 <H-Rhetor@msu.edu>.

For APA, the custom is to not include e-mail, listservs, and newsgroups in a reference list but rather to give a detailed in-text citation as follows: (S. Stockwell, posting to H-Rhetor@msu.edu, January 13, 1997).

However, if the content of the message is scholarly, many researchers do include messages in the references:

Stockwell, S. (1997, January 13). Rhetoric and democracy. Retrieved January 22, 1997, from e-mail: H-Rhetor@msu.edu

STUDENT SAMPLE: *A Research Paper (MLA Style)*

Following is student Patrick Pugh's research paper in MLA style.

Pugh 1

Last name, page number on each page

Patrick Pugh

English 1302

October 21, 2001

Professor Smith

Standard heading

Legalizing Euthanasia: A Means
to a More Comfortable Dying Process

Title centered; skip no lines between heading and first paragraph

All people are linked by one indisputable fact: Every human being dies. For some, death comes early, seeming to

Announces theme

Pugh 2

cut off life before many of its mysteries have even begun to unfold. For others, death is the conclusion to a lengthy and experience-filled existence. Death is life's one absolute certainty.

Paragraphs indented 5 character spaces or 1/2" ———

At issue, however, is the desire by some men and women, many of the most vocal of whom are in the medical profession, to intervene in what they describe as a heartless extension of the dying process. The term *euthanasia,* a Greek word whose literal translation is "good death," has been adopted by those who advocate legalizing certain measures to ensure a transition from life to death that is as comfortable and dignified as possible. One cannot help but agree with pioneer heart-transplant surgeon Dr. Christiaan Barnard that death should involve dignity and that society may have to accept the practice of euthanasia as a means to death with dignity (8). ——

No word breaks at ends of lines

Poses issue

Takes stance

Parenthetical page number only because author's name mentioned in text. Note: Page number goes before period.

To me, having watched both my grandfather and my aunt spend months dying slow, torturous deaths from incurable lung cancer, there can be little doubt that euthanasia would have provided a far more humane close to their lives than the painful and prolonged dying that the ultimately futile regimens of chemotherapy and radiation caused them to suffer. My family members' experiences were far too common, for "80 percent of Americans who die in hospitals are likely to meet their end [. . .] in a sedated or comatose state; betubed nasally, abdominally, and intravenously, far more like manipulated objects than moral subjects" (Minow 124).

Ties stance to personal experience

"Run in" quotation; use for shorter citations. Note brackets used with ellipses.

Both author and page number used because author not mentioned in sentence ———

Advocates of euthanasia can turn to history for support of their arguments. Robert Wennberg, a philosopher and Presbyterian minister, explains that "euthanasia is not an

Pugh 3

exclusively modern development, for it was widely endorsed in the ancient world. [It was] approved by such respected ancients as [. . .] Plato, Sophocles, [. . .] and Cicero" (1). The idea that we have a right to choose death was expressed by Seneca, a Stoic philosopher of Rome, who lived in the first century C.E.:

Identifies source unknown to audience; establishes authority of source

> Against all the injuries of life, I have the refuge of death. If I can choose between a death of torture and one that is simple and easy, why should I not select the latter? As I chose the ship in which I sail and the house which I inhabit, so will I choose the death by which I leave life. In no matter more than death should we act according to our desire. [. . .] Why should I endure the agonies of disease [. . .] when I can emancipate myself from all my torments? (qtd. in Wennberg 42–43)

Block quotation; use for longer citations. Note: No quotation marks; indented 10 character spaces or 1".

Note parenthetical citation. No end punctuation after block quote; contrast with "run in" quotation.

In a passage that echos Seneca, <u>Newsweek</u> writer Katrine Ames describes the modern viewpoint: "Most of us have some choices in how we live, certainly in how we conduct our lives. How we die is an equally profound choice, and, in the exhilarating and terrifying new world of medical technology, perhaps almost as important" (40).

Regardless of historical precedents and humane implications, euthanasia in both of its forms remains a controversial issue for many. In the first kind, known as passive or indirect euthanasia, death results from such measures as withholding or withdrawing life-support systems or life-sustaining medications. Passive euthanasia is often equated with simply "letting someone die," in contrast to the far more controversial active or direct euthanasia, in which life is ended by direct intervention, such as giving a

Makes important distinction

Pugh 4

patient a lethal dose of a drug or assisting a patient in his or her suicide.

During the past two decades, the so-called Right to Die movement has made great strides in the promotion of passive euthanasia as an acceptable alternative to the extension of impending death.

> There seems to be a clear consensus that the competent adult has the right to refuse treatments. [. . .] This legal recognition of the right to reject medical treatment is grounded in a respect for the bodily integrity of the individual, for the right of each person to determine when bodily invasions will take place. (Wennberg 116)

End of sentence plus omission from text; four spaced periods and brackets used.

Passive euthanasia, as an extension of the stated wishes of the dying patient, has become a widely accepted practice, a fact confirmed by medical ethicist and theologian Joseph Fletcher:

> What is called passive euthanasia, letting the patient die [. . .] is a daily event in hospitals. Hundreds of thousands of Living Wills have been recorded, appealing to doctors, families, pastors, and lawyers to stop treatment at some balance point of the pro-life, pro-death assessment. (47)

Three periods and brackets; omission from cited text only

The case for passive euthanasia has withstood, for the most part, the arguments of those who claim that life must be preserved and extended at all costs.

The euthanasia debate that is currently being waged focuses on active or direct euthanasia, where another person, notably a physician, assists a terminally ill patient in dying by lethal injection or provides the dying patient with the means to commit suicide. The case for active euthanasia is strong. For example, active euthanasia is preferable to passive

Pugh 5

euthanasia in cases of chronic and incurable diseases that promise the patient pain and suffering for the duration of his or her life. As Robert K. Landers explains, with the advance of AIDS and diseases such as Alzheimer's affecting our aging population, Americans are paying more attention to the idea of "giving death a hand" (555). Surely, many terminally ill patients whose only hope for release from agonizing pain or humiliating helplessness is death would welcome the more comfortable and dignified death that physician-assisted suicide can bring.

Restates stance, now focused on active euthanasia only

Still, there are those who argue that although passive euthanasia is moral, the active type is not. Ethically, is there a difference between passive and active euthanasia? Christiaan Barnard thinks not:

> Passive euthanasia is accepted in general by the medical profession, the major religions, and society at large. Therefore, when it is permissible for treatment to be stopped or not instituted in order to allow the patient to die, it makes for small mercy and less sense when the logical step of actively terminating life, and hence suffering, is not taken. Why, at that point, can life not be brought to an end, instead of extending the suffering of the patient by hours or days, or even weeks? [. . .] Procedurally, there is a difference between direct and indirect euthanasia, but ethically, they are the same. (68–69)

Argues that active euthanasia is ethical

Barnard's ethics are supported by Joseph Fletcher's definition of ethical action, which holds that the ethical value of any human action is not a quality inherent in the act itself but rather a judgment that we make about the act after examining the entire situation in which it takes place. We should decide what is moral and immoral on the basis of

Defines ethics in situational terms

Pugh 6

what is best for human well-being in any given set of circumstances (38–39).

Although Fletcher is an Episcopal theologian, many other Christians do make arguments against active euthanasia on religious grounds. However, according to ethicist James Rachels, even religious people ought to be able to see that these arguments may not be valid. For example, one of the most often-stated objections is that in the Ten Commandments God forbids killing. Rachels counters by pointing out that the Sixth Commandment is more accurately translated as "Thou shalt not commit murder." Because we define murder as "wrongful killing," we will not call some killing murder if we do not see it as wrong. Thus, the Sixth Commandment "is not normally taken to forbid killing in a just war; since such killing is (allegedly) justified" (161–62). Rachels points out that although the scriptures do not mention euthanasia and in fact affirm the "sanctity of human life," one also finds "exhortations to kindness and mercy" for fellow humans, principles that "support active euthanasia rather than condemn it" (162).

Takes up major objection; refutes the notion that mercy killing is murder

To those who claim that "[i]t is for God alone to decide when a person shall live and when he shall die," Rachels responds that "if it is for God alone to decide when we shall live and when we shall die, then we 'play God' just as much when we cure people as when we kill them" (163). He notes that philosopher David Hume made this argument over two hundred years ago.

Transitional sentences signal change of focus, allow smooth movement from paragraph to paragraph

A third common Christian argument is that because suffering is a part of God's plan for humans, we should not interrupt it by euthanasia. Rachels responds to this with the question, How can we then justify the use of any pain-relieving drugs and procedures? (165). He concludes that "[t]here is nothing in religious belief in general, or in Christian belief in particular, to preclude the acceptance of mercy killing as a humane response to some awful situations" (165).

In fact, the American public supports active euthanasia, specifically physician-assisted euthanasia, as an alternative to a lingering death for terminal patients. Polls show support running as high as 70 percent (ERGO). Support for assisted suicide may have leveled off recently, but polls still indicate that more Americans favor assisted suicide than oppose it (American Life League). Fifty percent of doctors also support it, with about 15 percent actually practicing it when a patient's dire situation warrants (ERGO).

Public support, however, has not translated into significant changes in the law. Only Oregon permits assisted suicides (ERGO). Maine rejected a measure similar to the Oregon law in the 2000 election ("Assisted Suicide"), and Attorney General John Ashcroft, reversing the stance of his predecessor, Janet Reno, has recently taken action to block implementation of Oregon's law (Vicini). Furthermore, the Supreme Court has ruled in two cases that the Constitution does not provide a right to die and therefore has upheld state laws against assisted suicide ("Physician"; Vacco v. Quill).

At this point, then, the law seems unresponsive to public opinion. There is no way to predict whether active euthanasia will be legalized in the near future. One thing is reasonably certain, however: Any compassionate person who has sat by helplessly as a fellow human being has spent his or her final days thrashing around on a sweat-soaked bed or who has observed a once-alert mind that has become darkened by the agony of inescapable pain will consider the eventual fate that awaits him or her. In times like these,

Forceful conclusion; avoids saying "in conclusion"

Pugh 8

frightened humans are united in the universal prayer, "God, spare me from this when my time comes," and even the most stubborn anti-euthanasia minds are opened to the option of an easier journey between life and death, an option that can be made a reality by the legalization of physician-assisted euthanasia.

Works Cited

American Life League, Inc. Legislative Guide to End-of-Life Issues. 11 Dec. 2001 <http://www.all.org/legislat/guide01.htm>.

Ames, Katrine. "Last Rights." Newsweek 26 Aug. 1991: 40–41.

"Assisted Suicide, Gay Rights, Lose in Maine." USA Today Network. 8 Nov. 2000. 11 Dec 2001 <http://www.usatoday.com/news/vote2000/me/main.htm>.

Barnard, Christiaan. Good Life, Good Death. Englewood Cliffs: Prentice, 1980.

ERGO (Euthanasia Research & Guidance Organization). "Frequently Asked Questions." Euthanasia World Directory. 11 Dec. 2001 <http://www.finalexit.org>.

Fletcher, Joseph. "In Defense of Suicide." Suicide and Euthanasia: The Rights of Personhood. Ed. Samuel E. Wallace and Albin Eser. Knoxville: U of Tennessee P, 1981. 38–50.

Landers, Robert. "Right to Die: Medical, Legal, and Moral Issues." Editorial Research Reports 1.36 (1990): 554–64.

Minow, Newton. "Communications in Medicine." Vital Speeches of the Day. 1 Dec. 1990: 121–25.

"Physician-Assisted Suicide: Vacco v. Quill; Washington v. Glucksberg." Supreme Court—Key Cases 1996–1997. Washington Post database. 11 Dec. 2001

Sources listed in alphabetical order

Author's last name first

Pugh 9

<http://www.washingtonpost.com/wp-dyn/
    politics>.

Rachels, James. <u>The End of Life</u>. Oxford: Oxford UP, 1987.

Vacco v. Quill. 95-1858. U.S. Supreme Ct. 1997. FindLaw
    Resources legal database. 11 Dec. 2001.
        <http://caselaw.lp.findlaw.com/us/000/95-1858.html>.

Vicini, James. "Doctor-Assisted Suicide Policy Reversed."
    <u>Excite Canada</u>. 6 Nov. 2001. 11 December 2001
    <http://www.excite.com>.

Wennberg, Robert N. <u>Terminal Choices: Euthanasia,
    Suicide, and the Right to Die</u>. Grand Rapids:
    Eerdmans, 1989.

Part Two The Aims of Argument

Part Two # The Aims of Argument

Chapter 6

Looking for Some Truth: Arguing to Inquire

To inquire is to look into something. Inquiry can be a police investigation or a doctor's attempt to diagnose a patient's illness, a scientist's experiment or an artist's attempt to see the world differently. According to singer and songwriter Lucinda Williams, one of the joys of life in this "sweet old world" is "looking for some truth."

It is satisfying to be able to say, "This is true." If we are religious, we find truth in the doctrines of our faith. But in our daily lives, we often must discern for ourselves what is true. We look for truth in messages from family and friends and lovers, in the study of nature, and in good art, music, and literature. Often, though, we have to work to decide what to believe, for even newspapers and textbooks sometimes offer differing versions of fact. The search for truth, then, is closely allied to the question, "What is knowledge?" The pursuit of both is inquiry.

INQUIRY AND INTERPRETATION IN ACADEMIC WRITING

Inquiry is an important part of college learning because college is where we learn that one "true" body of knowledge or set of objective facts about the world simply does not exist. Take, for example, something usually considered to be fact:

> Columbus discovered America in 1492.

If this statement were on a true/false test, would your answer be "true," "false," or "that depends"? With hardly any inquiry at all, we see that this "fact" depends upon:

- the calendar you use to mark time on this earth
- your definition of the word "discover"
- your definition of "America"

- whether your ancestors were here before Columbus
- whether you know anything about Vikings and other early explorers

So what we accept as fact, as truth, really is *an interpretation.* Most significant claims to truth are *efforts to understand and/or explain;* as such, they are interpretations that need defending. In college, we realize that knowledge is contested, as we read scholars' attempts to make the best cases for their interpretations. Later in this chapter, you will read several arguments, each claiming to know the truth about whether violence on television causes children to act out violently. The arguments offer data to prove their claims, but data itself is meaningless without interpretation. And interpretations are open to inquiry.

The current state of knowledge on any given topic depends on who is doing the interpreting, whether anyone pays attention to that person, and whether the observed data are of interest to people in a particular culture. Some facts remain unknown for centuries because for some reason no one thought they mattered. What one considers knowledge or truth, then, depends on the perspective of the interpreters, which in turn depends on the interpreters' social class, politics, religion, and a host of other factors that make up who they are and how they see the world. What you learn from research about a topic will depend on the perspectives of your sources.

Like the high school research paper, college writing requires research. Unlike the high school paper, which might have required only that you obtain some information, organize it, and restate in your own words the accepted knowledge about a topic, most college assignments will require that you *inquire* into your sources.

It's important to gather information and viewpoints. But research itself is not the goal of inquiry. The most important part of inquiry is the thinking you do before and after gathering sources. The quality of your paper will depend on the quality of your initial thinking as well as upon the quality of your sources and your understanding of them. Nothing is more vital to writing well than learning how to inquire well.

As we begin to inquire, it is important not to try to prove anything. Argument as inquiry is not confrontational; rather, it is conversational. It is part of our conversation with friends, family, and colleagues. We can have these kinds of conversations with ourselves, and we can ask and answer questions about the arguments we read.

To inquire well, we must question our initial viewpoints instead of holding onto them. We need to ask hard questions, even if the answers threaten our preconceptions and beliefs. Before Copernicus, "common sense" told people that the Earth was stationary, and religious beliefs reinforced this "truth." To question our truths makes us uncomfortable, to say the least. But for knowledge to advance, the willingness to hold a question open is essential. The scientist whose theory wins respect from other scientists must continue to test its truth rather than try to protect the idea from further inquiry.

Likewise, a college student needs to test the received wisdom from his or her past in order to grow intellectually. After inquiry, you may still hold the same belief, but because you have tested it, your belief will be a claim to truth that you have earned, not just received wisdom.

This chapter offers guidelines for inquiring and shows how writing plays a part in arguing to inquire. The writing project for inquiry is the exploratory essay, through which the following pages will guide you.

THE WRITING PROJECT: EXPLORATORY ESSAY, PART 1

The exploratory essay is a written account of your own inquiry. Your goal is to share with your readers the experience of questioning your opinions and the arguments of others on your chosen topic. The paper will be an intellectual journey; it will have a starting point, a tour of viewpoints on the issue, and a destination, some truth you feel you can defend. The essay will have three parts, one written before inquiry and the other two written after you have thoroughly explored the topic. In this informal paper, you will refer to yourself and your own thoughts and experiences. Feel free to write in first person.

In this chapter, we give specific, step-by-step advice about writing the paper; for now, though, here is an overview.

In Part 1, you will tell what question or issue interests you most about a given topic and express your initial opinion about or answer to this question.

Part 2 will be the exploration itself. The point of Part 2 is to open the question and keep it open, testing your opinions and exploring the issue through conversations and research that introduce you to a range of expert opinions. You are not trying to support your initial opinions but to test them. In Part 2, you will write about readings that confirm and contradict your thinking, and you'll evaluate these arguments with an open mind. You will use your critical-reading skills to discuss the strengths and weaknesses of the arguments you encounter.

Part 3, the conclusion of your paper, will be a statement of your thinking after the process of inquiry, an explanation of the truth you have found as a result of your conversations and readings. Think of exploration as the process of *arriving* at a claim. Ideally, in the conclusion of your exploratory essay, you will state a claim whose truth you have tested and earned.

Your instructor may follow up on this paper by asking you to read Chapter 7, "Making Your Case: Arguing to Convince," and to write an argument convincing others to assent to your claim. But in this paper, for the moment, you will explore an issue, not make a case for an opinion.

We illustrate the process of inquiry and the steps of writing the exploratory essay by exploring the topic of violence in the media and its relation to violence in our society. We show some students' initial thinking about this issue and take you through their exploration of it through dialogues and readings. For your own paper, you may continue to explore this topic or choose a different topic that interests you or your class.

Step 1: Choosing a Topic for Inquiry

If your instructor has not assigned a topic for inquiry, you might begin by looking at the newspapers. In a writing class focused on argumentation, current events are often topics, and they need interpretation. If you are familiar with some topic in the news, you probably already have an opinion about it, and that is a good place to begin inquiry. Because you are learning to write in an academic setting, it would make sense to pick a topic that is related to some part of the curriculum. The topic we've selected for illustration—violence in the media—is relevant to psychology, sociology, law, political science, courses in popular culture and film, and so on. We came upon our topic by noticing an op-ed column on the subject in the *New York Times*, but yours could come from a front-page story or an item on television.

Once you have selected a topic, consider what you already know about it and toward what smaller aspect of the topic your knowledge points. For example, violence in the media is a huge subject. There's violence in the sense of staged or *pretend violence*—the quarrels, muggings, rapes, fistfights, knifings, shootings, battlefield scenes, and so on of television and movie dramas. There's *virtual violence*—some computer games and Internet sites. There's also *actual violence*, the staple of broadcast news. "If it bleeds, it leads": Local TV news programs often start with an account of a brutal murder or a big traffic accident with injuries and fatalities.

You can find more needles in a small haystack than in a big one; the more you narrow your topic, the easier it will be to find issues to argue about and sources that converse with each other on these issues. For example, narrowing the topic of media violence to violence in video games or music lyrics will yield more perspectives and specific evidence that might be lost if you cast a wider net.

Step 2: Finding an Issue

An issue is a question the answer to which people disagree about. With our topic, we can begin to list such questions: Why do people find violence so engrossing, so entertaining? Why do we like to see violence in sports like football, hockey, and auto racing? Why do we go to movies that feature violence? Is it something in our nature or in our culture? Is it related to hormones, to gender roles?

These are worthwhile questions, but for purposes of systematic inquiry, most topics have one central or primary issue. In this instance, that issue is whether pretend violence can be connected to aggressive acts. This issue is central because most articles about the topic address it. It's also central because our answer largely determines what the other issues are.

Systematic inquiry recognizes order or hierarchy among issues; that is, the answer to one question leads to another question. *If* there is a link between fantasy violence and actual violence, *then* the next question is, How significant is the connection? We can't ask the second question until we answer the first. *If* we decide that pretend violence is a major contributor to actual aggression, *then* we must decide what action should be taken, if any—and this leads to issues of censorship, the First Amendment, and the freedom to create and consume violent entertainment. For our topic, then, we can list this hierarchy of issues:

- Is there a link between fantasy violence and real-world violence? If so, what is the nature of the link?
- How serious are the effects? Does media violence make people more aggressive and less sensitive to the suffering of others? Does it contribute to crimes such as murders and assaults?
- If the contribution is significant, can/should we consider censorship, or does Constitutional protection of free expression prohibit taking this kind of action?
- If censorship is out of the question, what other action(s) can we suggest to mitigate the negative effect?

Fortunately, locating the issues usually is not difficult. Often we can supply them from our own general knowledge and experience. We need only ask, What have we heard people arguing about when this topic came up? What have we ourselves argued about it? If we can't identify the issues before starting our research, the research will reveal them. In fact, once you begin reading what others have said about your topic, you may discover an issue you would not have considered but find more interesting than your initial question.

It is important to be conscious of issues, not just topics. A thorough exploration involves more than one issue, but the point is to inquire more deeply into one or two related questions rather than to broadly survey all issues surrounding a topic. And when you do research, be sure to select readings that address the same issues.

Following Through

In preparation for writing your exploratory paper, select a topic of current interest. What do you see as the main issue that people debate? With some answers to that question, draw up a chain of questions that follow one from another. Which are most interesting to you?

Following Through

Read an argument on a topic of current interest, perhaps on the topic you intend to explore. You can find such an argument in the newspaper, on the Internet, or elsewhere in this textbook. What issue does this argument primarily address? What is the central question it attempts to answer? What is the author's answer to this question—in other words, what is the author's claim? Try to restate it in your own words. What other issues are raised in the argument? Besides these, what *other* issues are raised in discussion of this topic?

Step 3: Stating Your Initial Opinions

In this step, you will write Part 1 of your exploratory essay, the part in which you state your initial ideas on the topic before inquiry. You may have read one or two articles about your topic or had a discussion with someone, but you should write this part of your paper before doing any serious research. Begin by introducing your topic and the issue or issues you have decided are most interesting. State your opinions on those issues, and explain your reasoning. Include some explanation of what, in your own experiences or observations, has contributed to your opinions.

Below is Part 1 of the essay of a student who is about to explore the connection between media violence and real-life violence.

STUDENT SAMPLE: *Exploratory Essay, Part 1*

Lauren's Initial Opinions

I have to admit that I am somewhat biased when it comes to the topic of the correlation between the entertainment industry and violence in children. Unfortunately, I have been involved in several life-altering experiences that even before this assignment made me feel very strongly that virtual violence and aggressive behavior in children are causally related. When I was in high school, a group of kids that I grew up with started getting mixed up in the whole "gangster" era. They listened to rap music that preached about murder, drugs, and human destruction. Ultimately, these boys decided to take the life of a fellow student at the McDonald's down the street from my school. They used an illegally purchased shotgun to murder him in a drug deal gone bad. Because I knew these kids when they were younger, I can say that when they were in the seventh grade, I would not have imagined they were capable of committing such a horrid act of violence. Did the rap music influence them to commit this heinous crime? We will never really know the truth, but they had to get the idea from somewhere, and I personally cannot think of another reasonable explanation.

Even though music cannot be the culprit that implants evil in the mind of a child, it can be the root of some problems. Throughout my senior year, I did a great deal of volunteer work at the Salvation Army recreation center. This rec center is located in the so-called "ghetto" of Lincoln, Nebraska. It is intended for children to walk to after school when their parents are working. It is like a daycare center, only it's free. Working here really opened up my eyes to how the future of America is growing up.

My first encounter was with a six-year-old boy who started calling me such profane names that I honestly couldn't imagine anyone ever using language like that. Not only was I verbally abused on several occasions, but I was also pushed, shoved, and kicked. Later, after discussing the situation with the young boy in time out, I found out that he had heard these names in an Eminem song that bashes women. Because of these experiences, I am interested in exploring this topic, but I am skeptical about whether my opinion will change.

Following Through

Draft Part 1 of your paper. In the opening paragraph or two, state what your opinions were before you researched the topic. In the case of violence in the media or entertainment, for instance, you might discuss the impact of violent entertainment on you or a younger sister or brother. If you seek out or avoid such entertainment, say so and explain why. Be specific. Describe and explain experiences that influenced your outlook. Refer to specific films or music or news broadcasts. If you've read or heard about the topic before or discussed it in school or elsewhere, try to recall both context and content and share them with your readers. Edit for clarity and correctness.

Step 4: Exploring an Issue

Once you have written Part 1 of your paper, turn to the task of exploring—reading and talking about your topic. Because you will eventually write about these experiences in Part 2 of your paper, use your writer's notebook and other writing, such as good annotations in the margins of what you read, to record your thoughts. These notes are the raw material from which you will eventually write the account of your exploration.

CONVERSATION AND DIALOGUE IN INQUIRY

A good way to begin inquiry is to talk through your position on an issue in serious conversation with a friend, family member, classmate, or teacher. More often than we might think, inquiry takes the form of discussion or conversation. Unsurprisingly, conversation is a big part of higher education. Many college classes are devoted to discussion rather than lectures; even lecturers break on occasion to allow the class to discuss controversial questions. Out of class, students often have the opportunity to talk with professors one-on-one as well as with each other.

As you know from watching talk shows, conversation is not always a search for truth. There is an art to productive conversation. In Chapter 2, we noted that critical reading depends on developing certain practices and habits of mind. Conversation aimed at finding some truth also depends on good practices and habits. The key to good conversation is this: Participants need to move beyond ordinary conversation, which is often just an exchange of opinions, to *dialogue*, which is a *questioning* of opinions.

Let's begin by looking at a conversation about the topic of violence in entertainment.

An Example Conversation

The conversation that follows took place shortly after the Columbine High School killings. It was recorded and transcribed, and an excerpt of it appeared in the May 17, 1999, issue of *Newsweek*. The conversation is neither especially good nor especially bad but rather typical, the sort of thing we encounter routinely in media-arranged talk. Just read it carefully. The comments that follow explain what we can learn from it.

Moving beyond the Blame Game
Jonathan Alter, Moderator

A month after the Littleton tragedy, the conversation continues — in schools, in homes and at this week's White House conference on youth violence. The theories of why Eric Harris and Dylan Klebold went on their rampage have given way to a broader discussion of the deeper sources of the problem and where to go from here. Obviously, there are no quick fixes; everything from more values [in] education to better supervision of antidepressant medication has been introduced into the debate. But Americans have singled out a few issues for special attention. According to the new *Newsweek* Poll, about half of all Americans want to see the movie industry, the TV industry, computer-game makers, Internet services and gun manufacturers and the NRA make major policy changes to help reduce teen violence. Slightly fewer want the music industry to change fundamentally. Younger Americans are less concerned about media violence than their elders are. On guns, there's a racial gap, with 72 percent of nonwhites and 41 percent of whites seeking major changes.

To further the conversation, *Newsweek* assembled a panel last week to explore the complexities. One after another, the people who actually make heavily violent movies, records and games declined to participate, just as they did when the White House called. This could be a sign that they are feeling the heat — or perhaps just avoiding it. Those who did take part in the *Newsweek* forum include Wayne LaPierre, executive director of the NRA; Jack Valenti, president of the Motion Picture Association of America; Hillary Rosen, president of the Recording Industry Association of America; Doug Lowenstein, president of the Interactive Digital Software Association; Marshall Herskovitz, TV and movie producer and director; and Jonah Green, a 15-year-old New York high-school student. *Newsweek*'s Jonathan Alter moderated the discussion.

Excerpts:

Alter: Youth shall be served, so I want to start with Jonah. You seem to think that there's [a] lot of scapegoating going on.

Green: Well, I have to say that America is very confused and scared. There's no one simple answer to teen violence. It's understandable because we're seeking answers, but right now people are focusing too much on putting the blame somewhere. We should be focusing on solutions.

Alter: Ok, Wayne, wouldn't making guns less easily accessible be at least a partial solution?   5

LaPierre: You can't talk about easy access to guns by people we all don't want to have guns without talking about the shameful secret that really hasn't been reported. Which is the complete collapse of enforcement of the existing firearm laws on the books by the Department of Justice [in] the last six years. The proof is in the statistics. Six thousand kids illegally brought guns to school the last two years. We've only had 13 [federal] prosecutions. And only 11 prosecutions for illegally transferring guns to juveniles.

Alter: Do you think that if an 11-year-old brings his father's gun to school, the child should be prosecuted?

LaPierre: Yes, I do. They did not prosecute Kip Kinkel out in Oregon after he was blowing up cats, threatening people. He walks into school with a gun. They do nothing to him except send him home. And he comes back to the school two days later with a gun and shoots those kids. I mean, the fact is we're either serious about this situation or we're not.

Alter: How about Clinton's gun-limit proposal? Why does anyone need to buy more than one gun a month?

LaPierre: That's just a sound bite.   10

Alter: Doug, some of your industry's games are a long way from Pac-Man, right?

Lowenstein: Oh, absolutely. There are some very violent videogames, although they represent only a small fraction of the market. There's a critical parental role here: It costs over $1,000 to own a computer. A hundred dollars plus to own a videogame machine. There's a very conscious choice involved in bringing this kind of entertainment into your home. And the parent needs the tools to make an informed choice.

Alter: You don't think it desensitizes kids to violence to play games over and over?

Green: Personally, I think some kids use videogames, especially the violent ones, just as some violent movies, as a vent. You know, they like to live vicariously and vent their anger through that. And Doug was right that we can't really map out everything a kid has and how they use it and what makes them able to kill somebody.

Alter: Hillary, MTV is doing a stop-the-violence campaign, but then they   15
air—and you supported—something like Eminem's song about stuffing a woman into the trunk of a car. Don't you see a contradiction here?

Rosen: Young people are so much smarter than anybody—the media or politicians or most adults, in fact—may give them credit for being. They understand the difference between fantasy and reality, and that's why giving them concrete steps to take when they face personal conflict or when they face a gang conflict or school bullying, or those sorts of things, are much more productive means for giving them tools to be nonviolent in their lives than taking away their culture.

Alter: Do you think that a music-rating system just makes it forbidden fruit and makes kids want to play or see it more?

Rosen: We've done surveys that show it doesn't encourage young people to buy artists. People buy music that they connect with, that they like, that has a good beat, that sounds good. The label is there for parents and for retailers.

Green: I actually think artists like Eminem are very sarcastic. It is more playful than hard core. I find rap being a little more human than it used to be. Gangsta rap isn't as big anymore, and now sampling is.

Rosen: It's true.   20

Green: Edgar Allan Poe talked about death—he was dark, but he was a celebrated poet. It's about having an edge, a hook. That can be violence.

Alter: You don't have any problem with Marilyn Manson naming himself after a serial killer?

Green: I think it's in bad taste. It was just stupid and controversial.

Alter: Hillary, how about you?

Rosen: Well, I agree with Jonah that it's bad taste, but that's the point. Mari-   25
lyn Manson in an act. It's an act that's sort of designed to create a persona
of empowering the geek. Unfortunately, Charles Manson was a real person.
People don't have to make up horrible tragedies in this world.

Green: Entertainment and the media were never really for getting across
good, moral messages like "I love my school and my mother." People rarely
feel they need to express bland feelings like that.

Rosen: But it is on some level, because Britney Spears sells more records
than Marilyn Manson. You know there's been a resurgence of young pop
music. B*Witched and the Dixie Chicks and Britney Spears and 'N Sync.
I mean, these artists are selling a hell of a lot more records than Marilyn
Manson.

Alter: Do you think that kids have kind of gotten that message and are
less interested in gratuitously violent lyrics than they used to be? Because
they've seen so much death, either in their own neighborhoods or on TV?

Rosen: Well, there's no question that what used to be known as gangsta rap
is definitely played out. Rap is much more light-hearted. It's about getting
money and getting women. The music has evolved.

Alter: Why is that?   30

Rosen: Well, this might be controversial, but I'm actually one of those people who believes that young people are a lot more positive about the world
today than most of the media is giving them credit for in the last couple of
weeks. Surveys have shown that young people are more optimistic about
their future, they're more positive, they're more connected to their parents
than they have been in generations. And these all speak to really good, positive things.

Alter: Marshall, what do you think are some of Hollywood's responsibilities in this area?

Herskovitz: I think we now have virtual reality available to people that is
nihilistic, anarchic and violent. And it is possible for a person to so completely live in that virtual reality that they come to confuse it for the real
world around them.

Alter: But you know from firsthand experience that violence sells.

Herskovitz: "Legends of the Fall" was a very violent movie. I think vio-   35
lence has a potentially strong part in any artistic venture. It's not something
I would ever want to talk about legislatively. I would like to talk about it in
terms of individual responsibility, yes.

Alter: So where should the thoughtful consumer of all of this draw the
line between gratuitous violence and necessary violence for dramatic
purposes?

Herskovitz: Oh, I think that's the point. The thoughtful consumers feel it in their gut. I think the problem in this culture is that thoughtful consumers are not particularly influencing their children.

Alter: But isn't it a little too easy to just say it's all the parent's responsibility?

Valenti: Well, I don't think the movie industry can stand *in loco parentis.* Over 30 years ago I put in place a movie-rating system, voluntary, which gives advanced cautionary warnings to parents so that parents can make their own judgments about what movies they want their children to see.

Alter: I think what a lot of parents wonder is, why is it that NC-17 is not applied to gratuitously violent movies?   40

Valenti: Well, it's because the definition of "gratuitous" is shrouded in subjectivity. There is no way to write down rules. I think Marshall can tell you that creative people can shoot a violent scene a hundred different ways. Sex and language are different, because there are few ways that you can couple on the screen that—there's only a few. And language is language. It's there or it isn't. But violence is far more difficult to pin down. It's like picking up mercury with a fork.

Alter: A movie director told me recently that he went to see "The Matrix," and there was a 5-year-old at the film with his mother. Isn't that a form of child abuse?

Valenti: If a parent says he wants his 5-year-old to be with him, who is to tell this parent he can't do it? Who is to tell him?

Alter: But if it was NC-17, that 5-year-old wouldn't be allowed to go, right?

Valenti: Well, that's right.   45

Alter: So why allow them in when it's R?

Valenti: Because the way our system is defined, we think there's a dividing line.

Alter: When parents aren't doing their job properly, where does the responsibility of everybody else begin?

LaPierre: I was talking with John Douglas, the FBI's criminal profiler. And he said, "Wayne, never underestimate the fact that there are some people that are just evil." And that includes young people. We go searching for solutions, and yet some people are just plain bad apples. You look around the country—the cities that are making progress across the board are really combining prevention and working with young people when you get the first warning signs. And making sure they find mentors. Making sure they're put into programs. And they're combining that with very, very tough enforcement of things like the gun laws.

Herskovitz: I have a fear that modern society, and in particular television,   50
may be beyond the ability of parents to really control. I think movies are different, because the kid has to go out of the house and go there. TV is a particular problem because it's in the house.

Alter: But Marshall, maybe that's because the values that are being propagated by the media, broadly speaking, are so much more powerful that parents can't compete as easily as they used to.

Herskovitz: I don't believe that. I accept a lot of responsibility for the picture the media create of the world. But I don't think there's a conflict between that and the responsibility of parents to simply sit down and talk with their children. Most violent crime is committed by males. Young men are not being educated in the values of masculinity by their fathers.

Alter: So why then let all of these boys see scenes of gratuitous violence that don't convey human values to them?

Valenti: There are only three places where a child learns what Marshall was talking about, values. You learn them in the church. You learn them in school. And you learn them at home. And if you don't have these moral shields built in you by the time you're 10 or 12 years old, forget it.

Alter: I'm not sure that people in Hollywood are thinking, "Is what we do part of the solution on this values question, or does it just contribute to the problem?"

Herskovitz: The answer is the people who aren't contributing to the problem are thinking about it a lot, and the people who are contributing to the problem are not thinking about it.

Valenti: Well, how does *Newsweek* then condone its putting on the cover of your magazine Monica Lewinsky? What kind of a value system does that convey?

Alter: Well, that's a separate discussion.

Valenti: Oh, I don't think it is.

Alter: Well, let me say this. We very explicitly did not put Dylan Klebold and Eric Harris on our cover the first week. We're wrong in these judgments sometimes, but we do at least try to think about the consequences of what we put out there, instead of just saying it's up to the parents. That seems to me a cop-out.

Lowenstein: What you're looking for is an elimination of any problematic content.

Alter: No, I'm not. I'm looking for a sense of shame and a sense of responsibility. I'm wondering where it is in all of the industries that we have represented here today.

Herskovitz: Most people, especially in electronic journalism, don't think at all about this, and their role is incredibly destructive, just like most people in the movie and television business don't think at all about this. And their role is destructive. I think there's a great need for shame. Most people I know and speak to are very ashamed, but unfortunately they're not the people who make violent movies.

Analysis of "Moving beyond the Blame Game"

It's obvious that the *Newsweek* excerpts are not part of a natural, spontaneous conversation, the sort of thing we might have with friends around a campfire, at a campus mixer, or at a bar or café after work. This conversation has been *arranged*. The participants didn't just happen to come together some place and start talking; they were invited. Furthermore, they knew why they were invited—each represents a group or industry implicated in teen violence. Even Jonah Green, the fifteen-year-old, is cast (that's the right word) as "youth," as if one young person could stand for all young people. Each participant knew his or her role in advance, then, and what was at stake. Except perhaps for Jonah Green, each had an agenda and an interest in protecting their reputations and the public image of their businesses and organizations. Therefore, unlike the conversations in which we ask you to engage, theirs from the start was something less than an open-minded search for truth. Even the moderator, Alter, takes a hit for his own magazine's covers. In a genuine dialogue for inquiry, people question each other in a friendly way and do not attack each other or become defensive.

In addition to its adversarial tone, this discussion falls short of good inquiry because it lacks depth. It is an extreme example of what tends to go wrong with *all* discussions, including many class discussions. In the classroom, the teacher plays Alter's role, trying, sometimes with more than a hint of desperation, to get students to talk. When a question from the podium is greeted by silence from the class, sometimes even teachers do what Alter does: solicit opinions by addressing questions to individuals who then have no choice but to answer. Often the instructor is happy to get any opinion, no matter how unconsidered, just to get things going. Once the ice is broken, students usually join in and opinions come forth. It can be stimulating just to hear what everybody else is thinking. Before long, we're caught up in the discussion and don't perceive what is happening: a superficial exchange of opinions, more or less like the *Newsweek* example. Much is said, but almost nothing is really discussed, that is, *examined, pursued, genuinely explored.*

Exactly what do we mean? Look at the first few exchanges in the *Newsweek* example. Alter addresses Jonah Green, the fifteen-year-old high school student, who had apparently talked enough previously to reveal an opinion. Alter summarizes that opinion: "There's a lot of scapegoating going on." Green himself immediately offers two more intelligent observations, better than anything we get from the adult participants: "There's no one simple answer to teen violence" and "we should be focusing on solutions" rather than on blame.

These statements merit our attention. But what happens? Alter must get the others into the discussion, so he turns to LaPierre and asks if better gun control might be part of the solution. *The secret of a good discussion is not to allow intelligent comments to go unquestioned.* Imagine, for example, what the following line of questioning might lead to. ("Q" stands for "questioner," who could be anyone involved in the discussion.)

> Green: There's a lot of scapegoating going on.
>
> Q: What do you mean by "scapegoating"?
>
> Green: A scapegoat is someone who gets blamed or punished for doing something everyone is guilty of or responsible for.
>
> Q: So you're saying that youth violence is a collective problem that everyone contributes to in one way or another. Is that right?
>
> Green: Yes.

Now that we know what Green's assertion actually means or implies, we can really discuss it, look for whatever truth it may convey. Are we *all* really implicated in youth violence? How exactly? If we are, what can each of us do?

We handle Green's comment about looking for solutions the same way. All we need to ask is, What might be part of the solution? It would be interesting to hear Jonathan's ideas. Maybe he has an idea how high schools could build more community or how parents could get involved. But no — the conversation moves away in a new direction.

Our intent is not to put down conversation. Exchanging opinions is one of the great pleasures of social life. For inquiry, however, we need genuine dialogue.

To help your conversations become dialogue, we offer "Questions for Inquiry" later in the chapter on pages 177–178. These same questions will help you inquire into written texts, such as the sources you might encounter in researching your topic. Most of the questions on this list can be traced back to the origins of dialogue in ancient Greece and have demonstrated their value in opening up arguments for about 2,500 years. Commit the list to memory, and practice asking these questions until they become second nature. There's no guarantee that this list will give you the best questions to ask of any given text, but you'll never be wholly at a loss when it's time to test the views you hear or read.

Following Through

Mark up the *Newsweek* dialogue. Use the "Questions for Inquiry" to probe the participants' comments. For example, one question suggests that you inquire about analogies and comparisons. We might ask Jonah if Edgar Allen Poe's "darkness" is truly comparable to the creations of Marilyn Manson. Aren't there some significant differences in the context in which these art forms present violence? Be ready to point out places where the discussants failed to answer questions directly or where you would have posed a good question if you had been there. Note places where the discussion moved toward dialogue and where it moved toward mere venting of opinion. Does Alter do a good job as moderator, or is he mainly concerned with moving on — going broader rather than deeper? Be ready to discuss your annotations in class.

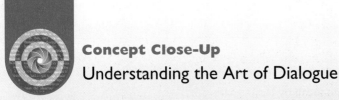

Concept Close-Up

Understanding the Art of Dialogue

To be useful for inquiry, conversations must become dialogues. They become dialogues when someone questions, in a nonhostile way, what someone else has said. Only then are we really discussing something, not just stating our opinion and talking for talking's sake.

Step 5: Engaging in a Dialogue about Your Initial Opinions

Earlier, you wrote Part 1 of your exploratory essay, a statement of your initial opinions on the topic you will explore. A good way to begin exploration is with what you said in Part 1. Exchanging these initial statements with a classmate and then asking each other questions will get you thinking more deeply about what you already know and believe. This exercise should be not just a conversation but also a true dialogue about each other's opinions.

Read the example below, which shows one student's first thoughts and the dialogue that he and another student had about his thoughts. These students used a software program that allowed them to record their conversation, and what follows is a transcript of a real-time chat on the subject of media violence and violence in society. They had hard-copy printouts of each other's initial opinions in front of them as they took turns being each other's friendly questioner. First, we read Matt's initial thoughts and then the dialogue he had with Lauren, whose own first thoughts we reproduced earlier. Note where the dialogue seems to be a conversation and where Lauren attempts to make it an inquiry. Where does it succeed as inquiry, and where does it not?

STUDENT SAMPLE: *Example Dialogue for Analysis—Matt's Initial Opinions*

I think the issue of violence in the media is way overdone. I believe that violence is a conscious act by people who are evil, not people who are motivated by what they have seen or heard in the media. There are simply some people who are violent, and they cannot be stopped from committing their crimes simply by depriving the media of their freedom to create false violence. Violence is an act of nature; it is an instinct all humans are born with, yet the majority of society is able to restrain themselves from acting on their impulse to be violent. Though I have seen and heard my share of violence in the media, I am not a violent person. Sure, sometimes after watching a violent movie, I think about what it would be like to do some of that stuff, but I am not stupid enough to act on my curiosity.

1. *Ask if you have understood the arguer's position on the issue.* The best way to do this is to restate, paraphrase, or summarize the thesis. (Face-to-face, you might say, "I believe that you are saying . . . Am I understanding you?") Be sure to note how strongly the claim is made. If you are inquiring into your own argument, ask if you have stated your own position clearly. Do you need to qualify it in any way?

2. *Ask about the meaning of any words that seem central to the argument.* You can do this at any point in a conversation and as often as it seems necessary. When dealing with a written text, try to discern the meaning from the context. For instance, if an author's case depends on the fairness of a proposed solution, you'll need to ask what "fair" means, because the word has a range of possible applications. You might ask, "Fair to whom?"

3. *Ask what reasons support the thesis.* Paraphrasing reasons is a good way to open up a conversation to further questions about assumptions, values, and definitions.

4. *Ask about the assumptions on which the thesis and reasons are based.* Most arguments are based on one or more unstated assumptions. For example, if a college recruiter argues that the school he or she represents is superior to most others (thesis) because its ratio of students to teachers is low (reason), the unstated assumptions are (1) that students there will get more attention and (2) that more attention results in a better education. As you inquire into an argument, note the assumptions, and ask if they are reasonable.

5. *Ask about the values expressed or implied by the argument.* For example, if you argue that closing a forest to logging operations is essential even at the cost of dozens of jobs, you are valuing environmental preservation over the livelihoods of the workers who must search for other jobs.

6. *Ask how well the reasons are supported.* Are they offered as opinions only, or are they supported with evidence? Is the evidence recent? sufficient? What kind of testimony is offered? Who are the authorities cited? What are their credentials and biases?

7. *Consider analogies and comparisons.* If the author makes an argument by analogy, does the comparison hold up? For example, advocates of animal rights draw an analogy with civil rights when they claim that just as we have come to recognize the immorality of exploiting human beings, so we should recognize the immorality of exploiting other species. But is this analogy sound?

8. *Ask about the arguer's biases and background.* What past experiences might have led the arguer to take this position? What does the holder

(continues)

of this position stand to gain? What might someone gain by challenging it?

9. *Ask about implications.* Where would the argument ultimately lead if we
accept what the speaker advocates? For example, if someone contends
that abortion is murder, asking about implications would lead to the
question, Are you willing to put women who get abortions on trial for
murder and, if they are convicted, to punish them as murderers are
usually punished?

10. *Ask whether the argument takes opposing views into account.* If it does,
are they presented fairly and clearly or with mockery and distortion?
Does the author take them seriously or dismiss them? Are they effectively refuted?

STUDENT SAMPLE: *Example*

Dialogue between Matt and Lauren

Lauren: You don't think there is any correlation between violence and the
entertainment industry?

Matt: Not really. I don't see how music could influence someone to the
point of violence.

Lauren: I kind of agree with you, but I don't know. I think that sometimes
it gives a person the mentality to do that kind of stuff when their friends
are—when people are impressionable like that, they will do a lot of stupid
things. When I was in high school, a group of kids I grew up with started
getting into the whole "gangster" era. They listened to rap talking about
murder, drugs, and destruction. They murdered a fellow student at the
McDonalds down the street from the school. Did the music make them do
this? We'll never know, but they had to get the idea from somewhere.

Matt: What happened to the guys that killed that person?

Lauren: They are all in jail now. Only one has gone to trial.

Matt: That's crazy. I listened to all kinds of music, and I am not violent.

Lauren: You can't assume everyone is like you. How do you explain kids
doing the kind of stuff they are doing?

Matt: There are just some violent, evil people. They just aren't right, if you
know what I mean.

Lauren: Do you mean they are crazy?

Matt: Yes, they're crazy.

Lauren: I think you said violence is an act of nature. Does that mean we
are born violent? Is it normal to be violent?

Matt: I think everyone has a violent side, but they act on it in different ways. I go play sports or work out to get rid of the aggression.

Lauren: But is violence the same thing as evil? Or aggression? Those kids at my school were evil, not natural. I think you need to think more about what you mean by violent when you say it's natural. Maybe it's natural for animals to have aggression and to attack and kill to stay alive, but is that evil? When you say people are "just not right," do you mean that they are natural or not natural?

Matt: OK, I think we are born violent, but some of us are also born evil.

Lauren: So are you saying that nothing good could change these people for the better, like having a good family or going to church? Are they just how they were born?

Matt: I'd have to think about that. They could maybe be taught.

Lauren: Well, I'm just saying, if they can be influenced for the better, why not for the worse? That the media could influence them to be worse.

Matt: I don't know.

Lauren: What about real life? When the media pays too much attention to one issue, like the school shooting in Columbine, do you think it makes other people want to do the same thing?

Matt: I don't know. I had a good friend of mine get kicked out of school for calling in a bomb threat. He probably wouldn't have done that if all that hadn't been on the news.

Following Through

Look at Lauren's initial opinion statement on pages 166–167. Use the "Questions for Inquiry" to suggest questions you would have asked her if you had been her partner.

Following Through

Writing should be a rhythm between "drawing in"—the solo act of composing—and "reaching out" through dialogues during every phase of the composing process.

Exchange initial opinion statements with a classmate. Take turns asking each other questions based on the "Questions for Inquiry" in the box on pages 177–178. Explore one person's thinking at a time. After twenty minutes, trade roles. If you do not have a software program that
(continues)

Following Through (continued)

allows you to record a transcript of the discussion, tape it, or simply take notes after each questioning session. Be ready to report on how the dialogue caused you to clarify or modify your thinking. What did the dialogue make you realize you need to think and read more about?

We should never think of dialogue as something distinct and unrelated to writing. We should think instead about how dialogue can help us write better, especially how it can reveal some truth. The notes and written records of these purposeful exchanges will provide material for your paper, so save them now as we turn to the next step, which is to read about the topic.

Step 6: Engaging in Dialogue with a Reading

Inquiry requires us to look into arguments that more knowledgeable people have written. Inquiry into a written text begins with a critical reading of the text, including attention to its rhetorical context, as we discussed in Chapter 2, "Reading an Argument" (pages 23–52). Sample the text quickly to see if it is worth your attention. If it is, read the text thoroughly and mark it up, noting its subdivisions and the structure of its argument. Mark claims and note evidence.

What we have just discussed about turning conversation into dialogue— posing questions about opinions—also applies to reading, but conversations and written arguments can't be approached the same way.

In conversations that don't reach the level of dialogue, we mostly encounter simple statements of opinion. People say what they think without much explanation or support unless someone asks for it. In sharp contrast, writers *argue* their opinions. That is, a written piece typically contains an opinion, sometimes called a *thesis* or *claim*. Then the claim is usually *explained*, and the claim is justified or defended with reasons and supported with evidence, because a text must stand on its own—the writer is not present to supply reasons and evidence in response to individual reader's questions. Instead, the writer must anticipate the questions an alert, critical reader will have and answer them in advance.

Consequently, whereas in conversation we can question simple statements of opinion as they occur, with written arguments we must question *entire cases*—claims, reasons, evidence, whatever the author uses to explain, justify, and defend his or her opinion. We need to look carefully at the "Questions for Inquiry" with special attention to recognizing the claim and its key terms, the reasons, and the evidence. We should note as well whether opposing views appear in the argument and how the author handles them. We can't know in advance all the questions to ask of any particular text; the best occur to us as we read the text thoughtfully or discuss it with others.

Example Dialogue with a Reading

As an example of how to engage in dialogue with a written text, we first look at the newspaper argument that got us thinking in the first place about violence in the entertainment industry. "Hollow Claims about Fantasy Violence," by Richard Rhodes, appeared September 17, 2000, in the *New York Times*. Rhodes is a nonfiction writer who has won awards for his books on the making of the atomic and hydrogen bombs. This essay appeared after the publication of his most recent book, *Why They Kill*, which is based on interviews with convicted murderers.

Hollow Claims about Fantasy Violence
Richard Rhodes

The moral entrepreneurs are at it again, pounding the entertainment industry for advertising its Grand Guignolesque confections to children. If exposure to this mock violence contributes to the development of violent behavior, then our political leadership is justified in its indignation at what the Federal Trade Commission has reported about the marketing of violent fare to children. Senators John McCain and Joseph Lieberman have been especially quick to fasten on the F.T.C. report as they make an issue of violent offerings to children.

But is there really a link between entertainment and violent behavior?

The American Medical Association, the American Psychological Association, the American Academy of Pediatrics and the National Institute of Mental Health all say yes. They base their claims on social science research that has been sharply criticized and disputed within the social science profession, especially outside the United States. In fact, no direct, causal link between exposure to mock violence in the media and subsequent violent behavior has ever been demonstrated, and the few claims of modest correlation have been contradicted by other findings, sometimes in the same studies.

History alone should call such a link into question. Private violence has been declining in the West since the media-barren late Middle Ages, when homicide rates are estimated to have been 10 times what they are in Western nations today. Historians attribute the decline to improving social controls over violence—police forces and common access to courts of law—and to a shift away from brutal physical punishment in child-rearing (a practice that still appears as a common factor in the background of violent criminals today).

The American Medical Association has based its endorsement of the media violence theory in major part on the studies of Brandon Centerwall, a psychiatrist in Seattle. Dr. Centerwall compared the murder rates for whites in three countries from 1945 to 1974 with numbers for television set ownership. Until 1975, television broadcasting was banned in South Africa, and "white homicide rates remained stable" there, Dr. Centerwall found, while corresponding rates in Canada and the United States doubled after television was introduced.

A spectacular finding, but it is meaningless. As Franklin E. Zimring and Gordon Hawkins of the University of California at Berkeley subsequently pointed out, homicide rates in France, Germany, Italy and Japan either failed to change with increasing television ownership in the same period or actually declined, and American homicide rates have more recently been sharply declining despite a proliferation of popular media outlets—not only movies and television, but also video games and the Internet.

Other social science that supposedly undergirds the theory, too, is marginal and problematic. Laboratory studies that expose children to se-lected incidents of televised mock violence and then assess changes in the children's behavior have sometimes found more "aggressive" behavior after the exposure—usually verbal, occasionally physical.

But sometimes the control group, shown incidents judged not to be vi-olent, behaves more aggressively afterward than the test group; sometimes comedy produces the more aggressive behavior; and sometimes there's no change. The only obvious conclusion is that sitting and watching television stimulates subsequent physical activity. Any kid could tell you that.

As for those who claim that entertainment promotes violent behavior by desensitizing people to violence, the British scholar Martin Barker offers this critique: "Their claim is that the materials they judge to be harmful can only influence us by trying to make us be the same as them. So horrible things will make us horrible—not horrified. Terrifying things will make us terrifying—not terrified. To see something aggressive makes us feel ag-gressive—not aggressed against. This idea is so odd, it is hard to know where to begin in challenging it."

Even more influential on national policy has been a 22-year study by two University of Michigan psychologists, Leonard D. Eron and L. Rowell Huesmann, of boys exposed to so-called violent media. The Telecommu-nications Act of 1996, which mandated the television V-chip, allowing parents to screen out unwanted programming, invoked these findings, as-serting, "Studies have shown that children exposed to violent video pro-gramming at a young age have a higher tendency for violent and aggres-sive behavior later in life than children not so exposed."

Well, not exactly. Following 875 children in upstate New York from third grade through high school, the psychologists found a correlation between a preference for violent television at age 8 and aggressiveness at age 18. The correlation — 0.31 — would mean television accounted for about 10 percent of the influences that led to this behavior. But the correlation only turned up in one of three measures of aggression: the assessment of students by their peers. It didn't show up in students' reports about themselves or in psychological testing. And for girls, there was no correlation at all.

Despite the lack of evidence, politicians can't resist blaming the media for violence. They can stake out the moral high ground confident that the First Amendment will protect them from having to actually write legislation that would be likely to alienate the entertainment industry. Some use the issue as a smokescreen to avoid having to confront gun control.

But violence isn't learned from mock violence. There is good evidence — causal evidence, not correlational — that it's learned in personal violent encounters, beginning with the brutalization of children by their parents or their peers.

The money spent on all the social science research I've described was diverted from the National Institute of Mental Health budget by reducing support for the construction of community mental health centers. To this day there is no standardized reporting system for emergency-room findings of physical child abuse. Violence is on the decline in America, but if we want to reduce it even further, protecting children from real violence in their real lives — not the pale shadow of mock violence — is the place to begin.

Inquiring into sources presents a special challenge: to overcome the authority the source projects. When ideas are in print, we tend to accept them too uncritically, especially when they support our own opinion. If the argument appears in a leading newspaper like the *New York Times,* as it does in this case, the piece can seem to have such authority that people just quote it and don't bother to assess it critically, especially when the author is as respected as Rhodes. We think, Who am I to question what he says? After all, I've gone to him to find out about fantasy violence. Shouldn't I just accept what he says, at least until I read other sources that oppose his view?

Our earlier chapters on reading and analyzing an argument show how we can overcome this natural tendency to be passive when we encounter an authoritative text. It's true that we are only inquirers, not experts, and so we cannot question Rhodes as another expert might. But we are hardly powerless. We can put into practice the critical-reading habits and skills discussed in Chapter 2. And we can use the "Questions for Inquiry" on pages 177–178 to open an argument to scrutiny.

A Dialogue with Rhodes

Looking at the "Questions for Inquiry," we noticed that some seemed like perfect entry points into Rhodes's argument. We have no problems

Following Through

After sampling Rhodes's essay and reading it through thoroughly, mark it up. What do you consider the introduction and the conclusion? Are there any other subsections besides the presentation of the reasoning? Do you see the claim, reasons, and evidence? (You might want to review Chapter 3, "Analyzing Arguments," pages 53–68.) Mark them with annotations. How does he present opposing views? Finally, use the "Questions for Inquiry" in the Best Practices box on pages 177–178 to open up the argument to inquiry. Make marginal annotations in response to Rhodes, and compare them with our discussion of the argument's strengths and weaknesses, following (pages 183–185).

Following Through

If you are working on a different topic, find an argument that addresses one of the topic's central issues. Read that argument critically (see the explanation and cross-references in the previous Following Through).

understanding his claim, but we might ask him about the second item on our list, "the meaning of any words that seem central to the argument." We wonder how he defines "violence." In this fourth, fifth, and sixth paragraphs, he refers to homicide rates having declined despite the proliferation of media violence. But when we think of violence today, we think of a lot of behavior that does not fall into the narrow category of homicide: date rape, child abuse and other domestic violence, bullying, and even aggressive driving and road rage.

Looking again at definitions, we could question the thinking of one of Rhodes's sources, Martin Barker, who says it is "odd" to assume that watching "horrible things will make us horrible — not horrified," that "terrifying things will make us terrifying — not terrified." What can he mean by "horrible" and "terrifying"? The terrorist attack on the World Trade Center made most of us terrified, not terrible, but there are many types of terrifying acts shown in the media, and some of them glorify models of terrible behavior or even make it seem funny. So Barker's nice-sounding language oversimplifies the problem.

We might also ask the sixth question for inquiry, which concerns evidence. In the third paragraph, Rhodes acknowledges that the American Medical Association, the American Psychological Association, the American Academy of Pediatrics, and the National Institute of Mental Health all affirm "a link between entertainment and violent behavior." Much of the rest of the article is an effort to undermine the science that claims to establish such a link. Is it likely that the AMA, APA, and the other institutions mentioned are *all* wrong? Is it likely that the AMA based its opinion "in major part" on only *one* study of fantasy violence, as Rhodes claims in paragraph five? Neither seems very likely, and so we should be suspicious. We could visit one of the Web sites for these organizations to find out more about the basis of their endorsements.

And we might question an assumption Rhodes makes, using question 4 as our inspiration. When he says that the rates of television ownership rose in France, Germany, Italy, and Japan while homicide rates did not change, is he assuming that the same shows were broadcast as in America and Canada, where homicide rates doubled in the same period? He seems to assume that the technology itself, rather than the programs, is an appropriate basis for comparison.

Finally, we might question his assumption that if one thing is not necessary for another thing to happen, it therefore cannot be a factor at all. For example, cell phone use is not necessary for a car wreck to occur; people are perfectly capable of having accidents without using cell phones while driving. So cell phone use alone is not a sufficient cause. However, cell phone use could—and does—*contribute* to automobile accidents. Rhodes claims that "violence isn't learned from mock violence. There is good evidence—causal evidence, not correlational—that it's learned in personal violent encounters, beginning with the brutalization of children by their parents or their peers." Does anyone doubt that real violence in children's lives contributes more than fantasy violence to aggressive behavior? Probably not. But that doesn't mean that fantasy violence contributes *nothing*. We can't dismiss something that might contribute to violent behavior just because other factors obviously contribute more. There may be no "proof" that fantasy violence is a necessary or sufficient cause of real-life violence, but it would not be logical to dismiss it as a factor. We could find examples of people abused as children who have not become violent, but would that make Rhode's own argument invalid?

Following Through

If you are inquiring into a topic of your own, use the "Questions for Inquiry" to open it up, as we have illustrated with Rhodes's essay. Do not try to pose every possible question; find questions that point to the areas of weakness in the argument.

Another Example of Dialogue with a Reading

We next inquired into a recent book on violent entertainment, Sissela Bok's *Mayhem* (1998). Following is one chapter from a section entitled "Opportunities," in which Bok assesses various ways to resist the destructive effects of media violence. The chapter reprinted here is especially interesting because it focuses on what children can do, guided by teachers and supported by parents, "to think for themselves and to become discriminating viewers."

Sissela Bok is professor of philosophy at Brandeis University and the author of numerous books and articles.

Media Literacy
Sissela Bok

How can children learn to take a more active and self-protective part in evaluating what they see? For an example of such learning, consider a class of second-graders in Oregon that Peter Jennings introduced on ABC's evening news in March 1995. With the help of their teacher, these children had arranged to study the role that television violence played in their lives: now they were presenting their "Declaration of Independence from Violence" to the rest of the student body. Their assignment had been to watch half an hour of television at home for several days running and to count the incidents of violence in each one—kicking, shooting, bombarding, killing. To their amazement, they had found nearly one such incident a minute in the programs they watched. The media mayhem they had taken for granted as part of their daily lives was suddenly put in question. One girl acknowledged that "before, I didn't even know what violence was."

The children then discussed the role of media violence in their own lives and concluded that what they saw on TV did affect them. Together, they considered different types of responses, often also discussing these choices in their homes. In their "Declaration of Independence from Violence," they addressed not only their school but the county board of education and community service organizations. Some pledged to limit their intake of violent programming and to refuse to watch certain shows; others wrote letters to television stations; a few organized a boycott of the products advertised on the programs they considered most violent.

These children were learning the rudiments of critical judgment and experiencing the pleasure of thinking for themselves about the messages beamed at them by advertisers and programmers. They were beginning to draw distinctions with respect to types of violence and their effects and to consider what might lie in their power to do in response. Throughout, they were learning to make active use of the media, including having their own initiative beamed to millions via the Jennings broadcast.

In so doing, the second-graders were participating in what has come to be called "media literacy education."[1] The media literacy movement, begun in Australia in the 1980s, views all media as offering scope for participants to learn not to submit passively to whatever comes along, but instead to examine offerings critically while recognizing the financial stakes of programmers and sponsors, to make informed personal and group choices, and to balance their own TV intake with participation in other activities. The hope is that children who become able to take such an approach will be more self-reliant, more informed, and correspondingly less fearful and passive, when it comes to their use of modern media. And since few adults have acquired critical viewing skills, such education is important at all ages.

Maturing, learning how to understand and deal with violence, coping   5
better with its presence on the screen as in the world, knowing its effects, and countering them to the extent possible involves exploring distinctions such as the following:

- between physical violence and psychological and other forms of violence
- between actual and threatened violence
- between direct and indirect violence
- between active violence and violence made possible by neglect or inaction
- between unwanted violence and, say, surgery, performed with consent
- between violence done to oneself and that done to others
- between seeing real violence and witnessing it on the screen
- between portrayals of "real" and fictional violence
- between violence conveyed as information and as entertainment
- between levels of violence in the media and in real life
- between oneself as viewer and as advertising or programming target
- between gratuitous portrayals of violence and others
- between violence glamorized or not

Learning to deal with violence involves sorting out such distinctions and categories and seeking to perceive when they overlap and interact and shade into one another. It is as inaccurate to view all these distinctions as utterly blurred as to imagine each category in a watertight compartment. Exploring these distinctions and their interactions is facilitated by talking them over with others and by seeing them illuminated, first in the simplest stories and pictures, later in literature and works of art.

Because the approach must be gradual and attuned to children's developmental stage, a film such as Steven Spielberg's *Schindler's List*, which offers searing insight into most of the distinctions listed above, is inappropriate for small children, who have not learned to make the necessary distinctions.[2] If they are exposed to such a film before they have learned to draw even rudimentary distinctions with respect to violence, they can respond with terror, numbing, sometimes even misplaced glee. As far as they are concerned, it is beside the point whether the horrors the film conveys are gratuitous or not, real or fictional, or meant as entertainment or not. They cannot tell the difference and should not be exposed to such material before they can do so. The film can be misunderstood, too, by those who would ordinarily be old enough to perceive such distinctions but whose capacity to respond to them has been thwarted or numbed, through personal experience, perhaps from violence in the home, or through overexposure to entertainment violence. The half-embarrassed, half-riotous laughter with which some high school audiences greeted the film troubled many: it was as if these students had lost their ability to make even the most basic distinctions.

A number of these distinctions are hard even for the most experienced media critics to pin down. Take the concept of "gratuitous" violence, violence not needed for purposes of the story being told but added for its shock or entertainment value. Some regard it as a characterization primarily in the eye of the beholder, while others insist that it can be clearly identified in particular films and television programs. Whatever the answer, there are borderline cases of violence where it is hard for anyone to be sure whether it is gratuitous or not. Works such as Spielberg's *Schindler's List* show instances of extreme cruelty that are necessary to convey the horror and inhumanity of the work's subject, and are thus not gratuitous in their own right; yet that film also explores how gratuitous violence is inflicted, even enjoyed, by its perpetrators. The film is about gratuitous violence, then, without in any sense exploiting it or representing an instance of it; and it is emphatically not meant as entertainment violence. Perhaps this is part of what Spielberg meant in saying that he made the film "thinking that if it did entertain, then I would have failed. It was important to me not to set out to please. Because I always had." [3]

Long before callous or uncomprehending ways of responding become ingrained, children can learn, much as the second-graders in the Jennings program were learning, to play a greater part in sorting out the distinctions regarding violence and media violence and to consider how they wish to respond. They can learn to think for themselves and to become discriminating viewers and active participants, rather than passive consumers of the entertainment violence beamed at them daily. Such learning helps, in turn, with the larger goal of achieving resilience — the ability to bounce back, to resist and overcome adversity.

Just as "Buyer beware" is an indispensable motto in today's media environment but far from sufficient, so is a fuller understanding of the role of violence in public entertainment. Individuals, families, and schools can do a great deal; but unless they can join in broader endeavors devoted to enhancing collective resilience, the many admirable personal efforts now under way will not begin to suffice. When neither families nor schools, churches, and neighborhoods can cope alone, what is the larger social responsibility?

10

Notes

1. See Neil Anderson, *Media Works* (Oxford: Oxford University Press, 1989); and Madeline Levine, *Viewing Violence* (New York: Doubleday, 1996).

2. When *Schindler's List* was about to be broadcast on television, Spielberg was quoted as saying that the film was not, in his opinion, one that should be shown to the very young. His own children, of elementary school age, had not seen it in 1997; but he would want them to once they were of high school age. See Caryn James, "Bringing Home the Horror of the Holocaust," *New York Times*, February 23, 1997, p. 36 H.

3. Steven Spielberg, quoted by Stephen Schiff in "Seriously Spielberg," *New Yorker*, March 21, 1994, p. 101.

Possibilities for Dialogue with "Media Literacy"

There is no one right way to have a dialogue, just as there is no magic question that will always unlock the text in front of us. But it's a good idea to begin with the first question on our "Questions for Inquiry" list, *What exactly is the arguer's position?* It's clear that Bok favors "media literacy education." She advocates it, but as only part of the solution to children's exposure to media violence. Her last paragraph implies that we will need other measures as well. And so we might ask, "Why is media education not the only solution?" or "Why isn't media education enough?" Can we tell what she thinks the limitations are?

Having begun with the first question, where we go from there *depends on the nature of the text*. In this case, we need to ask question 2, *What do certain key terms mean?* Paragraph 5 is about the kind of distinctions necessary to a mature understanding of violence. But are we ourselves sure about these distinctions? What is "psychological violence"? Bok doesn't say. How would we answer? If there are both physical and psychological forms of violence, what other forms are there? Again, Bok provides no explanation or examples. Can we? It's far from clear what she means. We must figure this out ourselves or work through these distinctions in class discussion.

We should also ask about assumptions and implications, questions 4 and 9 on our list. Bok admits that "a number of these distinctions are hard even for the most experienced media critics to pin down" (paragraph 8). As adults and college students, we're certainly having our troubles with them; how can we assume that the second-graders referred to in the first paragraph can make even the most rudimentary distinctions? Do they really understand whatever distinctions their teacher is helping them to make?

Once we question what the argument assumes—that young children (about seven or eight years old) can make meaningful distinctions and understand them—we begin to wonder about implications as well. For instance, the students present what they call a "Declaration of Independence from Violence" to "the rest of the student body." Does the declaration imply that violence is *not* part of the human condition? Are we ignoring reality or learning how to cope with it? More broadly, Bok's discussion implies that media education must continue as students grow up. Is this practical? realistic? Is it something our schools can or should undertake?

Following Through

In class discussion, continue the dialogue with "Media Literacy." What other questions are relevant from our list of "Questions for Inquiry"? What questions can we ask that do not appear on the list? Be sure to consider the rather unusual case of *Schindler's List*. Why might high school students laugh at it? Is the *only* explanation the one that Bok offers, that the students didn't understand the horror of Nazi violence against the Jews? Does a movie like *Schindler's List*, when audiences understand and react appropriately to it, help us in "achieving resilience—the ability to bounce back, to resist and overcome adversity"?

Following Through

As prewriting for Part 2 of your exploratory essay, read one substantial argument on the topic. The argument may or may not agree with your initial opinions. Write a brief summary of the argument, noting its claim and reasons. Then write a few paragraphs of response to it, as we have done with Rhodes's essay and Bok's chapter, showing how the "Questions for Inquiry" opened up that argument to closer inspection. How did the argument compare with your own initial opinions? Was your thinking changed in any way? Why or why not?

INQUIRY AGAIN: DIGGING DEEPER

Inquiry always leads to more inquiry. For example, if, after reading Bok, we doubt that media literacy can work, we can find out more about it, including what went on in Australia in the 1980s. If we question what second-graders can understand about media violence, we can research the cognitive development of young children. If we aren't sure about the impact of *Schindler's List*, we can watch it ourselves and/or read about Spielberg's making of the film and the popular and critical reception of it. There's nothing important in "Media Literacy" that can't be researched and explored further. Digging deeper means getting more information about the issue into which you are inquiring. But mere quantity is not your goal. Moving deeper into an issue means finding out what experts are saying. For example, Richard Rhodes is a journalist, not a social scientist. He consulted experts, social scientists, to write his argument. To evaluate Rhodes's claim to truth, we need to do the same. Digging deeper should take us closer to people who ought to know most.

Digging deeper also means sharpening the focus of inquiry. As we said earlier, the narrow but deep inquiry will produce a better argument than a broad survey of the topic. Be on the lookout for arguments and other informative sources that address exactly the same aspects of a topic. Ideally, you might find two or more arguments that directly debate each other.

What kinds of readings make good sources for a project like this, one for which you don't have an entire semester to do research? Your sources may be articles and arguments from periodicals, chapters from books, chapters or sections in reference books, newspaper reports, and newspaper columns, as long as they are substantial (more than 500 words) and reliable. Use sources from the Web only if you have checked their reliability and credibility.

To find good sources, read the discussion of finding and evaluating sources on pages 110–125. There are always resources for digging deeper into a question. Reference librarians are an excellent first stop once you have focused your line of inquiry. They can help you find the answers to your questions. They are experts at finding the experts.

When should you stop digging deeper? One answer is, when you have run out of allotted time for inquiring and have to start composing an argument. But suppose you had no deadline. You'll know when you're near the end of inquiry on a topic. You will be reading a lot but not finding much you haven't seen already. That's the time to stop—or, if you still aren't satisfied with what you know, to find another avenue for further research.

Most important, *seek out some sources with points of view that differ from your own*—sources that tell you things you didn't know and challenge your point of view. The whole point of inquiry is to seek out the new and different. *Remember: We are trying not to defend what we already think but to put it to the test.*

Following Through

Read pages 110–125 on finding and evaluating sources. Using the library and electronic indexes available, find at least five good articles and arguments about your chosen issue. Be sure to find sources that contain a variety of opinions but that all address the same issues. Read each carefully, and write notes and annotations based on the "Questions for Inquiry."

When the Experts Disagree

One of our own professors once advised his classes, "If you want to think you know something about a subject, read one book, because reading a second will just confuse you." The fact is, confusion is an unavoidable part of the process of exploring an issue. If you are digging deeply in the true spirit of inquiry, you will find sources that conflict. If you don't become confused, you are probably not looking hard enough into your issue. Instead of avoiding conflicting sources (our professor was mocking the "one-book expert"), seek out conflict and deal with it. Decide which sources to accept and which to reject. We illustrate some strategies for dealing with conflict in the following exploration of two articles by social scientists who assess in opposite ways the research linking fantasy violence to actual violence.

An Example of Experts Disagreeing

When we left Richard Rhodes, we still wondered how to answer the question, Does violent entertainment contribute to violence in our society? He made a good case against such a link, but we can't ignore all the experts he mentions who do take it seriously. Nor can we put aside the results of our own inquiry into the article, which gave us good reason to doubt his position. So we've decided to go to the social scientists themselves to see how they interpret the research. We've located the following exchange from the *Harvard Mental Health Letter* (1996). In the May issue, Jonathan L. Freedman, a professor of psychology at the University of Toronto, argues much as Rhodes did—that there's no proof linking fantasy violence to actual violence. In the June issue, L. Rowell Huesmann, a professor of psychology at the University of Michigan, and his graduate assistant, Jessica Moise, defend the link, based in part on their own research.

Now we have arguments on both sides of the question. Read the following articles and assess them on your own. Ask yourself, Who makes the better case? We should accept the position we think is the stronger.

Violence in the Mass Media and Violence in Society: The Link Is Unproven*
Jonathan L. Freedman

Imagine that the Food and Drug Administration (FDA) is presented with a series of studies testing the effectiveness of a new drug. There are some laboratory tests that produce fairly consistent positive effects, but the drug does not always work as expected and no attempt has been made to discover why. Most of the clinical tests are negative; there are also a few weak positive results and a few results suggesting that the drug is less effective than a placebo. Obviously the FDA would reject this application, yet the widely accepted evidence that watching television violence causes aggression is no more adequate.

In laboratory tests of this thesis, some children are shown violent programs, others are shown nonviolent programs, and their aggressiveness is measured immediately afterward. The results, although far from consistent, generally show some increase in aggression after a child watches a violent program. Like most laboratory studies of real-world conditions, however, these findings have limited value. In the first place, most of the studies have used dubious measures of aggression. In one experiment, for example, children were asked, "If I had a balloon, would you want me to prick it?" Other measures have been more plausible, but none is unimpeachable. Second, there is the problem of distinguishing effects of violence from effects of interest and excitement. In general, the violent films in these experiments are more arousing than the neutral films. Anyone who is aroused will display more of almost any behavior; there is nothing special about aggression in this respect. Finally and most important, these experiments are seriously contaminated by what psychologists call demand characteristics of the situation: the familiar fact that people try to do what the experimenter wants. Since the children know the experimenter has chosen the violent film, they may assume that they are being given permission to be aggressive.

Putting It to the Test

The simplest way to conduct a real-world study is to find out whether children who watch more violent television are also more aggressive. They are, but the correlations are small, accounting for only 1% to 10% of individual differences in children's aggressiveness. In any case, correlations do not prove causality. Boys watch more TV football than girls, and they play more football than girls, but no one, so far as I know, believes that television is what makes boys more interested in football. Probably personality characteristics that make children more aggressive also make them prefer violent television programs.

To control for the child's initial aggressiveness, some studies have measured children's TV viewing and their aggression at intervals of several years, using statistical techniques to judge the effect of early television viewing on later aggression. One such study found evidence of an effect, but most have found none.

For practical reasons, there have been only a few truly controlled experiments in which some children in a real-world environment are assigned to watch violent programs for a certain period of time and others are assigned to watch nonviolent programs. Two or three of these experiments indicated slight, short-lived effects of TV violence on aggression; one found a strong effect in the opposite of the expected direction, and most found no effect. All the positive results were obtained by a single research group, which conducted studies with very small numbers of children and used inappropriate statistics.

Scrutinizing the Evidence

An account of two studies will give some idea of how weak the research results are and how seriously they have been misinterpreted.

A study published by Lynette Friedrichs and Aletha Stein is often described (for example, in reports by the National Institute of Mental Health and the American Psychological Association) as having found that children who watched violent programs became more aggressive. What the study actually showed was quite different. In a first analysis the authors found that TV violence had no effect on physical aggression, verbal aggression, aggressive fantasy, or object aggression (competition for a toy or other object). Next they computed indexes statistically combining various kinds of aggression, a technique that greatly increases the likelihood of connections appearing purely by chance. Still they found nothing.

They then divided the children into two groups—those who were already aggressive and those who were not. They found that children originally lower in aggression seemed to become more aggressive and children originally higher in aggression seemed to become less aggressive no matter which type of program they watched. This is a well-known statistical artifact called regression toward the mean, and it has no substantive significance. Furthermore, the less aggressive children actually became more aggressive after watching the neutral program than after watching the violent program. The only comfort for the experimenters was that the level of aggression in highly aggressive children fell more when they watched a neutral program than when they watched a violent program. Somehow that was sufficient for the study to be widely cited as strong evidence that TV violence causes aggression.

An ambitious cross-national study was conducted by a team led by Rowell Huesmann and Leonard Eron and reported in 1986. In this widely cited research the effect of watching violent television on aggressiveness at a later age was observed in seven groups of boys and seven groups of girls in six countries. After controlling for initial aggressiveness, the researchers found no statistically significant effect for either sex in Australia, Finland, the Netherlands, Poland, or kibbutz children in Israel. The effect sought by the investigators was found only in the United States and among urban Israeli children, and the latter effect was so large, so far beyond the normal range for this kind of research and so incongruous with the results in other countries, that it must be regarded with suspicion. Nevertheless, the senior authors concluded that the pattern of results supported their position. The Netherlands researchers disagreed; they acknowledged that they had not been able to link TV violence to aggression, and they criticized the methods used by some of the other groups. The senior authors refused to include their chapter in the book that came out of the study, and they had to publish a separate report.

A Second Look

If the evidence is so inadequate, why have so many committees evaluating it concluded that the link exists? In the first place, these committees have   10 been composed largely of people chosen with the expectation of reaching that conclusion. Furthermore, committee members who were not already familiar with the research could not possibly have read it all themselves, and must have relied on what they were told by experts who were often biased. The reports of these committees are often seriously inadequate. The National Institute of Mental Health, for example, conducted a huge study but solicited only one review of the literature, from a strong advocate of the view that television violence causes aggression. The review was sketchy — it left out many important studies — and deeply flawed.

The belief that TV violence causes aggression has seemed plausible because it is intuitively obvious that this powerful medium has effects on children. After all, children imitate and learn from what they see. The question, however, is what they see on television and what they learn. We know that children tend to imitate actions that are rewarded and avoid actions that are punished. In most violent television programs villains start the fight and are punished. The programs also show heroes using violence to fight violence, but the heroes almost always have special legal or moral authority; they are police, other government agents, or protectors of society like Batman and the Power Rangers. If children are learning anything from these programs, it is that the forces of good will overcome evil assailants who are the first to use violence. That may be overoptimistic, but it hardly encourages the children themselves to initiate aggression.

Telling the Difference

Furthermore, these programs are fiction, and children know it as early as the age of five. Children watching Power Rangers do not think they can beam up to the command center, and children watching "Aladdin" do not believe in flying carpets. Similarly, children watching the retaliatory violence of the heroes in these programs do not come to believe they themselves could successfully act in the same way. (Researchers concerned about mass media violence should be more interested in the fights that occur during hockey and football games, which are real and therefore may be imitated by children who play those sports.)

Recently I testified before a Senate committee, and one Senator told me he knew TV made children aggressive because his own son had met him at the door with a karate kick after watching the Power Rangers. The Senator was confusing aggression with rough play, and imitation of specific actions with learning to be aggressive. Children do imitate what they see on television; this has strong effects on the way they play, and it may also influence the forms their real-life aggression takes. Children who watch the Ninja Turtles or Power Rangers may practice martial arts, just as years ago they might have been wielding toy guns, and long before that, wrestling or dueling with wooden swords. If there had been no television, the Senator's son might have butted him in the stomach or poked him in the ribs with a gun. The question is not whether the boy learned his karate kick from TV, but whether TV has made him more aggressive than he would have been otherwise.

Television is an easy target for the concern about violence in our society but a misleading one. We should no longer waste time worrying about this subject. Instead let us turn our attention to the obvious major causes of violence, which include poverty, racial conflict, drug abuse, and poor parenting.

Media Violence: A Demonstrated Public Health Threat to Children*
L. Rowell Huesmann and Jessica Moise

Imagine that the Surgeon General is presented with a series of studies on a widely distributed product. For 30 years well-controlled experiments have been showing that use of the product causes symptoms of a particular affliction. Many field surveys have shown that this affliction is always more common among people who use the product regularly. A smaller number of studies have examined the long-term effects of the product in different environments, and most have shown at least some evidence of harm, although it is difficult to disentangle effects of the product itself from the effects of factors that lead people to use it. Over all, the studies suggest that if a person with a 50% risk for the affliction uses the product, the risk rises to 60% or 70%. Furthermore, we have a fairly good understanding of how use of the product contributes to the affliction, which is persistent, difficult to cure, and sometimes lethal. The product is economically important, and its manufacturers spend large sums trying to disparage the scientific research. A few scientists who have never done any empirical work in the field regularly point out supposed flaws in the research and belittle its conclusions. The incidence of the affliction has increased dramatically since the product was first introduced. What should the Surgeon General do?

This description applies to the relationship between lung cancer and cigarettes. It also applies to the relationship between aggression and children's viewing of mass media violence. The Surgeon General has rightly come to the same conclusion in both cases and has issued similar warnings.

Cause and Effect

Dr. Freedman's highly selective reading of the research minimizes overwhelming evidence. First, there are the carefully controlled laboratory studies in which children are exposed to violent film clips and short-term changes in their behavior are observed. More than 100 such studies over the last 40 years have shown that at least some children exposed to visual depictions of dramatic violence behave more aggressively afterward both toward inanimate objects and toward other children. These results have been found in many countries among boys and girls of all social classes, races, ages, and levels of intelligence.

Freedman claims that these studies use "dubious measures of aggression." He cites only one example: asking children whether they would want the researcher to prick a balloon. But this measure is not at all representative. Most studies have used such evidence as physical attacks on other children and dolls. In one typical study Kaj Bjorkqvist exposed five- and six-year-old Finnish children to either violent or non-violent films. Observers who did not know which kind of film each child had seen then watched them play together. Children who had just seen a violent film were more likely to hit other children, scream at them, threaten them, and intentionally destroy their toys.

Freedman claims that these experiments confuse the effects of arousal   5
with the effects of violence. He argues that "anyone who is aroused will display more of almost any behavior." But most studies have shown that prosocial behavior decreases after children view an aggressive film. Finally, Freedman says the experiments are contaminated by demand characteristics. In other words, the children are only doing what they think the researchers want them to do. That conclusion is extremely implausible, considering the wide variety of experiments conducted in different countries by researchers with different points of view.

Large Body of Evidence

More than 50 field studies over the last 20 years have also shown that children who habitually watch more media violence behave more aggressively and accept aggression more readily as a way to solve problems. The relationship usually persists when researchers control for age, sex, social class, and previous level of aggression. Disbelievers often suggest that the correlation is statistically small. According to Freedman, it accounts for "only 1% to 10% of individual differences in children's aggressiveness." But an increase of that size (a more accurate figure would be 2% to 16%) has real social significance. No single factor has been found to explain more than 16% of individual differences in aggression.

Of course, correlations do not prove causality. That is the purpose of laboratory experiments. The two approaches are complementary. Experiments establish causal relationship, and field studies show that the relationship holds in a wide variety of real-world situations. The causal relationship is further confirmed by the finding that children who view TV violence at an early age are more likely to commit aggressive acts at a later age. In 1982 Eron and Huesmann found that boys who spent the most time viewing violent television shows at age eight were most likely to have criminal convictions at age 30. Most other long-term studies have come to similar conclusions, even after controlling for children's initial aggressiveness, social class, and education. A few studies have found no effect on some measures of violence, but almost all have found a significant effect on some measures.

Freedman singles out for criticism a study by Huesmann and his colleagues that was concluded in the late 1970s. He says we found "no statistically significant effect for either sex in Australia, Finland, the Netherlands, Poland, or kibbutz children in Israel." That is not true. We found that the television viewing habits of children [as] young as six or seven predicted subsequent increases in childhood aggression among boys in Finland and among both sexes in the United States, in Poland, and in Israeli cities. In Australia and on Israeli kibbutzim, television viewing habits were correlated with simultaneous aggression. Freedman also suggests that another study conducted in the Netherlands came to conclusions so different from ours that we banned it from a book we were writing. In fact, the results of that study were remarkably similar to our own, and we did not refuse to publish it. The Dutch researchers themselves chose to publish separately in a different format.

Cultural Differences

Freedman argues that the strongest results reported in the study, such as those for Israeli city children, are so incongruous that they arouse suspicion. He is wrong. Given the influence of culture and social learning on aggressive behavior, different results in different cultures are to be expected. In fact, the similarity of the findings in different countries is remarkable here. One reason we found no connection between television violence viewing and aggression among children on [kib]butzim is the strong cultural prohibition against intra-group aggression in those communities. Another reason is that kibbutz children usually watched television in a group and discussed the shows with an adult caretaker afterward.

Two recently published meta-analyses summarize the findings of many   10
studies conducted over the past 30 years. In an analysis of 217 experiments and field studies, Paik and Comstock concluded that the association between exposure to television violence and aggressive behavior is extremely strong, especially in the data accumulated over the last 15 years. In the other meta-analysis, Wood, Wong, and Chachere came to the same conclusion after combined analysis of 23 studies of unstructured social interaction.

We now have well-validated theoretical explanations of these results. Exposure to media violence leads to aggression in at least five ways. The first is imitation, or observational learning. Children imitate the actions of their parents, other children, and media heroes, especially when the action is rewarded and the child admires and identifies with the model. When generalized, this process creates what are sometimes called cognitive scripts for complex social problem-solving: internalized programs that guide everyday social behavior in an automatic way and are highly resistant to change.

Turning Off

Second, media violence stimulates aggression by desensitizing children to the effects of violence. The more televised violence a child watches, the more acceptable aggressive behavior becomes for that child. Furthermore, children who watch violent television become suspicious and expect others to act violently—an attributional bias that promotes aggressive behavior.

Justification is a third process by which media violence stimulates aggression. A child who has behaved aggressively watches violent television shows to relieve guilt and justify the aggression. The child then feels less inhibited about aggressing again.

A fourth process is cognitive priming or cueing—the activation of existing aggressive thoughts, feelings, and behavior. This explains why children observe one kind of aggression on television and commit another kind of aggressive act afterward. Even an innocuous object that has been associated with aggression may later stimulate violence. Josephson demonstrated this [. . .] in a study of schoolboy hockey players. She subjected the boys to frustration and then showed them either a violent or a non-violent television program. The aggressor in the violent program carried a walkie-talkie. Later, when the referee in a hockey game carried a similar walkie-talkie, the boys who had seen the violent film were more likely to start fights during the game.

A Numbing Effect

The fifth process by which media violence induces aggression is physiological arousal and desensitization. Boys who are heavy television watchers show lower than average physiological arousal in response to new scenes of violence. Similar short-term effects are found in laboratory studies. The arousal stimulated by viewing violence is unpleasant at first, but children who constantly watch violent television become habituated, and their emotional and physiological responses decline. Meanwhile the propensity to aggression is heightened by any pleasurable arousal, such as sexual feeling, that is associated with media violence.

Freedman argues that in violent TV shows, villains start the fight and are punished and the heroes "almost always have special legal or moral authority." Therefore, he concludes, children are learning from these programs that "the forces of good will overcome evil assailants." On the contrary, it is precisely because media heroes are admired and have special authority that children are likely to imitate their behavior and learn that aggression is an

15

acceptable solution to conflict. Freedman also claims that media violence has little effect because children can distinguish real life from fiction. But children under 11 do not make this distinction very well. Studies have shown that many of them think cartoons and other fantasy shows depict life as it really is.

The studies are conclusive. The evidence leaves no room for doubt that exposure to media violence stimulates aggression. It is time to move on and consider how best to inoculate our children against this insidious threat.

Commentary on the Experts' Disagreement

When experts disagree, the rest of us can respond in only a few ways. We can throw up our hands and say, "Who knows?" But this response doesn't work very well because expert disagreement is so common. We'd have to give up on most issues. Another response is to take seriously only those experts who endorse the opinion we favor, using them to make our case and ignoring the rest, a common tactic in debate, legal pleadings, business, and politics whenever the search for truth gives way to self-interest. We can also "go with our gut," opting for the opinion that "feels right" to us. But often these gut feelings amount to no more than our prejudices talking; in addition, such an approach to resolving conflict is not rational enough for inquiry. And so we are left with the only response appropriate to inquiry: rational assessment of the competing arguments. We should take as true the better or best case — at least until we encounter another more convincing. This is the way of genuine, honest inquiry.

We know, then, what we need to do, but how do we go about doing it? How can we decide which of two or several arguments is better or best?

In this instance, let's recognize that Huesmann and Moise have an advantage simply because they wrote second, after Freedman, who has no opportunity to respond to what they've said. Huesmann and Moise can *both* refute Freedman *and* make their own case without the possibility of rebuttal. Granting this, however, it's still hard to find Freedman's case more convincing. Why?

We'll offer only a few reasons for thinking that we must assent to the Huesmann–Moise argument. You and your class can carry out the analysis further — it's a good opportunity to practice critical reading and thinking.

Both articles begin with an analogy. Freedman compares the research on violent TV programs with the research required to approve a drug. Huesmann and Moise compare the research linking cigarettes to lung cancer with the research linking violent TV to aggressive behavior in children. The second comparison is better because the two instances of research compared are more nearly alike. Furthermore, the fact that the Surgeon General has issued warnings both for cigarettes and for violent entertainment's effect on children shows how seriously research on the latter is taken by qualified authorities. In fact, one of the more convincing aspects of the Huesmann–Moise case is the amount of support they claim for their position. They are specific about the numbers: "50 field studies over the last 20 years" (paragraph 6); "an analysis of 217 experiments and field studies" (paragraph 10)—all confirm their conclusion. If Freedman has evidence to rival this, he does not cite it. We must assume he doesn't because he doesn't have it.

Another strength of the Huesmann–Moise article is that they go beyond a review of the research linking TV violence to aggression; they offer five *explanations* for the negative impact of fantasy violence (paragraphs 11–15). We come away not only convinced that the link has been established but also with an understanding of why it exists. Freedman has no well-developed theoretical explanation to support his position. What he offers, such as the assertion that children know the difference between pretend and real violence, is refuted by Huesmann and Moise.

If you are thinking that the better or best case won't always be so easy to discern, you're right. Our point is certainly not that comparative assessment will always yield a clearly superior case. Often, we will argue with ourselves and others over whose case merits our support. Our point is this: When we encounter opposing positions in our sources, we should set aside our own prejudices and study the arguments they've made. We should resolve the conflict by taking the better or best case as the truth or the closest thing we have to the truth. We cannot just accept the argument that sides with our initial position. We must accept the better argument.

We think that, in most cases, the better or best argument will emerge as you think your way through the arguments and compare their strengths and weaknesses. What's hard is to let go of a position we're attracted to when another position has a better case. The real challenge of inquiry is to change or revise our own opinions as we encounter good arguments for positions different from our own.

Following Through

Even if they do not speak directly to each other, as our examples here do, find two sources that present conflicting data or information or conflicting interpretations of the same information. Write an evaluation of these arguments, telling which one seemed to present the best case. Explain why you think so. Did you find that comparing these arguments influenced your own thinking in any way? If so, how?

THE WRITING PROJECT: PART 2

By now, you have many notes that you can use as raw material for writing Part 2 of your essay. You have had a serious dialogue with at least one other person about your ideas. You should have notes about this dialogue and maybe even a recording or transcript of it. Look over this material, and make some more notes about how this conversation modified your ideas—by clarifying them, by presenting you with an idea you had not thought of, or by solidifying a belief you already held. If the conversations revealed conflicting opinions, to what would you attribute those differences?

You have also read several printed arguments and done some research. You have written some evaluations of these arguments and marked them up. Continue to do so, noting places where they touch upon the same points, whether in agreement or contrast. We suggest using highlighters to color-code passages that connect across the readings. Make some notes or draft paragraphs about what different experts have to say on the same question, and include an estimate of the effectiveness of their points and support in increasing your own knowledge about the issue. In which viewpoints did you feel you had found some truth, and why?

You are ready to draft the body of your paper. It should contain at least four well-developed paragraphs in which you describe your inquiry. Discuss the conversations you had and the materials you read, and show how these lines of inquiry influenced your thinking on the issue you explored. Assess the arguments you read, consider their rhetorical context, include the names of the authors and the biases they might have. Talk about why an author's argument was sound or not sound, why it influenced your initial opinion or why it did not.

Part 2 could be organized around a discussion of ideas that were strengthened by your research versus those that you have reconsidered because of it. Did a source offer new information that has caused you to reconsider part or all of what you thought? Tell what the information was, and explain why it's changed your outlook. Did you encounter a well-developed argument defending a position different from your own? How did you react? What aspects of the argument do you take seriously enough to consider modifying or changing your own opinion? Be sure to explain why. If you found sources or individual people who disagreed, which side did you find more convincing, and why?

Although some paragraphs could be devoted to a single source, others could compare an idea across two or three sources, and you could point out the ways in which they concur or disagree, showing how each contributed to the change in your opinion.

No matter how you organize your paper, be specific about what you have read. You will need to quote and paraphrase the ideas in your sources; when you refer to sources, do so very specifically. See our advice about using sources on pages 110–127. Paraphrase clearly and quote exactly. Use Modern Language Association (MLA) style for in-text citations (pages 139–143).

Be careful not to merely summarize your sources or use them in the conventional way of supporting and illustrating your own discussion or argument. You are evaluating the thinking expressed in the sources, so it is important not just to cite an author's name but also to include some information about that person's professional affiliation and point of view.

In other words, rhetorical context is vital here, and it should be part of your consideration of each source. Also, in the body of your paper, *be selective.* Select what struck you as particularly important in confirming or challenging your view. Explain what most strongly impressed you as strong or weak thinking and why. Obviously, your readers don't want to get bogged down in needless detail; they want the information that altered your understanding of the topic and the arguments that opened up new considerations. *The point is to show how your research-inquiry refined, modified, or changed your initial opinions and to explain why.* Anything that doesn't contribute significantly and directly to this end should not be in the final draft of your paper.

THE WRITING PROJECT: PART 3

In preparation for writing the conclusion of your essay, reread Part 1, the overview of your exploration. Decide whether you have found "some truth" about the issues you have explored. Can you arrive at a claim you want to defend in an essay to convince or persuade an audience to think differently? If so, what is it? Perhaps you're still unsure; what then? One option is to conclude your paper by explaining what you are unsure of and why, and what you'd like to learn from further research. An inconclusive but honest ending is better than a forced closing for the sake of making a claim.

Your goal, then, is to draft a conclusion for your paper in which you honestly discuss the results of your exploration, whatever they were. This section is about where you stand now, but it needn't be final or conclusive. If you have doubts, state them honestly, and indicate how you might resolve them through further research and inquiry.

AFTER DRAFTING YOUR ESSAY

Revise your draft to make sure each paragraph is unified around one point and to remove any unnecessary summarizing. You will quote and paraphrase from your sources, so check your work against the guidelines for incorporating source material in your own writing (pages 110–127).

Edit your paper for wordiness, repetition, and excessive passive voice. See the suggestions for editing in the appendix.

Proofread your paper. Read it aloud to catch omissions and errors of grammar and punctuation. You can ask for help with common errors such as comma splices or apostrophe problems. (But make sure your helper helps you see the problems and correct them yourself and doesn't do the job for you.)

STUDENT SAMPLE: *An Exploratory Essay*

EXPLORATORY ESSAY

Sydney Owens

Part 1

I think that the relationship between violence and the media is hard
to define. There is definitely some correlation between them, but to what
extent it is hard to say. Media itself is only one word, but it includes television, radio, CDs, video games, papers, books, the Internet, and more. It
is complicated, when you group them all together, to say that they cause
violence. Also you have to look at what kind of violence you are talking
about. Do media influence more aggressive behavior, such as killing? And
lastly, a child's environment, personality, parents, and media all have to be
considered. It is difficult to say why people do anything, let alone why they
commit acts of violence.

Each human is so unique that it seems too general to say that media
violence makes people more violent. One person could watch gruesome
violence every day and remain a very caring and loving person, whereas
another individual might see minimal violent media and then go out and
kill someone. Where do you draw the line? I guess you have to start taking
averages and define a norm. But then that norm only defines "normal"
people's reactions to violence seen or heard in the media. You might control the masses in this way, but this will not keep a person outside of the
norm from committing acts of violence.

When I see or hear violence in the media, I know that I am not inclined to do anything noticeably more violent than if I had not. Then again,
I do know that a high-action movie thriller has given me that feeling of
kick-ass satisfaction and that exposure to rap songs has caused me to
more readily use somewhat inappropriate language. Feelings and slang
are not acts of violence, but these examples do show that there is a connection between the media and undesirable effects on people.

Part 2

When I read "Violence in the Mass Media and Violence in Society:
The Link Is Unproven," I began to think that there really is not strong
enough evidence to say that media violence leads to violent behavior. The
author, Jonathan Freedman, argued that you could not prove the link because the "studies [. . .] used dubious measures of aggression," they could
not "distinguish effects of violence from effects of interest and excitement," and the studies were "seriously contaminated by [. . .] demand
characteristics of the situation." All of this made sense to me. I especially
agreed with the contamination of the demand characteristics because I
had just learned about this term in my psychology class. I was taught that
experimenters have to take into account the fact that many subjects alter

their own behavior to mirror what they think the experimenter is looking for.

Freedman also gave an example that really stuck out in my mind as proof that there is not a strong enough link to prove anything. He said to imagine that the FDA was testing out the effectiveness of a new drug. The results came out negative, weakly positive, and even less effective than a placebo. He said that obviously the FDA would reject this drug as having no effect and that, likewise, media should be rejected as having no effect on violence. This seemed to make perfect sense until I compared it to "Media Violence: A Demonstrated Public Health Threat to Children," an article by L. Rowell Huesmann and Jessica Moise that counters Freedman's position. The FDA analogy that had sounded so good now looked faulty compared with Huesmann's Surgeon General analogy. In Huesmann's analogy, he points out that if something has shown even the slightest negative effect, it is justifiable to put out a warning because it is always better to be safe than sorry. I agree with this reasoning. Freedman was right to say that we cannot prove for certain that media violence leads to violent behavior, but what he failed to acknowledge is that we should still put out the warning if any effects are negative. After contrasting these two articles, I had changed my mind and decided that media violence does induce violent behavior.

With this new state of mind, I read several other articles that reinforced the claim that media violence promotes more violent behavior. In the article "We Are Training Our Kids to Kill," Dave Grossman claims that "the desensitizing techniques used for training soldiers are being replicated in contemporary mass media movies, television, and video games, giving rise to the alarming rate of homicide and violence in our schools and communities." Not only was this article interesting, but it also made sense. Grossmann, who travels the world training medical, law enforcement, and U.S. military personnel about the realities of warfare, supported his claim by showing how classical and operant conditioning used in the military parallel the effects of violent media on young children. Grossman's article was simple and straightforward. I followed his argument and agreed that the desensitizing effects of media train our kids to kill.

To be sure that his argument was true, I tried looking for some evidence that would prove that desensitizing did not have an effect. The only text I could find that even attempted to counter that desensitizing techniques influence violent behavior was the article by Richard Rhodes, "Hollow Claims about Fantasy Violence." In this article, there is one short and very confusing paragraph (paragraph 9) in which Rhodes offers "a British scholar's" critique of the desensitization argument:

> [T]heir claim is that the materials they judge to be harmful can only influence us by trying to makes us be the same as them. So horrible

things will make us horrible—not horrified. . . . This idea is so odd, it is hard to know where to begin in challenging it.

After reading this, I felt like saying the same thing to Rhodes. His paragraph was so confusing I had a hard time knowing where to begin in challenging it. This was a very poor argument. In reality, it is not really an argument at all because Rhodes offers only a quote without any explanation. The quote lumps all forms of violence into one heap and ignores the fact that some violent entertainment is made to make us laugh. After realizing that this was a very poor argument, I stuck with my initial viewpoint that desensitization does promote violent behavior.

Part 3

After reading all of these articles and deciding that I definitely do think that media contributes to violent behavior, I began thinking about my own personal experiences again. I thought about that "kick-ass feeling" I get when I watch certain action movies, and I began feeling somewhat ashamed. As film producers Edward Zwick and Marshall Herskovitz pointed out in their *New York Times* column "When the Bodies Are Real" after the tragedies surrounding September 11, "perhaps what this event has revealed, with its real bodies blown to bits and real explosions bringing down buildings, is the true darkness behind so much of the product coming out of Hollywood today."

Annotated Bibliography

Freedman, Jonathan. "Violence in the Mass Media and Violence in Society: The Link Is Unproven." <u>Harvard Mental Health Letter</u> May 1996: 4–6.

This is an article for the general public that claims that there is not solid proof that mass media leads to violence. The author, Jonathan Freedman, proves his claim by showing that the studies have used dubious measures of aggression, by showing that it is hard to distinguish effects of violence from effects of excitement, and to separate either from the effects of demand characteristics. This would be a good article to use to prove that media does not influence aggressive behavior; however, I used the article's weak points to prove that media does lead to aggressive behavior.

Grossman, Dave. "We Are Training Our Kids to Kill". <u>Saturday Evening Post</u> July/Aug 1999: 64–70.

This is an article for the general public explaining the killings committed by America's youth as a result of media violence. First the author discusses how killing is unnatural. He then goes on to show how several military techniques for training soldiers mirror the ways in which the media interact with our children. This article gives logical support to the claim that media influences violent behavior.

Herskovitz, Marshall, and Edward Zwick. "When the Bodies Are Real".
Editorial. <u>New York Times</u>.
This is a short article written in response to the horrible tragedies
that befell the people of the United States on September 11. It is
written for the general public, but it focuses specifically on how the
media community will respond to this tragedy. The authors, Marshall
Herskovitz and Edward Zwick, are producers, directors, and writers.
Their most recent film was *Traffic*. They point out how this tragedy
has shamed Hollywood, along with all of us, to turn our eyes back
to ourselves and examine what is there.

Huesmann, L. Rowell, and Jessica Moise. "A Demonstrated Public Health
Threat to Children". <u>Harvard Mental Health Letter</u> June 1996: 5–7.
This is an article written in response to Jonathan Freedman's article,
"Violence in the Mass Media and Violence in Society: The Link Is
Unproven." The authors refute most of Freedman's article with re-
search. The article offers good support for the link between media
and real violence.

Rhodes, Richard. "Hollow Claims about Fantasy Violence.".Editorial. <u>New
York Times</u> 17 Sept. 2000.
This is an article that attempts to prove that there is not enough
evidence to claim that media violence leads to real violence. The author, Richard Rhodes, implies that people (in particular, politicians)
use media as a scapegoat for not looking to the real problems behind
violence. I used this source to prove that the media does induce violence because it contained a paragraph that made a very weak attempt at proving that desensitization does not make people more
violent.

Note: For a discussion of how to create an annotated bibliography, see Chapter 5, page 138.

INQUIRY: SUMMING UP THE AIM

In this chapter, we've introduced you to college-level inquiry. Here are the
key points:

- In college, we don't just ransack sources for information and quotes.
  We interact with them. "Interact" means both to be critical of sources
  and to allow them to influence, even change, our point of view.
- Informal conversation is a valuable medium of inquiry. But it becomes more valuable when we turn conversation into dialogue. *Assert opinions less, and question opinions more.* When a good question
  elicits a good response, follow it up with more questions.

- The best and most stimulating sources need dialogue. *Think of texts as something to "talk with."* Such dialogues will uncover more potential research possibilities. Pursue these, and you'll approach the depth of inquiry valued in college work and beyond, in graduate school and in the workplace.

Inquiry is learning. Inquiry is finding what we really think and therefore what we have to say. It's the most creative part of the writing process. Invest in it. It will repay your best efforts.

Chapter 7

Making Your Case: Arguing to Convince

The last chapter ended where inquiry ends—with the attempt to formulate a position, an opinion that we can assert with some confidence. Once our aim shifts from inquiring to convincing, everything changes.

The most significant change is in audience. In inquiry, our audience consists of our fellow inquirers—generally, friends, classmates, and teachers we can talk with face to face. We seek assurance that our position is at least plausible and defensible, a claim to truth that can be respected whether or not the audience agrees with it. In convincing, however, our audience consists of readers whose positions differ from our own or who have no position at all. The audience changes from a small, inside group that helps us develop our argument to a larger, public audience who will either accept or reject it.

As the audience changes, so does the situation or need for argument. Inquiry is a cooperative use of argument; it cannot take place unless people are willing to work together. Conversely, convincing is competitive. We pit our case against the case(s) of others in an effort to win the assent of readers who will compare the various arguments and ask, Who makes the best case? With whom should I agree? Our arguments now compete for "best or better" status, just as do the disagreeing arguments of experts.

Because of the change in audience and situation, our thinking also changes, becoming more strategic and calculated to influence the readers. In inquiry, we try to make a case we can believe in; in convincing, we must make a case that readers can believe in. What we find compelling in inquiry will sometimes also convince our readers, but in convincing we must adapt our reasoning to appeal to their beliefs, values, and self-interest. We will also likely offer reasons that did not occur to us at all in inquiry but that come as we attempt to imagine the people we hope to convince. Convincing, however, does not mean abandoning the work of inquiry. Our version of the truth, our convictions, must first be earned through inquiry before we seek to convince others.

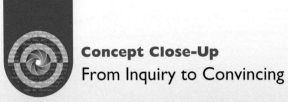

Concept Close-Up

From Inquiry to Convincing

Inquiry	→ Convincing
Intimate audience	Public readership
Cooperative	Competitive
Earns a conviction	Argues a thesis
Seeks a case convincing *to us*	Makes a case convincing *to them*, the readers

Essentially, we take the position we discovered through inquiry and turn it into a thesis supported by a case designed to gain the assent of a specific group of readers.

In this chapter, we look first at the structure and strategy of complete essays that aim to convince. Then we provide a step-by-step analysis of the kind of thinking necessary to produce such an essay.

THE NATURE OF CONVINCING: STRUCTURE AND STRATEGY

An argument is an assertion supported by a reason. To convince an audience, writers need to expand on this structure. They usually must offer more than one reason and support all reasons with evidence. In this chapter, we use the term **case structure** to describe a flexible plan for making *any argument to any audience* who expects sound reasoning. We use the term **case strategy** to describe the moves writers make *to shape a particular argument*—selecting reasons, ordering them, developing evidence, and linking the sections of the argument for maximum impact.

Case Structure

All cases have at least three levels of assertion. The first level is the thesis, or central claim, which everything else in the case supports. The second level is the reason or reasons the arguer advances for holding the thesis. The third level is the evidence offered to support each reason, typically drawn from some authoritative source.

In the abstract, then, cases look like this:

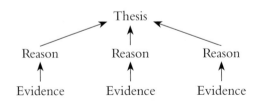

Figure 7.1

Our diagram shows three reasons, but good cases can be built with only one reason or with more than three.

Case Strategy

In Chapter 2, we explain that you can read an argument with greater comprehension if you begin with a sense of the rhetorical context in which the writer worked. Likewise, in preparing to write an argument, consider the "Key Questions for Case-Making" above.

By working out answers to these questions in your writer's notebook, you will create a rhetorical prospectus that will help you envision a context within which to write and a tentative plan to follow.

To demonstrate case strategy, we will look at "Arrested Development: The Conservative Case against Racial Profiling." The author, James Forman, Jr., is an educator and fellow at the New American Foundation in Washington, D.C. His article was published in *The New Republic,* September 10, 2001.

Thinking about Audience

To make an effective case for his position, Forman envisions an audience who favors racial profiling, and his strategy is to use reasons and evidence to convince readers who disagree with him. Therefore, he had to consider their likely responses. To develop a strategy, he posed questions like these:

- Who will my readers be?
- How will they be predisposed to view racial profiling?
- What will they have on their minds as soon as they see that my argument is against it?

Based on these questions, Forman assumes something like the following about the intended audience:

My conservative audience supports the police and approves or at least tolerates racial profiling as a tactic for apprehending criminals. I want to show them not only that profiling doesn't work but also, more important, that it violates fundamental conservative principles.

Strategy, then, must begin with thoughts about the audience, its values and preconceptions. Next, we examine how Forman shapes the elements of case structure—thesis, reasons, and evidence—to appeal to his readers.

Formulating the Thesis

Your thesis may not be explicitly stated in the text of your argument, but it must be *strongly implied* and clear to you and your reader. It must be clear to you because you must build a case around it. It must be clear to your readers so they know what you're claiming and what to expect from your case. Forman's thesis is implied and can be stated as follows: *Political conservatives, most of whom now support racial profiling, ought to oppose it.*

Choosing Reasons

Forman constructs his case around four reasons, all designed to appeal to his audience and undercut their support of racial profiling.

> *Thesis:* Political conservatives, most of whom now support racial profiling, ought to oppose it.
>
> *Reason 1:* Racial profiling is ineffective—it doesn't reliably identify criminals. (Strategy: Forman wants to take away the major justification for profiling, that it helps the police catch lawbreakers.)
>
> *Reason 2:* Racial profiling harasses law-abiding blacks just because they are black. (Strategy: Forman wants his readers, most of whom have not been stopped and frisked by the police, to appreciate how discriminatory profiling is and the damage it does to people's respect for authority.)
>
> *Reason 3:* Racial profiling violates the conservative principle that equates equal rights with equal responsibilities. (Strategy: Forman wants his readers to see that racial profiling contradicts his audience's values—in this instance, the relationship of individual achievement to full, equal participation in the community.)
>
> *Reason 4:* Racial profiling violates the conservative ideal of a color-blind society. (Strategy: Forman wants his audience to see that their reasons for opposing affirmative action apply with equal force to racial profiling.)

As you read Forman's argument, note how he arranges his reasons; the order of presentation matters. We have more to say later about his strategies for developing his reasons, especially his use of evidence.

Figure 7.2   Hulbert Waldroup, the artist who painted the controversial mural of Amadou Diallo in the Bronx near where Diallo was shot, signs his initials to his latest work, a painting on racial profiling, after unveiling it in Times Square, Tuesday, July 24, 2001, in New York. Waldroup says his work portrays racial profiling "through the eyes of a cop—what he sees, what he thinks, the stereotypes we are all responsible for." (AP Photo/Kathy Willens)

Arrested Development:
The Conservative Case against Racial Profiling
James Forman, Jr.

The Maya Angelou Public Charter School in Washington, D.C., is the kind of institution conservatives love—a place that offers opportunity but demands responsibility. Students are in school ten and a half hours per day, all year long, mostly studying core subjects like reading, writing, math, and history. When not in class, they work in student-run businesses, where they earn money and learn job skills. Those who achieve academically are held in high esteem not only by their teachers but by their peers. Those who disrupt class or otherwise violate the rules are subject to punishment, including expulsion, as determined by a panel of students and teachers.

The results have been impressive. Most Maya Angelou students had academic difficulty at their previous schools. In fact, more than one-half had stopped even attending school on a regular basis before they came to Maya

Angelou, while more than one-third had been in the juvenile court system. Yet more than 90 percent of its graduates go on to college, compared with a citywide rate of just 50 percent. This success stems in part from the school's small classes, innovative curriculum, and dedicated staff. But it is also due to its fundamentally conservative ethos: If you work hard and don't make excuses, society will give you a chance, no matter what your background is.

I can speak to this with some authority because I helped establish the school four years ago and still teach an elective there today. But, for all the school's accomplishments, we keep running up against one particularly debilitating problem. It's awfully hard to convince poor, African American kids that discrimination isn't an obstacle, that authority must be respected, and that individual identity matters more than racial identity when experiences beyond school walls repeatedly contradict it. And that's precisely what's happening today, thanks to a policy many conservatives condone: Racial profiling by the police.

The prevalence of racial profiling is no secret. Numerous statistical studies have shown that being black substantially raises the odds of a person being stopped and searched by the police — even though blacks who are stopped are no more likely than whites to be carrying drugs. As David Cole and John Lamberth recently pointed out in *The New York Times*, in Maryland "73 percent of those stopped and searched on a section of Interstate 95 were black, yet state police reported that equal percentages of the whites and blacks who were searched, statewide, had drugs or other contraband." Blacks were actually far less likely than whites to be found carrying drugs in New Jersey, a state whose police force has acknowledged the use of racial profiling. According to Cole and Lamberth, consensual searches "yielded contraband, mostly drugs, on 25 percent of whites, 13 percent of blacks and only 5 percent of Latinos."

Behind these statistics are hundreds if not thousands of well-chronicled   5
anecdotes, some from America's most prominent black citizens. Erroll McDonald, vice president and executive editor of Pantheon publishing, was driving a rented Jaguar in New Orleans when he was stopped — simply "to show cause why I shouldn't be deemed a problematic Negro in a possibly stolen car." [. . .]

Even off-duty black police frequently tell of being harassed by their unsuspecting white colleagues. Consider the case of Robert Byrd, an eleven-year veteran of the D.C. police, who was off duty and out of uniform when he tried to stop a carjacking and robbery in Southeast Washington last March. After witnessing the crime, Byrd used his police radio to alert a police dispatcher, then followed the stolen van in his own. Byrd got out of his van as marked police vehicles arrived. According to Byrd, white officers then began beating him in the belief that he was the African American suspect. The real perpetrators were caught later that night.

None of these stories would surprise the students at Maya Angelou. Almost weekly this past spring, officers arrived at the corner of 9th and

T Streets NW (in front of our school), threw our students against the wall, and searched them. As you might imagine, these are not polite encounters. They are an aggressive show of force in which children are required to "assume the position": legs spread, face against the wall or squad car, hands behind the head. Police officers then search them, feeling every area of their bodies. Last spring, a police officer chased one male student into the school, wrestled him to the ground, then drew his gun. Another time, when a student refused a police request to leave the corner in front of our school (where the student was taking a short break between classes, in complete compliance with school rules and D.C. law), the officer grabbed him, cuffed him, and started putting him into a police van, before a school official intervened. These students committed no crime other than standing outside a school in a high-drug-use neighborhood. Indeed, despite the numerous searches, no drugs have ever been discovered, and no student has ever been found in violation of the law.

Liberals generally decry such incidents; conservatives generally deny that they take place. "[T]he racial profiling we're all supposed to be outraged about doesn't actually happen very much," explained Jonah Goldberg in his *National Review Online* column last spring. And even those conservatives who admit the practice's frequency often still insist it does more good than harm. "The evidence suggests," William Tucker wrote in a recent issue of *The Weekly Standard*, "that racial profiling is an effective law enforcement tool, though it undeniably visits indignity on the innocent."

In other words, liberals—who are generally more concerned about individual rights and institutionalized racism—believe racial profiling contradicts their principles. Conservatives, on the other hand—who tolerate greater invasions of privacy in the name of law and order—consider racial profiling to be generally consistent with theirs. But conservatives are wrong—racial profiling profoundly violates core conservative principles.

It is conservatives, after all, who remind us that government policy   10
doesn't affect only resources; it affects values, which in turn affect people's behavior. This argument was at the heart of the conservative critique of welfare policy. For years, conservatives (along with some liberals) argued that welfare policies—like subsidizing unmarried, unemployed women with children—fostered a culture of dependency. Only by demanding that citizens take responsibility for their own fates, the argument went, could government effectively combat poverty.

But if sending out welfare checks with no strings attached sends the wrong message, so does racial profiling. For the conservative ethos about work and responsibility to resonate, black citizens must believe they are treated the same way as white citizens—that with equal responsibilities go equal rights. In *The Dream and the Nightmare*, which President Bush cites as one of the most influential books he has ever read, the conservative theorist Myron Magnet writes: "[W]hat underclass kids need most . . . is an authoritative link to traditional values of work, study, and self-improvement, and the assurance that these values can permit them to claim full membership in the larger community." Magnet quotes Eugene Lange, a businessman who promised scholarships to inner-city kids who graduated from high school: "It's important that [inner-city kids] grow up to recognize that they are not perpetuating a life of the pariah, but that the resources of the community are legitimately theirs to take advantage of and contribute to and be a part of."

Magnet is right. But random and degrading police searches radically undermine this message. They tell black kids that they are indeed pariahs — that, no matter how hard they study, they remain suspects. As one Maya Angelou first-year student explained to me: "We can be perfect, perfect, doing everything right, and they still treat us like dogs. No, worse than dogs, because criminals are treated worse than dogs." Or, as a junior asked me, noting the discrepancy between the message delivered by the school and the message delivered by the police: "How can you tell us we can be anything if they treat us like we're nothing?"

Indeed, people like myself — teachers, counselors, parents — try desperately to convince these often jaded kids that hard work really will pay off. In so doing, we are quite consciously pursuing an educational approach that conservatives have long advocated. We are addressing what conservative criminologist James Q. Wilson calls "intangible problems — problems of 'values,'" the problems that sometimes make "blacks less likely to take advantage of opportunities." But we are constantly fighting other people in the neighborhood who tell kids that bourgeois norms of work, family, and sexuality are irrelevant and impossible. Since the state will forever treat you as an outlaw, they say, you might as well act like one. Every time police single out a young black man for harassment, those other people sound more credible — and we sound like dupes.

Then there's that other vaunted conservative ideal: color-blindness. In recent years, conservatives have argued relentlessly for placing less emphasis on race. Since discrimination is on the wane, they suggest, government itself must stop making race an issue — i.e., no more affirmative action in admissions, no more set-asides in contracting, no more tailoring of government programs to favor particular racial or ethnic groups. In the words of affirmative action critics Abigail and Stephen Thernstrom, it's essential to fight the "politics of racial grievance" and counter the "suspicion that nothing fundamental [has] changed." Society, says Magnet, "needs to tell [blacks] that they can do it — not that, because of past victimization, they cannot."

But it's hard to tell young black men that they are not victims because of their race when police routinely make them victims because of their race. Students at Maya Angelou are acutely aware that the police do not treat young people the same way at Sidwell Friends and St. Albans, schools for Washington's overwhelmingly white elite. As another Maya Angelou first-year told me, "You think they would try that stuff with white kids? Never." Such knowledge makes them highly suspicious of the conservative asser-

15

tion that blacks should forego certain benefits—such as racial preferences in admissions—because of the moral value of color-blindness. Why, they wonder, aren't white people concerned about that principle when it hurts blacks as well as when it benefits them? And racial profiling makes them cynical about the conservative demand that blacks not see the world in racialized, group-identity terms. Why, they wonder, don't white people demand the same of the police?

Most conservatives who support racial profiling are not racist; they simply consider the practice an essential ingredient of effective law enforcement. But it isn't. Indeed, the great irony of conservative support for racial profiling is that conservative principles themselves explain why racial profiling actually makes law enforcement less effective.

[. . . D]iscriminatory police practices create unnecessary and unproductive hostility between police and the communities they serve. Imagine that you are 17, standing outside your school during a break from class, talking to friends, laughing, playing, and just relaxing. Imagine that squad cars pull up; officers jump out, shouting, guns drawn; and you are thrown against the wall, elbowed in the back, legs kicked apart, and violently searched. Your books are strewn on the ground. You ask what's going on, and you are told to "shut the fuck up" or you will be taken downtown. When it finally ends, the officers leave, giving no apology, no explanation, and you are left to fix your clothes, pick up your books, and gather your pride. Imagine that this is not the first time this has happened to you, that it has happened repeatedly, in one form or another, throughout your adolescence. Now imagine that, the day after the search, there is a crime in your neighborhood about which you hear a rumor. You know the police are looking for information, and you see one of the officers who searched you yesterday (or indeed any officer) asking questions about the crime. How likely are you to help? [. . .]

Arranging Reasons

Conservative support for racial profiling depends upon belief in its effectiveness, especially in combating the traffic in illegal drugs. Forman therefore challenges this belief first. If he can show that profiling doesn't produce the results claimed for it, his readers should then be more receptive to his other reasons, all of which establish its negative impact.

His second reason has force because no law-abiding citizen wants to be treated as if she or he were suspected of criminal activity. No matter who you are, however, and no matter what you are doing, you can be so treated if you fit the profile. Such harassment would not be tolerated by the conservative, mostly white audience Forman is trying to reach and so should not be condoned by that audience when directed toward other racial and ethnic groups. It's a matter of fairness.

Forman's first two reasons engage relatively concrete and easily grasped issues: Does racial profiling work? Are innocent people harassed when it's used? His third and fourth reasons are more abstract and depend on the reader's recognition of contradiction and desire to be consistent. If we oppose welfare because it encourages dependency and lack of personal responsibility, shouldn't we oppose racial profiling because it "tell[s] black kids that they are indeed pariahs—that, no matter how hard they study, they remain suspects"? Similarly, if we oppose affirmative action because it favors people because of their race, shouldn't we also oppose profiling because it, too, singles out race? Rational people want to be consistent; Forman shows his readers that they haven't been consistent—a powerful strategy after he's argued that profiling doesn't work and harasses innocent people.

Using Evidence

How well does Forman use the third level of case structure, the supporting evidence for each reason?

Note that he uses different *kinds* of evidence appropriately. To support his contention that racial profiling doesn't work, he cites *data*—in this case, statistical evidence—showing that blacks are no more likely, or even less so, than whites or Latinos to be caught with contraband (paragraph 4). Profiling blacks, therefore, makes no sense. Next, he uses *individual examples* to confirm that innocent people, including police officers, are treated as suspects simply because their skin is black. These individual examples may have more impact than statistics because they personalize the problem. Used together, individual examples and statistics complement each other.

Then, in paragraph 7, Forman draws on *personal experience*, what he himself has observed as evidence. He's seen police shake down students at the school where he teaches. He wants his readers to *feel* the sense of violation involved and so offers a graphic description. Clearly, personal experience can be a powerful source of evidence.

Finally, to back up his last two reasons, Forman cites *well-known authorities*, prominent conservatives such as Myron Magnet and Abigail and Stephen Thernstrom (paragraphs 11 and 14). He cites these sources, obviously, because his audience considers them representative of their own viewpoint and therefore voices meriting respect. Forman combines these authorities with the voices of his own students, who gain additional credibility simply by being cited along with the experts.

Forman's essay merits close attention for its use of evidence alone. He employs different kinds of evidence, combines different types well, and never forgets that evidence must appeal to his audience.

Introducing and Concluding the Argument

We have analyzed Forman's strategic use of the three levels of case structure—thesis, reasons, and evidence—to build an argument that should convince his audience not to support racial profiling. Arguing to convince also requires a writer to think strategically about ways to open and close the case.

The Introduction When you read Forman's essay the first time, you may have thought that somehow we had attached the wrong title to an essay about school reform. Not until the end of the third paragraph does the author announce his actual subject, racial profiling. Why this long introduction about the Maya Angelou Public Charter School?

The introduction accomplishes at least the following key purposes. Conservatives are strong supporters of alternatives to public schools. One of these is the charter school, and the author uses his story about a highly successful one to confirm conservative policy about educational reform. Note how he emphasizes the seriousness of the curriculum and other school activities. He also points to the strict rules and discipline and how the Maya Angelou school has turned around standard public school failures, including kids headed for serious trouble with the law. All of this is likely to sound good to conservatives.

The story also establishes the author's authority as someone who makes conservative ideas and values work. Later on, when he cites his students' words to confirm his points, we do not doubt their authenticity or his trustworthiness in representing black reactions to racial profiling. We can see, then, how crucial the introduction is to setting up the case.

Finally, the introduction anticipates the contradictions he'll address later, especially in reasons 3 and 4. The Maya Angelou school has succeeded in educating the kind of student that other schools often don't reach. Kids who could be a public danger now and adult criminals later are apparently becoming good citizens instead. But everything the school has accomplished can be undone by racial profiling. Thus, conservative educational reform clashes with conservative law enforcement policy. They don't fit together, and clearly the former is more important than the latter because the school is creating students who will stay on the right side of the law. Forman is already implying that racial profiling must go, which is the whole point of his essay.

The point for us is that introductions shouldn't be dashed off carelessly, thrown together just because we know we need one. Our introductions must prepare the way for our case.

The Conclusion Paragraphs 16 and 17 conclude his argument. What do they achieve?

Paragraph 16 states that most conservatives are not racists, that they just have been misled into thinking profiling works. In effect, these assertions release conservatives from the common accusation that they don't care about blacks and support policies that discriminate against them. Forman also reminds his readers that he has used *conservative principles* to explain why racial profiling diminishes police effectiveness.

Paragraph 17 explains in a concrete and memorable way how police tactics like profiling can interfere with law enforcement. He wants his readers to remember the harshness of the procedures and that the experience makes minorities suspicious of and uncooperative with police officers. We see the damage profiling does from the inside so to speak, and we cannot help but appreciate its negative consequences for law enforcement itself. The implied message is: If you value law and order, be against racial profiling. In this way, Forman advances his major point again but this time from another conservative vantage point — support for the police.

Like introductions, conclusions are not throwaways, not merely hasty summaries. Like introductions, they should do something, not just repeat what we've said already. The conclusion must clinch our case by ending it forcefully and memorably.

Following Through

A successful essay has smooth transitions between its opening and its first reason and between its last reason and its conclusion, as well as between each reason in the body of the essay. In your writer's notebook, describe how Forman (1) announces that he is moving from his introduction to the first reason, from the first reason to the second, and so on and (2) at the same time links each section to what has come before.

WRITING A CONVINCING ARGUMENT

Few people draft an essay sequentially, beginning with the first sentence of the first paragraph and ending with the last sentence of the last paragraph. But the final version of any essay must read as if it had been written sequentially with the writer fully in control throughout the process.

A well-written essay is like a series of moves in a chess game, in which each move is made to achieve some end or ends, to gain a strategic advantage, as part of an overall plan to win. In the case of convincing, the overall plan is to win the agreement of the reader.

Although readers may not be fully aware of the "moves" that make up a convincing argument, the writer probably created most of them more or less consciously. As we have seen in this chapter, we can learn much about how to convince by studying finished essays — polished arguments that convince. However, it is one thing to understand how something works and quite another to produce it ourselves. In part, the difficulty is that we cannot see from someone else's final product everything that went into making it work so well. Just as a movie audience typically cannot imagine all the rehearsals, the many takes, and the editing that make a scene powerful, so it is hard for us to imagine all the research and thinking, the many drafts, and the process of editing and proofreading that Forman must have gone through to make "Arrested Development" worth printing. Yet it is precisely this process you must understand and immerse yourself in if you are to go beyond appreciating the structure and strategies of someone else's writing to actually produce convincing arguments of your own.

1. Your thesis can be stated or implied, but **you and your readers must have no doubt about what you're contending.**
2. **Begin with your most important reason.** (For example, if your audience supports racial profiling because they think it works, begin your case against profiling by showing them that it doesn't.)
3. In general, **provide the kind of evidence each reason requires.** (For example, if you contend that helmet laws will reduce head injuries in motorcycle accidents, such a reason requires *data* for support. In contrast, if you contend that helmet laws do not seriously intrude upon personal freedom, data won't help—you must show that helmet laws are no more restrictive than other laws we accept as justified, such as seat belt or maximum speed laws.)
4. Use the **full range** of evidence available (data, individual examples, personal experience, expert opinion, etc.). When possible and appropriate, **mix different kinds of evidence to support a single reason.**
5. **Devote serious effort to introductions and conclusions.** They should accomplish definite tasks, such as generating interest at the beginning and leaving your reader with something memorable at the end. Avoid "throw-away," high school introductions that begin with "In this essay, I will discuss . . ." or "In conclusion . . ." conclusions.

The following discussion of the composing process assumes that the work of research (Chapter 5) and inquiry (Chapter 6) has already been done. It also assumes that you have worked out a rhetorical prospectus (see Chapter 1, page 21) to guide you in combining structure with strategy.

Preparing a Brief

Before you begin to draft, it is a good idea to prepare a brief. Recall that we defined *case structure* as the basic components of any case. In a brief, you adapt case structure to make a particular argument. The brief shows the thesis and reasons you plan to use and gives some indication of how you will support each reason with evidence. The brief ought to indicate a tentative plan for arranging the reasons, but that plan may change as you draft and revise.

Working toward a Position

First, we need to distinguish a position from a thesis. A **position** (or a stance or opinion) amounts to an overall, summarizing attitude or judgment about some issue. "Universities often exploit student athletes" is an example of a position. A **thesis** is not only more specific and precise but also more strategic, designed to appeal to readers and to be consistent with available evidence. For example, "Student athletes in revenue-generating sports ought to be paid for their services" is one possible thesis representing the preceding position, perhaps for an audience of college students. Because a case is nothing more than the reasons and evidence that support a thesis, we cannot construct a case without a thesis. But without a position, we do not know where we stand in general on an issue and so cannot experiment with various thesis formulations. So a position typically precedes a thesis.

The goal of inquiry is to earn an opinion, to find a stance that holds up in dialogue with other inquirers. What often happens in inquiry, however, is that we begin with a strong opinion, usually unearned, find it failing under scrutiny, discover other positions that do not fully satisfy us, and so emerge from inquiry uncertain about what we do think. Another common path in inquiry is to start out with no opinion at all, find ourselves attracted to several conflicting positions, and so wind up in much the same condition as the person whose strong initial position collapses under scrutiny—unsure, confused, even vexed because we can't decide what to think.

In such situations, resolve first to be patient with yourself. Certainty is often cheap and easy; the best, most mature positions typically come to us only after a struggle. Second, take out your writer's notebook and start making lists. Look over your research materials, especially the notecards on which you have recorded positions and evidence from your sources. Make lists in response to these questions:

What positions have you encountered in research and class discussion?
What seems strongest and weakest in each stance? What modifications might be made to eliminate or minimize the weak points? Are there other possible positions? What are their strong and weak points?
What evidence impressed you? What does each piece of evidence imply or suggest? What connections can you draw among the pieces of evidence given in various sources? If there is conflict in the implications of the evidence, what is that conflict?

While all this list-making at times may seem to be only doodling, you can often begin to see convergences as you begin to sort things out.

Bear in mind that although emotional commitment to ideas and values is important to a healthy life, it is often an impediment to clear thought and effective convincing. Sometimes we find our stance by relinquishing a strongly held opinion for which a case proves hard to make—perhaps for lack of compelling reasons or evidence that appeals to readers outside the group who already agrees with us. The more emotional the issue—abortion, pornography, affirmative action, among others—the more likely we are to cling to a position that is difficult to defend. When we sense deep conflict, when we want to argue a position even in the face of strong contradictory evidence and counter-arguments to which we cannot respond, it is time to reconsider our emotional commitments and perhaps even to change our minds.

Finally, if you find yourself holding out for the "perfect" position, the one that is all strength and no weakness, the best advice is to give up. Controversial issues are controversial precisely because no single stance convinces everyone, because there is always room for counterargument and for other positions that have their own power to convince.

Student Sample: Working toward a Position   Justin Spidel's class began by reading many arguments about homosexuality and discussing issues related to gay rights. Justin decided to investigate whether same-sex marriage should be legal. His initial perspective on the issue was that same-sex marriage ought to be legal because he thought that gays and lesbians should be treated as equals and that no harm would result. As he did research, he learned that a majority of Americans strongly oppose same-sex marriage, mainly because they believe its legalization would change a long-standing definition of marriage and alter its sacred bond. Justin read articles opposing gay marriage by such well-known public figures as William Bennett, but he also read many in favor. He found especially convincing the arguments by gays and lesbians who were in long-standing, loving, monogamous relationships but who were barred from marrying their partners. Justin's initial round of research led him to the position "Gays and lesbians should be able to marry."

During the inquiry stage, Justin discussed his position with his classmates and instructor. Knowing that gays and lesbians do sometimes get married in churches, Justin's classmates asked him to clarify the phrase "able to marry." Justin explained that he meant legal recognition of same-sex marriages by individual state governments and therefore all states, as marriage in any one state is usually recognized by the rest. When asked if other countries recognize same-sex marriage, Justin admitted that only Denmark does. He decided to argue for his position anyway on the grounds that the United States should take the lead in valuing equality and individual rights. He was asked about the implications of his position: Would granting legal status to same-sex marriage devalue the institution? Justin responded that the people who are fighting for legalization have the deepest respect for marriage and that marriage is about love and commitment rather than sexual orientation.

Following Through

Formulate a tentative position on a topic that you have researched and into which you have inquired. Write it up with a brief explanation of why you support this stand. Be prepared to defend your position in class or with a peer in a one-on-one exchange of position statements.

Analyzing the Audience

Before you decide on a thesis, give some thought to the rhetorical context of your argument. Who needs to hear it? What are their values? What common ground might you share with them? How might you have to qualify your position to influence their opinions?

To provoke thought, people occasionally make cases for theses that they know have little chance of winning significant assent. One example is the argument for legalizing all drug use; although reasonably good cases have been made for this position, most Americans find it too radical to be convincing. If you want to convince rather than provoke, you must formulate a thesis that both represents your position and creates as little resistance in your readers as possible. Instead of arguing for legalizing drugs, for example, you might argue that much of the staggering amount of money spent on enforcement, prosecution, and imprisonment should be diverted to rehabilitation and social problems connected with drug abuse. Because most positions allow for many possible theses, a writer should analyze the audience before settling on one.

Student Sample: Analyzing the Audience Justin knew that many people would view same-sex marriage as a very radical idea. Some possible audiences, such as conservative Christians, would never assent to it. So Justin targeted an audience he had some chance of convincing—people who opposed same-sex marriage but were not intolerant of homosexuals. Justin wrote the following audience profile:

> My audience would be heterosexual adults who accept that some people are homosexual or lesbian; they may know people who are. They would be among the nearly 47 percent of Americans who do not object to same-sex relationships between consenting adults. They may be fairly well educated and could belong to any age group, from college students to grandparents. They are not likely to have strong religious objections, so my argument will not have to go deeply into the debate about whether homosexuality is a sin. However, these readers oppose legalizing marriage between gays and lesbians because they think it would threaten the traditional role of marriage as the basis of family life. They think that marriage has come into enough trouble lately through divorce, and they want to preserve its meaning as much as possible. Their practical position would be that if same-sex couples want to live together and act like they're married, there is nothing to stop them, so they are really not being hurt by leaving things as they are. They believe in the value of heterosexual marriage for the individual and society, so I can appeal to that. They also hold to basic American principles of equal rights and the right to the "pursuit of happiness." But mainly I want to show my readers that gays and lesbians are missing out on some basic civil rights and that letting them marry would have benefits for everyone.

Following Through

Write a profile of the audience you hope to reach through an argument you are currently planning. Be as specific as possible; include any information—age, gender, economic status, and so forth—that may con-

(continues)

Following Through (continued)

tribute to your audience's outlook and attitudes. What interests, beliefs, and values might they hold? How might you have to alter your position or phrase your thesis to give your argument a chance of succeeding? What reasons might they be willing to consider? What would you have to rule out?

Developing a Thesis

A good thesis grows out of a combination of things: your position, your research, your exploration of reasons to support your position, and your understanding of the audience. During the process of drafting, you may refine the thesis by phrasing it more precisely, but for now you should concentrate only on stating a thesis that represents your position clearly and directly.

We advise against trying to make your thesis do more than simply present the claim. Naturally, your mind runs to reasons in support, but it makes more sense to save the reasons until you can present them thoroughly as the body of the paper unfolds.

Student Sample: Developing a Thesis   Justin's original statement, "Gays and lesbians should be able to marry," expresses a position, but it could be more precise and better directed toward the readers Justin defined in his audience profile. He already had some reasons to support his argument, and he wanted the thesis to represent his current position accurately without locking him into some rigid plan. He refined his position to the following:

A couple's right to marry should not be restricted because of sexual orientation.

This version emphasized that marriage is a right everyone should enjoy, but it did not go far enough in suggesting why the readers should care or recognize it as a right. Justin tried again:

Every couple who wishes to commit to each other in marriage should have the right to do so, regardless of sexual preference.

Justin was fairly satisfied with this version because it appealed to a basic family value — commitment.

He then started thinking about how committed relationships benefit society in general, an argument that would appeal to his readers. He wondered if he could point the thesis not just in the direction of rights for homosexuals and lesbians but also in the direction of benefits for everyone, which would broaden his appeal. It would also allow him to develop his essay further by using some good arguments he had encountered in his reading. He tried one more time and settled on the following thesis:

Everyone, gay and straight, will benefit from extending the basic human right of marriage to all couples, regardless of sexual preference.

Following Through

1. Write at least three versions of a tentative thesis for the essay on which you are currently working. For each version, write an evaluation of its strengths and weaknesses. Why is the best version the best?
2. As we saw in analyzing William May's case against assisted suicide (Chapter 3), sometimes a thesis needs to be qualified and exceptions to the thesis stated and clarified. Now is a good time to think about qualifications and exceptions.

You can handle qualifications and exceptions in two ways. First, you can add a phrase to your thesis that limits it, as William May did in his argument on assisted suicide: "*On the whole,* our social policy [. . .] should not regularize killing for mercy." May admits that a few extreme cases of suffering justify helping someone die. The other method is to word the thesis in such a way that exceptions or qualifications are implied rather than spelled out. As an example, consider the following thesis: "Life sentences with no parole are justifiable for all sane people found guilty of first-degree murder." Here the exceptions would be "those who are found insane" and "those tried on lesser charges."

Using your best thesis statement from the previous exercise, decide whether qualifications and exceptions are needed. If they are, determine how best to handle them.

Analyzing the Thesis

Once you have a thesis, your next task is to *unpack* it to determine what you must argue. To do this, put yourself in the place of your readers. To be won over, what must they find in your argument? Answering that question requires looking very closely at both what the thesis says and what it implies. It also requires thinking about the position and attitudes of your readers as you described them earlier in your audience profile.

Although many thesis sentences appear simple, analysis shows that they are quite complex. Let's consider a thesis on the issue of whether Mark Twain's *Huckleberry Finn* should be taught in the public schools. Some have argued that Twain's classic novel should be removed from required reading lists because a number of readers, especially African Americans, find its subject matter and language offensive. In fact, in some schools the novel is not assigned at all, whereas in others it may be assigned, but students have the option of choosing to study another novel of the same period instead. In our example thesis, the writer supports the teaching of the novel: "Mark Twain's *Huckleberry Finn* should be required reading for all high school students in the United States."

Unpacking this thesis, we see that the writer must first argue for *Huckleberry Finn* as *required* reading—not merely as a good book but also as one that is indispensable to an education in American literature. The writer must also argue that the book should be required at the high school level rather than in middle school or college. Finally, knowing that some people find certain passages offensive, the author must defend the novel from charges of racism, even though the thesis does not explicitly state, *"Huckleberry Finn* is not a racist book." Otherwise, these charges stand by default; to ignore them is to ignore the context of the issue.

Student Sample: Analyzing the Thesis   By analyzing his thesis—"Everyone, gay and straight, will benefit from extending the basic human right of marriage to all couples, regardless of sexual preference"—Justin realized that his main task was to explain specific benefits that would follow from allowing gays to marry. He knew that he would have to cite ways in which society, as well as those in same-sex relationships who want to marry, will be better off. He knew that his readers would agree that marriage is a "basic human right" for heterosexual adults, but he could not assume that they would see it that way for homosexual couples. Therefore, he had to make them see that same-sex couples have the same needs as other couples. He also wanted to make certain that his readers understood that he was arguing only that the law of the land should recognize such marriages, not that all churches and denominations should sanctify them.

Following Through

Unpack a tentative thesis of your own or one that your instructor gives you to see what key words and phrases an argument based on that thesis must address. Also consider what an audience would expect you to argue given a general knowledge about the topic and the current context of the dispute.

Finding Reasons

For the most part, no special effort goes into finding reasons to support a thesis. They come to us as we attempt to justify our opinions, as we listen to the arguments of our classmates, as we encounter written arguments in research, and as we think about how to reach the readers we hope to convince. Given good writing preparation, we seldom formulate a thesis without already having some idea of the reasons we will use to defend it. Our problem, rather, is usually selection—picking out the best reasons and shaping and stating them in a way that appeals to our readers. When we do find ourselves searching for reasons, however, it helps to be aware of their common sources.

The Audience's Belief System   Ask yourself, What notions of the real, the good, and the possible will my readers entertain? Readers will find any reason unconvincing if it is not consistent with their understanding of reality. For example, based on their particular culture's notions about disease, people will accept or reject arguments about how to treat illness. Likewise, people have differing notions of what is good. Some people think it is good to exploit natural resources so that we can live with more conveniences; those who place less value on conveniences see more good in preserving the environment. Finally, people disagree about what is possible. Those who believe it is not possible to change human nature will not accept arguments that certain types of criminals can be rehabilitated.

Special Rules or Principles   Good reasons can also be found in a community's accepted rules and principles. For example, in the United States, citizens accept the principle that a person is innocent until proven guilty. The Fourteenth Amendment states that no one may be "deprived of life, liberty, or property, without due process of law." We apply this principle in all sorts of nonlegal situations whenever we argue that someone should be given the benefit of the doubt.

The law is only one source of special rules or principles. We also find them in politics ("one person, one vote"), in business (the principle of seniority, which gives preference to employees who have been on a job longest), and even in the home, where each family formulates its own house rules. In other words, all human settings and activities have their own norms, and in any search for reasons we must ask ourselves what norms may apply to our particular topic or thesis.

Expert Opinion and Hard Evidence   Probably the next most common source of reasons is expert opinion, on which we must rely when we lack direct experience with a particular subject. Most readers respect the opinion of a trained professional with advanced degrees and prestige in his or her field. And when you can show that experts are in agreement, you have an even better reason.

Hard evidence can also provide good reasons. Readers generally respect the scientific method of gathering objective data upon which conclusions can be drawn. Research shows, for example, that wearing a bicycle helmet significantly reduces the incidence of head injuries from accidents. Therefore, we can support the thesis "Laws should require bicycle riders to wear helmets" with the reason "because statistics show that fewer serious head injuries occurred in bicycle accidents when the riders were wearing helmets than when no helmets were worn."

When you argue about any topic, you will be at a disadvantage if you don't have detailed, current information about it in the form of expert opinion and hard evidence.

Tradition   We can sometimes strengthen a position by citing or alluding to well-known sources that are part of our audience's cultural tradition — for example, the Bible, the Constitution, and the sayings or writings of people our readers recognize and respect. Although reasons drawn from tradition may lose their force if many audience members identify with different cultures or are suspicious of tradition itself, they will almost always be effective when readers revere the source.

Comparison   A reason based on similarity argues that what is true in one instance should be true in another. For example, we could make a case for legalizing marijuana by showing that it is similar in effect to alcohol, which is legal—and also a drug. The argument might look like this:

> *Thesis:* Marijuana use should be decriminalized.
>
> *Reason:* Marijuana is no more harmful than alcohol.

Many comparison arguments attempt to show that present situations are similar to past ones. For example, many who argue for the civil rights of gays and lesbians say that discrimination based on sexual preference should not be tolerated today just as discrimination based on race, common thirty years ago, is no longer tolerated.

A special kind of argument based on similarity is an *analogy*, which attempts to explain one thing, usually abstract, in terms of something else, usually more concrete. For example, in an argument opposing sharing the world's limited resources, philosopher Garrett Hardin reasons that requiring the wealthy nations of the world to feed the starving nations is analogous to requiring the occupants of a lifeboat filled to a safe capacity to take on board those still in the water until the lifeboat sinks and everyone perishes.

Arguments of comparison can also point to difference, showing how two things are not the same, not analogous. For example, many Americans supported participation in the 1992 Persian Gulf War by arguing that, unlike the disastrous conflict in Vietnam, this war was winnable. The argument went as follows:

> *Thesis:* America can defeat Iraq's military.
>
> *Reason:* Warfare in the deserts of Kuwait and Iraq is very different from warfare in the jungles of Vietnam.

The Probable or Likely   Of course, all reasoning about controversial issues relies on making a viewpoint seem probable or likely, but specific reasons drawn from the probable or likely may often come into play when we want to defend one account of events over another or when we want to attack or support a proposed policy. For example, defenders of Supreme Court nominee Clarence Thomas attempted to discredit Anita Hill's accusations of sexual harassment in a number of ways, all related to probability: Is it likely, they asked, that she would remember so clearly and in such detail events that happened as long as ten years ago? Is it probable that a woman who had been harassed would follow Thomas from one job to another, as Hill did?

Because a proposed policy may have no specific precedent, particularly if it is designed to deal with a new situation, sometimes all a writer can do who is arguing for or against the new policy is to speculate about its probable success or failure. For example, the collapse of communism in eastern Europe and the former Soviet Union has left the United States in the unusual position of having no serious military threat to its own or its allies' security. What, then, should we do—drastically reduce our armed forces, especially the nuclear arsenal? redirect part of what we once spent on defense into dealing with pressing domestic problems? Any proposal for confronting this new situation is defended and attacked based on what we are likely to face in the foreseeable future.

Cause and Effect   People generally agree that most circumstances result from some cause or causes, and they also agree that most changes in circumstances will result in some new effects. This human tendency to believe in cause-and-effect relationships can provide reasons for certain arguments. For example, environmentalists have successfully argued for reductions in the world's output of hydrofluorocarbons by showing that the chemicals damage the earth's ozone layer.

Cause-and-effect arguments are difficult to prove; witness the fact that cigarette manufacturers have argued for years that the connection between smoking and lung disease cannot be demonstrated. Responsible arguments from cause and effect depend on credible and adequate hard evidence and expert opinion. And they must always acknowledge the possible existence of hidden factors; smoking and lung disease, for example, may be influenced by genetic predisposition.

Definition   All arguments require definitions for clarification. However, a definition can often provide a reason in support of the thesis as well. If we define a term by placing it in a category, we are saying that whatever is true for the category is true for the term we are defining. For example, Elizabeth Cady Stanton's landmark 1892 argument for women's rights ("The Solitude of Self") was based on the definition "women are individuals":

> *Thesis:* Women must have suffrage, access to higher education, and sovereignty over their own minds and bodies.
>
> *Reason:* Women are individuals.

If Stanton's audience, the American Congress, accepted that all individuals are endowed with certain inalienable rights, Stanton's definition reminded them that women belong in the category of "individual" just as much as men do and so deserve the same rights.

Almost all good reasons come from one or some combination of these eight sources. However, simply knowing the sources will not automatically provide you with good reasons for your argument. Nothing can substitute for thoughtful research and determined inquiry. Approach each of these sources as an angle from which to think about your thesis statement and the results of your research and inquiry. They can help you generate reasons initially or find better reasons when the ones you have seem inadequate.

Finally, do not feel that quantity is crucial in finding good reasons. While it is good to brainstorm as many reasons as you can, focus on those that you think will appeal most to your audience and that you can develop thoroughly. A good argument is often based on just one or two good reasons.

Student Sample: Finding Reasons   Justin used the eight sources listed in this section to help find some of his reasons. He also considered his audience and the beliefs they would likely hold. Here are the possible reasons he found; note that each reason is stated as a complete sentence.

From the audience's belief system:
Marriage is primarily about love and commitment, not sex.
Marriage is a stabilizing influence in society.

From rules or principles the audience would likely subscribe to:
Everyone has an equal right to life, liberty, and the pursuit of happiness.

From expert opinion (in this case, a lawyer and some noted authors on gay rights):
Denying gays and lesbians the right to marry is an incredible act of discrimination.
Allowing gays and lesbians to marry will promote family values such as monogamy and the two-parent family.

From comparison or analogy:
Just as we once thought marriage between blacks and whites should be illegal, we now think same-sex marriage should be illegal.
Gay and lesbian couples can love each other just as devotedly as can heterosexual couples.

From cause and effect:
Marriage is a way for people to take care of each other rather than being a burden on society should they become ill or unemployed.

Justin now had far more ideas for his case than he needed. He now had to evaluate his list to check the fit between his thesis sentence and the reasons he thought were best.

Following Through

Here is one way to brainstorm for reasons. First, list the eight sources for finding reasons discussed on pages 227–230 in your writer's notebook, perhaps on the inside front cover or on the first or last page — someplace where you can easily find them. Practice using these sources by writing your current thesis at the top of another page and then going through the list, writing down reasons as they occur to you.

Selecting and Ordering Reasons

Selecting reasons from a number of possibilities depends primarily on two considerations: your thesis and your readers. Any thesis demands a certain line of reasoning. For example, the writer contending that *Huckleberry Finn* should be required reading in high school must offer a compelling reason for accepting no substitute — not even another novel by Mark Twain. Such a reason might be, "Because many critics and novelists see *Huckleberry Finn* as the inspiration for much subsequent American fiction, we cannot understand the American novel if we are not familiar with *Huckleberry Finn.*" A reason of this kind — one that focuses on the essential influence of the book — is likely to appeal to teachers or school administrators.

It is often difficult to see how to order reasons prior to drafting. Because we can easily reorder reasons as we write and rewrite, in developing our case we need only attempt to discover an order that seems right and satisfies us as an overall sequence. The writer advocating *Huckleberry Finn,* for example, should probably first defend the novel from the charge that it is racist. Readers unaware of the controversy will want to know why the book needs defending, and well-informed readers will expect an immediate response to the book's critics because it is these critics' efforts to remove the book from classrooms that has created the controversy. Once the charge of racism has been disposed of, readers will be prepared to hear the reasons for keeping the book on required-reading lists.

Besides thinking about what your readers need and expect and how one reason may gain force by following another one, keep in mind a simple fact about memory: We recall best what we read last; next best, what we read first. A good rule of thumb, therefore, is to begin and end your defense of a thesis with your strongest reasons, the ones you want to emphasize. A strong beginning also helps keep the reader reading; a strong conclusion avoids a sense of anticlimax.

Student Sample: Selecting and Ordering Reasons   Justin generated eight possible reasons to support his position on gay and lesbian marriage. To help decide which ones to use, he looked again at his audience profile. What had he said about the concerns of people who oppose same-sex marriage? Which of his potential reasons would best address these concerns?

Because his audience did not believe that the ban on same-sex marriage was a great loss to gays and lesbians, Justin decided to use the lawyer's point that the ban is discriminatory. The audience's other main concern was with the potential effect of gay marriage on the rest of society, particularly traditional marriage and family. Therefore, Justin decided to use the reasons about the benefits of same-sex marriage to society: that family values would be reinforced and that marriage keeps people from burdening society if they become unable to support themselves.

Justin noticed that some of his reasons overlapped one another. For example, the point that marriage is a stabilizing influence was merely a general statement that was better expressed in combination with his more specific reasons about economic benefits and family values. And his reason that mentioned discrimination overlapped his point that it is wrong to deny "life, liberty, and the pursuit of happiness." Overlapping is common because there are many ways of saying the same idea.

What is the best strategy for arranging these reasons? Initially, Justin wanted to begin with the point about discrimination, but then he decided to appeal to his audience's interests by listing the advantages first. Saving the argument about discrimination until the second half of his essay would let him end more strongly with an appeal to the readers' sympathy and sense of fairness.

Then Justin rechecked his thesis to confirm that the reasons really supported it. He decided that his readers might not accept that marriage is a "basic human right" for those of the same sex, so he decided to add one more reason in support of the similarities between heterosexuals and homosexuals.

Justin wrote up the following brief version of his argument:

> *Thesis:* Everyone, gay and straight, will benefit from extending the basic human right of marriage to all couples, regardless of sexual preference.
>
> *Reason:* It would reinforce family values such as monogamy and the two-parent family.
>
> *Reason:* It would help keep people from burdening society.
>
> *Reason:* Denying people the right to marry is discrimination.
>
> *Reason:* The love homosexuals have for each other is no different from love between heterosexuals.

Following Through

We call the case structure a flexible plan because as long as you maintain the three-level structure of thesis, reasons, and evidence, you can change everything else at will: throw out one thesis for another or alter its wording, add or take away reasons or evidence, or reorder both to achieve the desired impact. Therefore, when writing your brief, don't feel that the order in which you have found your reasons and evidence should determine their order in your essay. Rather, make your decisions based on the following questions:

What will my audience need or expect to read first?

Will one reason help set up another?

Which of my reasons are strongest? Can I begin and conclude my argument with the strongest reasons I have?

To a thesis you have already refined, now add the second level of your brief, the reason or reasons. Be ready to explain your decisions about selection and arrangement. Final decisions about ordering will often be made quite late in the drafting process—in a second or third writing. Spending a little time now, however, to think through possible orderings can save time later and make composing less difficult.

Using Evidence

The skillful use of evidence involves many complex judgments. Let's begin with some basic questions.

What Counts as Evidence?   Because science and technology rely on the hard data of quantified evidence—especially statistics—some people assume that hard data are the only really good source of evidence. Such a view, however, is far too narrow for our purposes. Besides hard data, evidence includes the following:

- Quotation from authorities: expert opinion, statements from people with special knowledge about an issue, and traditional or institutional authorities such as respected political leaders, philosophers, well-known authors, and people who hold positions of power and influence. Besides books and other printed sources, you can gather both data and quotations from interviews with experts or leaders on campus and in the local community.
- Constitutions, statutes, court rulings, organizational bylaws, company policy statements, and the like.
- Examples and case histories (that is, extended narratives about an individual's or an organization's experience).
- The results of questionnaires that you devise and administer.
- Personal experience.

In short, evidence includes anything that confirms a good reason or that might increase your readers' acceptance of a reason advanced to justify your thesis.

What Kind of Evidence Is Best?   What evidence is best depends on what particular reasons call for. To argue for bicycle helmet legislation, we need to cite facts and figures—hard data—to back up our claim that wearing helmets reduces the number of serious head injuries caused by bicycling accidents. To defend *Huckleberry Finn* by saying that it is an indictment of racism will require evidence of a different kind: quoted passages from the novel itself, statements from respected interpreters, and so forth.

When you have many pieces of evidence to choose from, what is best depends on the quality of the evidence itself and its likely impact on readers. In general—especially for hard data—the best evidence is the most recent. Also, the more trusted and prestigious the source, the more authority it will have for readers. Arguments about the AIDS epidemic in the United States, for example, often draw on data from the Centers for Disease Control in Atlanta, a respected research facility that specializes in the study of epidemics. And because the nature of the AIDS crisis changes relatively quickly, the most recent information is the most authoritative.

Finally, always look for evidence that will give you an edge in winning reader assent. For example, given the charge that *Huckleberry Finn* is offensive to blacks, its vigorous defense by an African-American literary scholar would ordinarily carry more weight than its defense by a white scholar.

How Much Evidence Is Needed?   The amount of evidence required depends on two judgments: (1) the more crucial a reason is to your case and (2) the more resistant readers are likely to be to a reason. Most cases have at least one pivotal reason, one point upon which the whole case is built and upon which, therefore, the whole case stands or falls. Forman's case against racial profiling turns on our accepting its unreliability for detecting criminals. Such a pivotal reason needs to be supported at length, regardless of the degree of reader resistance to it; about one-fourth of Forman's essay supports his contention that racial profiling is unreliable.

Of course, a pivotal reason may also be the reason to which readers will be most resistant. For instance, many arguments supporting women's right to abortion depend on the point that a fetus cannot be considered a human being until it reaches a certain stage of development and, therefore, does not qualify for protection under the law. This reason is obviously both pivotal and likely to be contested by many readers, so devoting much space to evidence for the reason would be a justified strategy.

Student Sample: Using Evidence   Justin took the brief showing his case so far and on a large table laid out all of his notecards and the material he had photocopied and marked up during his research. He needed to find the expert opinions, quotations, statistics, dates, and other hard evidence that would support the reasons he intended to use. Doing this before starting to draft is a good idea because it reveals where evidence is lacking or thin and what further research is necessary. If you have a lot of sources, it may help to use different-colored markers to indicate which passages will work with which of your reasons. Justin was now able to add the third level—evidence—to his case structure, including the sources from which he took it. For articles longer than one page, he included page numbers to turn to as he drafted his paper.

> *Thesis:* Everyone, gay and straight, will benefit from extending the basic human right of marriage to all couples, regardless of sexual preference.
>
> > *Reason:* It would reinforce family values such as monogamy and the two-parent family.
> >
> > > *Evidence:* Marriage stabilizes relationships. (Sources: Rauch 23; Dean 114)
> > > *Evidence:* Children of gays and lesbians should not be denied having two parents. (Sources: Dean 114; Sullivan; Salholz)
> > > *Evidence:* If gays can have and adopt children, they should be able to marry. (Source: Salholz)

Reason: It would provide a means of keeping people from burdening society.

> *Evidence:* Spouses take care of each other. (Source: Rauch)

Reason: Denying gays and lesbians the right to marry is discriminatory.

> *Evidence:* Marriage includes rights to legal benefits. (Source: Dean 112)
>
> *Evidence:* Domestic partnerships fail to provide these rights. (Sources: Dean 112; Salholz)
>
> *Evidence:* Barring these marriages violates many democratic principles. (Sources: "Declaration"; Dean 113; Salholz)

Reason: The love homosexuals have for each other is no different from love between heterosexuals.

> *Evidence:* Many gays and lesbians are in monogamous relationships. (Source: Ayers 5)
>
> *Evidence:* They have the same need to make a public, legal commitment. (Source: Sullivan)

Following Through

Prepare a complete brief for an argument. Include both reasons and some indication of the evidence you will use to support each one, along with a note about sources. Remember that a brief is a flexible plan, not an outline engraved in stone. The plan can change as you begin drafting.

From Brief to Draft

Turning a rough outline or brief of your argument into a piece of prose is never easy. Even if you know what points to bring up and in what order, you will have to (1) determine how much space to devote to each reason, (2) work in your evidence from sources, and (3) smoothly incorporate and correctly cite all quotations, summaries, and paraphrases. Furthermore, you will have to create parts of the essay that are not represented in the brief, such as an introduction that appeals to your audience and a conclusion that does not simply rehash all that you have said before. As you draft, you may also see a need for paragraphs that provide background on your topic, clarify or define an important term, or present and rebut an opposing argument. Following are some suggestions and examples that you may find helpful as you begin to draft.

1. A position or general outlook on a topic is not a thesis. A thesis is a carefully worded **claim** that your entire essay backs up with reasons and evidence. **Experiment with various ways of stating your thesis** until it says *exactly* what you want it to say and at the same time creates the least resistance in your readers.

2. Be willing to give up or modify significantly a thesis you find you cannot support with good reasons and strong evidence that appeal *to your readers*. **We must argue a thesis that fits the available evidence,** which may differ a little or a lot from what we really believe.

3. Take the time to create a specific **audience profile.** What is the age, gender, and economic status of your target audience? What interests, beliefs, and values might they bring to your topic and thesis? Remember: There is no such thing as a "general audience." **We are always trying to convince some definite group of possible readers.**

4. **Unpack your thesis** in an effort to discover what you must argue to uphold it adequately. If you say, for instance, that *Huckleberry Finn* should be *required* reading in high school, you must show why *this particular novel* should be an experience shared by all American high school students. It won't be enough just to argue that it's a good book.

5. Select your reasons based on what you must argue to defend your thesis combined with what you think you should say **given your audience's prior knowledge, preconceptions, prejudices, and interests.**

6. Be prepared to **try out different ways of ordering your reasons.** The order that seemed best in your brief might not work best as you draft and redraft your essay.

The Introduction

Some writers must work through a draft from start to finish, beginning every piece of writing with the introductory paragraph. They ask, How can you possibly write the middle unless you know what the beginning is like? Other writers feel they can't write the introduction until they have written the body of the argument. They ask, How can you introduce something until you know what it is you are introducing? Either approach will eventually get the job done, as long as the writer takes the rhetorical context and strategy into account when drafting the introduction and goes back to revise it when the draft is completed.

Introductions are among the hardest things to write well. Remember that an introduction need not be one paragraph; it is often two or even three short ones. A good introduction (1) meets the needs of the audience by setting up the topic with just enough background information and (2) goes right to the heart of the issue as it relates to the audience's concerns.

Should the introduction end with the thesis statement? This strategy works well in offering the easiest transition from brief to draft in that it immediately sets the stage for the reasons. However, the thesis need not be the last sentence in the introduction, and it need not appear explicitly until much later in the draft—or at all, provided that readers can tell what it is from the title or from reading the essay.

Student Sample: The Introduction   Our student writer Justin had to consider whether he needed to provide his readers with a detailed history of the institution of marriage and even whether people feel strongly about the value of marriage. Because they oppose same-sex marriage, he assumed that his readers were familiar with the traditions underpinning the institution. What would these readers need to be told in the introduction? Essentially that the gay and lesbian rights movement calls for extending to same-sex couples the legal right to marry and that Justin's argument supported its position.

For example, if Justin had opened with, "Americans' intolerant attitudes toward homosexuality are preventing a whole class of our citizens from exercising the right to marry," he would have been assuming that there are no valid reasons for denying same-sex marriage. Such a statement would offend his target audience members, who are not homophobic and might resent the implication that their arguments are based only on prejudice. Rather than confronting his readers, Justin's introduction attempts to establish some common ground with them:

> When two people fall deeply in love, they want to share every part of their lives with each other. For some, that could mean making a commitment, living together, and maybe having children together. But most people in love want more than that; they want to make their commitment public and legal through the ceremony of marriage, a tradition thousands of years old that has been part of almost every culture.
>
> But not everyone has the right to make that commitment. In this country and in most others, gays and lesbians are denied the right to marry. According to many Americans, allowing them to marry would destroy the institution and threaten traditional family values. Nevertheless, "advances in gay and lesbian civil rights [are] bringing awareness and newfound determination to many," and hundreds of same-sex couples are celebrating their commitment to each other in religious ceremonies (Ayers 6). These couples would like to make their unions legal, and we should not prohibit them. Everyone, gay and straight, will benefit from extending the basic human right of marriage to all couples, regardless of sexual orientation.

Justin's first paragraph builds common ground by offering an overview of marriage that his readers are likely to share. In the second paragraph, he goes on to introduce the conflict, showing his own awareness of the main objections offered by thoughtful critics of same-sex marriage. Notice the even tone with which he presents these views; this sort of care is what we define in Chapter 1 as paying attention to character—presenting yourself as fair and responsible. Finally, Justin builds common ground by showing the gay and lesbian community in a very positive light, as people who love and commit to each other just as heterosexuals do.

A good introduction attracts the reader's interest. To do this, writers use a number of techniques, some more dramatic than others. They may open with the story of a particular person whose experience illustrates some aspect of the topic. Or they may attempt to startle the reader with a surprising fact or opinion, as Jonathan Rauch, one of Justin's sources, did when he began his essay this way: "Whatever else marriage may or may not be, it is certainly falling apart." Generally, dictionary definitions are dull openers, but a *Newsweek* writer used one effectively to start her article on gay marriage: "Marry. 1 a) to join as husband and wife; unite in wedlock, b) to join (a man) to a woman as her husband, or (a woman) to a man as his wife." The technique works partly because the writer chose to use the definition not in an opening sentence but rather as an *epigraph*—words set off at the beginning of a piece of writing to introduce its theme. Pithy quotations work especially well as epigraphs. All of these are fairly dramatic techniques, but the best and most common bit of advice about openings is that specifics work better than generalizations at catching a reader's notice; this same *Newsweek* article had as its first sentence, "Say marriage and the mind turns to three-tiered cakes, bridal gowns, baby carriages."

How you choose to open depends on your audience. Popular periodicals like *Newsweek* are a more appropriate setting for high drama than are academic journals and college term papers, but every reader appreciates a writer's efforts to spark attention.

The Body: Presenting Reasons and Evidence

We now turn to drafting the body paragraphs of the argument. Although it is possible in a short argument for one paragraph to fully develop one reason, avoid thinking in terms of writing only one paragraph per reason. Multiple paragraphs are generally required to develop and support a reason.

The key thing to remember about paragraphs is that each one is a unit that performs some function in presenting the case. You ought to be able to say what the function of a given paragraph is—and your readers ought to be able to sense it. Does it introduce a reason? Does it define a term? Does it support a reason by setting up an analogy? Does another paragraph support the same reason by offering examples or some hard data or an illustrative case?

Not all paragraphs need topic sentences to announce their main point. Try instead to open each paragraph with some hints that allow readers to recognize the function of the paragraph. For example, some transitional word or phrase could announce to readers that you are turning from one reason to a new one. When you introduce a new reason, be sure that readers can see how it relates to the thesis. Repeating a key word or offering a synonym for one of the words in the thesis is a good idea.

Student Sample: Presenting Reasons and Evidence   As an example, let's look at how Justin developed the first reason in his case. Recall that he decided to put the two reasons about benefits to society ahead of his reasons about discrimination. Of the two benefits he planned to cite, strengthening family values seemed the stronger reason, so he decided to lead off with that one. Notice how Justin uses a transitional phrase to connect his first reason to the introductory material (printed earlier), which had mentioned opposing views. Observe how Justin develops his reason over a number of paragraphs, by drawing upon multiple sources, using both paraphrase and direct quotation. (Justin uses the Modern Language Association style for citing his sources. See Chapter 5 for guidelines on quoting and citing sources.)

In contrast to many critics' arguments, allowing gays and lesbians to marry actually promotes family values because it encourages monogamy and gives children a two-parent home. As Jonathan Rauch, a gay writer, explains, marriage stabilizes relationships:

> One of the main benefits of publicly recognized marriage is that it binds couples together not only in their own eyes but also in the eyes of society at large. Around the partners is woven a web of expectations that they will spend nights together, go to parties together, take out mortgages together, buy furniture at Ikea together, and so on—all of which helps tie them together and keep them off the streets and at home. (23)

Some people would say that gays and lesbians can have these things without marriage simply by living together, but if you argue that marriage is not necessary for commitment, you are saying marriage is not necessary for heterosexuals either. Many people think it is immoral to live together and not have the legal bond of marriage. If gays and lesbians could marry, they would be "morally correct" according to this viewpoint. Craig Dean, a Washington, D.C., lawyer and activist for gay marriage, says that it is "paradoxical that mainstream America stereotypes Gays and Lesbians as unable to maintain long-term relationships, while at the same time denying them the very institutions to stabilize such relationships" (114).

Furthermore, many homosexual couples have children from previous marriages or by adoption. According to a study by the American Bar Association, gay and lesbian families with children make up six percent of the population in the United States (Dean 114). A secure environment is very important for raising children, and allowing same-sex couples to marry would promote these children having two parents, not just one. It would also send these children the positive message that marriage is the foundation for family life. As Andrew Sullivan, a senior editor of *The New Republic*, asks, why should gays be denied the very same family values that many politicians are arguing everyone else should have? Why should their children be denied these values? *Newsweek* writer Eloise Salholz describes a paradox: If "more and more homosexual pairs are becoming parents [. . .] but cannot marry, what kind of bastardized definition of family is society imposing on their offspring?"

At this point, Justin is ready to take up his next reason: Marriage provides a system by which people take care of each other, lessening the burden on society. Justin's entire essay appears on pages 246–249. You may wish to look it over carefully before you begin to draft your own essay. Note which paragraphs bring in the remaining reasons and which paragraphs smoothly present and rebut some opposing views.

The Conclusion

Once you have presented your case, what else is there to say? You probably do not need to sum up your case; going over your reasons one more time is not generally a good strategy and will likely bore your readers. And yet you know that the conclusion is no place to introduce new issues.

Strategically, you want to end by saying, "Case made!" Here are some suggestions for doing so:

1. Look back at your introduction. Perhaps some idea you used there to attract your readers' attention could come into play again to frame the argument—a question you posed has an answer, or a problem you raised has a solution.
2. Think about the larger context into which your argument fits. For example, an argument that *Huckleberry Finn* should be taught in public high schools, even if some students are offended by its language, could end by pointing out that education becomes diluted and artificial when teachers and administrators design a curriculum that avoids all controversy.
3. If you end with a well-worded quotation, try to follow it up with some words of your own, as you normally would whenever you quote.
4. Be aware that too many conclusions run on after their natural endings. If you are dissatisfied with your conclusion, try lopping off the last one, two, or three sentences. You may uncover the real ending.
5. Pay attention to style, especially in the last sentence. An awkwardly worded sentence will not have a sound of finality, but one with some rhythmic punch or consciously repeated sounds can wrap up an essay neatly.

Student Sample: The Conclusion   Following is Justin's conclusion to his argument for same-sex marriage.

It's only natural for people in love to want to commit to each other; this desire is the same for homosexuals and lesbians as it is for heterosexuals. One recent survey showed that "over half of all lesbians and almost 40% of gay men" live in committed relationships and share a house together (Ayers 5). As Sullivan, who is gay, explains, "At some point in our lives, some of us are lucky enough to meet the person we truly love. And we want to commit to that person in front of family and country for the rest of our lives. It's the most simple, the most natural, the most human instinct in the world. How could anyone seek to oppose that?" And what does anyone gain when that right is denied? That's a question that everyone needs to ask themselves.

Justin's conclusion is unusual because although reasons usually appear in the body paragraphs of a written argument, Justin offers his fourth reason in the last paragraph: Gay and lesbian couples can love each other with the same devotion and commitment as can heterosexual couples. This reason and its development as a paragraph make an effective conclusion because they enable Justin to place the topic of same-sex marriage into the larger context of what marriage means and why anyone wishes to enter into it. Also, Justin was able to find a particularly moving quotation to convince his audience that this meaning is the same for homosexuals. The quotation could have ended the essay, but Justin wanted to conclude with words of his own that would make the readers think about their own positions.

Following Through

Using your brief as a guide, write a draft version of your argument to convince. In addition to the advice in this chapter, refer to Chapter 5, which covers paraphrasing, summarizing, quoting, incorporating, and documenting source material.

Revising the Draft

Too often, revising is confused with editing. Revising, however, implies making large changes in content and organization, not simply sentence-level corrections or even stylistic changes, which fall into the category of editing.

To get a sense of what is involved in revising, you should know that the brief of Justin Spidel's essay on pages 235–236 is actually a revised version. Justin had originally written a draft with his reasons presented in a different order and without three of the sources that now appear in his paper. When Justin exchanged drafts with another classmate who was writing on the same topic, he discovered that some of her sources would also help him develop more solidly his own case. The following paragraph was the original third paragraph of Justin's draft, immediately following the thesis. Read this draft version, and then note how in the revised essay, printed on pages 246–249, Justin improved this part of his argument by developing the point more thoroughly in two paragraphs and by placing them toward the end of the paper.

> Not to allow same-sex marriage is clearly discriminatory. The Human Rights Act of 1977 in the District of Columbia "prohibits discrimination based on sexual orientation. According to the Act, 'every individual shall have an equal opportunity to participate in the economic, cultural, and intellectual life of the District and have an *equal opportunity to participate in all aspects of life*'" (Dean 112). If politicians are going to make such laws, they need to recognize all their implications and follow them. Not allowing homosexuals to marry is denying the right to "participate" in an aspect of life that is important to every couple that has found love in each other. Also, the Constitution guarantees equality to every man and woman; that means nondiscrimination, something that is not happening for gays and lesbians in the present.

Reading Your Own Writing Critically

As we explained in Chapter 2, to be a critical reader of arguments means to be an analytical reader. In that chapter, we made suggestions for reading any argument; here we focus on what to look for in reading your own writing critically.

Read with an Eye to Structure   Remember, different parts of an argument perform different jobs. Read to see if you can divide your draft easily into its strategic parts, and be sure you can identify what role each group of paragraphs plays in the overall picture. The draft should reflect your brief, or you should be able to create a new brief from what you have written. If you have trouble identifying the working parts and the way they fit together, you need to see where points overlap, where you repeat yourself, or what distant parts actually belong together. This may be the time for scissors and tape, or electronic cutting and pasting if you are working at a computer.

Read with an Eye to Rhetorical Context   You may need to revise to make the rhetorical context clearer: Why are you writing, with what aim, and to whom? You establish this reader awareness in the introduction, and so you need to think about your readers' values and beliefs as well as any obvious personal data that might help explain their position on the issue—age, gender, race, occupation, economic status, and so on. You may need to revise your introduction now, finding a way to interest your readers in what you have to say. The more specific you can make your opening, the more likely you are to succeed.

Inquire into Your Own Writing Have a dialogue with yourself about your own writing. Some of the questions that we listed on pages 177–178 will be useful here:

1. Ask what you mean by the words that are central to the argument. Have you provided definitions when they are needed?
2. Find the reasons, and note their relation to the thesis. Be able to state the connection, ideally, with the word "because": *thesis* because *reason.*
3. Be able to state what assumptions lie behind your thesis and any of your reasons. Ask yourself, What else would someone have to believe to accept this as valid? If your audience is unlikely to share the assumption, then you must add an argument for it—or change your thesis.
4. Look at your comparisons and analogies. Are they persuasive?
5. Look at your evidence. Have you offered facts, expert opinion, illustrations, and so on? Have you presented these in a way that would not raise doubts but eliminate them?
6. Consider your own bias. What do you stand to gain from advocating the position you take? Is your argument self-serving or truth-serving?

Getting Feedback from Other Readers

Because it is hard to be objective about your own work, getting a reading from a friend, classmate, teacher, or family member is a good way to see where revision would help. An unfocused reading, however, usually isn't critical enough; casual readers may applaud the draft too readily if they agree with the thesis and condemn it if they disagree. Therefore, ask your readers to use a revision checklist, such as the one outlined in the "Reader's Checklist for Revision" on page 245.

Following Through

1. After you have written a draft of your own argument, revise it using the suggestions in the preceding section. Then exchange your revised draft for a classmate's, and use the "Reader's Checklist for Revision" to guide you in making suggestions for each other's drafts.
2. Read the final version of Justin Spidel's argument on pages 246–249. Then apply the questions for inquiry listed on pages 177–178 to inquire into the case presented in his argument.
3. You may or may not agree with Justin Spidel's views on same-sex marriage; however, if you were assigned to suggest ways to improve his written argument, what would you advise him to do? Reread his audience profile (page 224), and use the "Reader's Checklist for Revision" to help you decide how his presentation could be improved.

1. Be sure you understand the writer's intended audience, by either discussing it with the writer or reading any notes the writer has provided. Then read through the entire draft. It is helpful to number the paragraphs so you can refer to them by number later.
2. If you can find an explicit statement of the author's thesis, underline or highlight it. If you cannot find one, ask yourself whether it is necessary that the thesis be stated explicitly, or could any reader infer it easily? If the thesis is easily inferred, restate it in your own words at the top of the first page of the draft.
3. Think about how the thesis could be improved. Is it offensive, vague, too general? Does it have a single focus? Is it clearly stated? Suggest more concrete diction, if possible.
4. Circle the key terms of the thesis—that is, the words most central to the point. Could there be disagreement about the meaning of any of these terms? If so, has the author clarified what he or she means by these terms?
5. Look for the structure and strategy of the argument. Underline or highlight the sentences that most clearly present the reasons, and write "Reason 1," Reason 2," and so forth in the margin. If identifying the reasons is not easy, indicate this problem to the author. Also think about whether the author has arranged the reasons in the best order. Make suggestions for improvement.
6. Identify the author's best reason. Why would it appeal to the audience? Has the author placed it strategically in the best position for making his or her case?
7. Look for any weak parts in the argument. What reasons need more or better support? Next to any weakly supported reasons, write questions to let the author know what factual information seems lacking, what sources don't seem solid or credible, what statements sound too general, or what reasoning—such as analogies—seems shaky. Are there any reasons for which more research is in order?
8. Ask whether the author shows an awareness of opposing arguments. Where? If not, should this be added? Even if you agree with the argument, take the viewpoint of a member of the opposition: What are the best challenges you can make to anything the author has said?
9. Evaluate the introduction and conclusion.

Editing and Proofreading

The final steps of writing any argument are editing and proofreading, which we discuss in the appendix.

STUDENT SAMPLE: *An Essay Arguing to Convince*

WHO SHOULD HAVE THE RIGHT TO MARRY?

Justin Spidel

When two people fall deeply in love, they want to share every part of their lives with each other. For some, that could mean making a commitment, living together, and maybe having children together. But most people in love want more than that; they want to make their commitment public and legal through the ceremony of marriage, a tradition thousands of years old that has been part of almost every culture.

But not everyone has the right to make that commitment. In this country and in most others, gays and lesbians are denied the right to marry. According to many citizens and politicians, allowing them the right to marry would destroy the institution and threaten traditional family values. Nevertheless, "advances in gay and lesbian civil rights [are] bringing awareness and newfound determination to many," and hundreds of same-sex couples are celebrating their commitment to each other in religious ceremonies (Ayers 6). These couples would like to make their unions legal, and we should not prohibit them. Everyone, gay and straight, will benefit from extending the basic human right of marriage to all couples, regardless of sexual orientation.

In contrast to many critics' arguments, allowing gays and lesbians to marry actually promotes family values because it encourages monogamy and gives children a two-parent home. As Jonathan Rauch, a gay writer, explains, marriage stabilizes relationships:

> One of the main benefits of publicly recognized marriage is that it binds couples together not only in their own eyes but also in the eyes of society at large. Around the partners is woven a web of expectations that they will spend nights together, go to parties together, take out mortgages together, buy furniture at Ikea together, and so on—all of which helps tie them together and keep them off the streets and at home. (23)

Some people would say that gays and lesbians can have these things without marriage simply by living together, but if you argue that marriage is not necessary for commitment, you are saying marriage is not necessary for heterosexuals either. Many people think it is immoral to live together and not have the legal bond of marriage. If gays and lesbians could marry, they would be "morally correct" according to this viewpoint. Craig Dean, a Washington, D.C., lawyer and activist for gay marriage, says that it is "paradoxical that mainstream America stereotypes Gays and Lesbians as unable to maintain long-term relationships, while at the same time denying them the very institutions to stabilize such relationships" (114).

Furthermore, many homosexual couples have children from previous marriages or by adoption. According to a study by the American Bar Association, gay and lesbian families with children make up six percent of the population in the United States (Dean 114). A secure environment is very important for raising children, and allowing same-sex couples to marry would promote these children having two parents, not just one. It would also send these children the positive message that marriage is the foundation for family life. As Andrew Sullivan, a senior editor of *The New Republic,* asks, why should gays be denied the very same family values that many politicians are arguing everyone else should have? Why should their children be denied these values? *Newsweek* writer Eloise Salholz describes a paradox: If "more and more homosexual pairs are becoming parents [. . .] but cannot marry, what kind of bastardized definition of family is society imposing on their offspring?"

Also, binding people together in marriage benefits society because marriage provides a system for people to take care of each other. Marriage means that individuals are not a complete burden on society when they become sick, injured, old, or unemployed. Jonathan Rauch argues, "If marriage has any meaning at all, it is that when you collapse from a stroke, there will be at least one other person whose 'job' it is to drop everything and come to your aid" (22). Rauch's point is that this benefit of marriage would result from gay marriages as well as straight and in fact may be even more important for homosexuals and lesbians because their relationships with parents and other relatives may be strained, and they are also less likely than heterosexuals to have children to take care of them in their old age. Same-sex couples already show such devotion to each other; it's just that the public recognition of legal marriage helps keep all spouses together through hard times.

In spite of these benefits, many people say that same-sex marriage should not be allowed because it would upset our society's conventional definition of marriage as a bond between people of opposite sexes. As William Bennett has written, letting people of the same sex marry "would obscure marriage's enormously consequential function—procreation and childrearing." Procreation may be a consequence of marriage, but it is not the main reason anymore that people get married. Today "even for heterosexuals, marriage is becoming an emotional union and commitment rather than an arrangement to produce and protect children" ("Marriage" 770). And what about heterosexual couples who are sterile? No one would say that they should not be allowed to marry. If the right to marry is based on the possibility of having children, "then a post-menopausal woman who applies for a marriage license should be turned away at the courthouse door" (Rauch 22). No one would seriously expect every couple who gets married to prove that they are capable of having children and intend to do so. That would be a clear violation of their individual rights.

In the same way, to outlaw same-sex marriage is clearly discriminatory. According to Craig Dean, "Marriage is an important civil right because it gives societal recognition and legal protection to a relationship and confers numerous benefits to spouses" (112). Denying same-sex marriage means that gays and lesbians cannot enjoy material benefits such as health insurance through a spouse's employer, life insurance benefits, tax preferences, leaves for bereavement, and inheritance. In some states, laws about domestic partnership give same-sex couples some of these rights, but they are never guaranteed as they would be if the couple were legally next of kin. Thomas Stoddard, a lawyer, says that domestic partnership is the equivalent of "second-class citizenship" (qtd. in Salholz).

Aside from these concrete types of discrimination, denying same-sex marriage keeps gay and lesbian citizens from enjoying the basic human right to "life, liberty, and the pursuit of happiness." The Human Rights Act of 1977 in the District of Columbia makes one of the strongest stands against discrimination based on sexual orientation. According to the Act, "every individual shall have an equal opportunity to participate in the economic, cultural, and intellectual life of the District and have an equal opportunity to participate in all aspects of life" (qtd. in Dean 113). Not allowing homosexuals to marry does deny them the right to "participate" in an aspect of life that is important to almost every couple that has found love in each other. The Hawaii Supreme Court ruled in 1993 that the ban on gay marriage is probably in violation of the Constitution (Salholz).

Of course, many churches will never agree to perform these marriages because they believe that homosexuality is a sin. It is possible to debate the interpretations of the Bible passages that these people cite as evidence, and many religious leaders do. The separation of church and state allows all churches to follow their own doctrines, and many things that are legal in this country are disapproved of by some churches. My point is that the government should not deny the *legal* right to marry in relationships where couples want to express their love toward each other.

It's only natural for people in love to want to commit to each other; this desire is the same for homosexuals and lesbians as it is for heterosexuals. One recent survey showed that "over half of all lesbians and almost 40% of gay men" live in committed relationships and share a house together (Ayers 5). As Sullivan, who is gay, explains, "At some point in our lives, some of us are lucky enough to meet the person we truly love. And we want to commit to that person in front of family and country for the rest of our lives. It's the most simple, the most natural, the most human instinct in the world. How could anyone seek to oppose that?" And what does anyone gain when that right is denied? That's a question that everyone needs to ask themselves.

Works Cited

Ayers, Tess, and Paul Brown. The Essential Guide to Lesbian and Gay Weddings. San Francisco: Harper, 1994.

Bennett, William, "Leave Marriage Alone." Newsweek 3 June 1996: 27.

Dean, Craig R. "Gay Marriage: A Civil Right." The Journal of Homosexuality 27.3–4 (1994): 111–15.

"Marriage." <u>The Encyclopedia of Homosexuality</u>. Ed. Wayne R. Dynes. New York: Garland, 1990.

Rauch, Jonathan. "For Better or Worse?" <u>The New Republic</u> 6 May 1996: 18–23.

Salholz, Eloise. "For Better or For Worse." <u>Newsweek</u> 24 May 1993: 69.

Sullivan, Andrew. "Let Gays Marry." <u>Newsweek</u> 3 June 1996: 26.

Chapter 8

Motivating Action: Arguing to Persuade

In Chapter 1, we defined persuasion as "convincing *plus*" because, in addition to reason, three forms of appeal are required for persuasion: (1) appeal to the writer's character, (2) appeal to the emotions of the audience, and (3) appeal to style, the artful use of language itself. Building on what you learned about making cases in Chapter 7, this chapter's goal is to help you understand and control this wider range of appeals.

But shouldn't reason be enough? Perhaps it would be if human beings were completely rational creatures. But human beings are only sometimes rational—and even then imperfectly. We often agree with an argument but lack the courage or motivation to translate our assent into action.

Persuasion, then, aims to close the gap between assent and action. Because persuasion seeks a deeper and stronger commitment from readers, it appeals to the whole person, to our full humanity, not just to the mind. It offers reasons, of course, because people respond to good reasons. But it also encourages the reader to identify with the writer, to respond not only to the quality of an argument but also to the quality of the arguer. In addition, the persuader wants to stir the reader's emotions because strong feelings prompt the will to act; persuasion works on the heart as much as on the mind. Finally, style matters in persuasion because the response to what is said depends on how well it is said. (See the Concept Close-Up box on page 252.)

WHEN TO CONVINCE AND WHEN TO PERSUADE: A MATTER OF EMPHASIS

When should you aim to persuade rather than to convince? Always notice what an academic assignment calls for because the full range of persuasive appeal is not always appropriate for written arguments in college. In general, the more academic the audience or the more purely intellectual the issue, the

Concept Close-Up
The Four Forms of Appeal

Form	Function	Presence in Text
Reason	Logical cogency	Your case; any supported contention
Character	Personal appeal	Indications of author's status and values
Emotion	Appeals to feelings	Concrete descriptions, moving images
Style	Appeals through language	Word choice, sentence structure, metaphor

Essentially, persuasion differs from convincing in that it wants action, not just agreement; it seeks to integrate rational appeal with the full range of resources for influencing people.

less appropriate it is to appeal to the whole person. Often, philosophy or science papers require you to convince, but rarely will they require you to persuade. For those papers, you should confine yourself primarily to thesis, reasons, and evidence.

But when you are working with public issues, with matters of policy or questions of right and wrong, persuasion's fuller range of appeal is usually appropriate because such topics address a broader readership and involve a more inclusive community. Arguments in these areas affect not just how we think but also how we act, and the heightened urgency of persuasion goes further to spark action or change.

Convincing primarily requires that we control case making. But persuasion asks us to make conscious decisions about three other appeals as well: (1) We must gain our readers' confidence and respect through the deliberate projection of our good character; (2) We must touch our readers' emotions; and (3) We must focus on language itself as a means of affecting people's thoughts and behavior. The writer who aims to persuade integrates these other forms of appeal with a well-made case, deliberately crafting the essay so that they all work together.

As with convincing, writing a persuasive argument begins with inquiry and research — a patient search for the truth as preparation for earning a claim to truth. However, before you can move from a general idea of your own position to a specific thesis, you must think about the audience you seek to persuade.

ANALYZING YOUR READERS

Persuasion begins with difference and, when it works, ends with identity. That is, we expect that before reading our argument, our readers will differ from us not only in beliefs but also in attitudes and desires. A successful persuasive argument brings readers and writer together; it creates a sense of connection between parties who were previously separate in viewpoint. But what means can we use to overcome difference and create a sense of identity? First, we need to focus on our readers and attempt to understand their frames of mind by asking certain key questions.

Who Is the Audience, and How Do They View the Topic?

The first step is to identify possible appeals to your readership. Keep in mind that good persuaders are able to empathize and sympathize with other people, building bridges of commonality and solidarity. To aid your audience analysis, ask these questions:

- Who are my readers? How do I define them in terms of age, economic and social class, gender, education, and so forth?
- What typical attitudes or stances toward my topic do they have?
- What in their background or daily experiences helps explain their point of view?
- What are they likely to know about my topic?
- How might they be uninformed or misinformed about it?
- How would they like to see the problem, question, or issue resolved, answered, or handled? Why? That is, what personal stake do they have in the topic?
- In what larger framework—religious, ethical, political, economic— do they place my topic? That is, what general beliefs and values are involved?

What Are Our Differences?

Audience analysis is not complete until you can specify exactly what divides you from your readers. Sometimes specifying difference is difficult to do before formulating a detailed case; understanding exactly what divides you from your readers comes later, at the point of the first draft. But as soon as you can, you must clarify differences; knowing exactly what separates you from your readers tells you what to emphasize in making your case and in choosing other strategies of appeal. These questions can help:

- Is the difference a matter of assumptions? If so, how can I shake my readers' confidence in their assumptions and offer another set of assumptions favorable to my position?
- Is the difference a matter of principle, the application of general rules to specific cases? If so, should I dispute the principle itself and offer a competing one the audience will also value? Or should I show why the principle should not apply in some specific instance relevant to my case?
- Is the difference a matter of a hierarchy of values—that is, do we value the same things but to different degrees? If so, how might I restructure my readers' values?
- Is the difference a matter of ends or of means? If ends, how can I show that my vision of what ought to be is better or that realizing

my ends will also secure the ends my readers value? If a difference of means, how can I show that my methods are justified and effective, more likely to bear fruit than others?

- Is the difference a matter of interpretation? If so, how can I shake my readers' confidence in the traditional or common interpretation of something and show them that my interpretation is better, that it accounts more adequately for the facts?
- Is the difference a matter of implications or consequences? If so, how can I convince my readers that what they fear may happen will not happen, or that it will not be as bad as they think, or that other implications or consequences outweigh any negatives?

What Do We Have in Common?

In seeking to define the common ground you and your readers share, the key point to remember is that no matter how sharp the disagreements that divide you from those you hope to persuade, resources for identification always exist. Ask these sorts of questions:

- Do we have a shared local identity — as members of the same organization, for example, or as students at the same university?
- Do we share a more abstract, collective identity — as citizens of the same region or nation, as worshippers in the same religion, and so forth?
- Do we share a common cause — such as promoting the good of the community, preventing child abuse, or overcoming racial prejudice?
- Is there a shared experience or human activity — raising children, caring for aging parents, helping a friend in distress, struggling to make ends meet?
- Can we connect through a well-known event or cultural happening — a popular movie, a best-selling book, something in the news that would interest both you and your readers?
- Is there a historical event, person, or document that we both respect?

READING A PERSUASIVE ESSAY

To illustrate the importance of audience analysis, we turn to a classic essay of the twentieth century, Martin Luther King's "Letter from Birmingham Jail," a brilliant example of the art of persuasion. As we will see, King masterfully analyzed his audience and used the full range of appeals to suit that particular readership.

Background

To appreciate King's persuasive powers, we must first understand the events that led up to the "Letter" and also the actions King wanted to move his readers to take. In 1963, as president of the Southern Christian Leadership Con-

Concept Close-Up
Audience Analysis

To understand any audience we hope to persuade, we must know *both* what separates us from them *and* what common ground we share.

We may **differ** from our audience in:

Kind of Difference	Example
Assumptions	Western writers assume that separation of church and state is normal; some Muslim audiences do not make the distinction.
Principles	Most conservative writers believe in the principle of the open market; labor audiences often believe in protecting American jobs from foreign competition.
Value rankings	Some writers value personal freedom over duty and obligation; some audiences place duty and obligation above personal freedom.
Ends and means	Writer and audience may agree about purpose (for example, making America safe from terrorism) but disagree about what policies will best accomplish this end.
Interpretation	Some writers understood the September 11, 2001, attack as an act of war; some audiences saw it as a criminal act that demanded legal rather than military measures.
Consequences	Some writers think making divorce harder would keep more couples together; some audiences think it would only promote individual unhappiness.

We may **share** with our audience:

Kind of Identification	Example
Local identity	Students and teachers at the same university
Collective identity	Citizens of the same state or the same nation
Common cause	Improving the environment
Common experience	Pride in the success of American Olympic athletes
Common history	Respect for soldiers that have died defending the United States

Essentially, we must understand differences to discover how we need to argue; we must use the resources of identification to overcome differences separating us from our readers.

ference, a civil rights organization dedicated to nonviolent social change, King had been organizing and participating in demonstrations in Birmingham, Alabama. He was arrested, and while he was in jail, eight white Alabama clergymen of various denominations issued a public statement reacting to his activities. Published in a local newspaper, the statement deplored the illegal demonstrations of King and his organization as "unwise and untimely":

> We the undersigned clergymen are among those who, in January, issued "An Appeal for Law and Order and Common Sense," in dealing with racial problems in Alabama. We expressed understanding that honest convictions in racial

Figure 8.1   Rosa Parks, whose refusal to move to the back of a bus touched off the Montgomery bus boycott and the beginning of the civil rights movement, is fingerprinted by Deputy Sheriff D. H. Lackey in Montgomery, Alabama, February 22, 1956. She was among some 100 people charged with violating segregation laws. (AP Photo/Gene Herrick)

matters could properly be pursued in the courts, but urged that decisions of those courts should in the meantime be peacefully obeyed.

Since that time there had been some evidence of increased forbearance and a willingness to face facts. Responsible citizens have undertaken to work on various problems which cause racial friction and unrest. In Birmingham, recent public events have given indication that we all have opportunity for a new constructive and realistic approach to racial problems.

However, we are now confronted by a series of demonstrations by some of our Negro citizens, directed and led in part by outsiders. We recognize the natural impatience of people who feel that their hopes are slow in being realized. But we are convinced that these demonstrations are unwise and untimely.

We agree rather with certain local Negro leadership which has called for honest and open negotiation of racial issues in our area. And we believe this kind of facing of issues can best be accomplished by citizens of our own metropolitan area, white and Negro, meeting with their knowledge and experience of the local situation. All of us need to face that responsibility and find proper channels for its accomplishment.

Just as we formerly pointed out that "hatred and violence have no sanction in our religious and political traditions," we also point out that such actions as incite to hatred and violence, however technically peaceful those actions may be, have not contributed to the resolution of our local problems. We do not believe that these days of new hope are days when extreme measures are justified in Birmingham.

We commend the community as a whole, and the local news media and law enforcement officials in particular, on the calm manner in which these demonstrations have been handled. We urge the public to continue to show restraint should the demonstrations continue, and the law enforcement officials to remain calm and continue to protect our city from violence.

We further strongly urge our own Negro community to withdraw support from these demonstrations, and to unite locally in working peacefully for a better Birmingham. When rights are consistently denied, a cause should be pressed in the courts and in negotiations among local leaders, and not in the streets. We appeal to both our white and Negro citizenry to observe the principles of law and order and common sense.

Signed by:

C. C. J. Carpenter, D.D., LL.D., *Bishop of Alabama*

Joseph A. Durick, D.D., *Auxiliary Bishop, Diocese of Mobile, Birmingham*

Rabbi Milton L. Grafman, *Temple Emanu-El, Birmingham, Alabama*

Bishop Paul Hardin, *Bishop of the Alabama-West Florida Conference of the Methodist Church*

Bishop Nolan B. Harmon, *Bishop of the North Alabama Conference of the Methodist Church*

George M. Murray, D.D., LL.D., *Bishop Coadjutor, Episcopal Diocese of Alabama*

Edward V. Ramage, *Moderator, Synod of the Alabama Presbyterian Church in the United States*

Earl Stallings, *Pastor, First Baptist Church, Birmingham, Alabama*

In his cell, King began his letter on the margins of that newspaper page, addressing it specifically to the eight clergymen in the hope that he could move them from disapproval to support, from inaction to a recognition of the necessity of the demonstrations. As a public figure, King knew that his letter would reach a larger audience, including the demonstrators themselves, who were galvanized by its message when 50,000 copies were later distributed by his supporters. In the years since, King's letter has often been published, reaching a global audience with its argument for civil disobedience in the service of a higher moral law.

The Basic Message

King's letter is long; he even apologizes to his readers for having written so much. Its length is not due to its basic message, however, but to its persuasive appeals—to the way the main points are made. Before turning to King's "Letter from Birmingham Jail," read the following summary, which differs as greatly from King's prose as a nursery song differs from a Beethoven symphony.

Because I am the leader of an organization that fights injustice, it is most appropriate for me to be in Birmingham, where human rights are being violated. Our campaign of nonviolent civil disobedience was not rash and unpremeditated but the result of a history of failed negotiations and broken promises. We aim to increase tensions here until the city leaders realize that dialogue must occur. Our actions are not untimely but long overdue, given that blacks have been denied their civil rights in this country for over 340 years.

While we advocate breaking some laws, we distinguish between moral laws and immoral laws that degrade the human personality. The former must be obeyed, the latter disobeyed openly and lovingly. We may be extremists, but people who accomplish great things are often so labeled, and our nonviolent protests are preferable to inaction.

In failing to support us, white Southern religious leaders such as yourselves fail to meet the challenges of social injustice. You should not praise the police for their work at breaking up the demonstrations but rather praise the demonstrators for standing up for their human dignity.

Letter from Birmingham Jail
Martin Luther King, Jr.

April 16, 1963

My Dear Fellow Clergymen:

While confined here in the Birmingham city jail, I came across your recent statement calling my present activities "unwise and untimely." Seldom do I pause to answer criticism of my work and ideas. If I sought to answer all the criticisms that cross my desk, my secretaries would have little time for anything other than such correspondence in the course of the day, and I would have no time for constructive work. But since I feel that you are men of genuine good will and that your criticisms are sincerely set forth, I want to try to answer your statement in what I hope will be patient and reasonable terms.

I think I should indicate why I am here in Birmingham, since you have been influenced by the view which argues against "outsiders coming in." I have the honor of serving as president of the Southern Christian Leadership

Conference, an organization operating in every southern state, with head-quarters in Atlanta, Georgia. We have some eighty-five affiliated organizations across the South, and one of them is the Alabama Christian Movement for Human Rights. Frequently we share staff, educational, and financial resources with our affiliates. Several months ago the affiliate here in Birmingham asked us to be on call to engage in a nonviolent direct-action program if such were deemed necessary. We readily consented, and when the hour came we lived up to our promise. So I, along with several members of my staff, am here because I was invited here. I am here because I have organizational ties here.

But more basically, I am in Birmingham because injustice is here. Just as the prophets of the eighth century B.C. left their villages and carried their "thus saith the Lord" far beyond the boundaries of their home towns, and just as the Apostle Paul left his village of Tarsus and carried the gospel of Jesus Christ to the far corners of the Greco-Roman world, so am I compelled to carry the gospel of freedom beyond my own home town. Like Paul, I must constantly respond to the Macedonian call for aid.

Moreover, I am cognizant of the interrelatedness of all communities and states. I cannot sit idly by in Atlanta and not be concerned about what happens in Birmingham. Injustice anywhere is a threat to justice everywhere. We are caught in an inescapable network of mutuality, tied in a single garment of destiny. Whatever affects one directly, affects all indirectly. Never again can we afford to live with the narrow, provincial "outside agitator" idea. Anyone who lives inside the United States can never be considered an outsider anywhere within its bounds.

You deplore the demonstrations taking place in Birmingham. But your statement, I am sorry to say, fails to express a similar concern for the conditions that brought about the demonstrations. I am sure that none of you would want to rest content with the superficial kind of social analysis that deals merely with effects and does not grapple with underlying causes. It is unfortunate that demonstrations are taking place in Birmingham, but it is even more unfortunate that the city's white power structure left the Negro community with no alternative.

In any nonviolent campaign there are four basic steps: collection of the facts to determine whether injustices exist; negotiation; self-purification; and direct action. We have gone through all these steps in Birmingham. There can be no gainsaying the fact that racial injustice engulfs this community. Birmingham is probably the most thoroughly segregated city in the United States. Its ugly record of brutality is widely known. Negroes have experienced grossly unjust treatment in the courts. There have been more unsolved bombings of Negro homes and churches in Birmingham than in any other city in the nation. These are the hard, brutal facts of the case. On the basis of these conditions, Negro leaders sought to negotiate with the city fathers. But the latter consistently refused to engage in good-faith negotiation.

Then, last September, came the opportunity to talk with leaders of Birmingham's economic community. In the course of the negotiations, certain promises were made by the merchants—for example, to remove the stores' humiliating racial signs. On the basis of these promises, the Reverend Fred Shuttlesworth and the leaders of the Alabama Christian Movement for Human Rights agreed to a moratorium on all demonstrations. As the weeks and months went by, we realized that we were the victims of a broken promise. A few signs, briefly removed, returned; the others remained.

As in so many past experiences, our hopes had been blasted, and the shadow of deep disappointment settled upon us. We had no alternative except to prepare for direct action, whereby we would present our very bodies as a means of laying our case before the conscience of the local and the national community. Mindful of the difficulties involved, we decided to undertake a process of self-purification. We began a series of workshops on nonviolence, and we repeatedly asked ourselves: "Are you able to accept blows without retaliating?" "Are you able to endure the ordeal of jail?" We decided to schedule our direct-action program for the Easter season, realizing that except for Christmas, this is the main shopping period of the year. Knowing that a strong economic-withdrawal program would be the byproduct of direct action, we felt that this would be the best time to bring pressure to bear on the merchants for the needed change.

Then it occurred to us that Birmingham's mayoral election was coming up in March, and we speedily decided to postpone action until after election day. When we discovered that the Commissioner of Public Safety, Eugene "Bull" Connor, had piled up enough votes to be in the run-off, we decided again to postpone action until the day after the run-off so that the demonstrations could not be used to cloud the issues. Like many others, we waited to see Mr. Connor defeated, and to this end we endured postponement after postponement. Having aided in this community need, we felt that our direct-action program could be delayed no longer.

You may well ask: "Why direct action? Why sit-ins, marches and so forth? Isn't negotiation a better path?" You are quite right in calling for negotiation. Indeed, this is the very purpose of direct action. Nonviolent direct action seeks to create such a crisis and foster such a tension that a community which has constantly refused to negotiate is forced to confront the issue. It seeks so to dramatize the issue that it can no longer be ignored. My citing the creation of tension as part of the work of the nonviolent-resister may sound rather shocking. But I must confess that I am not afraid of the word "tension." I have earnestly opposed violent tension, but there is a type of constructive, nonviolent tension which is necessary for growth. Just as Socrates felt that it was necessary to create a tension in the mind so that individuals could rise from the bondage of myths and half-truths to the unfettered realm of creative analysis and objective appraisal, so must we see the need for nonviolent gadflies to create the kind of tension in society that will help men rise from the dark depths of prejudice and racism to the majestic heights of understanding and brotherhood.

10

The purpose of our direct-action program is to create a situation so crisis-packed that it will inevitably open the door to negotiation. I therefore concur with you in your call for negotiation. Too long has our beloved Southland been bogged down in a tragic effort to live in monologue rather than dialogue.

One of the basic points in your statement is that the action that I and my associates have taken in Birmingham is untimely. Some have asked: "Why didn't you give the new city administration time to act?" The only answer that I can give to this query is that the new Birmingham administration must be prodded about as much as the outgoing one, before it will act. We are sadly mistaken if we feel that the election of Albert Boutwell as mayor will bring the millennium to Birmingham. While Mr. Boutwell is a much more gentle person than Mr. Connor, they are both segregationists, dedicated to maintenance of the status quo. I have hope that Mr. Boutwell will be reasonable enough to see the futility of massive resistance to desegregation. But he will not see this without pressure from devotees of civil rights. My friends, I must say to you that we have not made a single gain in civil rights without determined legal and nonviolent pressure. Lamentably, it is an historical fact that privileged groups seldom give up their privileges voluntarily. Individuals may see the moral light and voluntarily give up their unjust posture; but, as Reinhold Niebuhr has reminded us, groups tend to be more immoral than individuals.

We know through painful experience that freedom is never voluntarily given by the oppressor; it must be demanded by the oppressed. Frankly, I have yet to engage in a direct-action campaign that was "well timed" in the view of those who have not suffered unduly from the disease of segregation. For years now I have heard the word "Wait!" It rings in the ear of every Negro with piercing familiarity. This "Wait" has almost always meant "Never." We must come to see, with one of our distinguished jurists, that "justice too long delayed is justice denied."

We have waited for more than 340 years for our constitutional God-given rights. The nations of Asia and Africa are moving with jetlike speed toward gaining political independence, but we still creep at horse-and-buggy pace toward gaining a cup of coffee at a lunch counter. Perhaps it is easy for those who have never felt the stinging darts of segregation to say, "Wait." But when you have seen vicious mobs lynch your mothers and fathers at will and drown your sisters and brothers at whim; when you have seen hate-filled policemen curse, kick, and even kill your black brothers and sisters; when you see the vast majority of your twenty million Negro brothers smothering in an airtight cage of poverty in the midst of an affluent society; when you suddenly find your tongue twisted and your speech stammering as you seek to explain to your six-year-old daughter why she can't go to the public amusement park that has just been advertised on television, and see tears welling up in her eyes when she is told that Funtown is closed to colored children, and see ominous clouds of inferiority beginning to form in her little mental sky, and see her beginning to distort her personality by developing an unconscious bitterness toward white people; when you have to concoct an answer for a five-year-old son who is asking: "Daddy, why do white people treat colored people so mean?"; when you take a cross-country drive and find it necessary to sleep night after night in the uncomfortable corners of your automobile because no motel will accept you; when you are humiliated day in and day out by nagging signs reading "white" and "colored"; when your first name becomes "nigger," your middle name becomes "boy" (however old you are), and your last name becomes "John," and your wife and mother are never given the respected title "Mrs."; when you are harried by day and haunted by night by the fact that you are a Negro, living constantly at tiptoe stance, never quite knowing what to expect next, and are plagued with inner fears and outer resentments; when you are forever fighting a degenerating sense of "nobodiness"—then you will understand why we find it difficult to wait. There comes a time when the cup of endurance runs over, and men are no longer willing to be plunged into the abyss of despair. I hope, sirs, you can understand our legitimate and unavoidable impatience.

You express a great deal of anxiety over our willingness to break laws. 15 This is certainly a legitimate concern. Since we so diligently urge people to obey the Supreme Court's decision of 1954 outlawing segregation in the public schools, at first glance it may seem rather paradoxical for us consciously to break laws. One may well ask: "How can you advocate breaking some laws and obeying others?" The answer lies in the fact that there are two types of laws: just and unjust. I would be the first to advocate obeying just laws. One has not only a legal but a moral responsibility to obey just laws. Conversely, one has a moral responsibility to disobey unjust laws. I would agree with St. Augustine that "an unjust law is no law at all."

Now, what is the difference between the two? How does one determine whether a law is just or unjust? A just law is a man-made code that squares with the moral law or the law of God. An unjust law is a code that is out of harmony with the moral law. To put it in the terms of St. Thomas Aquinas: An unjust law is a human law that is not rooted in eternal law and natural law. Any law that uplifts human personality is just. Any law that degrades human personality is unjust. All segregation statutes are unjust because segregation distorts the soul and damages the personality. It gives the segregator a false sense of superiority and the segregated a false sense of inferiority. Segregation, to use the terminology of the Jewish philosopher Martin Buber, substitutes an "I–it" relationship for an "I–thou" relationship and ends up relegating persons to the status of things. Hence, segregation is not only politically, economically, and sociologically unsound, it is morally wrong and sinful. Paul Tillich has said that sin is separation. Is not segregation an existential expression of man's tragic separation, his awful estrangement, his terrible sinfulness? Thus it is that I can urge men to obey the 1954 decision of the Supreme Court, for it is morally right; and I can urge them to disobey segregation ordinances, for they are morally wrong.

Let us consider a more concrete example of just and unjust laws. An unjust law is a code that a numerical or power majority group compels a minority group to obey but does not make binding on itself. This is *difference* made legal. By the same token, a just law is a code that a majority compels a minority to follow and that it is willing to follow itself. This is *sameness* made legal.

Let me give another explanation. A law is unjust if it is inflicted on a minority that, as a result of being denied the right to vote, had no part in enacting or devising the law. Who can say that the legislature of Alabama which set up that state's segregation laws was democratically elected? Throughout Alabama all sorts of devious methods are used to prevent Negroes from becoming registered voters, and there are some counties in which, even though Negroes constitute a majority of the population, not a single Negro is registered. Can any law enacted under such circumstances be considered democratically structured?

Sometimes a law is just on its face and unjust in its application. For instance, I have been arrested on a charge of parading without a permit. Now, there is nothing wrong in having an ordinance which requires a permit for a parade. But such an ordinance becomes unjust when it is used to maintain segregation and to deny citizens the First-Amendment privilege of peaceful assembly and protest.

I hope you are able to see the distinction I am trying to point out. In no sense do I advocate evading or defying the law, as would the rabid segregationist. That would lead to anarchy. One who breaks an unjust law must do so openly, lovingly, and with a willingness to accept the penalty. I submit that an individual who breaks a law that conscience tells him is unjust, and who willingly accepts the penalty of imprisonment in order to arouse the conscience of the community over its injustice, is in reality expressing the highest respect for law.

Of course, there is nothing new about this kind of civil disobedience. It was evidenced sublimely in the refusal of Shadrach, Meshach, and Abednego to obey the laws of Nebuchadnezzar, on the ground that a higher moral law was at stake. It was practiced superbly by the early Christians, who were willing to face hungry lions and the excruciating pain of chopping blocks rather than submit to certain unjust laws of the Roman Empire. To a degree, academic freedom is a reality today because Socrates practiced civil disobedience. In our own nation, the Boston Tea Party represented a massive act of civil disobedience.

We should never forget that everything Adolf Hitler did in Germany was "legal" and everything the Hungarian freedom fighters did in Hungary was "illegal." It was "illegal" to aid and comfort a Jew in Hitler's Germany. Even so, I am sure that, had I lived in Germany at the time, I would have aided and comforted my Jewish brothers. If today I lived in a Communist country where certain principles dear to the Christian faith are suppressed, I would openly advocate disobeying that country's antireligious laws.

20

I must make two honest confessions to you, my Christian and Jewish brothers. First, I must confess that over the past few years I have been gravely disappointed with the white moderate. I have almost reached the regrettable conclusion that the Negro's great stumbling block in his stride toward freedom is not the White Citizen's Counciler or the Ku Klux Klanner, but the white moderate, who is more devoted to "order" than to justice; who prefers a negative peace which is the presence of tension to a positive peace which is the presence of justice; who constantly says: "I agree with you in the goal you seek, but I cannot agree with your methods of direct action"; who paternalistically believes he can set the timetable for another man's freedom; who lives by a mythical concept of time and who constantly advises the Negro to wait for a "more convenient season." Shallow understanding from people of good will is more frustrating than absolute misunderstanding from people of ill will. Lukewarm acceptance is much more bewildering than outright rejection.

I had hoped that the white moderate would understand that law and order exist for the purpose of establishing justice and that when they fail in this purpose they become the dangerously structured dams that block the flow of social progress. I had hoped that the white moderate would understand that the present tension in the South is a necessary phase of the transition from an obnoxious negative peace, in which the Negro passively accepted his unjust plight, to a substantive and positive peace, in which all men will respect the dignity and worth of human personality. Actually, we who engage in nonviolent direct action are not the creators of tension. We merely bring to the surface the hidden tension that is already alive. We bring it out in the open, where it can be seen and dealt with. Like a boil that can never be cured so long as it is covered up but must be opened with all its ugliness to the natural medicines of air and light, injustice must be exposed, with all the tension its exposure creates, to the light of human conscience and the air of national opinion before it can be cured.

In your statement you assert that our actions, even though peaceful, must be condemned because they precipitate violence. But is this a logical assertion? Isn't this like condemning a robbed man because his possession of money precipitated the evil act of robbery? Isn't this like condemning Socrates because his unswerving commitment to truth and his philosophical inquiries precipitated the act by the misguided populace in which they made him drink hemlock? Isn't this like condemning Jesus because his unique God-consciousness and never-ceasing devotion to God's will precipitated the evil act of crucifixion? We must come to see that, as the federal courts have consistently affirmed, it is wrong to urge an individual to cease his efforts to gain his basic constitutional rights because the quest may precipitate violence. Society must protect the robbed and punish the robber.

I had also hoped that the white moderate would reject the myth concerning time in relation to the struggle for freedom. I have just received a letter from a white brother in Texas. He writes: "All Christians know that

25

the colored people will receive equal rights eventually, but it is possible that you are in too great a religious hurry. It has taken Christianity almost two thousand years to accomplish what it has. The teachings of Christ take time to come to earth." Such an attitude stems from a tragic misconception of time, from the strangely irrational notion that there is something in the very flow of time that will inevitably cure all ills. Actually, time itself is neutral; it can be used either destructively or constructively. More and more I feel that the people of ill will have used time much more effectively than have the people of good will. We will have to repent in this generation not merely for the hateful words and actions of the bad people but for the appalling silence of the good people. Human progress never rolls in on wheels of inevitability; it comes through the tireless efforts of men willing to be co-workers with God, and without this hard work, time itself becomes an ally of the forces of social stagnation. We must use time creatively, in the knowledge that the time is always ripe to do right. Now is the time to make real the promise of democracy and transform our pending national elegy into a creative psalm of brotherhood. Now is the time to lift our national policy from the quicksand of racial injustice to the solid rock of human dignity.

You speak of our activity in Birmingham as extreme. At first I was rather disappointed that fellow clergymen would see my nonviolent efforts as those of an extremist. I began thinking about the fact that I stand in the middle of two opposing forces in the Negro community. One is a force of complacency, made up in part of Negroes who, as a result of long years of oppression, are so drained of self-respect and a sense of "somebodiness" that they have adjusted to segregation; and in part of a few middle-class Negroes who, because of a degree of academic and economic security and because in some ways they profit by segregation, have become insensitive to the problems of the masses. The other force is one of bitterness and hatred, and it comes perilously close to advocating violence. It is expressed in the various black nationalist groups that are springing up across the nation, the largest and best-known being Elijah Muhammad's Muslim movement. Nourished by the Negro's frustration over the continued existence of racial discrimination, this movement is made up of people who have lost faith in America, who have absolutely repudiated Christianity, and who have concluded that the white man is an incorrigible "devil."

I have tried to stand between these two forces, saying that we need emulate neither the "do-nothingism" of the complacent nor the hatred and despair of the black nationalist. For there is the more excellent way of love and nonviolent protest. I am grateful to God that, through the influence of the Negro church, the way of nonviolence became an integral part of our struggle.

If this philosophy had not emerged, by now many streets of the South would, I am convinced, be flowing with blood. And I am further convinced that if our white brothers dismiss as "rabble-rousers" and "outside agitators" those of us who employ nonviolent direct action, and if they refuse to support our nonviolent efforts, millions of the Negroes will, out of frustration and despair, seek solace and security in black-nationalist ideologies—a development that would inevitably lead to a frightening racial nightmare.

Oppressed people cannot remain oppressed forever. The yearning for freedom eventually manifests itself, and that is what has happened to the American Negro. Something within has reminded him of his birthright of freedom, and something without has reminded him that it can be gained. Consciously or unconsciously, he has been caught up by the *Zeitgeist,* and with his black brothers of Africa and his brown and yellow brothers of Asia, South America, and the Caribbean, the United States Negro is moving with a sense of great urgency toward the promised land of racial justice. If one recognizes this vital urge that has engulfed the Negro community, one should readily understand why public demonstrations are taking place. The Negro has many pent-up resentments and latent frustrations, and he must release them. So let him march; let him make prayer pilgrimages to the city hall; let him go on freedom rides—and try to understand why he must do so. If his repressed emotions are not released in nonviolent ways, they will seek expression through violence; this is not a threat but a fact of history. So I have not said to my people: "Get rid of your discontent." Rather, I have tried to say that this normal and healthy discontent can be channeled into the creative outlet of nonviolent direct action. And now this approach is being termed extremist.

But though I was initially disappointed at being categorized as an extremist, as I continued to think about the matter I gradually gained a measure of satisfaction from the label. Was not Jesus an extremist for love: "Love your enemies, bless them that curse you, do good to them that hate you, and pray for them which despitefully use you, and persecute you." Was not Amos an extremist for justice: "Let justice roll down like waters and righteousness like an ever-flowing stream." Was not Paul an extremist for the Christian gospel: "I bear in my body the marks of the Lord Jesus." Was not Martin Luther an extremist: "Here I stand; I cannot do otherwise, so help me God." And John Bunyan: "I will stay in jail to the end of my days before I make a butchery of my conscience." And Abraham Lincoln: "This nation cannot survive half slave and half free." And Thomas Jefferson: "We hold these truths to be self-evident, that all men are created equal. . . ." So the question is not whether we will be extremists, but what kind of extremists we will be. Will we be extremists for hate or for love? Will we be extremists for the preservation of injustice or for the extension of justice? In that dramatic scene on Calvary's hill three men were crucified. We must never forget that all three were crucified for the same crime—the crime of extremism. Two were extremists for immorality, and thus fell below their environment. The other, Jesus Christ, was an extremist for love, truth and goodness, and thereby rose above his environment. Perhaps the South, the nation and the world are in dire need of creative extremists.

30

I had hoped that the white moderate would see this need. Perhaps I was too optimistic; perhaps I expected too much. I suppose I should have realized that few members of the oppressor race can understand the deep groans and passionate yearnings of the oppressed race, and still fewer have the vision to see that injustice must be rooted out by strong, persistent, and determined action. I am thankful, however, that some of our white brothers in the South have grasped the meaning of this social revolution and committed themselves to it. They are still all too few in quantity, but they are big in quality. Some—such as Ralph McGill, Lillian Smith, Harry Golden, James McBride Dabbs, Ann Braden, and Sarah Patton Boyle—have written about our struggle in eloquent and prophetic terms. Others have marched with us down nameless streets of the South. They have languished in filthy, roach-infested jails, suffering the abuse and brutality of policemen who view them as "dirty nigger-lovers." Unlike so many of their moderate brothers and sisters, they have recognized the urgency of the moment and sensed the need for powerful "action" antidotes to combat the disease of segregation.

Let me take note of my other major disappointment. I have been so greatly disappointed with the white church and its leadership. Of course, there are some notable exceptions. I am not unmindful of the fact that each of you has taken some significant stands on this issue. I commend you, Reverend Stallings, for your Christian stand on this past Sunday, in welcoming Negroes to your worship service on a nonsegregated basis. I commend the Catholic leaders of this state for integrating Spring Hill College several years ago.

But despite these notable exceptions, I must honestly reiterate that I have been disappointed with the church. I do not say this as one of those negative critics who can always find something wrong with the church. I say this as a minister of the gospel, who loves the church; who was nurtured in its bosom; who has been sustained by its spiritual blessings and who will remain true to it as long as the cord of life shall lengthen.

When I was suddenly catapulted into the leadership of the bus protest   35
in Montgomery, Alabama, a few years ago, I felt we would be supported by the white church. I felt that the white ministers, priests, and rabbis of the South would be among our strongest allies. Instead, some have been outright opponents, refusing to understand the freedom movement and misrepresenting its leaders; all too many others have been more cautious than courageous and have remained silent behind the anesthetizing security of stained-glass windows.

In spite of my shattered dreams, I came to Birmingham with the hope that the white religious leadership of this community would see the justice of our cause and, with deep moral concern, would serve as the channel through which our just grievances could reach the power structure. I had hoped that each of you would understand. But again I have been disappointed.

I have heard numerous southern religious leaders admonish their worshipers to comply with a desegregation decision because it is the law, but I have longed to hear white ministers declare: "Follow this decree because integration is morally right and because the Negro is your brother." In the midst of blatant injustices inflicted upon the Negro, I have watched white churchmen stand on the sideline and mouth pious irrelevancies and sanctimonious trivialities. In the midst of a mighty struggle to rid our nation of racial and economic injustice, I have heard many ministers say: "Those are social issues, with which the gospel has no real concern." And I have watched many churches commit themselves to a completely otherworldly religion which makes a strange, un-Biblical distinction between body and soul, between the sacred and the secular.

I have traveled the length and breadth of Alabama, Mississippi, and all the other southern states. On sweltering summer days and crisp autumn mornings I have looked at the South's beautiful churches with their lofty spires pointing heavenward. I have beheld the impressive outlines of her massive religious-education buildings. Over and over I have found myself asking: "What kind of people worship here? Who is their God? Where were their voices when the lips of Governor Barnett dripped with words of interposition and nullification? Where were they when Governor Wallace gave a clarion call for defiance and hatred? Where were their voices of support when bruised and weary Negro men and women decided to rise from the dark dungeons of complacency to the bright hills of creative protest?"

Yes, these questions are still in my mind. In deep disappointment I have wept over the laxity of the church. But be assured that my tears have been tears of love. There can be no deep disappointment where there is not deep love. Yes, I love the church. How could I do otherwise? I am in the rather unique position of being the son, the grandson, and the great-grandson of preachers. Yes, I see the church as the body of Christ. But, oh! How we have blemished and scarred that body through social neglect and through fear of being nonconformists.

There was a time when the church was very powerful—in the time when   40
the early Christians rejoiced at being deemed worthy to suffer for what they believed. In those days the church was not merely a thermometer that recorded the ideas and principles of popular opinion; it was a thermostat that transformed the mores of society. Whenever the early Christians entered a town, the people in power became disturbed and immediately sought to convict the Christians for being "disturbers of the peace" and "outside agitators." But the Christians pressed on, in the conviction that they were "a colony of heaven," called to obey God rather than man. Small in number, they were big in commitment. They were too God-intoxicated to be "astronomically intimidated." By their effort and example they brought an end to such ancient evils as infanticide and gladiatorial contests.

Things are different now. So often the contemporary church is a weak, ineffectual voice with an uncertain sound. So often it is an archdefender of the status quo. Far from being disturbed by the presence of the church, the power structure of the average community is consoled by the church's silent — and often even vocal — sanction of things as they are.

But the judgment of God is upon the church as never before. If today's church does not recapture the sacrificial spirit of the early church, it will lose its authenticity, forfeit the loyalty of millions, and be dismissed as an irrelevant social club with no meaning for the twentieth century. Every day I meet young people whose disappointment with the church has turned into outright disgust.

Perhaps I have once again been too optimistic. Is organized religion too inextricably bound to the status quo to save our nation and the world? Perhaps I must turn my faith to the inner spiritual church, the church within the church, as the true *ekklesia* and the hope of the world. But again I am thankful to God that some noble souls from the ranks of organized religion have broken loose from the paralyzing chains of conformity and joined us as active partners in the struggle for freedom. They have left their secure congregations and walked the streets of Albany, Georgia, with us. They have gone down the highways of the South on tortuous rides for freedom. Yes, they have gone to jail with us. Some have been dismissed from their churches, have lost the support of their bishops and fellow ministers. But they have acted in the faith that right defeated is stronger than evil triumphant. Their witness has been the spiritual salt that has preserved the true meaning of the gospel in these troubled times. They have carved a tunnel of hope through the dark mountain of disappointment.

I hope the church as a whole will meet the challenge of this decisive hour. But even if the church does not come to the aid of justice, I have no despair about the future. I have no fear about the outcome of our struggle in Birmingham, even if our motives are at present misunderstood. We will reach the goal of freedom in Birmingham and all over the nation, because the goal of America is freedom. Abused and scorned though we may be, our destiny is tied up with America's destiny. Before the pilgrims landed at Plymouth, we were here. Before the pen of Jefferson etched the majestic words of the Declaration of Independence across the pages of history, we were here. For more than two centuries our forebears labored in this country without wages; they made cotton king; they built the homes of their masters while suffering gross injustice and shameful humiliation — and yet out of a bottomless vitality they continued to thrive and develop. If the inexpressible cruelties of slavery could not stop us, the opposition we now face will surely fail. We will win our freedom because the sacred heritage of our nation and the eternal will of God are embodied in our echoing demands.

Before closing I feel impelled to mention one other point in your statement that has troubled me profoundly. You warmly commended the Birmingham police force for keeping "order" and "preventing violence." I doubt that you would have so warmly commended the police force if you had seen its dogs sinking their teeth into unarmed, nonviolent Negroes. I doubt

45

that you would so quickly commend the policemen if you were to observe their ugly and inhumane treatment of Negroes here in the city jail; if you were to watch them push and curse old Negro women and young Negro girls; if you were to see them slap and kick old Negro men and young boys; if you were to observe them, as they did on two occasions, refuse to give us food because we wanted to sing our grace together. I cannot join you in your praise of the Birmingham police department.

It is true that police have exercised a degree of discipline in handling the demonstrators. In this sense they have conducted themselves rather "nonviolently" in public. But for what purpose? To preserve the evil system of segregation. Over the past few years I have consistently preached that nonviolence demands that the means we use must be as pure as the ends we seek. I have tried to make clear that it is wrong to use immoral means to attain moral ends. But now I must affirm that it is just as wrong, or perhaps even more so, to use moral means to preserve immoral ends. Perhaps Mr. Connor and his policemen have been rather nonviolent in public, as was Chief Pritchett in Albany, Georgia, but they have used the moral means of nonviolence to maintain the immoral end of racial injustice. As T. S. Eliot has said: "The last temptation is the greatest treason: To do the right deed for the wrong reason."

I wish you had commended the Negro sit-inners and demonstrators of Birmingham for their sublime courage, their willingness to suffer and their amazing discipline in the midst of great provocation. One day the South will recognize its real heroes. They will be the James Merediths, with the noble sense of purpose that enables them to face jeering and hostile mobs, and with the agonizing loneliness that characterizes the life of the pioneer. They will be old, oppressed, battered Negro women, symbolized in a seventy-two-year-old woman in Montgomery, Alabama, who rose up with a sense of dignity and with her people decided not to ride segregated buses, and who responded with ungrammatical profundity to one who inquired about her weariness: "My feets is tired, but my soul is at rest." They will be the young high school and college students, the young ministers of the gospel and a host of their elders, courageously and nonviolently sitting in at lunch counters and willingly going to jail for conscience's sake. One day the South will know that when these disinherited children of God sat down at lunch counters, they were in reality standing up for what is best in the American dream and for the most sacred values in our Judaeo-Christian heritage, thereby bringing our nation back to those great wells of democracy which were dug deep by the founding fathers in their formulation of the Constitution and the Declaration of Independence.

Never before have I written so long a letter. I'm afraid it is much too long to take your precious time. I can assure you that it would have been much shorter if I had been writing from a comfortable desk, but what else can one do when he is alone in a narrow jail cell, other than write long letters, think long thoughts, and pray long prayers?

If I have said anything in this letter that overstates the truth and indicates an unreasonable impatience, I beg you to forgive me. If I have said anything that understates the truth and indicates my having a patience that allows me to settle for anything less than brotherhood, I beg God to forgive me.

I hope this letter finds you strong in faith. I also hope that circumstances will soon make it possible for me to meet each of you, not as an integrationist or a civil-rights leader but as a fellow clergyman and a Christian brother. Let us all hope that the dark clouds of racial prejudice will soon pass away and the deep fog of misunderstanding will be lifted from our fear-drenched communities, and in some not too distant tomorrow the radiant stars of love and brotherhood will shine over our great nation with all their scintillating beauty.

50

Yours for the cause of Peace and Brotherhood
MARTIN LUTHER KING, JR.

King's Analysis of His Audience: Identification and Overcoming Difference

King's letter is worth studying for his use of the resources of identification alone. For example, he appeals in his salutation to "My Dear Fellow Clergymen," which emphasizes at the outset that he and his readers share a similar role. Elsewhere he calls them "my friends" (paragraph 12) and "my Christian and Jewish brothers" (paragraph 23). In many other places, King alludes to the Bible and to other religious figures; these references put him on common ground with his readers.

King's letter also successfully deals with various kinds of difference between his readers and himself.

Assumptions

King's readers assumed that if black people waited long enough, their situation would naturally grow better. Therefore, they argued for patience. King, in paragraph 26, questions "the strangely irrational notion that [. . .] the very flow of time [. . .] will inevitably cure all ills." Against this common assumption that "time heals," King offers the view that "time itself is neutral," something that "can be used either destructively or constructively."

Principles

King's readers believed in the principle of always obeying the law, a principle blind to both intent and application. King substitutes another principle: Obey just laws, but disobey, openly and lovingly, unjust laws (paragraphs 15–22).

Hierarchy of Values

King's readers elevated the value of reducing racial tension over the value of securing racial justice. In paragraph 10, King's strategy is to talk about "constructive, nonviolent tension," clearly an effort to get his readers to see tension as not necessarily a bad thing but a condition for achieving social progress.

Ends and Means

King's audience seems to disagree with him not about the ends for which he was working but about the means. King, therefore, focuses not on justifying civil rights but on justifying civil disobedience.

Interpretation

King's audience interpreted extremism as always negative, never justifiable. King counters by showing, first, that he is actually a moderate, neither a "do-nothing" nor a militant (paragraph 28). But then he redefines their interpretation of extremism, arguing that extremism for good causes is justified and citing examples from history to support his point (paragraph 31).

Implications or Consequences

King's readers doubtless feared the consequences of supporting the struggle for civil rights too strongly—losing the support of more conservative members of their congregations. But as King warns, "If today's church does not recapture the sacrificial spirit of the early church, it will [. . .] be dismissed as an irrelevant social club" (paragraph 42). King's strategy is to turn his readers' attention away from short-term consequences and toward long-term consequences—the loss of the vitality and relevance of the church itself.

Following Through

As a class, look closely at one of the essays from an earlier chapter, and consider it in terms of audience analysis. What audience did the writer attempt to reach? How did the writer connect or fail to connect with the audience's experience, knowledge, and concerns? What exactly divides the author from his or her audience, and how did the writer attempt to overcome the division? How effective were the writer's strategies for achieving identification? What can you suggest that might have worked better?

USING THE FORMS OF APPEAL

We turn now to the forms of appeal in persuasion, noting how Martin Luther King, Jr., used them in his letter.

The Appeal to Reason

Persuasion, we have said, uses the same appeal to reason that we find in convincing; that is, the foundation of a persuasive argument is the case structure of thesis, reasons, and evidence. King, however, seems to have realized that an argument organized like a case would seem too formal and public for his purposes, so he chose instead to respond to the clergymen's statement with a personal letter, organized around their criticisms of him. In fact, most of King's letter amounts to self-defense and belongs to the rhetorical form known as *apologia*, from which our word "apology" derives. An **apologia** is an effort to explain and justify what one has done, or chosen not to do, in the face of condemnation or at least widespread disapproval or misunderstanding.

Although, strictly speaking, he does not present a case, King still relies heavily on reason. He uses a series of short arguments, occupying from one to as many as eight paragraphs, in responding to his readers' criticisms. These are the more important ones, in order of appearance:

> Refutation of the "outside agitator" concept (paragraphs 2–4)
> Defense of nonviolent civil disobedience (paragraphs 5–11)
> Definitions of "just" versus "unjust" laws (paragraphs 15–22)
> Refutation and defense of the label "extremist" (paragraphs 27–31)
> Rejection of the ministers' praise for the conduct of the police during
>   the Birmingham demonstration (paragraphs 45–47)

In addition to defending himself and his cause, King pursues an offensive strategy, advancing his own criticisms, most notably of the "white moderate" (paragraphs 23–26) and the "white church and its leadership" (paragraphs 33–44). This concentration on rational appeal is both effective and appropriate: It confirms King's character as a man of reason, and it appeals to an audience of well-educated professionals.

King also cites evidence that his readers must respect. In paragraph 16, for example, he cites the words of St. Thomas Aquinas, Martin Buber, and Paul Tillich—who represent, respectively, the Catholic, Jewish, and Protestant traditions—to defend his position on the nature of just and unjust laws. He has chosen these authorities carefully so that each of his eight accusers has someone from his own tradition with whom to identify. The implication, of course, is that King's distinction between just and unjust laws and the course of action that follows from this distinction is consistent with Judeo-Christian thought as a whole.

Following Through

1. Look at paragraphs 2–4 of King's letter. What reasons does King give to justify his presence in Birmingham? How well does he support each reason? How do his reasons and evidence reflect a strategy aimed at his clergy audience?

(continues)

Following Through (continued)

2. King's argument for civil disobedience (paragraphs 15–22) is based on one main reason. What is it, and how does he support it?
3. What are the two reasons King gives to refute his audience's charge that he is an extremist (paragraphs 27–31)?
4. Think about a time in your life when you did (or did not do) something for which you were unfairly criticized. Choose one or two of the criticisms, and attempt to defend yourself in a short case of your own. Remember that your argument must be persuasive to your accusers, not just to you. Ask yourself, as King did, How can I appeal to my readers? What will they find reasonable?

The Appeal to Character

In Chapter 7, our concern was how to make a good case. We did not discuss self-presentation explicitly there; but the fact is, when you formulate a clear and plausible thesis and defend it with good reasons and sufficient evidence, you are at the same time creating a positive impression of your own character. A good argument will always reveal the writer's values, intelligence, knowledge of the subject, grasp of the reader's needs and concerns, and so on. We tend to respect and trust a person who reasons well, even when we do not assent to his or her particular case.

In terms of the appeal to character, the difference between convincing and persuading is a matter of degree. In convincing, this appeal is implicit, indirect, and diffused throughout the argument; in persuading, the appeal to character is often quite explicit, direct, and concentrated in a specific section of the essay. The effect on readers is consequently rather different: In convincing, we are seldom consciously aware of the writer's character as such; in persuading, the writer's character assumes a major role in determining how we respond to the argument.

The perception of his character was a special problem for King when he wrote his letter. He was not a national hero in 1963 but rather a controversial civil rights leader whom many viewed as a troublemaker. Furthermore, of course, he wrote this now celebrated document while in jail—hardly a condition that inspires respect and trust in readers. Self-presentation, then, was very significant for King, something he concentrated on throughout his letter and especially at the beginning and end.

In his opening paragraph, King acknowledges the worst smirch on his character—that he is currently in jail. But he goes on to establish himself as a professional person like his readers, with secretaries, correspondence, and important work to do.

Just prior to his conclusion (paragraphs 48–50), King offers a strongly worded critique of the white moderate and the mainstream white church, taking the offensive in a way that his readers are certain to perceive as an attack.

In paragraph 48, however, he suddenly becomes self-deprecating and almost apologetic: "Never before have I written so long a letter." As unexpected as it is, this sudden shift of tone disarms the reader. Then, with gentle irony (the letter, he says, would have been shorter "if I had been writing from a comfortable desk"), King explains the length of his letter as the result of his having no other outlet for action. What can one do in jail but "write long letters, think long thoughts, and pray long prayers?" King paradoxically turns the negative of being in jail into a positive, an opportunity rather than a limitation on his freedom.

His next move is equally surprising, especially after the confident tone of his critique of the church. He begs forgiveness—from his readers if he has overstated his case and from God if he has understated his case or shown too much patience with injustice. This daring, dramatic penultimate paragraph is just the right touch, the perfect gesture of reconciliation. Because he asks so humbly, his readers must forgive him. What else can they do? The further subordination of his own will to God's is the stance of the sufferer and martyr in both the Jewish and Christian traditions.

Finally, King sets aside that which divides him from his readers—the issue of integration and his role as a civil rights leader—in favor of that which unifies him with his audience: All are men of God and brothers in faith. Like an Old Testament prophet, he envisions a time when the current conflicts will be over, when "the radiant stars of love and brotherhood will shine over our great nation." In other words, King holds out the possibility for transcendence, for rising above racial prejudice to a new age, a new America. In the end, his readers are encouraged to soar with him, to hope for the future.

Here King enlists the power of identification to overcome the differences separating writer and reader, invoking his status as a "fellow clergyman and a Christian brother" as a symbol of commonality. The key to identification is to reach beyond the individual self, associating one's character with something larger—the Christian community, the history of the struggle for freedom, national values, "spaceship Earth," or any appropriate cause or movement in which readers can also participate.

Following Through

We have already seen how King associates himself with the Christian community in the essay's final paragraph. Look at the list of questions for creating audience identification on pages 253–254. Find some examples in King's letter in which he employs some of these resources of identification. Which parts of the letter are most effective in creating a positive impression of character? Why? What methods does King use that any persuader might use?

The Appeal to Emotion

Educated people aware of the techniques of persuasion are often deeply suspicious of emotional appeal. Among college professors — those who will read and grade your work — this prejudice can be especially strong because all fields of academic study claim to value reason, dispassionate inquiry, and the critical analysis of data and conclusions. Many think of emotional appeal as an impediment to sound thinking and associate it with politicians who prey on our fears, with dictators and demagogues who exploit our prejudices, and with advertisers and televangelists who claim they will satisfy our dreams and prayers.

Of course, we can all cite examples of the destructive power of emotional appeal. But to condemn it wholesale, without qualification, is to exhibit a lack of self-awareness. Most scientists will concede, for instance, that they are passionately committed to the methods of their field, and mathematicians will confess that they are moved by the elegance of certain formulas and proofs. In fact, all human activity has some emotional dimension, a strongly felt adherence to a common set of values.

Moreover, we ought to have strong feelings about certain things: revulsion at the horrors of the Holocaust, pity and anger over the abuse of children, happiness when a war is concluded or when those kidnapped by terrorists are released, and so on. We cease to be human if we are not responsive to emotional appeal.

Clearly, however, we must distinguish between legitimate and illegitimate emotional appeals, condemning the latter and learning to use the former when appropriate. Distinguishing between the two is not always easy, but answering certain questions can help us do so:

Do the emotional appeals substitute for knowledge and reason?
Do they employ stereotypes and pit one group against another?
Do they offer a simple, unthinking reaction to a complex situation?

Whenever the answer is yes, our suspicions should be aroused.

Perhaps an even better test is to ask yourself, If I act on the basis of how I feel, who will benefit, and who will suffer? You may be saddened, for example, to see animals used in medical experiments, but an appeal showing only these animals and ignoring the benefits of experimentation for human life is pandering to the emotions.

In contrast, legitimate emotional appeal supplements argument rather than substituting for it, drawing on knowledge and often on first-hand experience. At its best, it can bring alienated groups together and create empathy or sympathy where these are lacking. Many examples could be cited from Martin Luther King's letter, but the most effective passage is surely paragraph 14:

> We have waited for more than 340 years for our constitutional God-given rights. The nations of Asia and Africa are moving with jetlike speed toward gaining political independence, but we still creep at horse-and-buggy pace toward gaining a cup of coffee at a lunch counter. Perhaps it is easy for those who have

never felt the stinging darts of segregation to say, "Wait." But when you have seen vicious mobs lynch your mothers and fathers at will and drown your sisters and brothers at whim; when you have seen hate-filled policemen curse, kick, and even kill your black brothers and sisters; when you see the vast majority of your twenty million Negro brothers smothering in an airtight cage of poverty in the midst of an affluent society; when you suddenly find your tongue twisted and your speech stammering as you seek to explain to your six-year-old daughter why she can't go to the public amusement park that has just been advertised on television, and see tears welling up in her eyes when she is told that Funtown is closed to colored children, and see ominous clouds of inferiority beginning to form in her little mental sky, and see her beginning to distort her personality by developing an unconscious bitterness toward white people; when you have to concoct an answer for a five-year-old son who is asking: "Daddy, why do white people treat colored people so mean?"; when you take a cross-country drive and find it necessary to sleep night after night in the uncomfortable corners of your automobile because no motel will accept you; when you are humiliated day in and day out by nagging signs reading "white" and "colored"; when your first name becomes "nigger," your middle name becomes "boy" (however old you are), and your last name becomes "John," and your wife and mother are never given the respected title "Mrs."; when you are harried by day and haunted by night by the fact that you are a Negro, living constantly at tiptoe stance, never quite knowing what to expect next, and are plagued with inner fears and outer resentments; when you are forever fighting a degenerating sense of "nobodiness"—then you will understand why we find it difficult to wait. There comes a time when the cup of endurance runs over, and men are no longer willing to be plunged into the abyss of despair. I hope, sirs, you can understand our legitimate and unavoidable impatience.

Just prior to this paragraph, King has concluded an argument justifying the use of direct action to dramatize social inequities and to demand the rights and justice denied to oppressed people. Direct-action programs are necessary, he says, because "freedom is never voluntarily given by the oppressor; it must be demanded by the oppressed." It is easy for those not oppressed to urge an underclass to wait. But "[t]his 'Wait' has almost always meant 'Never.'"

At this point King deliberately sets out to create in his readers a feeling of outrage. Having ended paragraph 13 by equating "wait" with "never," King next refers to a tragic historical fact: For 340 years, since the beginning of slavery in the American colonies, black people have been waiting for their freedom. He sharply contrasts the "jetlike speed" with which Africa is overcoming colonialism with the "horse-and-buggy pace" of integration in the United States. In African homelands, black people are gaining their political independence; but here, in the land of the free, they are denied even "a cup of coffee at a lunch counter." Clearly, this is legitimate emotional appeal, based on fact and reinforcing reason.

In the long and rhythmical sentence that takes up most of the rest of the paragraph, King unleashes the full force of emotional appeal in a series of concrete images designed to make his privileged white readers feel the anger, frustration, and humiliation of the oppressed. In rapid succession, King alludes to mob violence, police brutality, and economic discrimination — the more public evils of racial discrimination — and then moves to the personal, everyday experience of segregation, concentrating especially on what it does to the self-respect of innocent children. For any reader with even the least capacity for sympathy, these images must strike home, creating identification with the suffering of the oppressed and fueling impatience with the evil system that perpetuates this suffering. In short, through the use of telling detail drawn from his own experience, King succeeds in getting his audience to feel what he feels — feelings, in fact, that they ought to share, that are wholly appropriate to the problem of racial prejudice.

What have we learned from King about the available means of emotional appeal? Instead of telling his audience they should feel a particular emotion, he has brought forth that emotion using five specific rhetorical techniques:

Concrete examples
Personal experiences
Metaphors and similes
Sharp contrasts and comparisons
Sentence rhythm, particularly the use of intentional repetition

We next consider how style contributes to a persuasive argument.

Following Through

1. We have said that emotional appeals need to be both legitimate and appropriate — that is, honest and suitable for the subject matter, the audience, and the kind of discourse being written. Find examples of arguments from various publications — books, newspapers, magazines, and professional journals — and discuss the use or avoidance of emotional appeal in each. On the basis of this study, try to generalize about what kinds of subjects, audiences, and discourse allow direct emotional appeal and what kinds do not.

2. Write an essay analyzing the tactics of emotional appeal in the editorial columns of your campus or local newspaper. Compare the strategies with those used by King. Then evaluate the appeals. How effective are they in arousing your emotions? How well do they reinforce the reasoning offered? Be sure to discuss the way the appeals work and their legitimacy and appropriateness.

The Appeal through Style

By *style*, we mean the choices a writer makes at the level of words, phrases, and sentences. It would be a mistake to think of style as merely a final touch, something to "dress up" an argument. Style actually involves all of a writer's choices about what words to use and how to arrange them. Ideas and arguments do not develop apart from style, and all of the appeals discussed so far involve stylistic choices. For example, you are concerned with style when you consider what words will state a thesis most precisely or make yourself sound knowledgeable or provide your reader with a compelling image. The appeal of style works hand in hand with the appeals of reason, character, and emotion.

Furthermore, style makes what we say memorable. George Bush may wish he had never said it, but his statement, "Read my lips: No new taxes" was a message that generated high enthusiasm and, to the former president's dismay, remained in people's minds long after he had compromised himself on that issue. Because the persuasive effect we have on readers depends largely on what they remember, the appeal through style matters as much as the appeal to reason, character, and emotion.

Writers with effective style make conscious choices on many levels. One choice involves the degree of formality or familiarity they want to convey. You will notice that King strikes a fairly formal and professional tone throughout most of his letter, choosing words like *cognizant* (paragraph 4) rather than the more common *aware*. Writers also consider the **connotation** of words (what a word implies or what we associate it with) as much as their **denotation** (a word's literal meaning). For example, King opens his letter with the phrase "While confined here in the Birmingham city jail." The word *confined* denotes the same condition as *incarcerated* but has less unfavorable connotations, because people can also be *confined* in ways that evoke our sympathy.

Memorable writing often appeals to the senses of sight and sound. Concrete words can paint a picture; in paragraph 45, for example, King tells about "dogs sinking their teeth" into the nonviolent demonstrators. Writers may also evoke images through implied and explicit comparisons (respectively, metaphor and simile). King's "the stinging darts of segregation" (paragraph 14) is an example of metaphor. In this same paragraph King refers to the "airtight cage of poverty," the "clouds of inferiority" forming in his young daughter's "mental sky," and the "cup of endurance" that has run over for his people—each a metaphor with a powerful emotional effect.

Even when read silently, language has sound. Therefore, style includes the variation of sentence length and the use of rhythmic patterns as well. For example, a writer may emphasize a short, simple sentence by placing it at the end of a series of long sentences or a single long sentence, as King does in paragraph 14. One common rhythmic pattern is the repetition of certain phrases to emphasize a point or to play up a similarity or contrast; in the fourth sentence of paragraph 14, King repeats the phrase "when you" a number of times, piling up examples of racial discrimination and creating a powerful rhythm that carries readers through this unusually long sentence. Another common rhythmic pattern is parallelism. Note the following phrases, again from the fourth sentence of paragraph 14:

"lynch your mothers and fathers at will"

"drown your sisters and brothers at whim"

Here King uses similar words in the same places, even paralleling the number of syllables in each phrase. The parallelism here is further emphasized by King's choice of another stylistic device known as *alliteration*, the repetition of consonant sounds. In another passage from paragraph 14, King achieves a sound pattern that suggests violence when he describes the actions of police who "curse, kick, and even kill" black citizens. The repetition of the hard *k* sound, especially in words of one syllable, suggests the violence of the acts themselves.

Beyond the level of words, phrases, and sentences, the overall arrangement of an essay's main points or topics can also be considered a matter of style, for such arrangement determines how one point contrasts with another, how the tone changes, how the force of the argument builds. When we discuss style, we usually look at smaller units of an essay, but actually all the choices a writer makes contribute in some way to the essay's style.

Following Through

1. Analyze King's style in paragraphs 6, 8, 23, 24, 31, and 47. Compare what King does in these paragraphs with paragraph 14. How are they similar? How are they different? Why?
2. To some extent, style is a gift or talent that some people have more of than others. But it is also learned, acquired by imitating authors we admire. Use your writer's notebook to increase your stylistic options; whenever you hear or read something stated effectively, copy it down and analyze why it is effective. Try to make up a sentence of your own using the same techniques but with a different subject matter. In this way, you can begin to use analogy, metaphor, repetition, alliteration, parallelism, and other stylistic devices. Begin by imitating six or so sentences or phrases that you especially liked in King's letter.
3. Write an essay analyzing your own style in a previous essay. What would you do differently now? Why?

DRAFTING A PERSUASIVE ESSAY

Outside the classroom, persuasion begins, as Martin Luther King's letter did, with a real need to move people to action. In a writing course, you may have to create the circumstances for your argument. You should begin by thinking

The following list summarizes pages 280-288, "Drafting a Persuasive Essay."

1. Choose a **specific** audience whose characteristics you **know well** and who have some capacity for **taking action** or **influencing events.** Avoid writing to a "general audience" or seeking to persuade audiences whose opinions are unalterably opposed to yours.
2. Identify your audience **early** in the process.
3. In your case, show a **need** for action and emphasize **urgency.** Connect your proposal for action **directly and clearly** with the need you've established.
4. Your readers must feel that you are **well-informed, confident, fair, honest,** and have their **interests** and **values** in mind. **Avoid ridicule** of other positions. **Recognize** and **respond** to the **main** objections your readers are likely to have to your proposal.
5. Seek to arouse emotions that you **genuinely feel.** Concentrate on those feelings your audience may **lack** or not feel **strongly enough.** Use emotional appeal **sparingly,** and favor **middle to conclusion** locations in your essay for it.
6. Favor a **middle style** for persuasion, conversational without being too familiar or informal.

Essentially, you are making a case, just as you do when arguing to convince. To this, add careful attention to the impression you make on your audience, especially at the beginning of the essay. Add also descriptive and narrative detail designed to arouse emotions favorable to your case. Finally, work hard on style, especially in second and third drafts.

of an issue that calls for persuasion. Your argument must go beyond merely convincing your readers to believe as you do; now you must decide what action you want them to take and move them to take it.

Conceiving a Readership

Assuming that the task you have chosen or been assigned calls for persuasion, finding and analyzing your readership is your first concern. Because instructors evaluate the writing of their students, it is probably unavoidable that college writers, to some extent, tend to write for their instructors. However, real persuasion has a genuine readership, some definite group of people with a stake in the question or issue being addressed. Whatever you say must be adapted for this audience because moving the reader is the whole point of persuasion.

How can you go about conceiving a readership? First, you should throw out the whole notion of writing to the "general public." Such a "group" is a nearly meaningless abstraction, not defined enough to give you much guidance. Suppose, for example, you are arguing that sex education in public schools must include a moral dimension as well as the clinical facts of reproduction and venereal disease. You need to decide if you are addressing students, who may not want the moral lectures; school administrators, who may not want the added responsibility and curriculum changes; or parents, who may not want the schools to take over what they see as the responsibility of family or church.

Second, given the issue and the position you will probably take, you should ask who you would want to persuade. On the one hand, you do not need to persuade those who already agree with you; on the other, it would be futile to try to persuade those so committed to an opposing position that nothing you could say would make any difference. An argument against logging in old-growth forests, for example, would probably be aimed neither at staunch environmentalists nor at workers employed in the timber industry but rather at some readership between these extremes—say, people concerned in general about the environment but not focused specifically on the threat to mature forests.

Third, when you have a degree of choice among possible readerships, you should select your target audience based on two primary criteria. First, because persuasion is directly concerned with making decisions and taking action, seek above all to influence those readers best able to influence events. Second, when this group includes a range of readers (and it often will), also

Following Through

For a persuasive argument you are about to write, determine your audience; that is, decide who can make a difference with respect to this issue and what they can do to make a difference. Be sure that you go beyond the requirements of convincing when you make these decisions. For example, you may be able to make a good case that just as heterosexuals do not "choose" their attraction to the opposite sex, so homosexuality is also not voluntary. Based on this point, you could argue to a local readership of moderate-to-liberal voters that they should press state legislators to support a bill extending full citizens' rights to homosexuals. But with such a desire for action in mind, you would have to think even more about who your audience is and why they might resist such a measure or not care enough to support it strongly.

In your writer's notebook respond to the questions "Who is my audience?" and "What are our differences?" (refer to the lists of questions on pages 253–254 to help formulate answers). Use your responses to write an audience profile that is more detailed than the one you wrote for an argument to convince.

consider which of these readers you know the most about and can therefore appeal to best.

Because all appeals in persuasion are addressed to an audience, try to identify your reader early in the process. You can, of course, change your mind later on, but doing so will require considerable rethinking and rewriting. Devoting time at the outset to thinking carefully about your intended audience can save much time and effort in the long run.

Discovering the Resources of Appeal

With an audience firmly in mind, you are ready to begin thinking about how to appeal to them. Before and during the drafting stage, you will be making choices about the following:

How to formulate a case and support it with research, as needed
How to present yourself
How to arouse your readers' emotions
How to make the style of your writing contribute to the argument's effectiveness

All of these decisions will be influenced by your understanding of your readers' needs and interests.

Appealing through Reason

In both convincing and persuading, rational appeal amounts to making a case or cases—advancing a thesis or theses and providing supporting reasons and evidence. What you learned in Chapter 7 about case-making applies here as well, so you may want to review that chapter as you work on rational appeal for a persuasive paper. Of course, research (Chapter 5) and inquiry into the truth (Chapter 6) are as relevant to persuasion as they are to convincing.

One difference between convincing and persuading, however, is that in persuasion you will devote much of your argument to defending a course of action. The steps here are basically a matter of common sense:

1. Show that there is a need for action.
2. If your audience, like that for Martin Luther King's letter, is inclined to inactivity, show urgency as well as need—we must act and act now.
3. Satisfy the need, showing that your proposal for action meets the need or will solve the problem. One way to do this is to compare your course of action with other proposals or solutions, indicating why yours is better than the others.

Sometimes your goal will be to persuade your audience *not* to act because what they want to do is wrong or inappropriate or because the time is not right. Need is still the main issue. The difference, obviously, is the goal of showing that no need exists or that it is better to await other developments before a proposed action will be appropriate or effective.

Following Through

Prepare a brief of your argument (see Chapter 7). Be ready to present an overview of your audience and to defend your brief, either before the class or in small groups. Pay special attention to how well the argument establishes a need for your defined audience or motivation to act (or shows that there is no need for action). If some action is called for, assess the solution in the context of other, common proposals: Will the proposed action meet the need? Is it realistic—that is, can it be done?

Appealing through Character

A reader who finishes your essay should have the following impressions:

> The author is well-informed about the topic.
> The author is confident about his or her own position and sincere in advocating it.
> The author has been fair and balanced in dealing with other positions.
> The author understands my concerns and objections and has dealt with them.
> The author is honest.
> The author values what I value; his or her heart is in the right place.

What can you do to communicate these impressions? Basically, you must earn these impressions, just as you must earn a conviction and a good argument. There are no shortcuts, and educated readers are seldom fooled.

To *seem* well informed, you must *be* well informed. This requires that you dig into the topic, thinking about it carefully, researching it thoroughly and taking good notes, discussing the topic and your research with other students, consulting campus experts, and so on. This work will provide you with the following hallmarks of being well informed:

> The ability to make passing references to relevant events and people connected with the issue now or recently
> The ability to create a context or provide background information, which may include comments on the history of the question or issue
> The ability to produce sufficient high-quality evidence to back up contentions

Just as digging in will make you well informed, so inquiry (struggling to find the truth) and convincing (making a case for your conviction about the truth) will lend your argument sincerity and confidence. Draw upon personal experience when it has played a role in determining your position, and don't be reluctant to reveal your own stake in the issue. Make your case boldly, qualifying it as little as possible. If you have prepared yourself with good research, genuine inquiry, and careful case-making, you have earned authority; what remains is to claim your authority, which is essential in arguing to persuade.

Represent other positions accurately and fairly; then present evidence that refutes those positions, or show that the reasoning is inadequate or inconsistent. Don't be afraid to agree with parts of other opinions when they are consistent with your own. Such partial agreements can play a major role in overcoming reader resistance to your own position.

It is generally not a good idea to subject other positions to ridicule. Some of your readers may sympathize with all or part of the position you are attacking and take offense. Even readers gratified by your attack may feel that you have gone too far. Concentrate on the merits of your own case rather than the faults of others.

Coping with your readers' concerns and objections should present no special problems, assuming that you have found an appropriate audience and thought seriously about both the common ground you share and the way their outlook differs from yours. You can ultimately handle concerns and objections in one of two ways: (1) by adjusting your case—your thesis and supporting reasons—so that the concerns or objections do not arise or (2) by taking up the more significant objections one by one and responding to them in a way that reduces reader resistance. Of course, doing one does not preclude doing the other: You can adjust your case and also raise and answer whatever objections remain. What matters is that you never ignore any likely and weighty objection to what you are advocating.

Responding to objections patiently and reasonably will also help with the last and perhaps most important impression that readers have of you—that you value what they value. Sensitivity to the reasoning and moral and emotional commitments of others is one of those values you can and must share with your readers.

If you are to have any chance of persuading at all, your readers must feel that you would not deceive them, so you must conform to the standards of honesty readers will expect. Leaving readers with the impression of your honesty requires much more than simply not lying. Rather, honesty requires (1) reporting evidence accurately and with regard for the original context; (2) acknowledging significant counterevidence for your case, pointing to its existence and explaining why it does not change your argument; and (3) pointing out areas of doubt and uncertainty that must await future events or study.

Following Through

The "Following Through" assignment on page 284 asked you to prepare an audience profile and explore your key areas of difference. Now use the results of that work to help you think through how you could appeal to these readers. Use the questions on page 254 to help establish commonality with your audience and formulate strategies for bringing you and your readers closer together.

Appealing to Emotion

In both convincing and persuading, your case determines largely what you have to say and how you order your presentation. As in King's essay, argument is the center, the framework, while emotional appeal plays a supporting role to rational appeal, taking center stage only occasionally. Consequently, your decisions must take the following into account:

> What emotions to arouse and by what means
> How frequent and intense the emotional appeals should be
> Where to introduce emotional appeals

The first of these decisions is usually the easiest. Try to arouse emotions that you yourself have genuinely felt; whatever moved you will probably also move your readers. If your emotions come from direct experience, draw upon that experience for concrete descriptive detail, as King did. Study whatever you heard or read that moved you; you can probably adapt your sources' tactics for your own purposes. (The best strategy for arousing emotions is often to avoid emotionalism yourself. Let the facts, the descriptive detail, the concrete examples do the work, just as King did.)

Deciding how often, at what length, and how intensely to make emotional appeals presents a more difficult challenge. Much depends on the topic, the audience, and your own range and intensity of feeling. In every case, you must estimate as best you can what will be appropriate, but the following suggestions may help.

As always in persuasion, your primary consideration is your audience. What attitudes and feelings do they have already? Which of these lend emotional support to your case? Which work against your purposes? Emphasize those feelings that are consistent with your position, and show why any others are understandable but inappropriate.

Then ask a further question: What does my audience not feel or not feel strongly enough that they must feel or feel more strongly if I am to succeed in persuading them? King, for example, decided that his readers' greatest emotional deficit was their inability to feel what victims of racial discrimination feel—hence paragraph 14, the most intense emotional appeal in his letter. Simply put, devote space and intensity to arousing emotions central to your case that are lacking or only weakly felt by your readers.

The questions of how often and where to include emotional appeals are both worth careful consideration. Regarding frequency, the best principle is to take your shots sparingly, getting as much as you can out of each effort. Positioning emotional appeals depends on pacing: Use them to lead into or to clinch a key point. So positioned, they temporarily relieve the audience of the intellectual effort required to follow your argument.

It is generally not a good idea to begin an essay with your most involved and most intense emotional appeal; you don't want to peak too early. Besides that, in your introduction you need to concentrate on establishing your tone and authority, providing needed background information, and clearly and forcefully stating your thesis. The conclusion can be an effective position for emotional appeals because your audience is left with something memorable to carry away from the reading. In most cases, however, it is best to concentrate emotional appeals in the middle or near the end of an essay.

Following Through

After you have a first draft of your essay, reread it with an eye to emotional appeal. Highlight the places where you have deliberately sought to arouse the audience's emotions. (You might also ask a friend to read the draft or exchange drafts with another student in your class.)

Decide if you need to devote more attention to your emotional appeal through additional concrete examples, direct quotations, or something else. Consider also how you could make each appeal more effective and intense and whether each appeal is in the best possible location in the essay.

Appealing through Style

As we have seen, the style of your argument evolves with every choice you make, even in the prewriting stages. As you draft, think consciously about how stylistic choices can work for you, but don't agonize over them. In successive revisions, you will be able to make refinements and experiment for different effects.

In the first draft, however, set an appropriate level of formality. Most persuasive writing is neither chatty and familiar nor stiff and distant. Rather, persuasive prose is like dignified conversation — the way people talk when they care about and respect one another but do not know each other well. We can see some of the hallmarks of persuasive prose in King's letter:

- It uses *I, you,* and *we.*
- It avoids both technical jargon and slang.
- It inclines toward strong action verbs.
- It chooses examples and images familiar to the reader.
- It connects sentence to sentence and paragraph to paragraph with transitional words and phrases like *however, moreover,* and *for instance.*

All of these and many other features characterize the **middle style** of most persuasive writing.

As we discovered in King's letter, this middle style can cover quite a range of choices. King varies his style from section to section, depending on his purpose. Notice how King sounds highly formal in his introduction (paragraphs 1–5), where he wants to establish authority, but more plainspoken when he narrates the difficulties he and other black leaders had in their efforts to negotiate with the city's leaders (paragraphs 6–9). Notice as well how his sentences and paragraphs shorten, on average, in the passage comparing just and unjust laws (paragraphs 15–22). And we have already noted the use of sound and imagery in the passages of highest emotional appeal, such as paragraphs 14 and 47.

Just as King matches style with function, so you need to vary your style based on what each part of your essay is doing. This variation creates *pacing*, or the sense of overall rhythm in your essay. Readers need places where they can relax a bit between points of higher intensity such as lengthy arguments and passionate pleas.

As you prepare to write your first draft, then, concern yourself with matching your style to your purpose from section to section, depending on whether you are providing background information, telling a story, developing a reason in your case, mounting an emotional appeal, or doing something else. Save detailed attention to style (as explained in the appendix) for later in the process while editing a second or third draft.

Following Through

Once you have completed the first draft of an argument to persuade, select one paragraph in which you have consciously made stylistic choices to create images, connotations, sound patterns, and so on. It may be the introduction, the conclusion, or a body paragraph where you are striving for emotional effect. Be ready to share the paragraph with your class, describing your choices as we have done with many passages from Martin Luther King's letter.

Following Through

Read the following argument, and be ready to discuss its effectiveness as persuasion. You might build your evaluation around the suggestions listed in the "Reader's Checklist for Revising a Persuasive Essay" on page 289.

STUDENT SAMPLE: *An Essay Arguing to Persuade*

The following essay was written in response to an assignment for a first-year rhetoric course. The intended readers were other students, eighteen to twenty-two years old and for the most part middle-class, who attended the same large, private university as the writer. Within this group, Shanks was trying to reach those who might sit in class and disagree with the opinions of more

The following list will direct you to specific features of a good persuasive essay. You and a peer may want to exchange drafts; having someone else give your paper a critical reading often helps identify weaknesses you may have overlooked. After you have revised your draft, use the suggestions in the appendix to edit for style and check for errors at the sentence level.

- ☐ Read the audience profile for this essay. Then read the draft all the way through, projecting yourself as much as possible into the role of the target audience. After reading the draft, find and mark the essay's natural divisions. You may also want to number the paragraph so that you can refer to them easily.

- ☐ Recall that persuasive arguments must be based on careful inquiry and strategic case making. Inspect the case first. Begin by underlining the thesis and marking the main reasons in support. You might write "Reason 1," "Reason 2," and so forth in the margins. Circle any words that need clearer definition. Also note any reasons that need more evidence or other support, such as illustrations or analogies.

- ☐ Evaluate the plan for organizing the case. Are the reasons presented in a compelling and logical order? Does the argument build to a strong conclusion? Can you envision an alternative arrangement? Make suggestions for improvement, referring to paragraphs by number.

- ☐ Remember that persuasion requires the writer to make an effort to present him- or herself as worthy of the reader's trust and respect. Reread the draft with a highlighter or pen in hand, marking specific places where the writer has sought identification with the target audience. Has the writer made an effort to find common ground with readers by using any of the ideas listed on page 254? Make suggestions for improvement.

- ☐ Be aware that persuasion also requires the writer to make a conscious effort to gain the audience's emotional support through concrete examples and imagery, analogies and metaphors, first-person reporting, quotations, and so on. How many instances of conscious emotional appeal are there? Are the efforts at emotional appeal uniformly successful? What improvements can you suggest? Has the writer gone too far with emotional appeal? Or should more be done?

- ☐ Add conscious stylistic appeals later, in the editing stage, because style involves refinements in word choice and sentence patterns. However, look now to see if the draft exhibits a middle style appropriate to the targeted audience. Mark any instances of the following:

  Poor transitions between sentences or paragraphs

  Wordy passages, especially those containing the passive voice (see the section "Editing for Clarity and Conciseness" in the appendix)

(continues)

Awkward sentences

Poor diction—that is, the use of incorrect or inappropriate words

☐ Note any examples of effective style—good use of metaphor, repetition, or parallelism, for example.

☐ Describe the general tone. Does it change from section to section? How appropriate and effective is the tone in general and in specific sections of the essay?

☐ After studying the argument, ask whether you are sure what the writer wants or expects of the audience. Has the writer succeeded in persuading the audience? Why or why not?

outspoken students but, for whatever reasons, refrain from expressing their own dissenting viewpoints.

AN UNCOMFORTABLE POSITION

Joey Shanks

I sat quietly in my uncomfortable chair. Perhaps it was my position, I thought, and not the poly-wood seat that tormented me; so I sat upright, realizing then that both the chair and my position were probably responsible for my disposition. But I could do nothing to correct the problem.

Or maybe it was the conversation. I sat quietly, only for a lack of words. Usually I rambled on any subject, even if I knew nothing about it. No one in my rhetoric class would ever accuse me of lacking words, but today I was silent. The opinions of my classmates flew steadily across the room with occasional "I agree's" and "that's the truth's." My teacher shook her head in frustration.

She mediated the debate, if it was a debate. I could not imagine that a group of white college students angrily confessing that we all were constantly victims of reverse racism could provide much of a debate. For our generalizations to have formed a legitimate debate, there should have been two opposing sides, but the power of the majority had triumphed again. I sat quietly, knowing that what I heard was wrong. The little I said only fueled the ignorance and the guarded, David Duke–like articulations.

Did everyone in the class really think America had achieved equal opportunity? I could only hope that someone else in the classroom felt the same intimidation that I felt. I feared the majority. If I spoke my mind, I would only give the majority a minority to screw with.

But what about the young woman who sat next to me? She was Hispanic, with glasses and no name or voice that I knew of. She was the visible minority in a class full of Greek letters and blond hair. She must have been more uncomfortable than I was. She sat quietly every day.

The individual in society must possess the courage and the confidence to challenge and oppose the majority if he or she feels it necessary. In the classroom, I had not seen this individualism. My classmates may have had different backgrounds and interests, but eventually, in every discussion, a majority opinion dominated the debate and all personalities were lost in a mob mentality. In rhetoric class, we read and discussed material designed to stimulate a debate with many sides; however, the debate was rendered useless because the power of the majority stifled open discussion and bullied the individual to submit or stay quiet.

Tocqueville wrote of the dangerous power of the majority in his book *Democracy in America:* "The moral authority of the majority is partly based upon the notion that there is more intelligence and wisdom in a number of men united than in a single individual" (113). Tocqueville illustrated a point that I witnessed in class and that history has witnessed for ages. The majority rules through the power of numbers. No matter how wrong, an opinion with many advocates becomes the majority opinion and is difficult to oppose. The majority makes the rules; therefore, we accept that "might makes right."

The true moral authority, however, lies in the fundamental acceptance that right and wrong are universal and not relative to time and place. Thomas Nagel, a contemporary philosopher, states, "Many things that you probably think are wrong have been accepted as morally correct by large groups of people in the past" (71). The majority is not right simply because it is a large group. An individual is responsible for knowing right from wrong, no matter how large the group appears. Ancient philosophers such as Aristotle and Socrates have defied generations of majorities. They preached that morality is universal and that the majority is not always right.

In our classroom, after the first week all the students chose their chairs in particular areas. Certain mentalities aligned, acknowledging similar philosophies on politics, hunting, sports, African Americans, welfare, and women. Debate on *The Awakening* awoke the beefcake majority with confused exclamations: "She's crazy! Why did the chick kill herself?" The majority either misunderstood the book or was not willing to accept another opinion.

Mark Twain, a pioneer of American literature, fought an empire of slavery with his book *The Adventures of Huckleberry Finn.* Twain saw through the cruelty of racism and spoke against a nation that treated men and women like animals because of the color of their skin. Twain possessed the confidence and individualism to fight the majority, despite its power. Mark Twain protected individualism when he opposed racism and the institution of slavery. He proved that the single individual is sometimes more intelligent than men united.

Ramsey Clark, a former attorney general and now a political activist, expressed a great deal of distress over the Persian Gulf war. He spoke for the minority, a position of peace. In an interview in *The Progressive,* Clark stated, "We really believe that might makes right, and that leads us to perpetual war" (qtd. in Dreifus 32). Clark was referring to the United States' foreign policy of peace through intimidation, but his words can be taken on a universal level. We will never accomplish anything if might makes right and humanity is in a perpetual war of opinions. Clark is an example of individualism against the majority, though he will never be considered an American hero; few may remember his words, but like Mark Twain, he fought the majority's "moral authority."

In the classroom, or in the post-slavery South, or in the deserts of the Middle East, the majority has the power, and whoever has the power controls the world and may even seem to control all the opinions in it. As a country, we abuse the power of the majority. America, the spokesperson for the world majority, manipulates its position while flexing and growling, "Might makes right!" This situation is a large-scale version of a rhetoric seminar in which students too frequently align with or submit to the majority opinion. In rhetoric seminar, we lack champions, individuals who see wrong and cry, "Foul!" Maybe the young Hispanic woman who quietly sits is just waiting for the right moment. Perhaps I had my chance and lost it, or maybe the majority has scared all the individuals into sitting quietly in their uncomfortable chairs.

Works Cited

Dreifus, Claudia. "An Interview with Ramsey Clark." The Progressive Apr. 1991: 32–35.

Nagel, Thomas. What Does It All Mean? Oxford: Oxford UP, 1987.

Tocqueville, Alexis de. Democracy in America. 1835. New York: Penguin, 1956.

Chapter 9

Resolving Conflict: Arguing to Negotiate and Mediate

Argument to convince and persuade is a healthy force within a community. Whatever the issue, people hold a range of positions, and debate among advocates of these various positions serves to inform the public and draw attention to problems that need solution. Yet, although some issues seem to be debated endlessly—the death penalty, abortion, gun control, the U.S. role in the affairs of other nations—a time comes when the conflict must be resolved and a particular course of action pursued.

But what happens after each side has made its best effort to convince and persuade, yet no one position has won general assent? If the conflicting parties have equal power, the result can be an impasse, a stalemate. More often, however, one party has greater authority and is able to impose its will, as, for example, when a university dean or president imposes a policy decision on students or faculty. But imposing power can be costly—especially in terms of the worsened relationships—and it is often temporary. Foes of abortion, for example, have been able to influence policy significantly under conservative administrations, only to see their policy gains eroded when more liberal politicians gain power. If conflicts are going to be resolved—and stay resolved—each side needs to move beyond advocating its own position and argue with a new aim in mind: negotiation.

Arguing to negotiate aims to resolve, or at least reduce, conflict to the mutual satisfaction of all parties involved. But negotiation involves more than simply making a deal in which each side offers a few concessions while retaining a few of its initial demands. As this chapter shows, through the process of negotiating, opposing sides come to a greater understanding of their differing interests, backgrounds, and values; ideally, negotiation builds consensus and repairs strained relationships.

CONFLICT RESOLUTION AND
THE OTHER AIMS OF ARGUMENT

You may find it difficult to think of negotiation and mediation as argument if you see argument only as presenting a case for a particular position or as persuading an audience to act in accordance with that position. Both of these aims clearly involve advocating one position and addressing the argument to those with different viewpoints. But recall that one definition of *argue* is "to make clear." As we discussed in Chapter 6, sometimes we argue in order to learn what we should think; that is, we argue to inquire, trying out an argument, examining it critically and with as little bias as possible with an audience of nonthreatening partners in conversation such as friends or family.

Arguing to mediate or negotiate shares many of the characteristics of arguing to inquire. Like inquiry, negotiation most often takes the form of dialogue, although writing plays an important role in the process. Also, whether the negotiator is a party in the conflict or an outside mediator among the various parties, he or she must inquire into the positions of all sides. Furthermore, someone who agrees to enter into negotiation, especially someone who is a party to the conflict, must acknowledge his or her bias and remain open to the positions and interests of others, just as the inquirer does. Negotiation differs from inquiry, however, in that negotiation must find a mediating position that accommodates at least some of the interests of all sides. The best position in negotiation is the one all sides will accept.

As we will see in more detail, argument as mediation draws upon the strategies of the other aims of argument as well. Like convincing, negotiation requires an understanding of case structure, as negotiators must analyze the cases each side puts forth, and mediators often need to build a case of their own for a position acceptable to all. And like persuasion, negotiation recognizes the role of human character and emotions both in the creation of conflict and in its resolution.

To illustrate the benefits to be gained through the process of negotiation, in this chapter we concentrate on one of the most heated conflicts in the United States today: the debate over abortion. A wide range of positions exists on this issue. Extremists for fetal rights, who sometimes engage in violent acts of civil disobedience, and extremists for the absolute rights of women, who argue that a woman should be able to terminate a pregnancy at any time and for any reason, may not be amenable to negotiation. However, between these poles lie the viewpoints of most Americans, whose differences possibly can be resolved.

Negotiation has a chance only among people who have reasoned through their own positions through inquiry and who have attempted to defend their positions not through force but through convincing and persuasive argumentation. And mediation has a chance only when people see that the divisions caused by their conflict are counterproductive. They must be ready to listen to each other. They must be willing to negotiate.

Concept Close-Up

Characteristics of Negotiation

1. Aims to **resolve conflict** between opposing and usually **hardened** positions, often because action of some kind must be taken.
2. Aims to reduce hostility and promote understanding between or among conflicting parties; **preserving human relationships and promoting communication** are paramount.
3. Like inquiry, negotiation **involves dialogue** and requires that one understand all positions and strive for an **open mind.**
4. Like convincing, negotiation involves taking stances and making cases, but negotiation involves making a case that **appeals to all parties in the controversy.**
5. Like persuasion, negotiation depends on the **good character** of the negotiator and on sharing **values and feelings.**
6. Negotiation depends on conflicting parties' desire to **find solutions to overcome counterproductive stalemates.**

Essentially, negotiation comes into play when convincing and persuading have resulted in sharply differing viewpoints. The task is first to understand the positions of all parties involved and second to uncover a mediating position capable of producing consensus and a reduction in hostility.

THE PROCESS OF NEGOTIATION AND MEDIATION

As a student in a writing class, you can practice the process of negotiation in at least two ways. You and several other students who have written conflicting arguments on a common topic may negotiate among yourselves to find a resolution acceptable to all, perhaps bringing in a disinterested student to serve as a mediator. Or your class as a whole may mediate a dispute among writers whose printed arguments offer conflicting viewpoints on the same issue. Here we illustrate the mediator approach, which can be adapted easily to the more direct experience of face-to-face negotiation.

Understanding the Spirit of Negotiation and Mediation

In arguing issues of public concern, it is a mistake to think of negotiation as the same thing as negotiating the price of a car or a house or even a collective bargaining agreement. In a dialogue between buyer and seller, both sides typically begin by asking for much more than they seriously hope to get, and the process involves displays of will and power as each side tries to force the other to back down on its demands. Negotiation as rhetorical argument, however, is less adversarial; in fact, it is more like collaborative problem solving in which various opposing parties work together not to rebut one another's arguments but to understand them. Negotiation leads to the most permanent resolution of conflict when it is based on an increased understanding of difference rather than on a mere exchange of concessions. Negotiators must let go of the whole notion of proving one side right and other sides wrong. Rather, the negotiator says, "I see what you are demanding, and you see what I am demanding. Now let's sit down and find out *why* we hold these positions. What are our interests in this issue? Maybe together we can work out a solution that will address these interests." Unlike negotiators, mediators are impartial, and if they have a personal viewpoint on the issue, they must suppress it and be careful not to favor either side.

Understanding the Opposing Positions

Resolving conflict begins with a close look at opposing views. As in inquiry, the first stage of the process is an analysis of the positions, the thesis statements, and the supporting reasons and evidence offered on all sides. It is a good idea for each party to write a brief of his or her case, as described on pages 221–236 and 312–313. These briefs should indicate how the reasons are supported so that disputants can see where they agree or disagree about data.

The mediator also must begin by inquiring into the arguments presented by the parties in dispute. To illustrate, we look at two reasoned arguments representing opposing views on the value of the Supreme Court's *Roe v. Wade* decision. In that decision, which was handed down in 1973, the Court ruled that the Constitution does grant to citizens a zone of personal privacy, which for women includes the decision regarding whether to terminate a pregnancy. The Court stipulated, however, that the right to abortion was not unqualified and that states could regulate abortions to protect the fetus after viability.

The first argument, "Living with *Roe v. Wade*," is by Margaret Liu McConnell, a writer and mother of three, who herself had an abortion while she was in college. This experience led McConnell to decide that abortion on demand should not have become a constitutional right. To those who applaud abortion rights, McConnell argues that *Roe v. Wade* has had serious social and moral consequences for our nation. She does not call for the decision to be overturned, but she does want abortion rights supporters to take a closer look at the issue and recognize that abortion is fundamentally an immoral choice, one that should result in a sense of guilt. This essay originally appeared in 1990 in *Commentary*, a journal published by the American Jewish Committee.

The second argument is by Ellen Willis, also a mother who once had an abortion. For Willis, abortion is very much a right; in fact, it is the foundation of women's equality with men. Willis defends *Roe v. Wade* as the "cutting edge of feminism." Her audience consists of liberals who oppose abortion — "the left wing of the right-to-life movement" — specifically, the editors of *Com-

Figure 9.1   In a familiar scene, angry pro-choice and pro-life activists confront each other at a pro-choice demonstration. Although abortion remains one of the most contentious issues of our time, some of its proponents and opponents remain committed to working toward reconciling their differences.

monweal, a liberal Catholic journal. Her audience could also include people like Margaret Liu McConnell, who see abortion as a moral question rather than as a political question framed in terms of equal rights. Willis' "Putting Women Back into the Abortion Debate" originally appeared in the left-leaning *Village Voice* in 1985.

Living with *Roe v. Wade*
Margaret Liu McConnell

There is something decidedly unappealing to me about the pro-life activists seen on the evening news as they are dragged away from the entrances to abortion clinics across the country. Perhaps it is that their poses remind me of sulky two-year-olds, sinking to their knees as their frazzled mothers try to haul them from the playground. Or perhaps it is because I am a little hard put to believe, when one of them cries out, often with a Southern twang, "Ma'am, don't keel your baby," that he or she could really care that deeply about a stranger's fetus. After all, there are limits to compassion and such concern seems excessive, suspect.

Besides, as pro-choice adherents like to point out, the fact that abortion is legal does not mean that someone who is against abortion will be forced to have one against her wishes. It is a private matter, so they say, between a woman and her doctor. From this it would follow that those opposed to abortion are no more than obnoxious busybodies animated by their own inner pathologies to interfere in the private lives of strangers.

Certainly this is the impression conveyed by those news clips of anti-abortion blockades being broken up by the police. We pity the woman, head sunk and afraid, humiliated in the ancient shame that all around her know she is carrying an unwanted child. Precisely because she is pregnant, our hearts go out to her in her vulnerability. It would seem that those workers from the abortion clinic, shielding arms around her shoulders, their identification vests giving them the benign look of school-crossing guards, are her protectors. They are guiding her through a hostile, irrational crowd to the cool and orderly safety of the clinic and the medical attention she needs.

But is it possible that this impression is mistaken? Is it possible that those who guide the woman along the path to the abortionist's table are not truly her protectors, shoring her up on the road to a dignified life in which she will best be able to exercise her intellectual and physical faculties free from any kind of oppression? Is it possible that they are serving, albeit often unwittingly, to keep her and millions of other women on a demeaning and rather lonely treadmill — a treadmill on which these women trudge through cycles of sex without commitment, unwanted pregnancy, and abortion, all in the name of equal opportunity and free choice?

Consider yet again the woman on the path to an abortion. She is already   5
a victim of many forces. She is living in a social climate in which she is expected to view sex as practically a form of recreation that all healthy women should pursue eagerly. She has been conditioned to fear having a child, particularly in her younger years, as an unthinkable threat to her standard of living and to the career through which she defines herself as a "real" person. Finally, since 1973, when the Supreme Court in *Roe v. Wade* declared access to abortion a constitutional right, she has been invited, in the event that she does become pregnant, not only to have an abortion, but to do so without sorrow and with no moral misgivings. As the highly vocal proabortion movement cheers her on with rallying cries of "Freedom of Choice," she may find herself wondering: "Is this the great freedom we've been fighting for? The freedom to sleep with men who don't care for us, the freedom to scorn the chance to raise a child? The freedom to let doctors siphon from our bodies that most precious gift which women alone are made to receive: a life to nurture?"

My goal here is not to persuade militant pro-choicers that abortion is wrong. Instead, it is to establish that abortion cannot and should not be seen as strictly a matter between a woman and her doctor. For the knowledge that the law allows free access to abortion affects all of us directly and indirectly by the way it shapes the social climate. Most directly and most easy to illustrate, the realization that any pregnancy, intended or accidental, may be aborted at will affects women in their so-called childbearing years. The indirect effects are more difficult to pinpoint. I would like tentatively to suggest that *Roe v. Wade* gives approval, at the highest level of judgment in this country, to certain attitudes which, when manifest at the lowest economic levels, have extremely destructive consequences.

But to begin with the simpler task of examining *Roe*'s questionable effect on the world women inhabit: I—who at thirty-two am of the age to have "benefited" from *Roe*'s protections for all my adult years—offer here some examples of those "benefits."

It was my first year at college, my first year away from my rather strict, first-generation American home. I had a boyfriend from high school whom I liked and admired but was not in love with, and I was perfectly satisfied with the stage of heavy-duty necking we had managed, skillfully avoiding the suspicious eyes of my mother. But once I got to college I could think of no good reason not to go farther. For far from perceiving any constraints around me, I encountered all manner of encouragement to become "sexually active"—from the health center, from newspapers, books, and magazines, from the behavior of other students, even from the approval of other students' parents of their children's "liberated" sexual conduct.

Yet the truth is that I longed for the days I knew only from old movies and novels, those pre-60's days when boyfriends visiting from other colleges stayed in hotels (!) and dates ended with a lingering kiss at the door. I lived in an apartment-style dormitory, six women sharing three bedrooms and a kitchen. Needless to say, visiting boyfriends did not stay in hotels. By the end of my freshman year three out of the six of us would have had abortions.

How did it come to pass that so many of us got pregnant? How has it come to pass that more than one-and-one-half million women each year get pregnant in this country, only to have abortions? Nowadays it is impossible to go into a drugstore without bumping into the condoms on display above the checkout counters. And even when I was in college, contraception was freely available, and everyone knew that the health center, open from nine to four, was ready to equip us with the contraceptive armament we were sure to need.

Nevertheless, thanks to *Roe v. Wade*, we all understood as well that if anything went wrong, there would be no threat of a shotgun marriage, or of being sent away in shame to bear a child, or of a dangerous back-alley abortion. Perhaps the incredible number of "accidental" pregnancies, both at college and throughout the country, finds its explanation in just that understanding. Analogies are difficult to construct in arguments about abortion, for there is nothing quite analogous to terminating a pregnancy. That said, consider this one anyway. If children are sent out to play ball in a yard near a house, a responsible adult, knowing that every once in a while a window will get broken, will still tell them to be very careful not to break any. But what if the children are sent into the yard and told something like this: "Go out and play, and don't worry about breaking any windows. It's bound to happen, and when it does, no problem: it will be taken care of." How many more windows will be shattered?

There were, here and there, some women who seemed able to live outside these pressures. Within my apartment one was an Orthodox Jewish freshman from Queens, another a junior from Brooklyn, also Jewish, who was in the process of becoming Orthodox. They kept kosher as far as was possible in our common kitchen, and on Friday afternoons would cook supper for a group of friends, both men and women. As darkness fell they would light candles and sing and eat and laugh in a circle of light. I remember looking in at their evenings from the doorway to the kitchen, wishing vainly that I could belong to such a group, a group with a code of behavior that would provide shelter from the free-for-all I saw elsewhere. But the only group I felt I belonged to was, generically, "young American woman," and as far as I could see, the norm of behavior for a young American woman was to enjoy a healthy sex life, with or without commitment.

A few months later, again thanks to *Roe v. Wade*, I discovered that the logistics of having an abortion were, as promised, extremely simple. The school health center was again at my service. After a few perfunctory questions and sympathetic nods of the head I was given directions to the nearest abortion clinic.

A strange thing has happened since that great freedom-of-choice victory in 1973. Abortion has become the only viable alternative many women feel they have open to them when they become pregnant by accident. Young men no longer feel obligated to offer to "do the right thing." Pregnancy is most often confirmed in a medical setting. Even though it is a perfectly normal and healthy state, in an unwanted pregnancy a woman feels distressed. The situation thus becomes that of a distressed woman looking to trusted medical personnel for relief. Abortion presents itself as the simple, legal, medical solution to her distress. A woman may have private reservations, but she gets the distinct impression that if she does not take advantage of her right to an abortion she is of her own accord refusing a simple solution to her troubles.

That is certainly how it was for me, sitting across from the counselor at   15
the health center, clutching a wad of damp tissues, my heart in my throat. The feeling was exactly parallel to the feeling I had had at the beginning of the school year: I could be defiantly old-fashioned and refuse to behave like a normal American woman, or I could exercise my sexual liberation. Here, six weeks pregnant, I could be troublesome, perverse, and somehow manage to keep the baby, causing tremendous inconvenience to everyone, or I could take the simple route of having an abortion and not even miss a single class. The choice was already made.

Physically, also, abortion has become quite a routine procedure. As one of my grosser roommates put it, comforting me with talk of her own experiences, it was about as bad as going to the dentist. My only memory of the

operation is of coming out of the general anesthesia to the sound of sobbing all around. I, too, was sobbing, without thought, hard and uncontrol-
lably, as though somehow, deep below the conscious level, below whatever
superficial concerns had layered themselves in the day-to-day mind of a
busy young woman, I had come to realize what I had done, and what
could never be undone.

I have since had three children, and at the beginning of each pregnancy
I was presented with the opportunity to have an abortion without even
having to ask. For professional reasons my husband and I have moved several times, and each of our children was born in a different city with a different set of obstetrical personnel. In every case I was offered the unsolic-
ited luxury of "keeping my options open": of choosing whether to continue
the pregnancy or end it. The polite way of posing the question, after a positive pregnancy test, seems to be for the doctor to ask noncommittally, "And
how are we treating this pregnancy?"

Each one of those pregnancies, each one of those expendable bunches
of tissue, has grown into a child, each one different from the other. I cannot
escape the haunting fact that if I had had an abortion, one of my children
would be missing. Not just a generic little bundle in swaddling clothes in-
terchangeable with any other, but a specific child.

I still carry in my mind a picture of that other child who was never born,
a picture which changes as the years go by, and I imagine him growing up.
For some reason I usually do imagine a boy, tall and with dark hair and
eyes. This is speculation, of course, based on my coloring and build and on
that of the young man involved. Such speculation seems maudlin and mor-
bid and I do not engage in it on purpose. But whether I like it or not, every
now and then my mind returns to that ghost of a child and to the certainty
that for seven weeks I carried the beginnings of a being whose coloring and
build and, to a large extent, personality were already determined. Buoyant
green-eyed girl or shy, dark-haired boy, I wonder. Whoever, a child would
have been twelve this spring.

I am not in the habit of exposing this innermost regret, this endless re-   20
morse to which I woke too late. I do so only to show that in the wake of
Roe v. Wade abortion has become casual, commonplace, and very hard to
resist as an easy way out of an unintended pregnancy, and that more unintended pregnancies are likely to occur when everyone knows there is an
easy way out of them. Abortion has become an option offered to women,
married as well as unmarried, including those who are financially, physically, and emotionally able to care for a child. This is what *Roe v. Wade*
guarantees. For all the pro-choice lobby's talk of abortion as a deep personal moral decision, casting abortion as a right takes the weight of morality out of the balance. For, by definition, a right is something one need not
feel guilty exercising.

I do not wish a return to the days when a truly desperate woman unable to get a safe legal abortion would risk her life at the hands of an illegal

abortionist. Neither could I ever condemn a woman whose own grip on life is so fragile as to render her incapable of taking on the full responsibility for another life, helpless and demanding. But raising abortion to the plane of a constitutional right in order to ensure its accessibility to any woman for any reason makes abortion too easy a solution to an age-old problem.

Human beings have always coupled outside the bounds deemed proper by the societies in which they lived. But the inevitable unexpected pregnancies often served a social purpose. There was a time when many young couples found in the startling new life they had created an undeniable reason to settle down seriously to the tasks of earning a living and making a home. That might have meant taking on a nine-to-five job and assuming a mortgage, a prospect which sounds like death to many baby boomers intent on prolonging adolescence well into middle age. But everyone knows anecdotally if not from straight statistics that many of these same baby boomers owe their own lives to such happy (for them) accidents.

When I became pregnant in college, I never seriously considered getting married and trying to raise a child, although it certainly would have been possible to do so. Why should I have, when the road to an abortion was so free and unencumbered, and when the very operation itself had been presented as a step on the march to women's equality?

I know that no one forced me to do anything, that I was perfectly free to step back at any time and live by my own moral code if I chose to, much as my Orthodox Jewish acquaintances did. But this is awfully hard when the society you consider yourself part of presents abortion as a legal, morally acceptable solution. And what kind of a world would it be if all those in need of a moral structure stepped back to insulate themselves, alone or in groups—ethnic, religious, or economic—each with its own exclusive moral code, leaving behind a chaos at the center? It sounds like New York City on a bad day.

This is not, of course, to ascribe the chaos reigning in our cities directly to *Roe v. Wade*. That chaos is caused by a growing and tenacious underclass defined by incredibly high rates of drug abuse, and dependence on either crime or welfare for financial support. But sometimes it does seem as though the same attitude behind abortion on demand lies behind the abandonment of parental responsibility which is the most pervasive feature of life in the underclass and the most determinative of its terrible condition.

Parental responsibility can be defined as providing one's offspring at every level of development with that which they need to grow eventually into independent beings capable of supporting themselves emotionally and financially. Different parents will, of course, have different ideas about what is best for a child, and different parents will have different resources to draw upon to provide for their children. But whatever the differences may be, responsible parents will try, to the best of their ability and in accordance with their own rights, to raise their children properly. It is tedious, expensive, and takes a long, long time. For it is not a question of fetal weeks before a hu-

25

man being reaches any meaningful stage of "viability" (how "viable" is a two-year-old left to his own devices? A five-year-old?). It is a question of years, somewhere in the neighborhood of eighteen.

Why does any parent take on such a long, hard task? Because life is a miracle that cannot be denied? Because it is the right thing to do? Because there is a certain kind of love a parent bears a child that does not require a calculated return on investment? Because we would hate ourselves otherwise? All these factors enter into the powerful force that compels parents to give up years of their free time and much of their money to bring up their children. Yet the cool, clinical approach *Roe v. Wade* allows all of us—men no less than women—in deciding whether or not we are "ready" to accept the responsibility of an established pregnancy seems to undermine an already weakening cultural expectation that parents simply have a duty to take care of their children.

A middle- or upper-class woman may have high expectations of what she will achieve so long as she is not saddled with a baby. When she finds herself pregnant she is guaranteed the right under *Roe v. Wade* to opt out of that long and tedious responsibility, and does so by the hundreds of thousands each year. By contrast, a woman in the underclass who finds herself pregnant is not likely to have great expectations of what life would be like were she free of the burden of her child; abortion would not broaden her horizons and is not usually her choice. Yet she often lacks the maternal will and the resources to take full responsibility for the well-being of her child until adulthood.

To be sure, these two forms of refusing parental responsibility have vastly different effects. But how can the government hope to devise policies that will encourage parental responsibility in the underclass when at the highest level of judgment, that of the Supreme Court, the freedom to opt out of parental responsibility is protected as a right? Or, to put the point another way, perhaps the weakening of the sense of duty toward one's own offspring is a systemic problem in America, present in all classes, with only its most visible manifestation in the underclass.

The federal Family Support Act of 1988 was the result of much study and debate on how to reform the welfare system to correct policies which have tended to make it easier for poor families to qualify for aid if the father is not part of the household. Among other provisions intended to help keep families from breaking up, states are now required to pay cash benefits to two-parent families and to step up child-support payments from absent fathers. New York City, for example, has this year begun to provide its Department of Health with information, including Social Security numbers, on the parents of every child born in the city. Should the mother ever apply for aid, the father can be tracked down and child-support payments can be deducted from his paycheck. Such a strict enforcement of child-support obligations is a powerful and exciting legal method for society to show that it will not tolerate the willful abandonment of children by their fathers.

It is evident that there is a compelling state interest in promoting the responsibility of both parents toward their child. The compelling interest is that it takes a great deal of money to care for a child whose parents do not undertake the responsibility themselves. For whatever else we may have lost of our humanity over the last several decades, however hardened we have been by violence and by the degradation witnessed daily in the lost lives on the street, we still retain a basic decent instinct to care for innocent babies and children in need.

It is also evident that parental responsibility begins well before the child is born. Thus, the Appellate Division of the State Supreme Court of New York in May of this year ruled that a woman who uses drugs during pregnancy and whose newborn has drugs in its system may be brought before Family Court for a hearing on neglect. Yet how can we condemn a woman under law for harming her unborn child while at the same time protecting her right to destroy that child absolutely, for any reason, through abortion? Is the only difference that the first instance entails a monetary cost to society while the second does not?

There is another kind of behavior implicitly condoned by *Roe v. Wade*, which involves the value of life itself, and which also has its most frightening and threatening manifestation in the underclass. Consensus on when human life begins has yet to be established and perhaps never will be. What is clear, however, is that abortion cuts short the development of a specific human life; it wipes out the future years of a human being, years we can know nothing about. Generally we have no trouble conceiving of lost future years as real loss. Lawsuits routinely place value on lost future income and lost future enjoyment, and we consider the death of a child or a young person to be particularly tragic in lost potential, in the waste of idealized years to come. Yet under *Roe v. Wade* the value of the future years of life of the fetus is determined by an individual taking into account only her own well-being.

Back in 1965, justifying his discovery of a constitutional right to privacy which is nowhere mentioned in the Constitution itself, and which helped lay the groundwork for *Roe v. Wade*, Justice William O. Douglas invoked the concept of "penumbras, formed by emanations" of constitutional amendments. Is it far-fetched to say that there are "penumbras, formed by emanations" of *Roe v. Wade* that grant the right to consider life in relative terms and to place one's own interest above any others? This same "right" when exercised by criminals is a terrifying phenomenon: these are people who feel no guilt in taking a victim's life, who value the future years of that life as nothing compared with their own interest in the victim's property. Of course, one might argue that a fetus is not yet cognizant of its own beingness and that, further, it feels no pain. Yet if a killer creeps up behind you and blows your head off with a semi-automatic, you will feel no pain either, nor will you be cognizant of your death.

Roe v. Wade was a great victory for the women's movement. It seemed to promote equality of opportunity for women in all their endeavors by free-

35

ing them from the burden of years of caring for children conceived unintentionally. But perhaps support for *Roe v. Wade* should be reconsidered in light of the damage wrought by the kind of behavior that has become common in a world in which pregnancy is no longer seen as the momentous beginning of a new life, and life, by extension, is no longer held as sacred.

At any rate, even if one rejects my speculation that *Roe v. Wade* has at least some indirect connection with the degree to which life on our streets has become so cheap, surely there can be no denying the direct connection between *Roe v. Wade* and the degree to which sex has become so casual. Surely, for example, *Roe v. Wade* will make it harder for my two daughters to grow gracefully into womanhood without being encouraged to think of sex as a kind of sport played with a partner who need feel no further responsibility toward them once the game is over.

For me, that is reason enough not to support this elevation of abortion to the status of a constitutional right.

Putting Women Back into the Abortion Debate
Ellen Willis

Some years ago I attended a New York Institute for the Humanities seminar on the new right. We were a fairly heterogeneous group of liberals and lefties, feminists and gay activists, but on one point nearly all of us agreed: The right-to-life movement was a dangerous antifeminist crusade. At one session I argued that the attack on abortion had significance far beyond itself, that it was the linchpin of the right's social agenda. I got a lot of supporting comments and approving nods. It was too much for Peter Steinfels, a liberal Catholic, author of *The Neoconservatives,* and executive editor of *Commonweal.* Right-to-lifers were not all right-wing fanatics, he protested. "You have to understand," he said plaintively, "that many of us see abortion as a *human life issue.*" What I remember best was his air of frustrated isolation. I don't think he came back to the seminar after that.

Things are different now. I often feel isolated when I insist that abortion is, above all, a *feminist issue.* Once people took for granted that abortion was an issue of sexual politics and morality. Now, abortion is most often discussed as a question of "life" in the abstract. Public concern over abortion centers almost exclusively on fetuses; women and their bodies are merely the stage on which the drama of fetal life and death takes place. Debate about abortion—if not its reality—has become sexlessly scholastic. And the people most responsible for this turn of events are, like Peter Steinfels, on the left.

The left wing of the right-to-life movement is a small, seemingly eccentric minority in both "progressive" and antiabortion camps. Yet it has played a critical role in the movement: By arguing that opposition to abortion can be separated from the right's antifeminist program, it has given antiabortion sentiment legitimacy in left-symp[1] and (putatively) profeminist circles. While left antiabortionists are hardly alone in emphasizing fetal life, their innovation has been to claim that a consistent "pro-life" stand involves opposing capital punishment, supporting disarmament, demanding government programs to end poverty, and so on. This is of course a leap the right is neither able nor willing to make. It's been liberals—from Garry Wills to the Catholic bishops—who have supplied the mass media with the idea that prohibiting abortion is part of a "seamless garment" of respect for human life.

Having invented this countercontext for the abortion controversy, left antiabortionists are trying to impose it as the only legitimate context for debate. Those of us who won't accept their terms and persist in seeing opposition to abortion, antifeminism, sexual repression, and religious sectarianism as the real seamless garment have been accused of obscuring the issue with demagoguery. Last year *Commonweal*—perhaps the most important current forum for left antiabortion opinion—ran an editorial demanding that we shape up: "Those who hold that abortion is immoral believe that the biological dividing lines of birth or viability should no more determine whether a developing member of the species is denied or accorded essential rights than should the biological dividing lines of sex or race or disability or old age. This argument is open to challenge. Perhaps the dividing lines are sufficiently different. Pro-choice advocates should state their reasons for believing so. They should meet the argument on its own grounds. . . ."

In other words, the only question we're allowed to debate—or the only one *Commonweal* is willing to entertain—is "Are fetuses the moral equivalent of born human beings?" And I can't meet the argument on its own grounds because I don't agree that this is the key question, whose answer determines whether one supports abortion or opposes it. I don't doubt that fetuses are alive, or that they're biologically human—what else would they be? I do consider the life of a fertilized egg less precious than the well-being of a woman with feelings, self-consciousness, a history, social ties; and I think fetuses get closer to being human in a moral sense as they come closer to birth. But to me these propositions are intuitively self-evident. I wouldn't know how to justify them to a "nonbeliever," nor do I see the point of trying.

I believe the debate has to start in a different place—with the recognition that fertilized eggs develop into infants inside the bodies of women. Pregnancy and birth are active processes in which a woman's body shelters, nourishes, and expels a new life; for nine months she is immersed in the most intimate possible relationship with another being. The growing fetus makes considerable demands on her physical and emotional resources, cul-

5

---

[1] *Left-symp:* sympathetic to the left.

minating in the cataclysmic experience of birth. And child-bearing has un-predictable consequences; it always entails some risk of injury or death.

For me all this has a new concreteness: I had a baby last year. My much-desired and relatively easy pregnancy was full of what antiabortionists like to call "inconveniences." I was always tired, short of breath; my digestion was never right; for three months I endured a state of hormonal siege; later I had pains in my fingers, swelling feet, numb spots on my legs, the dread hemorrhoids. I had to think about everything I ate. I developed borderline glucose intolerance. I gained fifty pounds and am still overweight; my shape has changed in other ways that may well be permanent. Psychologically, my pregnancy consumed me — though I'd happily bought the seat on the roller coaster, I was still terrified to be so out of control of my normally tractable body. It was all bearable, even interesting — even, at times, tran-scendent — because I wanted a baby. Birth was painful, exhausting, and wonderful. If I hadn't wanted a baby it would only have been painful and exhausting — or worse. I can hardly imagine what it's like to have your body and mind taken over in this way when you not only don't look forward to the result, but positively dread it. The thought appalls me. So as I see it, the key question is "Can it be moral, under any circumstances, to make a woman bear a child against her will?"

From this vantage point, *Commonweal*'s argument is irrelevant, for in a society that respects the individual, no "member of the species" in *any* stage of development has an "essential right" to make use of someone else's body, let alone in such all-encompassing fashion, without that person's consent. You can't make a case against abortion by applying a general principle about everybody's human rights; you have to show exactly the opposite — that the relationship between fetus and pregnant woman is an exception, one that justifies depriving women of their right to bodily integrity. And in fact all antiabortion ideology rests on the premise — acknowledged or sim-ply assumed — that women's unique capacity to bring life into the world carries with it a unique obligation that women cannot be allowed to "play God" and launch only the lives they welcome.

Yet the alternative to allowing women this power is to make them im-potent. Criminalizing abortion doesn't just harm individual women with unwanted pregnancies, it affects all women's sense of themselves. Without control of our fertility we can never envision ourselves as free, for our biol-ogy makes us constantly vulnerable. Simply because we are female our physical integrity can be violated, our lives disrupted and transformed, at any time. Our ability to act in the world is hopelessly compromised by our sexual being.

Ah, sex — it does have a way of coming up in these discussions, despite all. When pressed, right-to-lifers of whatever political persuasion invariably point out that pregnancy doesn't happen by itself. The leftists often give patronizing lectures on contraception (though some find only "natural birth control" acceptable), but remain unmoved when reminded that

10

contraceptives fail. Openly or implicitly they argue that people shouldn't have sex unless they're prepared to procreate. (They are quick to profess a single standard—men as well as women should be sexually "responsible." Yes, and the rich as well as the poor should be allowed to sleep under bridges.) Which amounts to saying that if women want to lead heterosexual lives they must give up any claim to self-determination, and that they have no right to sexual pleasure without fear.

Opposing abortion, then, means accepting that women must suffer sexual disempowerment and a radical loss of autonomy relative to men: If fetal life is sacred, the self-denial basic to women's oppression is also basic to the moral order. Opposing abortion means embracing a conservative sexual morality, one that subordinates pleasure to reproduction: If fetal life is sacred, there is no room for the view that sexual passion—or even sexual love—for its own sake is a human need and a human right. Opposing abortion means tolerating the inevitable double standard, by which men may accept or reject sexual restrictions in accordance with their beliefs, while women must bow to them out of fear . . . or defy them at great risk. However much *Commonweal*'s editors and those of like mind want to believe their opposition to abortion is simply about saving lives, the truth is that in the real world they are shoring up a particular sexual culture, whose rules are stacked against women. I have yet to hear any left right-to-lifers take full responsibility for that fact or deal seriously with its political implications.

Unfortunately, their fuzziness has not lessened their appeal—if anything it's done the opposite. In increasing numbers liberals and leftists, while opposing antiabortion laws, have come to view abortion as an "agonizing moral issue" with some justice on both sides, rather than an issue—however emotionally complex—of freedom versus repression, or equality versus hierarchy, that affects their political self-definition. This above-the-battle stance is attractive to leftists who want to be feminist good guys but are uneasy or ambivalent about sexual issues, not to mention those who want to ally with "progressive" factions of the Catholic church on Central America, nuclear disarmament, or populist economics without that sticky abortion question getting in the way.

Such neutrality is a way of avoiding the painful conflict over cultural issues that continually smolders on the left. It can also be a way of coping with the contradictions of personal life at a time when liberation is a dream deferred. To me the fight for abortion has always been the cutting edge of feminism, precisely because it denies that anatomy is destiny, that female biology dictates women's subordinate status. Yet recently I've found it hard to focus on the issue, let alone summon up the militance needed to stop the antiabortion tanks. In part that has to do with second-round weariness—do we really have to go through all these things twice?—in part with my life now.

Since my daughter's birth my feelings about abortion—not as a political demand but as a personal choice—have changed. In this society, the dif-

ference between the situation of a childless woman and of a mother is immense; the fear that having a child will dislodge one's tenuous hold on a
nontraditional life is excruciating. This terror of being forced into the sea-
change of motherhood gave a special edge to my convictions about abortion. Since I've made that plunge voluntarily, with consequences still un-
folding, the terror is gone; I might not want another child, for all sorts of
reasons, but I will never again feel that my identity is at stake. Different bat-
tles with the culture absorb my energy now. Besides, since I've experienced
the primal, sensual passion of caring for an infant, there will always be part
of me that does want another. If I had an abortion today, it would be with
conflict and sadness unknown to me when I had an abortion a decade ago.
And the antiabortionists' imagery of dead babies hits me with new force.
Do many women—left, feminist women—have such feelings? Is this the
sort of "ambivalence about abortion" that in the present atmosphere slides
so easily into self-flagellating guilt?

Some left antiabortionists, mainly pacifists—Juli Loesch, Mary Meehan,   15
and other "feminists for life"; Jim Wallis and various writers for Wallis's radical evangelical journal *Sojourners*—have tried to square their position with
concern for women. They blame the prevalence of abortion on oppressive
conditions—economic injustice, lack of child care and other social supports for mothers, the devaluation of childrearing, men's exploitative sexual
behavior and refusal to take equal responsibility for children. They disagree
on whether to criminalize abortion now (since murder is intolerable no
matter what the cause) or to build a long-term moral consensus (since
stopping abortion requires a general social transformation), but they all
regard abortion as a desperate solution to desperate problems, and the
women who resort to it as more sinned against than sinning.

This analysis grasps an essential feminist truth: that in a male-
supremacist society no choice a woman makes is genuinely free or entirely
in her interest. Certainly many women have had abortions they didn't want
or wouldn't have wanted if they had any plausible means of caring for a
child; and countless others wouldn't have gotten pregnant in the first place
were it not for inadequate contraception, sexual confusion and guilt, male
pressure, and other stigmata of female powerlessness. Yet forcing a woman
to bear a child she doesn't want can only add injury to insult, while refusing to go through with such a pregnancy can be a woman's first step toward
taking hold of her life. And many women who have abortions are "victims"
only of ordinary human miscalculation, technological failure, or the vaga-
ries of passion, all bound to exist in any society, however utopian. There
will always be women who, at any given moment, want sex but don't want
a child; some of these women will get pregnant; some of them will have
abortions. Behind the victim theory of abortion is the implicit belief that
women are always ready to be mothers, if only conditions are right, and
that sex for pleasure rather than procreation is not only "irresponsible"
(i.e., bad) but something men impose on women, never something women

actively seek. Ironically, left right-to-lifers see abortion as always coerced (it's "exploitation" and "violence against women"), yet regard mother-hood—which for most women throughout history has been inescapable, and is still our most socially approved role—as a positive choice. The anal-ogy to the feminist antipornography movement goes beyond borrowed rhetoric: the antiporners, too, see active female lust as surrender to male domination and traditionally feminine sexual attitudes as expressions of women's true nature.

This Orwellian version of feminism, which glorifies "female values" and dismisses women's struggles for freedom—particularly sexual free-dom—as a male plot, has become all too familiar in recent years. But its use in the abortion debate has been especially muddleheaded. Somehow we're supposed to leap from an oppressive patriarchal society to the egali-tarian one that will supposedly make abortion obsolete without ever allow-ing women to see themselves as people entitled to control their reproduc-tive function rather than be controlled by it. How women who have no power in this most personal of areas can effectively fight for power in the larger society is left to our imagination. A "New Zealand feminist" quoted by Mary Meehan in a 1980 article in *The Progressive* says, "Accepting short-term solutions like abortion only delays the implementation of real re-forms like decent maternity and paternity leaves, job protection, high-quality child care, community responsibility for dependent people of all ages, and recognition of the economic contribution of childminders"—as if these causes were progressing nicely before legal abortion came along. On the contrary, the fight for reproductive freedom is the foundation of all the others, which is why antifeminists resist it so fiercely.

As "pro-life" pacifists have been particularly concerned with refuting charges of misogyny, the liberal Catholics at *Commonweal* are most exer-cised by the claim that antiabortion laws violate religious freedom. The edi-torial quoted above hurled another challenge at the proabortion forces:

> It is time, finally, for the pro-choice advocates and editorial writers to aban-don, once and for all, the argument that abortion is a religious "doctrine" of a single or several churches being imposed on those of other persuasions in vio-lation of the First Amendment. . . . Catholics and their bishops are accused of imposing their "doctrine" on abortion, but not their "doctrine" on the needs of the poor, or their "doctrine" on the arms race, or their "doctrine" on human rights in Central America. . . .
>
> The briefest investigation into Catholic teaching would show that the church's case against abortion is utterly unlike, say, its belief in the Real Presence, known with the eyes of faith alone, or its insistence on a Sunday obligation, applicable only to the faithful. The church's moral teaching on abortion . . . is for the most part like its teaching on racism, warfare, and capital punishment, based on ordinary reasoning common to believers and nonbelievers. . . .

This is one more example of right-to-lifers' tendency to ignore the sexual ideology underlying their stand. Interesting, isn't it, how the editorial neglects to mention that the church's moral teaching on abortion jibes neatly with its teaching on birth control, sex, divorce, and the role of women. The traditional, patriarchal sexual morality common to these teachings is explicitly religious, and its chief defenders in modern times have been the more conservative churches. The Catholic and evangelical Christian churches are the backbone of the organized right-to-life movement and—a few Nathansons and Hentoffs notwithstanding—have provided most of the movement's activists and spokespeople.

Furthermore, the Catholic hierarchy has made opposition to abortion   20
a litmus test of loyalty to the church in a way it has done with no other political issue—witness Archbishop O'Connor's harassment of Geraldine Ferraro during her vice-presidential campaign. It's unthinkable that a Catholic bishop would publicly excoriate a Catholic officeholder or candidate for taking a hawkish position on the arms race or Central America or capital punishment. Nor do I notice anyone trying to read William F. Buckley out of the church for his views on welfare. The fact is there is no accepted Catholic "doctrine" on these matters comparable to the church's absolutist condemnation of abortion. While differing attitudes toward war, racism, and poverty cut across religious and secular lines, the sexual values that mandate opposition to abortion are the bedrock of the traditional religious world view, and the source of the most bitter conflict with secular and religious modernists. When churches devote their considerable political power, organizational resources, and money to translating those values into law, I call that imposing their religious beliefs on me—whether or not they're technically violating the First Amendment.

Statistical studies have repeatedly shown that people's views on abortion are best predicted by their opinions on sex and "family" issues, not on "life" issues like nuclear weapons or the death penalty. That's not because we're inconsistent but because we comprehend what's really at stake in the abortion fight. It's the antiabortion left that refuses to face the contradiction in its own position: you can't be wholeheartedly for "life"—or for such progressive aspirations as freedom, democracy, equality—and condone the subjugation of women. The seamless garment is full of holes.

Analysis of the Writers' Positions

These essays by McConnell and Willis represent the two sides on which most Americans fall regarding the issue of legalized abortion. Because abortion is likely to stay legal, what is the point of trying to reconcile these positions? One benefit is that doing so might help put to rest the controversy surrounding abortion—a controversy that rages at abortion clinics and in the media, distracting Americans from other issues of importance and causing divisiveness and distrust, and that also rages within millions of Americans who want abortion to remain legal but at the same time disapprove of it. In addition, reaching some consensus on abortion might resolve the contradiction of its being legal but unavailable to many women, as extremist opponents have caused many doctors to refuse to perform abortions and restrictions on public funding for abortion have limited the access of poor women. Finally, some consensus on abortion will be necessary to formulate decisions of public policy: What restrictions, if any, are appropriate? Should parental notification or consent be required for women under eighteen? Should public funds be available for an abortion when a woman cannot otherwise afford one?

We have said that the first step in resolving conflict is to understand what the parties in conflict are claiming and why. Using the following outline form, or brief, we can describe the positions of each side:

McConnell's position: She is against unrestricted abortion as a woman's right.

Claim (or thesis): The right to abortion has hurt the moral and social climate of our nation.

> *Reason:* It has put pressure on young single women to adopt a "liberated" lifestyle of sex without commitment.
>> *Evidence:* Her own college experiences.
>
> *Reason:* It has caused an increase in unintended pregnancies.
>> *Evidence:* The analogy of children playing ball.
>
> *Reason:* It has taken questions about morality out of the decision to end a pregnancy.
>> *Evidence:* Her own experiences with doctors and clinics.
>
> *Reason:* It has allowed middle- and upper-class men and women to avoid the consequences of their sex lives and to evade the responsibilities of parenthood.
>> *Evidence:* None offered.
>
> *Reason:* It has reduced people's sense of duty toward their offspring, most noticeably in the lower classes.
>> *Evidence:* Legislation has become necessary to make fathers provide financial support for their children and to hold women legally culpable for harming their fetuses through drug use.

Willis's position: She is for unrestricted abortion as a woman's right.

Claim (or thesis): The right to abortion is an essential part of feminism.

> *Reason:* Without control of their reproductive lives, women constantly fear having their lives disrupted.
>> *Evidence:* A fetus makes immense demands on a woman's physical and mental resources. Her own pregnancy is an example.

Reason: Without abortion, women must live according to a sexual double standard.
Evidence: Sex always carries the risk of pregnancy. The fear of pregnancy puts restrictions on women's ability to enjoy sex for pleasure or passion rather than procreation.

Following Through

If you and some of your classmates have written arguments taking opposing views on the same issue, prepare briefs of your respective positions to share with one another. (You might also create briefs of your opponents' positions to see how well you have understood one another's written arguments.)

Alternatively, write briefs summarizing the opposing positions offered in several published arguments as a first step toward mediating these viewpoints.

Locating the Areas of Disagreement

Areas of disagreement generally involve differences over facts and differences in interests.

Differences over Facts

Any parties involved in negotiation, as well as any mediator in a dispute, should consider both the reasons and evidence offered on all sides in order to locate areas of factual agreement and particularly disagreement. Parties genuinely interested in finding the best solution to a conflict rather than in advocating their own positions ought to be able to recognize when more evidence is needed, no matter the side. Negotiators and mediators should also consider the currency and the authority of any sources. If new or better research could help resolve factual disparities, the parties should do it collaboratively rather than independently.

Following Through

In the preceding arguments on abortion, the writers do not present much factual evidence, as their arguments are relatively abstract. Are there any facts on which they agree? Would more facts make a difference in getting either side to reconsider her position? How could you gather more solid evidence or hard data?

Differences in Interests

Experts in negotiation have found that conflicts most often result from interpretive differences rather than from factual differences; that is, people in conflict look at the same situation differently depending on their values, their beliefs, and their interests. McConnell opens her argument with this very point
by showing how most women's rights advocates would interpret the scene at
a typical antiabortion protest and then by offering a second perspective, affected by her view that legalized abortion has victimized women.

What kinds of subjective differences cause people to draw conflicting
conclusions from the same evidence? To identify these differences, we can ask
the same questions that are useful in persuasion to identify what divides us
from our audience (see the box "Questions for Understanding Difference,"
page 317). In negotiation and mediation, these questions can help uncover
the real interests that any resolution must address. It is in identifying these
interests that the dialogue of negotiation begins, because only when the interests that underlie opposing positions are identified can creative solutions
be formulated. Often, uncovering each party's real interests leads to the discovery of previously ignored common ground. Finding these interests should
be a collaborative project, one that negotiation experts compare to problem
solving through teamwork.

Here we apply the questions about difference to McConnell's and Willis's
positions on abortion rights.

Is the Difference a Matter of Assumptions?   Both arguments make the assumption that legalizing abortion removed constraints on women's sexuality. McConnell blames abortion for this presumed effect, but Willis credits
abortion with enabling women to enjoy sex as men have traditionally been
able to do. A mediator might begin by pointing out that this assumption itself could be wrong, that it is possible, for example, that the introduction of
birth control pills and the political liberalism of the 1970s contributed more
to the increased sexual activity of women. McConnell wants young women
not to feel pressured to have sex, while Willis's interest is in freeing women
from a sexual double standard.

McConnell also assumes that abortion becomes guilt free for most
women because it is legal. Willis insists that women should not feel guilty. A
mediator might ask what interest McConnell has in making women feel
guilty and what Willis means when she says she would now feel "conflict and
sadness" (paragraph 14) over choosing an abortion. What is the difference
between "conflict and sadness" and "guilt"?

The main assumption these writers do not share concerns the motives of
those who cast abortion as a moral issue. Willis assumes that any question
about the morality of abortion is part of an effort to repress and subordinate
women. This assumption makes Willis see those who disagree with her as a
threat to her chief interest—women's rights. McConnell, on the other hand,
challenges the feminist assumption that abortion has liberated women. To

her, the legalization of abortion, rather than protecting women's rights, has actually contributed to the further exploitation of women sexually, which she sees as immoral.

Is the Difference a Matter of Principle?   The principle of equal rights for all individuals is featured in both arguments but in different ways. Willis is interested in equal rights among men and women. McConnell is concerned with the equal rights of the fetus as a potential human being.

Is the Difference a Matter of Values or Priorities?   The question of priorities brings us to a key difference underlying the positions of McConnell and Willis. Willis puts the value of a woman's well-being above the value of a fetus's life (paragraph 5). In paragraph 8, she states, "in a society that respects the individual, no [fetus] in *any* stage of development has an 'essential right' to make use of someone else's body [. . .] without that person's consent." For Willis, it is immoral to force any woman to bear a child against her will. For McConnell, however, the fetus counts too. Denying rights to the unborn is denying life itself (paragraph 33).

In addition, these two writers have very different values regarding sex. For McConnell, sex for pleasure, without commitment, is demeaning to women, something to which they acquiesce only because they have been told that it is normal and healthy. For Willis, sexual passion "for its own sake is a human need and a human right" (paragraph 11); she seems to be responding directly to McConnell in paragraph 16: "Behind the victim theory of abortion is the implicit belief [. . .] that sex for pleasure is not only 'irresponsible' (i.e., bad) but something men impose on women, never something women actively seek."

Is the Difference a Matter of Ends or Means?   McConnell and Willis both claim to have the same end in mind—a society in which women are truly free and equal, able to live dignified and uncompromised lives. However, they differ over legalized abortion as a means to this end. McConnell does not argue that *Roe v. Wade* should be overturned; rather, she wants her audience to recognize that abortion has cheapened both sex and life, allowing women to be victimized by men who want sex without commitment and encouraging a society that wants rights without responsibilities. Her ultimate goal is higher moral standards for the community. Willis, on the other hand, wants to make sure that freedom and equality for women stay in the forefront of the abortion debate. She resists any compromise on the abortion issue—even the concession that women should feel guilt about having abortions—because she sees the issue of morality as a slope down which women could slide back into a subordinate societal role.

Is the Difference a Matter of Interpretation?   These two writers interpret abortion from polar extremes. McConnell sees it as totally negative; to her, abortion is a convenience, a way of avoiding responsibility after an act of sexual carelessness. Willis's definition of abortion stresses its positive political value; it is the "cutting edge of feminism" because it guarantees to women absolute reproductive freedom. Furthermore, as we have seen, they interpret individualism differently: for Willis, individualism is positive, the autonomy and freedom to reach one's goals; for McConnell it is more negative, with connotations of selfishness and immaturity.

Is the Difference a Matter of Implications or Consequences?   Both writers are concerned with consequences, but neither entertains the other's concerns. Willis sees the result of legalized abortion as a more just society. McConnell argues that the positive consequences Willis claims for women are illusory and that women have been harmed by the easy availability of abortion.

Is the Difference a Result of Personal Background, Basic Human Needs, or Emotions?   In their arguments about abortion, both writers are fairly open about some of their emotions. McConnell is quite frank about her "remorse" over her abortion in her first year of college. In her description of that experience, she suggests that she was coerced by the university's health counselors. Notice, too, that she describes herself as the child of "first-generation" Americans with strict moral standards, a fact that surely influenced her perception of liberated sexual morals.

Willis expresses anger that the arena of debate over abortion has moved from its original focus on women's rights to a new focus on the rights of the fetus. She fears that hard-won ground for women's rights could be slipping. Yet, in discussing her own child, she reveals an emotional vulnerability that could possibly make her rethink her position on the morality of abortion. Note, for example, that she mentions her own abortion only once, in paragraph 14.

In face-to-face negotiation and mediation, having a conversation about underlying differences can go a long way toward helping opposing parties understand each other. Each side must "try on" the position of those who see the issue from a different perspective. They may still not agree or change their positions, but at this point each side ought to be able to say to the other, "I see what your concerns are." Progress toward resolution begins when people start talking about their underlying concerns or interests rather than their positions.

As a student mediating among written texts, you must decide what you could say to help each side see other viewpoints and to loosen the commitment each side has to its own position. (See the Best Practices box on page 317.)

Defining the Problem in Terms of the Real Interests

As we have said, although it is important in negotiating to see clearly what each side is demanding, successful negotiation looks for a solution that addresses the interests that underlie the positions of each side. Uncovering

1. Is the difference a matter of *assumptions*? As we discussed in Chapter 3 on the Toulmin method of analysis and in Chapter 6 on inquiry, all arguments are based on some assumptions.
2. Is the difference a matter of *principle*? Are some parties to the dispute following different principles, or general rules, from others?
3. Is the difference a matter of *values* or a matter of having the same values but giving them different *priorities*?
4. Is the difference a matter of *ends* or *means*? That is, do people want to achieve different goals, or do they have the same goals in mind but disagree on the means to achieve them?
5. Is the difference a matter of *interpretation*?
6. Is the difference a matter of *implications* or *consequences*?
7. Is the difference a result of *personal background, basic human needs,* or *emotions*?

To our list of questions about difference in persuasive writing, we add this last question because negotiation requires the parties involved to look not just at one another's arguments but also at one another as people with histories and feelings. It is not realistic to think that human problems can be solved without taking human factors into consideration. Negotiators must be open about their emotions and such basic human needs as personal security, economic well-being, and a sense of belonging, recognition, and control over their own lives. They can be open with one another about such matters only if their dialogue up to this point has established trust between them. If you are mediating among printed texts, you must use the texts themselves as evidence of these human factors.

Following Through

If you are negotiating between your own position and the arguments of classmates, form groups and use the questions in the Best Practices box above to identify the interests of each party. You may ask a student outside the group to mediate the discussion. As a group, prepare a report on your conversation: What are the main interests of each party?

If you are mediating among printed arguments, write an analysis based on applying the questions to two or more arguments. You could write out your analysis in list form, as we did in analyzing the differences between McConnell and Willis, or you could treat it as an exploratory essay.

As a creative variation for your analysis, write a dialogue with yourself as mediator, posing questions to each of the opposing parties. Have each side respond to your questions just as we demonstrated in our sample dialogue on pages 178–179.

those interests is the first step. The next is summing them up, recognizing the most important ones a solution must address. Meeting these underlying interests is the task that negotiators undertake collaboratively.

To illustrate, let's look at the two arguments about legalized abortion. Although McConnell criticizes abortion and those who choose it, she admits that she would keep it legal. Her real interest is in reducing what she sees as the consequences of legalized abortion: irresponsible sex and a disregard for life.

Willis is not totally unwilling to consider the moral value of the fetus as human life, admitting that it begins to acquire moral value as it comes to term; her problem with the moral question is the possibility that considering it at all will endanger women's right to choose for—or against—having an abortion. Her real interest is in equality of the sexes.

A mediator between these two positions would have to help resolve the conflict in a way that guarantees women's autonomy and control over their reproductive lives and that promotes responsibility and respect for the value of life. Any resolution here must ensure both the rights of the individual and the good of the community.

Following Through

For the conflict among classmates' positions that you have been negotiating or the conflict among written texts that you have been mediating, write a description of the problem that a resolution must solve: What are the key interests that must be addressed? If you are negotiating, write a statement collaboratively.

Inventing Creative Options

Parties can work toward solutions to a problem in collaboration, each party can brainstorm solutions alone, or an individual mediator can take on this task. Collaboration can help or hinder the invention process, depending on the relationship of the negotiators. Because coming up with possible solutions means making some concessions, you might want to do so privately rather than state publicly what you would be willing to give up. Whether you are a mediator or a negotiator, this is the stage for exploring options, for entertaining wild ideas, for experimenting without making judgments.

With respect to the abortion issue, Willis might be willing to consider counseling for women contemplating abortion and admit that the issue inevitably involves some ethical concerns. McConnell might be willing to take a less judgmental position and concede that it is not really fair to impose either motherhood or guilt on every woman who has an unwanted pregnancy.

Following Through

1. Think about a possible compromise on the issue of legalized abortion. Your ideas should address the interests of both Willis and McConnell. How likely is it that they would accept your compromise?
2. For a class assignment on negotiating or mediating a dispute, brainstorm possible solutions either independently or collaboratively. Try to make your list of options as long as you can.

Gathering More Data

Once a mediator has proposed a solution or negotiators have created a tentative resolution, some or all of the parties might think they could accept it if only they had a little more information. For example, one side in the abortion issue might want to know not only that there are approximately 1.5 million abortions performed each year in the United States but also that many of them are second or third abortions for the same women. If Willis learned that many women have abortions repeatedly, she might agree that the right is being abused — and that some counseling might help. If McConnell were to find out that most women have only a single abortion, she might decide that women do not interpret the right to abortion as nonchalantly as she had imagined. Professional negotiators suggest that information gathering at this point be done collaboratively. However, the trust and spirit of collaboration built so far can be damaged if each side tries to gather data favorable to its own original position.

Following Through

1. If you have an idea for a compromise that would address the interests of Willis and McConnell, what additional data do you think either or both of these authors would want to have before accepting your solution?
2. If you have come up with a proposal for resolving a conflict that you and some classmates have been negotiating or that you have been mediating, decide together if additional information could help you reach consensus. What questions need to be answered? Try to answer these questions collaboratively with a joint visit to the library.

Reaching a Solution Based on Agreed-Upon Principles

The kind of negotiation we have been discussing in this chapter is not the "I give a little, you give a little" sort that occurs between a buyer and seller or in a hostage situation when terrorists offer to trade a number of hostages for an equal number of released prisoners. Such a resolution involves no real principle other than that concessions ought to be of equal value. It brings the opposing sides no closer to understanding why they differed in the first place.

Instead, negotiated settlements on matters of public policy such as abortion or sexual harassment or gun control ought to involve some principles that both sides agree are fair. For example, Willis might agree that abortion ought to be a real choice, not something a woman is railroaded into as McConnell feels she was at age eighteen. Based on this principle, Willis might agree that professional counseling about ethics and options at least ought to be available to women considering abortion.

Following Through

If you have been mediating or negotiating a conflict with classmates, formalize your resolution if possible. Be ready to explain what principles you have agreed on as the basis for the compromise.

THE MEDIATORY ESSAY

Arguments that appear in newspapers and popular magazines usually seek to convince or persuade an audience to accept the author's position. Sometimes, however, the writer assumes the role of mediator and attempts to negotiate a solution acceptable to the opposing sides. This writer moves beyond the stated positions and the facts of the dispute to expose the underlying interests, values, and beliefs of those in opposition. The goal is to show what interests they may have in common, to increase each side's understanding of the other, and to propose a solution to the dispute, a new position based on interests and values that will be acceptable to both sides. The following essay by Roger Rosenblatt aims to mediate one of the most deeply entrenched conflicts of our day—the issue of legalized abortion. As you read it, keep in mind the arguments of Margaret Liu McConnell and Ellen Willis. Do you think that reading this mediatory essay might bring them closer to some consensus on the question of how to live with legalized abortion?

How to End the Abortion War
Roger Rosenblatt

Roger Rosenblatt is a writer who regularly contributes to the New York Times Magazine, *in which this essay originally appeared.*

The veins in his forehead bulged so prominently they might have been blue worms that had worked their way under the surface of his skin. His eyes bulged, too, capillaries zigzagging from the pupils in all directions. His face was pulled tight about the jaw, which thrust forward like a snowplow attachment on the grille of a truck. From the flattened O of his mouth, the word "murderer" erupted in a regular rhythm, the repetition of the r's giving the word the sound of an outboard motor that failed to catch.

She, for her part, paced up and down directly in front of him, saying nothing. Instead, she held high a large cardboard sign on a stick, showing the cartoonish drawing of a bloody coat hanger over the caption, "Never again." Like his, her face was taut with fury, her lips pressed together so tightly they folded under and vanished. Whenever she drew close to him, she would deliberately lower the sign and turn it toward him, so that he would be yelling his "murderer" at the picture of the coat hanger.

For nearly twenty years these two have been at each other with all the hatred they can unearth. Sometimes the man is a woman, sometimes the woman a man. They are black, white, Hispanic, Asian; they make their homes in Missouri or New Jersey; they are teenagers and pharmacists and college professors; Catholic, Baptist, Jew. They have exploded at each other on the steps of the Capitol in Washington, in front of abortion clinics, hospitals, and politicians' homes, on village greens and the avenues of cities. Their rage is tireless; at every decision of the United States Supreme Court or of the President or of the state legislatures, it rises like a missile seeking only the heat of its counterpart.

This is where America is these days on the matter of abortion, or where it seems to be. In fact, it is very hard to tell how the country really feels about abortion, because those feelings are almost always displayed in political arenas. Most ordinary people do not speak of abortion. Friends who gladly debate other volatile issues — political philosophy, war, race — shy away from the subject. It is too private, too personal, too bound up with one's faith or spiritual identity. Give abortion five seconds of thought, and it quickly spirals down in the mind to the most basic questions about human life, to the mysteries of birth and our relationship with our souls.

We simply will not talk about it. We will march in demonstrations, shout and carry placards, but we will not talk about it. In the Presidential election of 1992, we will cast votes for a national leader based in part on his or her position on abortion. Still, we will not talk about it.

The oddity in this unnatural silence is that most of us actually know what we feel about abortion. But because those feelings are mixed and complicated, we have decided that they are intractable. I believe the opposite is true: that we are more prepared than we realize to reach a common, reasonable understanding on this subject, and if we were to vent our mixed feelings and begin to make use of them, a resolution would be at hand.

Seventy-three percent of Americans polled in 1990 were in favor of abortion rights. Seventy-seven percent polled also regard abortion as a kind of killing. (Forty-nine percent see abortion as outright murder, 28 percent solely as the taking of human life.) These figures represent the findings of the Harris and Gallup polls, respectively, and contain certain nuances of opinion within both attitudes. But the general conclusions are widely considered valid. In other words, most Americans are both for the choice of abortion as a principle and against abortion for themselves. One has to know nothing else to realize how conflicted a problem we have before and within us.

The fact that abortion entails conflict, however, does not mean that the country is bound to be locked in combat forever. In other contexts, living with conflict is not only normal to America, it is often the only way to function honestly. We are for both Federal assistance and states' autonomy; we are for both the First Amendment and normal standards of propriety; we are for both the rights of privacy and the needs of public health. Our most productive thinking usually contains an inner confession of mixed feelings. Our least productive thinking, a nebulous irritation resulting from a refusal to come to terms with disturbing and patently irreconcilable ideas.

Yet acknowledging and living with ambivalence is, in a way, what America was invented to do. To create a society in which abortion is permitted and its gravity appreciated is to create but another of the many useful frictions of a democratic society. Such a society does not devalue life by allowing abortion; it takes life with utmost seriousness and is, by the depth of its conflicts and by the richness of its difficulties, a reflection of life itself.

Why, then, are we stuck in political warfare on this issue? Why can we not make use of our ambivalence and move on? 10

The answer has to do with America's peculiar place in the history of abortion, and also with the country's special defining characteristics, both ancient and modern, with which abortion has collided. In the 4,000-year-old history extending from the Greeks and Romans through the Middle Ages and into the present, every civilization has taken abortion with utmost seriousness. Yet ours seems to be the only civilization to have engaged in an emotional and intellectual civil war over the issue.

There are several reasons for this. The more obvious include the general lack of consensus in the country since the mid-60's, which has promoted bitter divisions over many social issues — race, crime, war, and abortion, too. The sexual revolution of the 60's resulted in the heightened activity of people who declared themselves "pro-choice" *and* "pro-life" — misleading terms used here principally for convenience. The pro-life movement began in 1967, six years before *Roe v. Wade*. The women's movement, also revitalized during the 60's, gave an impetus for self-assertion to women on both sides of the abortion issue.

But there are less obvious reasons, central to America's special character, which have helped to make abortion an explosive issue in this country.

Religiosity. America is, and always has been, a religious country, even though it spreads its religiosity among many different religions. Perry Miller, the great historian of American religious thought, established that the New England colonists arrived with a ready-made religious mission, which they cultivated and sustained through all its manifestations, from charity to intolerance. The Virginia settlement, too, was energized by God's glory. Nothing changed in this attitude by the time the nation was invented. If anything, the creation of the United States of America made the desire to receive redemption in the New World more intense.

Yet individuals sought something in American religion that was different, more emotional than the religion practiced in England. One member of an early congregation explained that the reason he made the long journey to America was "I thought I should find feelings." This personalized sense of religion, which has endured to the present, has an odd but telling relationship with the national attitude toward religion. Officially, America is an a-religious country; the separation of church and state is so rooted in the democracy it has become a cliché. Yet that same separation has created and intensified a hidden national feeling about faith and God, a sort of secret, undercurrent religion, which, perhaps because of its subterranean nature, is often more deeply felt and volatile than that of countries with official or state religions.

The Catholic Church seems more steadily impassioned about abortion in America than anywhere else, even in a country like Poland—so agitated, in fact, that it has entered into an unlikely, if not unholy, alliance with evangelical churches in the pro-life camp. In Catholic countries like Italy, France, and Ireland, religion is often so fluidly mixed with social life that rules are bent more quietly, without our personal sort of moral upheaval.

Americans are moral worriers. We tend to treat every political dispute that arises as a test of our national soul. The smallest incident, like the burning of the flag, can bring our hidden religion to the surface. The largest and most complex moral problem, like abortion, can confound it for decades.

Individualism. Two basic and antithetical views of individualism have grown up with the country. Emerson, the evangelist of self-reliance and nonconformity, had a quasi-mystical sense of the value of the individual self.[1] He described man as a self-sufficient microcosm: "The lightning which explodes and fashions planets, maker of planets and suns, is in him." Tocqueville had a more prosaic and practical view.[2] He worried about the tendency of Americans to withdraw into themselves at the expense of the public good, confusing self-assertion with self-absorption.

Abortion hits both of these views of the individual head on, of course; but both views are open to antipodal interpretations. The Emersonian

[1] Ralph Waldo Emerson (1803–1882) was an essayist and leader of New England transcendentalism.
[2] Alexis de Tocqueville (1805–1859) was a French aristocrat and magistrate who toured the United States in 1831 to study the effects of democracy. His classic work *Democracy in America* was first published in 1835.

celebration of the individual may be shared by the pro-choice advocate who sees in individualism one's right to privacy. It may be seen equally by a pro-life advocate as a justification for taking an individual stance — an anti-liberal stance to boot — on a matter of conscience.

The idea of the independent individual may also be embraced by the pro-life position as the condition of life on which the unborn have a claim immediately after conception. Pro-life advocates see the pregnant woman as two individuals, each with an equal claim to the riches that American individualism offers.

20

Tocqueville's concern with individualism as selfishness is also available for adoption by both camps. The pro-life people claim that the pro-choice advocates are placing their individual rights above those of society, and one of the fundamental rights of American society is the right to life. Even the Supreme Court, when it passed *Roe v. Wade*, concluded that abortion "is not unqualified and must be considered against important state interests in regulation."

To those who believe in abortion rights, the "public good" consists of a society in which people, collectively, have the right to privacy and individual choice. Their vision of an unselfish, unself-centered America is one in which the collective sustains its strength by encouraging the independence of those who comprise it. Logically, both camps rail against the individual imposing his or her individual views on society at large, each feeling the same, if opposite, passion about both what society and the individual ought to be. Passion on this subject has led to rage.

Optimism. The American characteristic of optimism, like that of individualism, is affected by abortion in contradictory ways. People favoring the pro-life position see optimism exactly as they read individual rights: Every American, born or unborn, is entitled to look forward to a state of infinite hope and progress. The process of birth is itself an optimistic activity.

Taking the opposite view, those favoring abortion rights interpret the ideas of hope and progress as a consequence of one's entitlement to free choice in all things, abortion definitely included. If the individual woman wishes to pursue her manifest destiny unencumbered by children she does not want, that is not only her business but her glory. The issue is national as well as personal. The pro-choice reasoning goes: The country may only reach its ideal goals if women, along with men, are allowed to achieve their highest potential as citizens, unburdened by limitations that are not of their own choosing.

Even the element of American "can-do" ingenuity applies. The invention of abortion, like other instruments of American optimism, supports both the pro-life and pro-choice stands. Hail the procedure for allowing women to realize full control over their invented selves. Or damn the procedure for destroying forever the possibility of a new life inventing itself. As with all else pertaining to this issue, one's moral position depends on the direction

25

in which one is looking. Yet both directions are heaving with optimism, and both see life in America as the best of choices.

Sexuality. The connection of abortion with American attitudes toward sexuality is both economic and social. The American way with sex is directly related to the country's original desire to become a society of the middle class, and thus to cast off the extremes of luxury and poverty that characterized Europe and the Old World. The structure of English society, in particular, was something the new nation sought to avoid. Not for Puritan America was the rigid English class system, which not only fixed people into economically immobile slots but allowed and encouraged free-wheeling sexual behavior at both the highest and lowest strata.

At the top of the English classes was a self-indulgent minority rich enough to ignore middle-class moral codes and idle enough to spend their time seducing servants. At the opposite end of the system, the poor also felt free to do whatever they wished with their bodies, since the world offered them so little. The masses of urban poor, created by the Industrial Revolution, had little or no hope of bettering their lot. Many of them wallowed in a kind of sexual Pandemonium,[1] producing babies wantonly and routinely engaging in rape and incest. Between the two class extremes stood the staunch English middle class, with its hands on its hips, outraged at the behavior both above and below them, but powerless to insist on, much less enforce, bourgeois values.

This was not to be the case in America, where bourgeois values were to become the standards and the moral engine of the country. Puritanism, a mere aberrant religion to the English, who were able to get rid of it in 1660 after a brief eighteen years, was the force that dominated American social life for a century and a half. Since there has been a natural progression from Puritanism to Victorianism and from Victorianism to modern forms of fundamentalism in terms of social values, it may be said that the Puritans have really never loosened their headlock on American thinking. The Puritans offered a perfect context for America's desire to create a ruling middle class, which was to be known equally for infinite mobility (geographic, social, economic) and the severest forms of repression.

Abortion fits into such thinking more by what the issue implies than by what it is. In the 1800's and the early 1900's, Americans were able to live with abortion, even during periods of intense national prudery, as long as the practice was considered the exception that proved the rule. The rule was that abortion was legally and morally discouraged. Indeed, most every modern civilization has adopted that attitude, which, put simply, is an attitude of looking the other way in a difficult human situation, which often cannot and should not be avoided. For all its adamant middle-classedness,

---

[1] In *Paradise Lost*, John Milton's name for the capital of Hell. From Greek *para* ("all") and *daimon* ("demon")—hence, a place of wild disorder.

it was not uncomfortable for Americans to look the other way, either—at least until recently.

When abortion was no longer allowed to be a private, albeit danger-   30
ous, business, however, especially during the sexual revolution of the 60's, America's basic middle-classedness asserted itself loudly. Who was having all these abortions? The upper classes, who were behaving irresponsibly, and the lower orders, who had nothing to lose. Abortion, in other words, was a sign of careless sexuality and was thus an offense to the bourgeois dream.

The complaint was, and is, that abortion contradicts middle-class val-ues, which dictate the rules of sexual conduct. Abortion, it is assumed, is the practice of the socially irresponsible, those who defy the solid norms that keep America intact. When *Roe v. Wade* was ruled upon, it sent the harshest message to the American middle class, including those who did not oppose abortion themselves but did oppose the disruption of conform-ity and stability. If they—certainly the middle-class majority—did not ob-ject to *Roe v. Wade* specifically, they did very much object to the atmosphere of lawlessness or unruliness that they felt the law encouraged. Thus the out-cry; thus the warfare.

There may be one other reason for abortion's traumatic effect on the country in recent years. Since the end of the Second World War, American society, not unlike modern Western societies in general, has shifted intellec-tually from a humanistic to a social science culture; that is, from a culture used to dealing with contrarieties to one that demands definite, provable answers. The nature of social science is that it tends not only to identify, but to create issues that must be solved. Often these issues are the most signifi-cant to the country's future—civil rights, for example.

What social science thinking does not encourage is human sympathy. By that I do not mean the sentimental feeling that acknowledges another's pain or discomfort; I mean the intellectual sympathy that accepts another's views as both interesting and potentially valid, that deliberately goes to the heart of the thinking of the opposition and spends some time there. That sort of humanistic thinking may or may not be humane, but it does offer the opportunity to arrive at a humane understanding outside the realm and rules of politics. In a way, it is a literary sort of thinking, gone now from a post-literary age, a "reading" of events to determine layers of depth, com-plication, and confusion and to learn to live with them.

Everything that has happened in the abortion debate has been within the polarities that social science thinking creates. The quest to determine when life begins is a typical exercise of social science—the attempt to im-pose objective precision on a subjective area of speculation. Arguments over the mother's rights versus the rights of the unborn child are social sci-ence arguments, too. The social sciences are far more interested in rights than in how one arrives at what is right—that is, both their strength and weakness. Thus the abortion debate has been political from the start.

A good many pro-choice advocates, in fact, came to lament the political   35
character of the abortion debate when it first began in the 60's. At that time,
political thinking in America was largely and conventionally liberal. The
liberals had the numbers; therefore, they felt that they could set the national agenda without taking into account the valid feelings or objections
of the conservative opposition. When, in the Presidential election of 1980,
it became glaringly apparent that the feelings of the conservative opposition were not only valid but were politically ascendant, many liberals reconsidered the idea that abortion was purely a rights issue. They expressed
appreciation of a more emotionally complicated attitude, one they realized
that they shared themselves, however they might vote.

If the abortion debate had risen in a humanistic environment, it might
never have achieved the definition and clarity of the *Roe v. Wade* decision,
yet it might have moved toward a greater public consensus. One has to
guess at such things through hindsight, of course. But in a world in which
humanistic thought predominated, abortion might have been taken up
more in its human terms and the debate might have focused more on such
unscientific and apolitical components as human guilt, human choice and
human mystery.

If we could find the way to retrieve this kind of conflicted thinking,
and find a way to apply it to the country's needs, we might be on our way
toward a common understanding on abortion, and perhaps toward a common good. Abortion requires us to think one way and another way simultaneously. Americans these days could make very good use of this bifur-
cated way of thinking.

This brings me back to the concern I voiced at the beginning: Americans are not speaking their true minds about abortion because their minds
are in conflict. Yet living with conflict is normal in America, and our reluc-
tance to do so openly in this matter, while understandable in an atmosphere of easy polarities, may help create a false image of our country in
which we do not recognize ourselves. An America that declares abortion legal and says nothing more about it would be just as distorted as one that
prohibited the practice. The ideal situation, in my view, would consist of a
combination of laws, attitudes, and actions that would go toward satisfying
both the rights of citizens and the doubts held by most of them.

Achieving this goal is, I believe, within reach. I know how odd that
must sound when one considers the violent explosions that have occurred
in places like Wichita as recently as August of last year,[1] or when one sees
the pro-life and pro-choice camps amassing ammunition for this year's
Presidential campaign. But for the ordinary private citizen, the elements
of a reasonably satisfying resolution are already in place. I return to the fact
that the great majority of Americans both favor abortion rights and disapprove of abortion. Were that conflict of thought to be openly expressed,

[1] That is, 1991.

and were certain social remedies to come from it, we would not find a middle of the road on this issue — logically there is no middle of the road. But we might well establish a wider road, which would accommodate a broad range of beliefs and opinions and allow us to move on to more important social concerns.

What most Americans want to do with abortion is to permit but discourage it. Even those with the most pronounced political stands on the subject reveal this duality in the things they say; while making strong defenses of their positions, they nonetheless, if given time to work out their thoughts, allow for opposing views. I discovered this in a great many interviews over the past three years. 40

Pro-choice advocates are often surprised to hear themselves speak of the immorality of taking a life. Pro-life people are surprised to hear themselves defend individual rights, especially women's rights. And both sides might be surprised to learn how similar are their visions of a society that makes abortion less necessary through sex education, help for unwanted babies, programs to shore up disintegrating families and moral values, and other forms of constructive community action. Such visions may appear Panglossian,[1] but they have been realized before, and the effort is itself salutary.

If one combines that sense of social responsibility with the advocacy of individual rights, the permit-but-discourage formula could work. By "discourage," I mean the implementation of social programs that help to create an atmosphere of discouragement. I do not mean ideas like parental consent or notification, already the law in some states, which, however well-intentioned, only whittle away at individual freedoms. The "discourage" part is the easier to find agreement on, of course, but when one places the "permit" question in the realm of respect for private values, even that may become more palatable.

Already 73 percent of America finds abortion acceptable. Even more may find it so if they can tolerate living in a country in which they may exercise the individual right not to have an abortion themselves or to argue against others having one, yet still go along with the majority who want the practice continued. The key element for all is to create social conditions in which abortion will be increasingly unnecessary. It is right that we have the choice, but it would be better if we did not have to make it.

Were this balance of thought and attitude to be expressed publicly, it might serve some of the country's wider purposes as well, especially these days when there is so much anguish over how we have lost our national identity and character. The character we lost, it seems to me, was one that exalted the individual for what the individual did for the community. It honored and embodied both privacy and selflessness. A balanced attitude on abortion would also do both. It would make a splendid irony if this

---

[1] Ideal, utopian. A reference to Dr. Pangloss is Voltaire's *Candide;* as Candide's tutor, he taught that "all is for the best in this best of possible worlds."

most painful and troublesome issue could be converted into a building block for a renewed national pride based on good will.

For that to happen, the country's leaders—Presidential candidates come to mind—have to express themselves as well. As for Congress, it hardly seems too much to expect our representatives to say something representative about the issue. Should *Roe v. Wade* be overturned, as may well happen, the country could be blown apart. To leave the matter to the states would lead to mayhem, a balkanization of what ought to be standard American rights. Congress used to pass laws, remember? I think it is time for Congress to make a law like *Roe v. Wade* that fully protects abortion rights, but legislates the kind of community help, like sex education, that would diminish the practice.

Taking a stand against abortion while allowing for its existence can turn out to be a progressive philosophy. It both speaks for moral seriousness and moves in the direction of ameliorating conditions of ignorance, poverty, the social self-destruction of fragmented families, and the loss of spiritual values in general. What started as a debate as to when life begins might lead to making life better.

The effort to reduce the necessity of abortion, then, is to choose life as wholeheartedly as it is to be "pro-life." By such an effort, one is choosing life for millions who do not want to be, who do not deserve to be, forever hobbled by an accident, a mistake or by miseducation. By such an effort, one is also choosing a different sort of life for the country as a whole—a more sympathetic life in which we acknowledge, privileged and unprivileged alike, that we have the same doubts and mysteries and hopes for one another.

Earlier, I noted America's obsessive moral character, our tendency to treat every question that comes before us as a test of our national soul. The permit-but-discourage formula on abortion offers the chance to test our national soul by appealing to its basic egalitarian impulse. Were we once again to work actively toward creating a country where everyone had the same health care, the same sex education, the same opportunity for economic survival, the same sense of personal dignity and worth, we would see both fewer abortions and a more respectable America.

Analyzing a Mediatory Essay

Rosenblatt's argument poses a possible resolution of the abortion controversy and in so doing analyzes the opposing positions and interests, as all mediation must. The following analysis shows how Rosenblatt takes his readers through the process of mediation.

Understanding the Spirit of Negotiation

A mediator has to be concerned with his or her own ethos, as well as with helping the opposing parties achieve an attitude that will enable negotiation to begin. The mediator must sound fair and evenhanded; the opposing parties must be open-minded.

Rosenblatt, interestingly, opens his essay in a way that invites commentary. In his first two paragraphs, he portrays both sides at their worst, as extremists in no frame of mind to negotiate—and, in fact, in no frame of mind even to speak to each other. In his third paragraph he relates the history of their debate, describing their emotions with words like *hatred* and *rage* and their behavior with metaphors of war and destruction. Readers who see themselves as reasonable will disassociate themselves from the people in these portraits.

Following Through

Do you think Rosenblatt's introduction is a good mediation strategy? In your writer's notebook, describe your initial response to Rosenblatt's opening. Having read the whole essay, do you think it is an effective opening? Once he has presented these warriors on both sides, do you think he goes on to discuss the opposing positions and their values in an evenhanded, neutral way? Can you cite some passages where you see either fairness or bias on his part?

Understanding the Opposing Positions

Rosenblatt establishes the opposing positions, already well known, in the first two paragraphs: the "pro-life" position that abortion is murder, the "pro-choice" position that outlawing abortion violates women's rights. Interestingly, Rosenblatt does not wait until the close of the essay to suggest his compromise position. Rather, he presents it in paragraph 9, although he goes into more detail about the solution later in the essay.

Following Through

In your writer's notebook, paraphrase Rosenblatt's compromise position on abortion. Do you think this essay would have been more effective if Rosenblatt had postponed presenting his solution?

Locating Areas of Disagreement over Facts

Rosenblatt points out that both sides' focus on the facts alone is what has made the issue intractable. As he points out in paragraph 34, the opposing sides have adopted the "objective precision" of the social sciences: The pro-life side has focused on establishing the precise moment of the beginning of life; the pro-choice side has focused on the absolute rights of women, ignoring the emotions of their conservative opponents.

Following Through

Reread paragraph 33. In your writer's notebook, paraphrase Rosenblatt's point about humanistic thinking as opposed to social science thinking. If you have taken social science courses, what is your opinion?

Locating Areas of Disagreement in Interests

Rosenblatt perceives that the disagreement over abortion may in fact be a disagreement over certain underlying interests and emotions held by each side, involving their perceptions about what life should be like in America. His aim is to help the two sides understand how these "less obvious reasons" have kept them from reaching any agreement. At the same time, he points out that many of the differences that seem to put them at odds are tied to common values deeply rooted in American culture. Thus, Rosenblatt attempts to show each side that the other is not a threat to its interests and perceptions of the American way of life.

Rosenblatt notes that both sides share an assumption that is keeping them apart: They both assume that there is one answer to the question of abortion rights rather than a solution that accepts ambivalence. He locates the source of this assumption in what he calls "social science thinking," which leads both sides to think that problems can be objectively studied and solved apart from human subjectivity. Thus, both sides are ignoring the very thing that is so vital to the process of negotiation and mediation.

Rosenblatt further shows how different principles underlie the arguments of each side. One side bases its argument on the right to privacy and free choice, whereas the other bases its argument on the right to life. Both principles are fundamental to American society—and neither is completely unqualified.

In addition, Rosenblatt shows how each side values the rights of the individual but interprets these rights differently. For example, antiabortion advocates see the fetus as an individual with the right to life, whereas pro-choice advocates argue for the individual right of the mother to privacy. In paragraphs 18–22, Rosenblatt shows how two perceptions or interpretations of individualism, one positive (emphasizing self-reliance) and one more critical (emphasizing selfishness), are traceable throughout American culture. In fact, he shows how both sides embrace individualism as an element of their arguments.

In addressing the main difference between the opposing parties over values, Rosenblatt shows how legalized abortion could be perceived as a threat to traditional middle-class economic and social values, and he traces middle-class sexual repression back to the Puritans. Rosenblatt may be stepping outside of the neutral stance of a mediator here, as he suggests that antiabortionists are somewhat prudish. He makes no corresponding remarks about the sexual values of the pro-choice side.

Rosenblatt points out that both sides see different consequences of legalizing abortion. Antiabortion advocates see abortion as destabilizing society and undermining the middle-class American way of life. These people worry not merely about abortion but about an "unruly" society. Pro-choice advocates, on the other hand, see abortion as the route to a better society; as Rosenblatt paraphrases their vision, "The country may only reach its ideal goals if women, along with men, are allowed to achieve their highest potential as citizens [. . .]" (paragraph 24).

In addressing the emotional characteristics of those involved in the dispute over abortion, Rosenblatt points to the role of religion in America. He explains that Americans historically have been more emotional about religion and morality than people of other nations, even ones where Catholicism is a state religion.

Following Through

Recall the chief areas of difference between Ellen Willis and Margaret Liu McConnell in their respective arguments on the value of abortion rights. In your writer's notebook, indicate which of their stated concerns correspond to points in Rosenblatt's analysis of the differences that fuel the abortion war. Does Rosenblatt say anything that might help bring Willis and McConnell closer together?

Defining the Problem in Terms of the Real Interests

Rosenblatt finds the real issue in the abortion controversy to be not whether abortion should be legal or illegal but rather how fundamental, conflicting interests in American society can be addressed. In other words, how can we create laws and institutions that reflect the ambivalence most Americans feel on the topic of abortion? How do we permit abortion legally, in order to satisfy our traditional values for privacy and individual rights, but also discourage it morally, in order to satisfy the American religious tradition that values life, respects fetal rights, and disapproves of casual and promiscuous sex?

Following Through

In your writer's notebook, give your opinion of whether Rosenblatt has defined the abortion debate in terms of the opposing sides' real interests. Would his definition of the problem affect related issues, such as making the "abortion pill," or RU 486, available in the United States?

Inventing Creative Options

Rosenblatt's solution is based on what he calls humanistic thinking, that is, thinking that permits conflict and rejects simple solutions to complicated human problems. He shows that many Americans think that abortion is both right and wrong but cannot even talk about their feelings because they are so contradictory. His creative option is for us to accept this ambivalence as a society and pass legislation that would satisfy both "the rights of citizens and the doubts held by most of them" (paragraph 38). In paragraph 45, Rosenblatt suggests that Congress pass a law legalizing abortion but at the same time requiring various activities, such as sex education, that over time promote respect for life and strengthen community moral standards.

Following Through

Reread paragraphs 39–48, and explore in your writer's notebook your opinion of Rosenblatt's proposed solution. Should he have made it more specific?

Gathering More Data

Before opposing sides can reach an agreement based on the real issues, they often need to get more information. Rosenblatt's mediatory argument is short on actual data. In response to his proposed solution, the antiabortion side might have severe doubts that the social programs proposed could in fact reduce the number of abortions performed.

Following Through

In your writer's notebook, suggest what kinds of evidence Rosenblatt might have to offer to convince the antiabortion side that sex education and other social programs could reduce the number of abortions performed.

Reaching a Solution Based on Agreed-Upon Principles

Rosenblatt attempts to get those who support abortion rights and those who oppose them to reduce their differences by accepting the "permit but discourage" principle. This is a principle that American society applies to other areas, such as marital infidelity, which is legal but certainly discouraged through social institutions and customs.

Following Through

1. Reread, if necessary, the two arguments on abortion by McConnell and Willis. Would each writer accept the principle of "permit but discourage"?
2. Draft a letter to the editor of the *New York Times Magazine,* in which Rosenblatt's argument originally appeared. In no more than three paragraphs, evaluate the argument as an attempt at mediation. Then read the following letters to the magazine, written in response to Rosenblatt's essay.

   Alternatively, write a letter or letters to the editor of the *New York Times,* playing the role of either Willis or McConnell, or both, responding as you think each would.

Three Readers' Responses to Rosenblatt

Roger Rosenblatt's essay on abortion is timely and welcome ("How to End the Abortion War," Jan. 19). However, his belief that Americans can coalesce on a policy that "discourages" abortion without making it illegal is probably too optimistic. The polarization of Americans on this issue results from some pretty deep differences. Differences in life style, for one thing, can dictate profound political polarization. Many American women derive their most fundamental sense of self-worth from child-rearing and care of the family; many others find theirs in lives that include participation in the larger society, particularly the work place. For women in "traditional" families (and their husbands), untrammeled access to abortion constitutes a form of permissiveness that threatens the things they hold most dear. For women whose identities are tied to work outside the home, the right to control reproductive lives is essential.

So I'm afraid these wars will continue. Rosenblatt and others should not tire in their efforts to find middle ground, but it would be unrealistic to think that we will be able to occupy it together anytime soon.

—PHILIP D. HARVEY, Cabin John, MD

I don't want to "permit but discourage" abortion. I want to stop abortion the way the abolitionists wanted to stop slavery. I believe slavery is wrong: that no one has the right to assure his or her quality of life by owning another. In the same way, and for the same reasons, I believe abortion is wrong: that no one has the right to assure her quality of life by aborting another.

—ANITA JANDA, Kew Gardens, Queens

Your article states that "most of us actually know what we feel about abortion." It is true that most people have a position on abortion, but that position is seldom an informed one in this era of the 10-second sound bite and the oversimplification of issues.

Few people understand that *Roe v. Wade* gives the interests of the woman precedence over those of the embryo early in the pregnancy, but allows Government to favor the fetus once it has attained viability.

Were a poll to propose full freedom of choice for women during the early stages of pregnancy, and prohibition of abortion during the later stages, except in cases of fetal deformity or a threat to a woman's life, I believe that the response of the American public would be overwhelmingly positive. Rosenblatt is right on the mark in saying that the public "simply will not talk about abortion." With thoughtful and dispassionate discussion, we might lay aside the all-or-nothing attitude that currently prevails.

—RICHARD A. KELLEY, Rumson, NJ

Following Through

Analyze the three letters to the *New York Times Magazine* critiquing Rosenblatt's article. What values does each contribute to the debate? How might Rosenblatt respond to each?

Writing a Mediatory Essay

Prewriting

If you have been mediating the positions of two or more groups of classmates or two or more authors of published arguments, you may be assigned to write a mediatory essay in which you argue for a compromise position, appealing to an audience of people on all sides. In preparing to write such an essay, you should work through the steps of negotiation and mediation as described on pages 295–320. In your writer's notebook, prepare briefs of the various conflicting positions, and note areas of disagreement; think hard about the differing interests of the conflicting parties, and respond to the questions about difference on page 317.

If possible, give some thought to each party's background—age, race, gender, and so forth—and how it might contribute to his or her viewpoint on the issue. For example, in a debate about whether *Huckleberry Finn* should be taught and read aloud in U.S. high schools, an African-American parent whose child is the only minority student in her English class might well have a different perspective from that of a white teacher. Can the white teacher be made to understand the embarrassment that a sole black child might feel when the white characters speak with derision about "niggers"?

In your writer's notebook, also describe the conflict in terms of the opposing sides' real interests rather than the superficial demands each side might be stating. For example, considering the controversy over *Huckleberry Finn*, you might find some arguments in favor of teaching it anytime, others opposed to teaching it at all, others suggesting that it be an optional text for reading outside of class, and still others proposing that it be taught only in twelfth grade, when students are mature enough to understand Twain's satire. However, none of these suggestions addresses the problem in terms of the real interests involved: a desire to teach the classics of American literature for what they tell us about the human condition and our country's history and values; a desire to promote respect for African-American students; a desire to ensure a comfortable learning climate for all students; and so on. You may be able to see that people's real interests are not as far apart as they might seem. For example, those who advocate teaching *Huckleberry Finn* and those who are opposed may both have in mind the goal of eliminating racial prejudice.

At this point in the prewriting process, think of some solutions that would satisfy at least some of the real interests on all sides. It might be necessary for you to do some additional research. What do you think any of the opposing parties might want to know more about in order to accept your solution?

Finally, write up a clear statement of your compromise. Can you explain what principles it is based on? In the *Huckleberry Finn* debate, we might propose that the novel be taught at any grade level provided that it is presented as part of a curriculum to educate students about the African-American experience with the involvement of African-American faculty or visiting lecturers.

Drafting

There is no set form for the mediatory essay. In fact, it is an unusual, even somewhat experimental, form of writing. As with any argument, the important thing is to have a plan for arranging your points and to provide clear signals to your readers. One logical way to organize a mediatory essay is in three parts:

Overview of the conflict. Describe the conflict and the opposing positions in the introductory paragraphs.

Discussion of differences underlying the conflict. Here your goal is to make all sides more sympathetic to one another and to sort out the important real interests that must be addressed by the solution.

Proposed solution. Here you make a case for your compromise position, giving reasons why it should be acceptable to all—that is, showing that it does serve at least some of their interests.

Revising

When revising a mediatory essay, you should look for the usual problems of organization and development that you would be looking for in any essay to convince or persuade. Be sure that you have inquired carefully and fairly into the conflict and that you have clearly presented the cases for all sides, including your proposed solution. At this point, you also need to consider how well you have used the persuasive appeals:

The appeal to character. Think about what kind of character you have projected as a mediator. Have you maintained neutrality? Do you model open-mindedness and genuine concern for the sensitivities of all sides?

The appeal to emotions. To arouse sympathy and empathy, which are needed in negotiation, you should take into account the emotional appeals discussed on pages 276–278. Your mediatory essay should be a moving argument for understanding and overcoming difference.

The appeal through style. As in persuasion, you should put the power of language to work. Pay attention to concrete word choice, striking metaphors, and phrases that stand out because of repeated sounds and rhythms.

For suggestions about editing and proofreading, see the appendix.

STUDENT SAMPLE: *An Essay Arguing to Mediate*

The following mediatory essay was written by Angi Grellhesl, a first-year student at Southern Methodist University. Her essay examines opposing written views on the institution of speech codes at various U.S. colleges and its effect on freedom of speech.

MEDIATING THE SPEECH CODE CONTROVERSY

Angi Grellhesl

The right to free speech has raised many controversies over the years. Explicit lyrics in rap music and marches by the Ku Klux Klan are just some examples that test the power of the First Amendment. Now, students and administrators are questioning if, in fact, free speech ought to be limited on university campuses. Many schools have instituted speech codes to protect specified groups from harassing speech.

Both sides in the debate, the speech code advocates and the free speech advocates, have presented their cases in recent books and articles. Columnist Nat Hentoff argues strongly against the speech codes, his main reason being that the codes violate students' First Amendment rights. Hentoff links the right to free speech with the values of higher education. In support, he quotes Yale president Benno Schmidt, who says, "Freedom of thought must be Yale's central commitment [. . .] [U]niversities cannot censor or suppress speech, no matter how obnoxious in content, without violating their justification for existence [. . .]" (qtd. in Hentoff 223). Another reason Hentoff offers against speech codes is that universities must teach students to defend themselves in preparation for the real world, where such codes cannot shield them. Finally, he suggests that most codes are too vaguely worded; students may not even know they are violating the codes (216).

Two writers in favor of speech codes are Richard Perry and Patricia Williams. They see speech codes as a necessary and fair limitation on free speech. Perry and Williams argue that speech codes promote multicultural awareness, making students more sensitive to the differences that are out there in the real world. These authors do not think that the codes violate First Amendment rights, and they are suspicious of the motives of those who say they do. As Perry and Williams put it, those who feel free speech rights are being threatened "are apparently unable to distinguish between a liberty interest on the one hand and, on the other, a quite specific interest in being able to spout racist, sexist, and homophobic epithets completely unchallenged—without, in other words, the terrible inconvenience of feeling bad about it" (228).

Perhaps if both sides trusted each other a little more, they could see that their goals are not contradictory. Everyone agrees that students' rights should be protected. Hentoff wishes to ensure that students have the right to speak their minds. He and others on his side are concerned about freedom. Defenders of the codes argue that students have the right not to be harassed, especially while they are getting an education. They are concerned about opportunity. Would either side really deny that the other's goal had value?

Also, both sides want to create the best possible educational environment. Here the difference rests on the interpretation of what benefits the students. Is the best environment one most like the real world, where prejudice and harassment occur? Or does the university have an obligation to provide an atmosphere where potential victims can thrive and participate freely without intimidation?

I think it is possible to reach a solution that everyone can agree on. Most citizens want to protect constitutional rights; but they also agree that those rights have limitations, the ultimate limit being when one person infringes on the rights of others to live in peace. All sides should agree that a person ought to be able to speak out about his or her convictions, values, and beliefs. And most people can see a difference between that protected speech and the kind that is intended to harass and intimidate. For example, there is a clear difference between expressing one's view that Jews are mistaken in not accepting Christ as the son of God, on the one hand, and yelling anti-Jewish threats at a particular person in the middle of the night, on the other. Could a code not be worded in such a way as to distinguish between these two kinds of speech?

Also, I don't believe either side would want the university to be an artificial world. Codes should not attempt to ensure that no one is criticized or even offended. Students should not be afraid to say controversial things. But universities do help to shape the future of the real world, so shouldn't they at least take a stand against harassment? Can a code be worded that would protect free speech and prevent harassment?

The current speech code at Southern Methodist University is a compromise that ought to satisfy free speech advocates and speech code advocates. It prohibits hate speech at the same time that it protects an individual's First Amendment rights.

First, it upholds the First Amendment by including a section that reads, "due to the University's commitment to freedom of speech and expression, harassment is more than mere insensitivity or offensive conduct which creates an uncomfortable situation for certain members of the community" (*Peruna* 92). The code therefore should satisfy those, like Hentoff, who place a high value on the basic rights our nation was built upon. Secondly, whether or not there is a need for protection, the current code protects potential victims from hate speech or "any words or acts deliberately designed to disregard the safety or rights of another, and which intimidate, degrade, demean, threaten, haze, or otherwise interfere with another person's rightful action" (*Peruna* 92). This part of the code should satisfy those who recognize that some hurts cannot be overcome. Finally, the current code outlines specific acts that constitute harassment: "Physical, psychological, verbal and/or written acts directed toward an individual or group of individuals which rise to the level of 'fighting words' are prohibited" (*Peruna* 92).

The SMU code protects our citizens from hurt and from unconstitutional censorship. Those merely taking a position can express it, even if it hurts. On the other hand, those who are spreading hatred will be limited as to what harm they may inflict. Therefore, all sides should respect the code as a safeguard for those who use free speech but a limitation for those who abuse it.

Works Cited

Hentoff, Nat. "Speech Codes on the Campus and Problems of Free Speech." <u>Debating P.C.</u> Ed. Paul Berman. New York: Bantam, 1992. 215–24.

Perry, Richard, and Patricia Williams. "Freedom of Speech." <u>Debating P.C.</u> Ed. Paul Berman. New York: Bantam, 1992. 225–30.

<u>Peruna Express 1993–1994</u>. Dallas: Southern Methodist U, 1993.

Appendix

A Short Guide to Editing and Proofreading

Editing and proofreading are the final steps in creating a finished piece of writing. Too often, however, these steps are rushed as writers race to meet a deadline. Ideally, you should distinguish between the acts of revising, editing, and proofreading. Because each step requires that you pay attention to something different, you cannot reasonably expect to do them well if you try to do them all at once.

Our suggestions for revising appear in each of Chapters 6–9 on the aims of argument. Revising means shaping and developing the whole argument with an eye to audience and purpose; when you revise, you are ensuring that you have accomplished your aim. Editing, on the other hand, means making smaller changes within paragraphs and sentences. When you edit, you are thinking about whether your prose will be a pleasure to read. Editing improves the sound and rhythm of your voice. It makes complicated ideas more accessible to readers and usually makes your writing more concise. Finally, proofreading means eliminating errors. When you proofread, you correct everything you find that will annoy readers, such as misspellings, punctuation mistakes, and faulty grammar.

In this appendix, we offer some basic advice on what to look for when editing and proofreading. For more detailed help, consult a handbook on grammar and punctuation and a good book on style, such as Joseph Williams's *Ten Lessons in Clarity and Grace* or Richard Lanham's *Revising Prose*. Both of these texts guided our thinking in the advice that follows.

EDITING

Most ideas can be phrased in a number of ways, each of which gives the idea a slightly distinctive twist. Consider the following examples:

In New York City, about 74,000 people die each year.

In New York City, death comes to one in a hundred people each year.

Death comes to one in a hundred New Yorkers each year.

To begin an article on what becomes of the unknown and unclaimed dead in New York, Edward Conlon wrote the final of these three sentences. We can only speculate about the possible variations he considered, but because openings are so crucial, he almost certainly cast these words quite deliberately.

For most writers, such deliberation over matters of style occurs during editing. In this late stage of the writing process, writers examine choices made earlier, perhaps unconsciously, while drafting and revising. They listen to how sentences sound, to patterns of rhythm both within and among sentences. Editing is like an art or craft; it can provide you the satisfaction of knowing you've said something gracefully and effectively. To focus on language this closely, you will need to set aside enough time following the revision step.

In this section, we discuss some things to look for when editing your own writing. Don't forget, though, that editing does not always mean looking for weaknesses. You should also recognize passages that work well just as you wrote them, that you can leave alone or play up more by editing passages that surround them.

Editing for Clarity and Conciseness

Even drafts revised several times may have wordy and awkward passages; these are often places where a writer struggled with uncertainty or felt less than confident about the point being made. Introductions often contain such passages. In editing, you have one more opportunity to clarify and sharpen your ideas.

Express Main Ideas Forcefully

Emphasize the main idea of a sentence by stating it as directly as possible, using the two key sentence parts (*subject* and *verb*) to convey the two key parts of the idea (*agent* and *act*).

As you edit, first look for sentences that state ideas indirectly rather than directly; such sentences may include (1) overuse of the verb *to be* in its various forms (*is, was, will have been,* and so forth), (2) the opening words "There is . . ." or "It is . . . ," (3) strings of prepositional phrases, or (4) many vague nouns. Then ask, "What is my true subject here, and what is that subject's action?" Here is an example of a weak, indirect sentence:

> It is a fact that the effects of pollution are more evident in lower-class neighborhoods than in middle-class ones.

The writer's subject is pollution. What is the pollution's action? Limply, the sentence tells us its "effects" are "evident." The following edited version makes pollution the agent that performs the action of a livelier verb, "fouls." The edited sentence is more specific—without being longer.

> *Pollution* more frequently *fouls* the air, soil, and water of lower-class neighborhoods than of middle-class ones.

Editing Practice

The following passage about a plan for creating low-income housing contains two weak sentences. In this case, the weakness results from wordiness. (Note the overuse of vague nouns and prepositional phrases.) Decide what the true subject is for each sentence, and make that word the subject of the verb. Your edited version should be much shorter.

> As in every program, there will be the presence of a few who abuse the system. However, as in other social programs, the numbers would not be sufficient to justify the rejection of the program on the basis that one person in a thousand will try to cheat.

Choose Carefully between Active and Passive Voice

Active voice and passive voice indicate different relationships between subjects and verbs. As we have noted, ideas are usually clearest when the writer's true subject is also the subject of the verb in the sentence — that is, when it is the agent of the action. In the passive voice, however, the agent of the action appears in the predicate or not at all. Rather than acting as agent, the subject of the sentence *receives* the action of the verb.

The following sentence is in the passive voice:

> The air of poor neighborhoods is often fouled by pollution.

There is nothing incorrect about the use of the passive voice in this sentence, and in the context of a whole paragraph, passive voice can be the most emphatic way to make a point. (Here, for example, it allows the word *pollution* to fall at the end of the sentence, a strong position.) But, often, use of the passive voice is not a deliberate choice at all but rather a vague and unspecific way of stating a point.

Consider the following sentences, in which the main verbs have no agents:

> It *is believed* that dumping garbage at sea is not as harmful to the environment as *was* once *thought.*

> Ronald Reagan *was considered* the "Great Communicator."

Who thinks such dumping is not so harmful? environmental scientists? industrial producers? Who considered former president Reagan a great communicator? speech professors? news commentators? Such sentences are clearer when they are written in the active voice:

> Some environmentalists believe that dumping garbage at sea is not as harmful to the environment as they used to think.

> Media commentators considered Ronald Reagan the "Great Communicator."

In editing for the passive voice, look over your verbs. Passive voice is easily recognized because it always contains (1) some form of *to be* as a helping verb and (2) the main verb in its past participle form (which ends in -*ed*, -*d*, -*t*, -*en*, or -*n*, or in some cases may be irregular: *drunk, sung, lain,* and so on).

When you find a sentence phrased in the passive voice, decide who or what is performing the action; the agent may appear after the verb or not at all. Then decide if changing the sentence to the active voice will improve the sentence as well as the surrounding passage.

Editing Practice

1. The following paragraph from a student's argument needs to be edited for emphasis. It is choking with excess nouns and forms of the verb *to be*, some as part of passive constructions. You need not eliminate all passive voice, but do look for wording that is vague and ineffective. Your edited version should be not only stronger but shorter.

   > Although emergency shelters are needed in some cases (for example, a mother fleeing domestic violence), they are an inefficient means of dealing with the massive numbers of people they are bombarded with each day. The members of a homeless family are in need of a home, not a temporary shelter into which they and others like them are herded, only to be shuffled out when their thirty-day stay is over to make room for the next incoming herd. Emergency shelters would be sufficient if we did not have a low-income housing shortage, but what is needed most at present is an increase in availability of affordable housing for the poor.

2. Select a paragraph of your own writing to edit; focus on using strong verbs and subjects to carry the main idea of your sentences.

Editing for Emphasis

When you edit for emphasis, you make sure that your main ideas stand out so that your reader will take notice. Following are some suggestions to help.

Emphasize Main Ideas by Subordinating Less Important Ones

Subordination refers to distinctions in rank or order of importance. Think of the chain of command at an office: the boss is at the top of the ladder, the middle management is on a lower (subordinate) rung, the support staff is at an even lower rung, and so on.

In writing, subordination means placing less important ideas in less important positions in sentences in order to emphasize the main ideas that should stand out. Writing that lacks subordination treats all ideas equally; each idea may consist of a sentence of its own or may be joined to another idea by a coordinator (*and, but,* and *or*). Such a passage follows with its sentences numbered for reference purposes.

> (1) It has been over a century since slavery was abolished and a few decades since lawful, systematic segregation came to an unwilling halt. (2) Truly, blacks

have come a long way from the darker days that lasted for more than three centuries. (3) Many blacks have entered the mainstream, and there is a proportionately large contingent of middle-class blacks. (4) Yet an even greater percentage of blacks are immersed in truly pathetic conditions. (5) The inner-city black poor are enmeshed in devastating socioeconomic problems. (6) Unemployment among inner-city black youths has become much worse than it was even five years ago.

Three main ideas are important here—that blacks have been free for some time, that some have made economic progress, and that others are trapped in poverty—and of these three, the last is probably intended to be the most important. Yet, as we read the passage, these key ideas do not stand out. In fact, each point receives equal emphasis and sounds about the same, with the repeated subject-verb-object syntax. The result seems monotonous, even apathetic, though the writer is probably truly disturbed about the subject. The following edited version, which subordinates some of the points, is more emphatic. We have italicized the main points.

> *Blacks have come a long way* in the century since slavery was abolished and in the decades since lawful, systematic segregation came to an unwilling halt. Yet, although many blacks have entered the mainstream and the middle class, *an even greater percentage is immersed in truly pathetic conditions.* To give just one example of these devastating socioeconomic problems, *unemployment among inner-city black youths is much worse now than it was even five years ago.*

Although different editing choices are possible, this version plays down sentences 1, 3, and 5 in the original so that sentences 2, 4, and 6 stand out.

As you edit, look for passages that sound wordy and flat because all the ideas are expressed with equal weight in the same subject-verb-object pattern. Then single out your most important points, and try out some options for subordinating the less important ones. The key is to put main ideas in main clauses and modifying ideas in modifying clauses or phrases.

Modifying Clauses   Like simple sentences, modifying clauses contain a subject and verb. They are formed in two ways: (1) with relative pronouns and (2) with subordinating conjunctions.

Relative pronouns introduce clauses that modify nouns, with the relative pronoun relating the clause to the noun it modifies. There are five relative pronouns: *that, which, who, whose,* and *whom.* The following sentence contains a relative clause:

> Alcohol advertisers are trying to sell a product *that is by its very nature harmful to users.*
>
> —JASON RATH (student)

Relative pronouns may also be implied:

> I have returned the library book [that] *you loaned me.*

Relative pronouns may also be preceded by prepositions, such as *on, in, to,* or *during:*

> Drug hysteria has created an atmosphere *in which civil rights are disregarded.*

Subordinating conjunctions show relationships among ideas. It is impossible to provide a complete list of subordinating conjunctions in this short space, but here are the most common and the kinds of modifying roles they perform:

> To show time: *after, as, before, since, until, when, while*
> To show place: *where, wherever*
> To show contrast: *although, though, whereas, while*
> To show cause and effect: *because, since, so that*
> To show condition: *if, unless, whether, provided that*
> To show manner: *how, as though*

By introducing it with a subordinating conjunction, you can convert one sentence into a dependent clause that can modify another sentence. Consider the following two versions of the same idea:

> Pain is a state of consciousness, a "mental event." It can never be directly observed.

> *Since pain is a state of consciousness, a "mental event,"* it can never be directly observed.
>
> —PETER SINGER, "Animal Liberation"

Modifying Phrases   Unlike clauses, phrases do not have a subject and a verb. Prepositional phrases and infinitive phrases are most likely already in your repertoire of modifiers. (Consult a handbook if you need to review these.) Here, we remind you of two other useful types of phrases: (1) participial phrases and (2) appositives.

Participial phrases modify nouns. Participles are created from verbs, so it is not surprising that the two varieties represent two verb tenses. The first is present participles ending in *-ing:*

> *Hoping to eliminate harassment on campus,* many universities have tried to institute codes for speech and behavior.

> The desperate Haitians fled here in boats, *risking all.*
>
> —CARMEN HAZAN-COHEN (student)

The second is past participles ending in *-ed, -en, -d, -t,* or *-n:*

> Women themselves became a resource, *acquired by men much as the land was acquired by men.*
>
> —GERDA LERNER

> *Linked more to the Third World and Asia than to the Europe of America's racial and cultural roots,* Los Angeles and Southern California will enter the 21st century as a multi-racial and multicultural society.
>
> —RYSZARD KAPUSCINSKI

Notice that modifying phrases should immediately precede the nouns they modify.

An *appositive* is a noun or noun phrase that restates another noun, usually in a more specific way. Appositives can be highly emphatic, but more often they are tucked into the middle of a sentence or added to the end, allowing a subordinate idea to be slipped in. When used like this, appositives are usually set off with commas:

> Rick Halperin, *a professor at Southern Methodist University,* noted that Ted Bundy's execution cost Florida taxpayers over six million dollars.
> —DIANE MILLER (student)

Editing Practice

1. Edit the following passage as needed for emphasis, clarity, and conciseness, using subordinate clauses, relative clauses, participial phrases, appositives, and any other options that occur to you. If some parts are effective as they are, leave them alone.

   > The monetary implications of drug legalization are not the only reason it is worth consideration. There is reason to believe that the United States would be a safer place to live if drugs were legalized. A large amount of what the media has named "drug-related" violence is really prohibition-related violence. Included in this are random shootings and murders associated with black-market transactions. Estimates indicate that at least 40 percent of all property crime in the United States is committed by drug users so they can maintain their habits. That amounts to a total of 4 million crimes per year and $7.5 billion in stolen property. Legalizing drugs would be a step toward reducing this wave of crime.

2. Edit a paragraph of your own writing with an eye to subordinating less important ideas through the use of modifying phrases and clauses.

Vary Sentence Length and Pattern

Even when read silently, your writing has a sound. If your sentences are all about the same length (typically fifteen to twenty words) and all structured according to a subject-verb-object pattern, they will roll along with the monotonous rhythm of an assembly line. Obviously, one solution to this problem is to open some of your sentences with modifying phrases and clauses, as we discuss in the previous section. Here we offer some other strategies, all of which add emphasis by introducing something unexpected.

1. Use a short sentence after several long ones.

   > [A] population's general mortality is affected by a great many factors over which doctors and hospitals have little influence. For those diseases and injuries for which modern medicine can affect the outcome, however, which country the patient lives in really matters. Life expectancy is not the same among developed countries for premature babies, for children

> born with spina bifida, or for people who have cancer, a brain tumor, heart disease, or chronic renal failure. *Their chances of survival are best in the United States.*
>
> —JOHN GOODMAN

2. Interrupt a sentence.

> The position of women in that hippie counterculture was, *as a young black male leader preached succinctly,* "prone."
>
> —BETTY FRIEDAN

> Symbols and myths—*when emerging uncorrupted from human experience*—are precious. Then it is the poetic voice and vision that informs and infuses—*the poet-warrior's, the prophet-seer's, the dreamer's*—reassuring us that truth is as real as falsehood. And ultimately stronger.
>
> —OSSIE DAVIS

3. Use an intentional sentence fragment. The concluding fragment in the previous passage by Ossie Davis is a good example.
4. Invert the order of subject-verb-object.

> Further complicating negotiations is the difficulty of obtaining relevant financial statements.
>
> —REGINA HERZLINGER

> This creature, with scarcely two thirds of man's cranial capacity, was a fire user. Of what it meant to him beyond warmth and shelter, we know nothing; with what rites, ghastly or benighted, it was struck or maintained, no word remains.
>
> —LOREN EISELY

Use Special Effects for Emphasis

Especially in persuasive argumentation, you will want to make some of your points in deliberately dramatic ways. Remember that just as the crescendos stand out in music because the surrounding passages are less intense, so the special effects work best in rhetoric when you use them sparingly.

Repetition   Deliberately repeating words, phrases, or sentence patterns has the effect of building up to a climactic point. In Chapter 8, we noted how Martin Luther King, Jr., in the emotional high point of his "Letter from Birmingham Jail," used repeated subordinate clauses beginning with the phrase "when you" to build up to his main point: "[. . .] then you will understand why we find it difficult to wait" (paragraph 14, pages 261–262). Here is another example, from the conclusion of an argument linking women's rights with environmental reforms:

> Environmental justice goes much further than environmental protection, a passive and paternalistic phrase. *Justice requires that* industrial nations pay back the environmental debt incurred in building their wealth by using less of nature's resources. *Justice prescribes that* governments stop siting hazardous waste facili-

ties in cash-poor rural and urban neighborhoods and now in the developing world. *Justice insists that* the subordination of women and nature by men is not only a hazard; it is a crime. *Justice reminds us that* the Earth does not belong to us; even when we "own" a piece of it, we belong to the Earth.

—H. PATRICIA HYNES

Paired Coordinators Coordinators are conjunctions that pair words, word groups, and sentences in a way that gives them equal emphasis and that also shows a relationship between them, such as contrast, consequence, or addition. In grade school, you may have learned the coordinators through the mnemonic *FANBOYS*, standing for *for, and, nor, but, or, yet, so.*

Paired coordinators emphasize the relationship between coordinated elements; the first coordinator signals that a corresponding coordinator will follow. Some paired coordinators are:

both _____ and _____

not _____ but _____

not only _____ but also _____

either _____ or _____

neither _____ nor _____

The key to effective paired coordination is to keep the words that follow the marker words as grammatically similar as possible. Pair nouns with nouns, verbs with verbs, prepositional phrases with prepositional phrases, and whole sentences with whole sentences. (Think of paired coordination as a variation on repetition.) Here are some examples:

Feminist anger, or any form of social outrage, is dismissed breezily—*not* because it lacks substance *but* because it lacks "style."

—SUSAN FALUDI

Alcohol ads that emphasize "success" in the business and social worlds are useful examples *not only* of how advertisers appeal to people's envy *but also* of how ads perpetuate gender stereotypes.

—JASON RATH (student)

Emphatic Appositives While an appositive (a noun or noun phrase that restates another noun) can subordinate an idea, it can also emphasize an idea if it is placed at the beginning or the end of a sentence, where it will command attention. Here are some examples:

The poorest nation in the Western hemisphere, Haiti is populated by six million people, many of whom cannot obtain adequate food, water, or shelter.

—SNEED B. COLLARD III

[Feminists] made a simple, though serious, ideological error when they applied the same political rhetoric to their own situation as women versus men: *too literal an analogy with class warfare, racial oppression.*

—BETTY FRIEDAN

Note that at the end of a sentence, an appositive may be set off with a colon or a dash.

Emphatic Word Order   The opening and closing positions of a sentence are high-profile spots, not to be wasted on weak words. The following sentence, for example, begins weakly with the filler phrase "there are":

> *There are* several distinctions, all of them false, that are commonly made between rape and date rape.

A better version would read:

> My opponents make several distinctions between rape and date rape; all of these are false.

Even more important are the final words of every paragraph and the opening and closing of the entire argument.

Editing Practice

1. Select one or two paragraphs from a piece of published writing you have recently read and admired. Be ready to share it with the class, explaining how the writer has crafted the passage to make it work.
2. Take a paragraph or two from one of your previous essays, perhaps even an essay from another course, and edit it to improve clarity, conciseness, and emphasis.

Editing for Coherence

Coherence refers to what some people call the "flow" of writing; writing flows when the ideas connect smoothly, one to the next. In contrast, when writing is incoherent, the reader must work to see how ideas connect and must infer points that the writer, for whatever reason, has left unstated.

Incoherence is a particular problem with writing that contains an abundance of direct or indirect quotations. In using sources, be careful always to lead into the quotation with some words of your own, showing clearly how this new idea connects with what has come before.

Because finding incoherent passages in your own writing can be difficult, ask a friend to read your draft to look for gaps in the presentation of ideas. Here are some additional suggestions for improving coherence.

Move from Old Information to New Information

Coherent writing is easy to follow because the connections between old information and new information are clear. Sentences refer back to previously introduced information and set up reader expectations for new information to come. Notice how every sentence fulfills your expectations in the following excerpts from an argument on animal rights by Steven Zak.

> The credibility of the animal-rights viewpoint [. . .] need not stand or fall with the "marginal human beings" argument.

Next, you would expect to hear why animals do not have to be classed as "marginal human beings"—and you do:

> Lives don't have to be qualitatively the same to be worthy of equal respect.

At this point you might ask upon what else we should base our respect. Zak answers this question in the next sentence:

> One's perception that another life has value comes as much from an appreciation of its uniqueness as from the recognition that it has characteristics that are shared by one's own life.

Not only do these sentences fulfill reader expectations, but each also makes a clear connection by referring specifically to the key idea in the sentence before it, forming an unbroken chain of thought. We have italicized the words that accomplish this linkage and connected them with arrows.

> The credibility of the animal rights viewpoint [. . .] need not stand or fall with the *"marginal human beings"* argument.
>
> Lives don't have to be *qualitatively the same* to be worthy of *equal respect.*
>
> One's perception that *another life has value* comes as much from an *appreciation of its uniqueness* as from the recognition that it has characteristics that are shared by one's own life.
>
> One can imagine that the lives of various kinds of animals *differ radically.* [. . .]

In the following paragraph, reader expectations are not so well fulfilled:

> We are presently witness to the greatest number of homeless families since the Great Depression of the 1930s. The cause of this phenomenon is a shortage of low-income housing. Mothers with children as young as two weeks are forced to live on the street because there is no room for them in homeless shelters.

While these sentences are all on the subject of homelessness, the second leads us to expect that the third will take up the topic of shortages of low-income housing. Instead, it takes us back to the subject of the first sentence and offers a different cause—no room in the shelters.

Looking for ways to link old information with new information will help you find problems of coherence in your own writing.

Editing Practice

1. In the following paragraph, underline the words or phrases that make the connections back to the previous sentence and forward to the next, as we did earlier with the passage from Zak.

> The affluent, educated, liberated women of the First World, who can en-
> joy freedoms unavailable to any women ever before, do not feel as free
> as they want to. And they can no longer restrict to the subconscious their
> sense that this lack of freedom has something to do with—with appar-
> ently frivolous issues, things that really should not matter. Many are
> ashamed to admit that such trivial concerns—to do with physical ap-
> pearance, bodies, faces, hair, clothes—matter so much. But in spite of
> shame, guilt, and denial, more and more women are wondering if it isn't
> that they are entirely neurotic alone but rather that something important
> is indeed at stake that has to do with the relationship between female
> liberation and female beauty.
>
> —NAOMI WOLF

2. The following student paragraph lacks coherence. Read through it,
   and put a slash (/) between sentences expressing unconnected ideas.
   You may try to rewrite the paragraph, rearranging sentences and adding ideas to make the connections tighter.

   > Students may know what AIDS is and how it is transmitted, but most are
   > not concerned about AIDS and do not perceive themselves to be at risk.
   > But college-age heterosexuals are the number-one high-risk group for
   > this disease (Gray and Sacarino 258). "Students already know about
   > AIDS. Condom distribution, public or not, is not going to help. It just
   > butts into my personal life," said one student surveyed. College is a time
   > for exploration and that includes the discovery of sexual freedom. Stu-
   > dents, away from home and free to make their own decisions for maybe
   > the first time in their lives, have a "bigger than life" attitude. The thought
   > of dying is the farthest from their minds. Yet at this point in their lives,
   > they are most in need of this information.

Use Transitions to Show Relationships between Ideas

Coherence has to be built into a piece of writing; as we discussed earlier, the
ideas between sentences must first cohere. However, sometimes readers need
help in making the transition from one idea to the next, so you must provide
signposts to help them see the connections more readily. For example, a transitional word like *however* can prepare readers for an idea in contrast to the
one before it, as in the second sentence in this paragraph. Transitional words
can also highlight the structure of an argument ("These data will show three
things: first . . . , second . . . , and third . . ."), almost forming a verbal path for
the reader to follow. Following are examples of transitional words and
phrases and their purposes:

To show order: *first, second, next, then, last, finally*
To show contrast: *however, yet, but, nevertheless*
To show cause and effect: *therefore, consequently, as a result, then*
To show importance: *moreover, significantly*

To show an added point: *as well, also, too*
To show an example: *for example, for instance*
To show concession: *admittedly*
To show conclusion: *in sum, in conclusion*

The key to using transitional words is similar to the key to using special effects for emphasis: Don't overdo it. To avoid choking your writing with these words, anticipate where your reader will genuinely need them, and limit their use to these instances.

Editing Practice

Underline the transitional words and phrases in the following passage of published writing:

> When people believe that their problems can be solved, they tend to get busy solving them.
>
> On the other hand, when people believe that their problems are beyond solution, they tend to position themselves so as to avoid blame. Take the woeful inadequacy of education in the predominantly black central cities. Does the black leadership see the ascendancy of black teachers, school administrators, and politicians as an asset to be used in improving those dreadful schools? Rarely. You are more likely to hear charges of white abandonment, white resistance to integration, conspiracies to isolate black children, even when the schools are officially desegregated. In short, white people are accused of being responsible for the problem. But if the youngsters manage to survive those awful school systems and achieve success, leaders want to claim credit. They don't hesitate to attribute that success to the glorious Civil Rights movement.
>
> —WILLIAM RASPBERRY

PROOFREADING

Proofreading is truly the final step in writing a paper. After proofreading, you ought to be able to print your paper out one more time; but if you do not have time, most instructors will be perfectly happy to see the necessary corrections done neatly in ink on the final draft.

Following are some suggestions for proofreading.

Spelling Errors

If you have used a word processor, you may have a program that will check your spelling. If not, you will have to check your spelling by reading through again carefully with a dictionary at hand. Consult the dictionary whenever you feel uncertain. You might consider devoting a special part of your writer's notebook to your habitual spelling errors: some students always misspell *athlete*, for example, whereas others leave the second *n* out of *environment*.

Omissions and Jumbled Passages

Read your paper out loud. Physically shaping your lips around the words can help locate missing words, typos (*saw* instead of *was*), or the remnants of some earlier version of a sentence that did not get fully deleted. Place a caret (∧) in the sentence and write the correction or addition above the line, or draw a line through unnecessary text.

Punctuation Problems

Apostrophes and commas give writers the most trouble. If you have habitual problems with these, you should record your errors in your writer's notebook.

Apostrophes

Apostrophe problems usually occur in forming possessives, not contractions, so here we discuss only the former. If you have problems with possessives, you may also want to consult a good handbook or seek a private tutorial with your instructor or your school's writing center.

Here are the basic principles to remember.

1. Possessive pronouns — *his, hers, yours, theirs, its* — never take an apostrophe.
2. Singular nouns become possessive by adding -'s.

   A single parent's life is hard.

   A society's values change.

   Do you like Mr. Voss's new car?

3. Plural nouns ending in -s become possessive by simply adding an apostrophe.

   Her parents' marriage is faltering.

   Many cities' air is badly polluted.

   The Joneses' house is up for sale.

4. Plural nouns that do not end in -s become possessive by adding -'s.

   Show me the women's (men's) room.

   The people's voice was heard.

If you err by using apostrophes where they don't belong in nonpossessive words ending in -s, remember that a possessive will always have a noun after it, not some other part of speech such as a verb or a preposition. You may even need to read each line of print with a ruler under it to help you focus more intently on each word.

Commas

Because commas indicate a pause, reading your paper aloud is a good way to decide where to add or delete them. A good handbook will elaborate on the following basic principles. The example sentences have been adapted from an argument by Mary Meehan, who opposes abortion.

1. Use a comma when you join two or more main clauses with a coordinating conjunction.

   Main clause, conjunction (and, but, or, nor, so, yet) *main clause.*

   Feminists want to have men participate more in the care of children, but abortion allows a man to shift total responsibility to the woman.

2. Use a comma after an introductory phrase or dependent clause.

   Introductory phrase or clause, main clause.

   To save the smallest children, the Left should speak out against abortion.

3. Use commas around modifiers such as relative clauses and appositives unless they are essential to the noun's meaning. Be sure to put the comma at both ends of the modifier.

   _____, *appositive,* _____

   _____, *relative clause,* _____

   One member of the 1972 Presidential commission on population growth was Graciela Olivarez, a Chicana who was active in civil rights and anti-poverty work. Olivarez, who later was named to head the Federal Government's Community Services Administration, had known poverty in her youth in the Southwest.

4. Use commas with a series.

   ____x___ , ___y___ , and ___z___ ,

   The traditional mark of the Left has been its protection of the underdog, the weak, and the poor.

Semicolons

Think of a semicolon as a strong comma. It has two main uses.

1. Use a semicolon to join two main clauses when you choose not to use a conjunction. This works well when the two main clauses are closely related or parallel in structure.

   Main clause; main clause.

   Pro-life activists did not want abortion to be a class issue; they wanted to end abortion everywhere, for all classes.

As a variation, you may wish to add a transitional adverb to the second main clause. The adverb indicates the relationship between the main clauses, but it is not a conjunction, so a comma preceding it would not be correct.

Main clause; transitional adverb (however, therefore, thus, moreover, con-sequently)*, main clause.*

When speaking with counselors at the abortion clinic, many women change their minds and decide against abortion; however, a woman who is accompanied by a husband or boyfriend often does not feel free to talk with the counselor.

2. Use semicolons between items in a series if any of the items them-selves contain commas.

_____ , _____ ; _____ , _____ ; _____ , _____

A few liberals who have spoken out against abortion are Jesse Jackson, a Civil Rights leader; Richard Neuhaus, a theologian; the comedian Dick Gregory; and politicians Mark Hatfield and Mary Rose Oakar.

Colons

The colon has two common uses.

1. Use a colon to introduce a quotation when both your own lead-in and the words quoted are complete sentences that can stand alone. (See the section in Chapter 5 entitled "Incorporating and Docu-menting Source Material in the Text of Your Argument" for more on introducing quotations.)

   Main clause in your words: "Quoted sentence(s)."

   Mary Meehan criticizes liberals who have been silent on abortion: "If much of the leadership of the pro-life movement is right-wing, that is due largely to the default of the Left."

2. Use a colon before an appositive that comes dramatically at the end of a sentence, especially if the appositive contains more than one item.

   Main clause: appositive, appositive, and appositive.

   Meehan argues that many pro-choice advocates see abortion as a way to hold down the population of certain minorities: blacks, Puerto Ricans, and other Latins.

Grammatical Errors

Grammatical mistakes can be hard to find, but once again we suggest reading aloud as one method of proofing for them; grammatical errors tend not to "sound right" even if they look like good prose. Another suggestion is to rec-ognize your habitual errors and then look for particular grammatical struc-tures that lead you into error.

Introductory Participial Phrases

Constructions such as these often lead writers to create dangling modifiers. To avoid this pitfall, see the discussion of participial phrases earlier in this appendix. Remember that an introductory phrase dangles if it is not immediately followed by the noun it modifies.

> *Incorrect:* Using her conscience as a guide, our society has granted each woman the right to decide if a fetus is truly a "person" with rights equal to her own.

(Notice that the implied subject of the participial phrase is "each woman," when in fact the subject of the main clause is "our society"; thus, the participial phrase does not modify the subject.)

> *Corrected:* Using her conscience as a guide, each woman in our society has the right to decide if a fetus is truly a "person" with rights equal to her own.

Paired Coordinators

If the words that follow each of the coordinators are not of the same grammatical structure, then an error known as nonparallelism has occurred. To correct this error, line up the paired items one over the other. You will see that the correction often involves simply adding a word or two to, or deleting some words from, one side of the paired coordinators.

> not only _____ but also _____
>
> *Incorrect:* Legal abortion not only protects women's lives, but also their health.
>
> *Corrected:* Legal abortion protects not only women's lives but also their health.

Split Subjects and Verbs

If the subject of a sentence contains long modifying phrases or clauses, by the time you get to the verb you may make an error in agreement (using a plural verb, for example, when the subject is singular) or even in logic (for example, having a subject that is not capable of being the agent that performs the action of the verb). Following are some typical errors:

> The *goal* of the courses grouped under the rubric of "Encountering Non-Western Cultures" *are* . . .

Here the writer forgot that *goal*, the subject, is singular.

> During 1992, *the Refugee Act of 1980*, with the help of President Bush and Congress, *accepted* 114,000 immigrants into our nation.

The writer here should have realized that the agent doing the accepting would have to be the Bush administration, not the Refugee Act. A better version would read:

During 1992, the Bush administration accepted 114,000 immigrants into our nation under the terms of the Refugee Act of 1980.

Proofreading Practice

Proofread the following passage for errors of grammar and punctuation.

The citizens of Zurich, Switzerland tired of problems associated with drug abuse, experimented with legalization. The plan was to open a central park, Platzspitz, where drugs and drug use would be permitted. Many European experts felt, that it was the illegal drug business rather than the actual use of drugs that had caused many of the cities problems. While the citizens had hoped to isolate the drug problem, foster rehabilitation, and curb the AIDS epidemic, the actual outcome of the Platzspitz experiment did not create the desired results. Instead, violence increased. Drug-related deaths doubled. And drug users were drawn from not only all over Switzerland, but from all over Europe as well. With thousands of discarded syringe packets lying around, one can only speculate as to whether the spread of AIDS was curbed. The park itself was ruined and finally on February 10, 1992, it was barred up and closed. After studying the Swiss peoples' experience with Platzspitz, it is hard to believe that some advocates of drug legalization in the United States are urging us to participate in the same kind of experiment.

Glossary

agent-action: Technical term for a sentence in "who-does-what" form.

alliteration: The repetition of consonant sounds.

annotation: A brief critical commentary on a text or section of text.

apologia: An effort to explain and justify what one has done, or chosen not to do, in the face of condemnation or at least widespread disapproval or misunderstanding.

argument: Mature reasoning; a considered opinion backed by a reason or reasons.

bibliography: A list of works on a particular topic.

case strategy: The moves a writer makes to shape a particular argument, including selecting reasons, ordering them, developing evidence, and linking the sections of the argument for maximum impact.

case structure: A flexible plan for making any argument to any audience; it consists of one or more theses, each of which is supported by one or more reasons, each of which is supported by evidence.

claim: In argument, what the author wants the audience to believe or to do.

connotation: What a word implies or what we associate it with; see also *denotation*.

conviction: An earned opinion achieved through careful thought, research, and discussion.

convincing: One of the four aims of argument; to use reasoning to secure the assent of people who do not share the author's conviction.

critical reading: A close reading involving analyzing and evaluating a text.

denotation: A word's literal meaning; see also *connotation*.

dialectic: Dialogue or serious conversation; the ancient Greeks' term for argument as inquiry.

graphics: Visual supplements to a longer text such as an essay, article, or manual.

identification: A strong linking of the readers' interests and values with an image, which represents something desired or potentially desirable.

implied question: A question that is inherent in an argument but not explicitly stated; all statements of opinion are answers to questions, usually implied ones.

inquiry: One of the four aims of argument; to use reasoning to determine the best position on an issue.

issue: An aspect of a topic that presents a problem, the solution to which people disagree about.

middle style: A style of persuasive writing that is neither stiff and formal nor chatty and familiar.

negotiation: One of the four aims of argument; using reason and understanding to bring about consensus among disagreeing parties or positions.

paraphrase: To restate someone else's writing or speech in one's own words.

persuasion: One of the four aims of argument; persuasion uses both rational and emotional appeals to influence not just thinking but also behavior.

plagiarism: The act of presenting someone else's words and/or ideas as one's own, without acknowledging the source.

position: An overall, summarizing attitude or judgment about some issue.

rhetoric: The art of argument as mature reasoning.

rhetorical context: The circumstances surrounding the text as an act of communication: the time and place in which it was written; its place of publication; its author and his or her values; the ongoing, historical debate to which it contributes.

rhetorical prospectus: A plan for proposed writing that includes a statement of the thesis, aim, audience, speaker's persona, subject matter, and organizational plan.

sampling: A fast, superficial, not necessarily sequential reading of a text, not to learn all that a text has to say but to get a feeling for the territory it covers.

thesis: In argumentation, a very specific position statement that is strategically designed to appeal to readers and to be consistent with available evidence.

topic: A subject or aspect of a subject; see also *issue*.

visual rhetoric: The use of images, sometimes coupled with sound or appeals to the other senses, to make an argument or persuade one's audience to act as the image-maker would have them act.

Credits

Text Credits

Photo Credits

Index